THE CAMBRIDGE COMPANION TO
PENTECOSTALISM

Pentecostalism is one of the fastest-growing religious movements in the world. Groups in the United States dominated early pentecostal historics, but recent global manifestations have expanded and complicated the definition of Pentecostalism. This volume provides a nuanced overview of Pentecostalism's various manifestations and explores what it means to be pentecostal from the perspectives of both insiders and outsiders. Leading scholars in the field use a multidisciplinary approach to analyze the historical, economic, political, cultural, anthropological, sociological, and theological aspects of the movement. They address controversies, such as the Oneness-Trinity dispute, introduce new theories, and chart trajectories for future research. *The Cambridge Companion to Pentecostalism* will enable beginners to familiarize themselves with the important issues and debates surrounding the global movement, while also offering experienced scholars a valuable handbook for reference.

Cecil M. Robeck, Jr. is Professor of Church History and Ecumenics and director of the David J. DuPlessis Center for Christian Spirituality at Fuller Theological Seminary in California. He served as the editor of *Pneuma: The Journal of the Society for Pentecostal Studies* for nine years and is the author of *The Azusa Street Mission and Revival: The Birth of the Global Pentecostal Movement* (2006) and *Prophecy at Carthage: Perpetua, Tertullian, and Cyprian* (1992).

Amos Yong is Professor of Theology and Mission and director of the Center for Missiological Research at Fuller Theological Seminary in Pasadena, California. He has authored or edited more than two dozen books, many relating to pentecostal theology, including *Pentecostalism and Prosperity: The Socioeconomics of the Global Charismatic Movement* (2012) and *The Spirit of Creation: Modern Science and Divine Action in the Pentecostal-Charismatic Imagination* (2011).

CAMBRIDGE COMPANIONS TO RELIGION
A series of companions to major topics and key figures in theology and religious studies. Each volume contains specially commissioned chapters by international scholars that provide an accessible and stimulating introduction to the subject for new readers and nonspecialists.

Titles in the Series

(continued after Index)

THE CAMBRIDGE COMPANION TO

PENTECOSTALISM

Edited by

Cecil M. Robeck, Jr.
Fuller Theological Seminary, California

Amos Yong
Fuller Theological Seminary, California

CAMBRIDGE
UNIVERSITY PRESS

CAMBRIDGE
UNIVERSITY PRESS

32 Avenue of the Americas, New York, NY 10013-2473, USA

Cambridge University Press is part of the University of Cambridge.

It furthers the University's mission by disseminating knowledge in the pursuit of education, learning, and research at the highest international levels of excellence.

www.cambridge.org
Information on this title: www.cambridge.org/9781107007093

© Cambridge University Press 2014

First published 2014

A catalog record for this publication is available from the British Library.

Library of Congress Cataloging in Publication data
The Cambridge companion to Pentecostalism / edited by Cecil M. Robeck, Jr., Fuller Theological Seminary, California, Amos Yong, Fuller Theological Seminary, California.
   pages   cm. – (Cambridge companions to religion)
Includes bibliographical references and index.
ISBN 978-1-107-00709-3 (hardback) – ISBN 978-0-521-18838-8 (pbk.)
 1. Pentecostalism.   I. Robeck, Cecil M., editor of compilation.
BR1644.C325   2014
270.8'2–dc23   2014002504

ISBN 978-1-107-00709-3 Hardback
ISBN 978-0-521-18838-8 Paperback

Contents

Contributors

Daniel E. Albrecht (PhD Graduate Theological Union) is academic director and professor at William Jessup University-BAC, San Jose, California. He has published *Rites in the Spirit: A Ritual Approach to Pentecostal/Charismatic Spirituality* (1999) and other essays in pentecostal spirituality, liturgy, and theology.

Mark J. Cartledge (PhD University of Wales) is Senior Lecturer in Pentecostal and Charismatic Theology and director of the Centre for Pentecostal and Charismatic Studies, University of Birmingham. He has authored or edited many books on pentecostal and charismatic studies, one of the most recent being *Testimony in the Spirit: Rescripting Ordinary Pentecostal Theology* (2010).

David D. Daniels III (PhD Union Theological Seminary) is Professor of Church History at McCormick Theological Seminary. He has published numerous scholarly articles and book chapters on African-American Pentecostalism in global context.

André Droogers (PhD VU University Amsterdam) is Professor Emeritus of Cultural Anthropology at VU University Amsterdam. He is the author of several publications on Pentecostalism, including (as coeditor) *More than Opium: An Anthropological Approach to Latin American and Caribbean Pentecostal Praxis* (1998), *Studying Global Pentecostalism: Theories and Methods* (2009), and *Play and Power in Religion* (2012).

Evan B. Howard (PhD Graduate Theological Union) is the founder and director of Spirituality Shoppe: An Evangelical Center for the Study of Christian Spirituality. He has published *The Brazos Introduction to Christian Spirituality* (2008) and other books and articles on Christian spirituality.

Veli-Matti Kärkkäinen (Dr. Theol.Habil. University of Helsinki) is Professor of Systematic Theology at Fuller Theological Seminary and Docent of Ecumenics at University of Helsinki, Finland. He is the author and editor of numerous works on pentecostal theology and ecumenism including *The Spirit in the World: Emerging Pentecostal Theologies in Global Contexts* (2009).

Wonsuk Ma (PhD Fuller Theological Seminary) is executive director and David Yonggi Cho Research Tutor of Global Christianity at the Oxford Centre for Mission Studies. He served as founding editor of the *Asian Journal of Pentecostal Studies* and has edited many books on Pentecostalism in general and on Asian Pentecostalism in particular, including (with J. Ma) *Mission in the Spirit: Towards a Pentecostal/Charismatic Missiology* (2011).

Michael J. McClymond (PhD University of Chicago) is Clarence Louis and Helen Irene Steber Professor of Theological Studies at Saint Louis University. He is the editor of *Embodying the Spirit: New Perspectives on North American Revivalism* (2004) and *Encyclopaedia of Religious Revivals in America*, 2 vols. (2007), among other books.

Cephas N. Omenyo (PhD University of Utrecht) is professor and dean of the Faculty of Arts at the University of Ghana. He has written *Pentecost Outside Pentecostalism: A Study of the Development of Charismatic Renewal in the Mainline Churches in Ghana* (2002) and other essays on African Pentecostalism.

Jean-Daniel Plüss (PhD Catholic University of Louvain) is chairman of the European Pentecostal and Charismatic Research Association in Zurich. He has published *Therapeutic and Prophetic Narratives in Worship: A Hermeneutic Study of Testimonies and Visions – Their Potential Significance for Christian Worship and Secular Society* (1988), as well as numerous other essays on pentecostal history and thought.

Daniel Ramirez (PhD Duke University) is assistant professor of North American Religious History at the University of Michigan, Ann Arbor, and co-chair of the History of Christianity section of the American Academy of Religion. His numerous publications and current book project, *Migrating Faith: Pentecostalism in the United States and Mexico, 1906–1966*, reflect his interest in the intersections of migration, culture, and Pentecostalism.

David A. Reed (PhD Boston University) is Professor Emeritus of Pastoral Theology and Research Professor at Wycliffe College, University of Toronto. He is the author of the award-winning volume, *"In Jesus' Name": The History and Beliefs of Oneness Pentecostals* (2008), and other essays on pentecostal and charismatic history and theology and is currently working on two book projects: the True Jesus Church (China) and Global Oneness Pentecostalism.

Cecil M. Robeck, Jr. (PhD Fuller Theological Seminary), is Professor of Church History and Ecumenics and director of the David du Plessis Center for Christian Spirituality, Fuller Theological Seminary. He is the author of the highly acclaimed *The Azusa Street Mission and Revival: The Birth of the Classical Pentecostal Movement* (2006), among many other works on pentecostal and charismatic history.

Calvin L. Smith (PhD University of Birmingham) is principal at King's Evangelical Divinity School, United Kingdom. He is the author and editor of several works, including *Revolution, Revival, and Religious Conflict in Sandinista Nicaragua* (2007) and *Pentecostal Power: Expressions, Impact and Faith of Latin American Pentecostalism* (2011).

Wolfgang Vondey (PhD Marquette University) is associate professor of Systematic Theology and director of the Center for Renewal Studies at the Regent University School of Divinity, Virginia Beach, Virginia. He is the author and editor of several works on pentecostal theology and ecumenism including, most recently, *Pentecostalism: A Guide for the Perplexed* (2013) and two volumes on *Pentecostalism and Christian Unity*: vol. 1, *Ecumenical Documents and Critical Assessments* (2010), and vol. 2, *Continuing and Building Relationships* (2013).

Michael Wilkinson (PhD University of Ottawa) is Professor of Sociology, director of the Religion in Canada Institute, and coordinator of the Canadian Pentecostal Research Network at Trinity Western University, Langley, British Columbia. His most recent publications include *Global Pentecostal Movements: Migration, Mission, and Public Religion* (2012) and *Catch the Fire: Soaking Prayer and Charismatic Renewal* (2014), as well as numerous articles and chapters on globalization and Pentecostalism.

Amos Yong (PhD Boston University) is Professor of Theology and Mission and director of the Center for Missiological Research at Fuller Theological Seminary in Pasadena, California, and the author or editor of more than two dozen books.

Preface

This project has been a long time in coming to fruition. The editors are grateful to the various contributors for agreeing to write a chapter, for working with us to keep it within the word constraints established by the Press, and for their patience. There were a number of others who were approached and invited to be a part of this – the editors being sensitive especially to the need to recruit authors from a variety of ethnic, gender, and disciplinary perspectives in order to address a global phenomenon as diverse as Pentecostalism – but these were unable to participate for different reasons. Thanks also to Laura Morris and her colleagues at Cambridge University Press for their enthusiastic embrace of the proposal, patience with the many unexpected developments that delayed the volume's submission, and expert guidance throughout the process. Vince Le and Enoch Charles, Amos's graduate assistants, helped with the formatting and indexing (respectively) of the book.

Amos is indebted to the support of his former dean Michael Palmer for the space to pursue scholarly projects such as this one. Mel wishes to thank Dr. Richard Mouw, the generous sabbatical policy of Fuller Theological Seminary, and Mel's gifted colleagues in the Church History department, Drs. James Bradley, John Thompson, Nate Feldmeth, Charlie Scalise, and Grayson Carter, for their collegiality, continuing support, and encouragement through the years.

Generally, the volume will capitalize "Charismatic," "Pentecostal," "Pentecostalism," and so forth when used as nouns or when they appear as part of proper names; otherwise, we leave "charismatic," "pentecostal," and their cognates uncapitalized when used adjectivally.

Global Pentecostalism: An Introduction to an Introduction

CECIL M. ROBECK, JR. AND AMOS YONG

Where does one begin when introducing a book that attempts to provide a scholarly introduction to a phenomenon as complex as is global Pentecostalism? Part of the challenge relates to how to define Pentecostalism, and the complexity of this question derives in part from debates about its history, including its origins. Lingering for a moment over some of the historiographic issues will illuminate this contested scholarly terrain.

Although the modern pentecostal movement is barely a century old, discussions surrounding its historiography – that is, how its history has been written and, more importantly, how its origins have been or are being interpreted – have become increasingly complex. There are several reasons for this. First, in recent years significant changes have taken place in the writing of pentecostal history. Voices from around the world, voices that have not been heard from previously or have been ignored by earlier pentecostal historians, are increasingly involved in these discussions. Regional histories are emerging with the result that the findings of earlier, more general histories, originating mainly from the United States, are being challenged and in some cases set aside. Pentecostal history writing and pentecostal historiography are now worldwide discussions, no longer dominated solely by voices from the United States.[1]

Second, the definition of what it means to be "Pentecostal" has become nearly as elusive as a grain of sand in a desert windstorm. Probably because the writing of pentecostal history and pentecostal theology was controlled for so long by American pentecostal denominations and the authors whose salaries they paid, the Pentecostals who wrote and published earlier works believed that the definition of a Pentecostal, and hence the meaning of Pentecostalism, was rightfully defined solely by them. It was understood to be a movement defined by an encounter with the Holy Spirit called "baptism in the Holy Spirit" that was evidenced by speaking in tongues.[2] As a result of the many works now being published throughout the world, that assumption is no longer taken for granted. Those who thought that they knew who Pentecostals were increasingly fail to recognize themselves in the various definitions being demanded by the greater inclusiveness now given to the term "Pentecostal."[3]

Third, for a generation Pentecostalism has become the focus of studies in a growing number of nonhistorical (in the technical sense) but related disciplines such as theology, sociology, anthropology, economics, and political science. These disciplines are frequently combined with history (e.g., social, economic, or political history, historical theology, among other variations) and provide important insights into our understanding of Pentecostalism. They have also raised new questions that deserve thoughtful responses. Because Pentecostalism is currently one of the more popular fields in the study of religion on the global level, it is now being defined by an increasing number of external observers working in these and related fields as much as it is by Pentecostals.[4] This has contributed to the broadening understandings of what it means to be Pentecostal, sometimes without any reference to speaking in tongues.[5] As a result, some have pointed to this as the dilution of what it means to be Pentecostal. Whether or not that claim is accurate, the range of possibilities given to the term Pentecostal has in many cases become a source of confusion.[6]

Fourth, the growing complexity of the term Pentecostal and its modifiers has led a number of historians to observe that no single definition for the term may any longer be possible. One must now think of pentecostal movements (plural) with multiple definitions.[7] This concession has been useful because it enables differentiation between various types of pentecostal groups that otherwise display unique characteristics, especially against a postmodern backdrop. While the term Pentecostal helps identify what they hold in common, its modifiers allow such groups also to claim their unique contributions. However, this concession to a growing number of adjectives also contributes to the growing fragmentation of Pentecostalism. A generation ago they might have been content with the simple designation Pentecostal, but now they appeal to one of these many adjectives (e.g., classical, holiness, finished work, Oneness, deliverance, word of faith, neo-, and others) to establish their independent existence *over against* other Pentecostals from whom, for whatever reason, they wish to differentiate themselves. There is, for instance, remarkably little difference between the teachings of Igreja Universal do Reino de Deus as set forth by its founder, Bishop Edir Macedo, and which views itself as a neo-pentecostal church, and those taught by the Assemblies of God, a classical Pentecostal church.[8]

At times, it has been argued that "The Church is Charismatic"[9] or even "pentecostal," and today, we hear much about the pentecostalization, even charismatization, of the church.[10] The editors have given the authors a free hand to use the term P/pentecostal in the way or ways that best helps them to describe the realities that they have been assigned. As a result, the term is used in a manner that is sufficiently broad, and a few members of some groups described as pentecostal may raise voices that do not readily approve. The ways that the various authors have understood their specific assignments, however, are fully in keeping with the task as it was envisioned by the editors. The breadth as well as the depth of what it means to be or how a group may be described as Pentecostal is explored in ways that are fully consistent with the historical, theological, and/or praxiological realities that these groups manifest. That being said, it is not the intention of either the editors or the authors of the various chapters to be or act in a triumphalistic manner. That the term Pentecostal has been or may be used to describe movements that do not always see eye to eye on all aspects of their history, theology, or praxis does not in itself disqualify them from the core realities that make them Pentecostal.

How then to situate the topic in a manageable manner without dismissing the important issues but yet also without getting bogged down in any one or another debate? The editors of this volume have adopted a framework for the book that holds together three commitments: first, it adopts a historical method that observes how and why the current debates have emerged; second, it expands on the discussion both through regional and thematic/disciplinary approaches that enable registration of the family resemblances as well as differences related to the contemporary global phenomenon; and third, the ensuing discussion provides numerous occasions for both insiders and outsiders to the movement – however such is defined – to appreciate and engage the issues. The rest of this introductory chapter explicates on these matters via comments on the three parts of the book.

Part I allows readers to trace, at least in broad strokes, the emergence of the dominant streams of twentieth-century pentecostal and charismatic renewal while also observing how critical scholarship on these movements has emerged. Cecil M. Robeck frequently writes as a social historian or as an historical theologian. In this case, his chapter focuses on the first generation of Pentecostalism, particularly in North America, although he places it into a larger narrative structure that takes seriously the global horizon. Even here, although portraying both the complexity and coherence of the early pentecostal movement clearly, there is already a contested diversity amid a recognizable unity. However, the plurality that seems from the beginning to have bubbled perennially under the pentecostal banner unfolds – even explodes – with the neo-pentecostal movement starting in the late 1940s. Picking up at this point, historical theologian Michael McClymond expertly traces the main lines of charismatic renewal through the mainline Protestant, Roman Catholic, and other churches not only through the early twentieth-century pentecostal streams but also through the mid-twentieth-century Latter Rain Revivals and other related currents. Read together, Robeck's and MyClymond's chapters say much about why we can talk about Pentecostalism as if it were a homogeneous phenomenon on the one hand, and also why it simultaneously makes sense to refer to Pentecostalisms as disparate phenomena (vis-à-vis their differences) that nevertheless hold loosely together (vis-à-vis the non-Pentecostalisms with which such might be contrasted).

The third chapter in this part of the book both sets in relief as well as prominently foregrounds the issues of pentecostal unity and diversity through a focused analysis of Oneness Pentecostalism. Whereas the preceding two chapters do not neglect the Oneness tradition – or traditions, as the case might be – there are important historical and theological differences at stake that merit a separate discussion within the overall framework of this companion. Of course, the divide between Oneness and Trinitarian Pentecostalism is specifically theological, not only with regard to the doctrine of God but also with regard to the understandings of salvation and the baptism of the Spirit, not to mention holiness codes of conduct and behavior. However, David Reed's historical and theological assessment – he is equally at home in both disciplines – spotlights both the unity and diversity of Pentecostalism writ large: there is no denying the theological similarities and even practices across the full range of Oneness Pentecostalism, just as there is also no doubt about the vast differences that separate white Oneness groups and churches from black and other ethnic versions across the global apostolic landscape (even movements). In short, Reed's chapter can be read as providing parallel depiction, even commentary, on Robeck's and McClymond's chapters in ways that illuminate the (contested) origins, growth, and development of Pentecostalism while also showing why diversity has been a central part of these narratives from the very beginning.

The second part of the book seeks to register regional developments, trends, and distinctives. We have divided things in just this way largely for pragmatic reasons – in particular, those things that related to the existing scholarly literature deserving of coverage in books published in such a companion series. This means that there is no explicit or sustained focus on Pentecostalism in Oceania or even the Middle East, for instance, except in passing. It also means that each contributor has had to make difficult choices about what to include and exclude within the word constraints established by the publisher. However, what does emerge in this part of the book is two features that build on but yet also add to the three essays in Part I: first, a deeper portrait that specifies what can only be discussed in more abstract terms in the initial set of essays, and second, a set of comparative lenses that illuminate the real life issues and the scholarly conflicts about how to interpret the global pentecostal movement.

Historian David Daniels's chapter, for instance, shows how the Day of Pentecostal narrative central to the modern pentecostal revival can function heuristically as an interpretive lens. Without denying the specifically theological value of tongues-speech as a pentecostal identity marker, Daniels's analysis highlights also how the visitation of the Spirit brought about observable effects in race and gender relations, both indicated in the Acts account as impacted by the pentecostal outpouring of the Spirit. To the same degree that pentecostal movements have not only included charismatic leaders but also empowered lay ministers in almost every arena, Daniels' chapter elaborates on pentecostal expressions in both ecclesial and civic domains. Similarly, theologian Jean-Daniel Plüss's chapter illustrates the diversity of ethnic Pentecostalisms across the European and Eurasian landmass, albeit not usually in ways that threaten to dissolve this category for understanding. The broader European sociopolitical and religious contexts both set in relief how North American and continental manifestations can be recognizably pentecostal on the one hand and clarify how scholarly analysis inevitably diverges in multiple trajectories on the other.

The next three chapters on Latin American, African, and Asian Pentecostalisms can be profitably overviewed together. These are three very different continents, each with a large variety of pentecostal churches, traditions, and movements. The three chapters differ firstly because of their methodologies. Daniel Ramirez works primarily as a cultural historian, whereas Cephas Omenyo is a theologian, and Wonsuk Ma is trained in biblical studies but has long published on Asian Pentecostalism. Further, Ramirez's home is within a secular religious studies department, while both Omenyo and Ma operate as theological educators engaged in missiological endeavors. Part of the result is that the chapter on Latin America explicates more of the cultural-historical factors, whereas that on Africa is more extensively theological. Ma, in part because of the overwhelming diversity of Pentecostalisms across the Asian continent, helpfully utilizes a case study approach that invites other more concrete investigations.

What is common to the three chapters is a grappling with the unity and the diversity of the movement/s, precisely what is laid out in Part I. Ramirez does this through historiographic and periodization analyses – certainly to be expected from his vantage point as a historian – but this is enriched through the interdisciplinary methods that inform his study. Omenyo focuses on the terminological, typological, and taxonomic debates regarding African Pentecostalism and attempts to come to grips with the many indigenous forms that have led scholars to include "pentecostal-type" in their efforts. As already noted, Ma decides that the way forward through the conflicted terrain is by describing three very different types of Asian Pentecostalism. Each can be seen to be grappling with how to understand the nature of Pentecostalism, even if in nonessentialist ways, while appreciating how a diversified approach can be helpful rather than debilitating.

Similarly, all three scholars deal with the theological aspects of Pentecostalism in their respective regions. Ramirez, as a cultural historian, focuses on how migration and globalization dynamics impinge on missiological and theologies of culture discourses. The African context presses soteriological (related to the doctrine of salvation) questions, the complex interfaces between missiology and public life, and the nature of the "Africanness" of Pentecostalism in that part of the world. The Asian case studies prompt similar questions about the indigenous character of Pentecostalism across that continent and also about the charismatic character of its various levels of manifestation.

If the five chapters in Part II of this volume provide greater depth for and expand our understanding of contemporary global Pentecostalism and its various vicissitudes, then the contributions that the third and final part of this companion provide further cross-disciplinary perspectives. These go from the more social-scientific to the more theological. However, the former are not oblivious to the explicitly religious and even theological aspects of the movement, while the latter are also methodologically interdisciplinary and sophisticated in their approach.

Chapters 9 through 11 are on the political-economic (Calvin Smith), cultural-anthropological (André Droogers), and sociological (Michael Wilkinson) facets of global Pentecostalisms. Each relies on personal ethnographical and empirical research while at the same time superbly drawing from the breadth and depth of the extant literature in these areas. They also take up contested questions in their various fields of study – that is, how Pentecostalism contributes, if at all, to the debate about religion's capacity to motivate socioeconomic uplift and political engagement (Smith); how pentecostal conversion facilitates cultural rupture in personal identities (Droogers); and how Pentecostalism exemplifies or undermines the dominant secularization narrative in the sociology of religion (Wilkinson) – in each case demonstrating the difference the pentecostal perspective and focus make in the discussion.

Methodologically with regard to these various disciplines, each chapter also suggests how the study of pentecostal movements advances theoretical discussion in the field. Smith's political overview depicts what political scientists and even politicians are gradually becoming aware of: that there is a political potential to modern Pentecostalism awaiting harness. Droogers shows how pentecostal religiosity does not allow dismissal of the transcendental domain in considering the repertoire of available behaviors and practices, while Wilkinson depicts how current social network theory is being expanded through a constructivist model informed by the centrality of testimony in the pentecostal social imaginary. In each case, then, the various disciplinary angles open up new vistas for understanding, but simultaneously, the focus on pentecostal movements precipitates new questions for methodological and theoretical consideration within these domains of inquiry.

The chapter by Daniel Albrecht and Evan Howard shifts from nonreligious to religious and theological methods of analysis. Their approach utilizes ritual theory and spirituality studies, both as deployed within the religious and theological studies domains. In that sense, this chapter straddles the insider-outsider issue in multiple ways – for example, via assessment of pentecostal beliefs and practices from both angles, even as Albrecht does so as a pentecostal insider while Howard locates himself more within the charismatic renewal tradition. Our two authors conclude via a consideration of the normative question about if and how Pentecostalism is to be considered a revitalization or renewal movement, which itself partakes of multiple discursive fields of discourse.

The last three chapters are explicitly theological in orientation. We make no apologies for including these chapters because the discipline of religious studies itself is increasingly recognizing that the understanding of religious phenomenon is reductionistic if the religious and theological self-understanding of its devotees and practitioners are neglected. The inclusion of these specifically theological analyses intends to register how pentecostal commitments make a difference not only to pentecostal praxis and ways of life but also to the understanding of such, for both insiders and outsiders. In each case, however, our authors are expert navigators of the scholarly enterprise that respects but yet is not uncritical about the confessional gaze.

How do they attain a measure of objectivity amid their writing from a confessional location? Mark Cartledge's Anglican charismatic orientation is measured by his training in the social sciences, and this shapes his work as a practical theologian in the continental sense that prizes empirical methodologies: his chapter thus skillfully surveys the contemporary pentecostal theological frontline and does so in ways that highlight its lived, practical, and empirical bases. Wolfgang Vondey's pentecostal commitments are balanced against his ecumenical sensibilities and training: his chapter not only maps the ecumenical character of Pentecostalism but also exemplifies the ecumenical methodology and its capacity to chart a way forward for competing faith communities. Last but not least, Veli-Matti Kärkkäinen is an ecumenical and systematic theologian but, here, brings this background into service of chronicling Pentecostalism as a missionary movement, especially in the interfaith encounter. Readers – theologians and otherwise, inside and outside the movement – will learn much about pentecostal self-understanding from attending to its missiological dynamics in particular, not to mention its ecumenical and broader theological vanguard as unfolded in these three chapters. The concluding chapter by Amos Yong will pick up on various theological themes and anticipate next steps in the many theoretical, disciplinary, and methodological discussions initiated in and through the study of Pentecostalism.

The preceding overview is designed primarily to register how the organization and execution of this companion takes seriously the insider-outsider issue in the study of religion but does so by confronting head on its challenges rather than take one or the other side in response. This has led to the organizational structure of the volume (which rationale has been here briefly unpacked), even as it has motivated invitation of different confessional, disciplinary, and majority world vantage points. In each of these ways, the editors trust that the coherence and diversity of Pentecostalism on the historically diachronic and globally synchronic scales can be appreciated. More can and ought to be said, and readers who come away inspired about the next research project in contemporary global Pentecostalism will have received the proper spirit in which this companion is being released.

Notes

1   See for example, **Asia**: Michael Bergunder, *The South Indian Pentecostal Movement in the Twentieth Century* (Grand Rapids: William B. Eerdmans Publishing Company, 2008), and Allan Anderson and Edmond Tang, eds., *Asian and Pentecostal: The Charismatic Face of Christianity in Asia* (Oxford: Regnum Books International and APTS Press, 2005); **Africa**: Ogbu Kalu, *African Pentecostalism: An Introduction* (Oxford: Oxford University Press, 2008); **Latin America**: Karl Wilhelm-Westmeier, *Protestant Pentecostalism in Latin America: A Study in the Dynamics of Missions* (Madison, NJ: Farleigh Dickinson University Press, 1999); **Europe:** William K. Kay and Anne E. Dyer, eds., *European Pentecostalism* (Leiden, Netherlands: Brill, 2011); and **North America:** Joe Creech, "Visions of Glory: The Place of the Azusa Street Revival in Pentecostal History," *Church History* 65 (1996), 405–24, and Adam Stewart, "A Canadian Azusa? The Implications of the Hebden Mission for Pentecostal Historiography," in Michael Wilkinson and Peter Althouse, eds., *Winds from the North: Canadian Contributions to the Pentecostal Movement* (Leiden: Brill, 2010), 17–37.

2   Gary B. McGee, ed., *Initial Evidence: Historical and Biblical Perspectives on the Pentecostal Doctrine of Spirit Baptism* (Peabody: Hendrickson Publishers, 1991).

3   See for instance the discussion of Gary McGee, "Pentecostal Missiology: Moving beyond Triumphalism to Face the Issues," *Pneuma: The Journal of the Society for Pentecostal Studies* 16:2 (1994), 277, and Boo-Woong Yoo, *Korean Pentecostalism: Its History and Theology* (Frankfurt am Main: Peter Lang, 1988).

4   See for example, **Anthropology:** Karla Poewe, ed., *Charismatic Christianity as a Global Culture* (Columbia: University of South Carolina Press, 1994), Barbara Boudewijnse, André Droogers, and Frans Kamsteeg, eds., *More than Opium: An Anthropological Approach to Latin American and Caribbean Pentecostal Praxis* (Lanham, MD: Scarecrow Press, 1998), and Sturla J. Stålsett, ed., *Spirits of Globalization: The Growth of Pentecostalism and Experiential Spiritualities in a Global Age* (London: SCM Press, 2006); **Sociology**: Emilio Willems, *Followers of the New Faith: Culture Change and the Rise of Pentecostalism in Brazil and Chile* (Nashville, TN: Vanderbilt University Press, 1967), Benjamin F. Gutierrez and Dennis A. Smith, eds., *In the Power of the Spirit: The Pentecostal Challenge to Historic Churches in Latin America* (Mexico City: AIPRAL, Guatemala City: CELEP, and Louisville: Presbyterian Church USA, Worldwide Ministries Division, 1996), and Stephen Hunt, Malcolm Hamilton, and Tony Walker, eds., *Charismatic Christianity: Sociological Perspectives* (London: Macmillan, and New York: St. Martin's Press, 1997); **Economics:** R. Andrew Chesnut, *Competitive Spirits: Latin America's New Religious Economy* (New York: Oxford University Press, 2003), David Martin, *Tongues of Fire: The Explosion of Protestantism in Latin America* (Oxford: Basil Blackwell, 1990), and Dana Freeman, ed., *Pentecostalism and Development: Churches, NGOs and Social Change in Africa* (New York: Palgrave Macmillan, 2012); **Politics:** Edward L. Cleary and Hannah Stewart-Gambino, eds., *Power, Politics, and Pentecostals in Latin America* (Boulder, CO: Westview Press, 1996), Paul Freston, *Evangelicals*

and Politics in Asia, Africa and Latin America (Cambridge: Cambridge University Press, 2001), and Timothy J. Steigenga, The Politics of the Spirit: The Political Implications of Pentecostalized Religion in Costa Rica and Guatemala (Lanham, MD: Lexington Books, 2001).

5 E.g., Tony Campolo, How to Be Pentecostal without Speaking in Tongues (Dallas, TX: Word Publishing, 1991).

6 See Gary B. McGee, "'More than Evangelical': The Challenge of the Evolving Theological Identity of the Assemblies of God," Pneuma: The Journal of the Society for Pentecostal Studies 25:2 (2003), 289–300, and James K. Bridges, "The Full Consummation of the Baptism in the Holy Spirit," Enrichment: A Journal of Pentecostal Ministry 5:4 (Fall 2000), 92.

7 See Allan Anderson, An Introduction to Pentecostalism: Global Charismatic Christianity (Cambridge: Cambridge University Press, 2004), 10.

8 Cf. Bishop Edir Macedo, Doutrinas da Igreja Universal do Reino de Deus, 2 vols. (Rio de Janeiro: Universal, 1998), and the Minutes of the 54th Session of the General Council of the Assemblies of God Convened in Phoenix, Arizona August 1–5, 2011 with Constitution and Bylaws, (Springfield, MO, 2011), Article V "Statement of Fundamental Truths," 90–94. The difference between these two denominations lies largely in their approach to political involvement and their teachings regarding exorcism and prosperity. Cf. Leonildo Silveira Campos, Teatro, Templo e Mercado: Organização e marketing de um empreendimento Neopentecostal (Petrópolis: Editora Vozes, São Paulo: Simpósio Editora, and São Bernardo do Campo: UMESP, 1999), 329n2. The beliefs of the Rhema churches of southern Africa and Deus es Amor in Brazil are also similar to those of the Assemblies of God.

9 Arnold Bittlinger, The Church is Charismatic (Geneva: World Council of Churches, 1981).

10 Russell P. Spittler speaks of Evangelicals in "Are Pentecostals and Charismatics Fundamentalists? A Review of American Uses of these Categories," in Karla Poewe, ed., Charismatic Christianity as a Global Culture (Columbia: University of South Carolina Press, 1994), 112–13; John Allen speaks of Catholics in The Future Church: How Ten Trends Are Revolutionizing the Church (New York: Doubleday, 2009), 375–413.

Part I

Historical Considerations

1 The Origins of Modern Pentecostalism: Some Historiographical Issues

CECIL M. ROBECK, JR.

INTRODUCTION

The historiography of pentecostal origins is currently hotly debated. To set in relief the major issues, this chapter will focus on the first generation of source material, from 1900 through 1926. We begin by overviewing recent historiographical proposals and then shift to early understandings of pentecostal history. Within these latter discussions, several competing narratives are identified, and the complexities attending to earlier outpourings as well as to those outside North America are registered. The conclusion notes the theological complications that carry over from this first generation into more recent historiographical and identity debates.

RECENT HISTORIOGRAPHICAL OVERVIEWS

The best assessments of pentecostal historiography to date have appeared in *The New International Dictionary of Pentecostal Charismatic Movements*. There Augustus Cerillo and Grant Wacker summarized and assessed the historiographical issues viewed from the perspective of American historians.[1] They began by recording the complexity and tensions that early pentecostal understandings of history represented – a mix of concerns over the relationship between divine initiative and human response, the linear or cyclical directions embraced in pentecostal historical thought, the limits on historicist assumptions in light of claims to supernatural intervention, how the movement should be defined, who should receive credit for the revival, and the significance of the movement for God's ultimate plan. Each of these discussions holds implications for what claims could be made regarding the movement's unique place in history.

After noting these preliminary factors, Cerillo and Wacker identified four primary approaches to pentecostal historiography. The "providential approach," which acknowledges the role of God in the governance of history, was most common among early writers. This approach is found less frequently today in any overt form, although it is still found in various denominational histories, largely the works of untrained historians. The "genetic approach," which attempts to root the movement in historical movements of the nineteenth century, is currently the most popular approach. It is useful for showing the relationship between Pentecostalism and other Christian movements. The holiness movement (Wesleyan and Keswick), reformed evangelical thought, and dispensational teaching have each been identified among the most common contributors to this line of thinking. One must also add the influence of Pietism if Europe is to be taken seriously,[2] and given the impact of early Pentecostals such as Frank Bartleman and A. J. Tomlinson, one might add aspects of Quaker thought. Over the past four decades, the "multicultural approach," which especially represents the concerns of various ethnic minorities within the United States, in particular African Americans and Hispanics, has raised new questions to be addressed, although the claims of its proponents, while significant, are still in a developmental stage. Finally, they identified what they called the "functional approach" that comes closer to responding to questions being raised by adjacent disciplines such as sociology, anthropology, economics, and political science. It explores why and how the movement appealed to those who ultimately joined it. This approach is most often employed by social scientists.

In the same volume, David Bundy sketched a global overview of pentecostal historiography.[3] The strength of this article lies in his analysis of western European perspectives, especially those originating in Scandinavia and from Latin America. Bundy noted several important historiographical concerns that first emerged in the study of Pentecostalism in Latin America. They include the claims that Pentecostalism is (1) a *response to social alienation*, (2) is best understood in relation to *sect theory* or (3) *deprivation theory*, (4) has been the *subject* of sociological and anthropological research, (5) been typified as a form of *folk* or *popular religion*, or even (6) as a *North American Fundamentalist export*. When these issues are viewed in light of the four approaches outlined by Cerillo and Wacker, most of them are consistent with the kinds of issues raised by the functional approach.

Since the publication of these essays, others have augmented the discussion. Allan Anderson, for instance, has set forth a clear account of the biases that earlier historians have brought to the task of writing pentecostal history, most of which have been limited by the narrow body of source materials they have used.[4] Most early sources and histories still extant were written in English or in some other western European language. Most American historians of Pentecostalism have not studied any of the available sources outside of the English language. Many, although not all, early sources were collected and published by men – pastors, evangelists, missionaries, and laity. When these factors are placed alongside the fact that many early resources from other parts of the world have not been as diligently preserved as European and American resources have, it becomes clear that writing a complete and objective account of the early pentecostal period is extremely difficult, if not impossible. It is biased in favour of the West, in favour of the United States, and in favour of males, especially white males. Many of those who carried the message, women and indigenous people, those who transformed it into something indigenous to various cultures, have been overlooked, marginalized, or forgotten altogether.[5] Thus, it has become incumbent on historians of early Pentecostalism to collaborate with others around the world in an attempt to overcome these deficiencies.

EARLY PENTECOSTAL UNDERSTANDINGS OF HISTORY

Multiple narratives may be found within virtually all early pentecostal historical sources – ecclesial continuity as opposed to the restoration of something lost, the leadership of Charles Parham as opposed to that of William Seymour or of no one at all, the priority given to white folk over against that given to people of colour, the claim that the movement originated in North America or that it emerged simultaneously or even spontaneously in different places around the world with little or no North American influence, and responses to the question of whether it appeared as a direct result of divine intervention or in an evolutionary fashion through the development of thought that was shared between established human networks are all present. Some of these narratives are easily distilled from the early sources, whereas others are more subtle, especially those that may conceal factors related to race or ethnicity. Some writers favour only one narrative, whereas others embrace a dominant historiographical approach but supplement it with other approaches as well. Questions of where Pentecostalism began, who should be credited with its early founding or its leadership, and how it became global are not new, but they have always been politicized.[6]

The earliest sources of pentecostal history are the hundreds of individual testimonies published in diaries, tracts, pamphlets, and religious papers around the world.[7] Occasionally, secular newspapers joined them, providing short overviews of the movement as it developed.[8] Before long, a few testimonies appeared in serial form.[9] These accounts were written by ordinary people, not trained historians, who recorded their personal impressions of the churches they visited and the experiences they had. They were piecemeal at best, often competing with counternarratives, and many of them were little more than self-serving promotional pieces.[10]

In 1906, Minnie Abrams wrote a brief account of her experience in the Mukti, India, revival.[11] G. F. Taylor's autobiographical theology, *The Spirit and the Bride*, gave a nine-page account of the movement as he understood it in 1908.[12] Frank Bartleman's *My Story: "The Latter Rain"* and T. B. Barratt's *In the Days of the Latter Rain* were first published in 1909 as small autobiographical accounts to which sequels were later added.[13] A. J. Tomlinson published his testimony, explaining the coming of "Pentecost" to the Church of God (Cleveland, TN) in *The Last Great Conflict*, published in 1913.[14] Aimee Semple McPherson skipped the serial format and published her first book-length autobiographical account, *This Is That*, in 1919.[15]

Some testimonies were collected to form larger, edited, historical narratives that became the first history books of the movement. B. F. Lawrence offered a regular historical column in the *Weekly Evangel* of the Assemblies of God between January 1 and April 15, 1916. The column included several apologetic pieces as well as testimonies outlining recent events. In May 1916, the Assemblies of God published this collection as a 120-page booklet titled *The Apostolic Faith Restored*.[16] It was introduced by John W. Welch, chairman of the Assemblies of God, who reflected a providential historiographical understanding when he claimed that those testimonies documented that "God's time-piece" had "reached the dispensational hour" and "the last times" were being ushered in.[17] Lawrence concurred, noting as a result that Pentecostals were "indifferent" to church history.[18] All that counted were what God had done in the New Testament and what God was doing in this new movement. For months, this booklet, which ironically contained a chapter on "Tongues in History" was touted in a full-page ad on the back cover of the *Weekly Evangel* – "Over 100 pages of the most important information ever gathered together of the rise and progress of the Apostolic Movement" – whose reading, it promised, would result in "the greatest and most fruitful service of your ministry."[19] Thus, the knowledge of recent pentecostal history was used to motivate pentecostal evangelistic and missionary efforts.

In subsequent weeks, Lawrence offered a new column. During that time, the editor of the *Weekly Evangel* intervened in the column to include several instalments of Andrew D. Urshan's testimony based on his recent journey to Persia (Iran) and Russia. The accounts of this popular evangelist were ultimately published in January 1918 as *The Story of My Life*, and like Lawrence's work, it followed the providential approach.[20] Lawrence officially resigned from further involvement in the column on December 16, 1916, and the column disappeared from the paper.[21]

Three years later, in 1919, a Swedish Baptist from Minneapolis, Minnesota, August Andrew Holmgren published *Pingströrelsen och dess Förkunnelse (Pentecostalism and Its Preaching)*,[22] which he contended was the first substantial study of this new global movement. Holmgren was greatly influenced by what he had observed in the pentecostal movement because it reminded him of the Baptists in Sweden. Although technically he never left the Baptist church, he did join the independent, Swedish-based, Filadelfia Church in Minneapolis, and for a number of years he served as the secretary covering their South American missionary work.

With the number of publications growing that criticized the movement, Holmgren decided that it was time for a broader, more positive assessment to be made. His would also be an edited volume, and although he drew much of his historical material (nine chapters) from Lawrence, he added several others. He was almost apologetic for the historical part of the book, because the events recounted were so recent. Still, half of Holmgren's work may be safely counted as history. To this historical material he added a number of "sermons, speeches and articles by writers in different countries," although many stemmed from the Upper Midwest. Some were Pentecostals, although a few were outsiders sympathetic to the movement.[23] In the end, Holmgren hoped that his work, which once again took the providential approach to historiography, would function as an apology for Pentecostalism in which he would demonstrate that the movement compared favourably alongside the account of the early church described in the New Testament.

The significance of this volume lies in the fact that it became an important resource for understanding the movement and the assessments made regarding the movement in several of the earliest scientific studies of Pentecostalism, all of them undertaken in Sweden. Efraim Briem, who wrote on the historical, organizational, and psychological dimensions of the movement, cited Holmgren several times as he set up the story of the movement's development beginning from the United States.[24] Emanuel Linderholm, who evaluated the movement as a contemporary example of folk religiosity with both ecstatic and apocalyptic elements, recognized Holmgren's limitations but announced that although the volume might be a "muddled" resource, it was nevertheless "sufficient to establish the main features of the movement" in the United States.[25] G. E. Söderholm, who produced a major two-volume set that became the first history of Pentecostalism in Sweden, cited it as well, suggesting that it was a corrective to Linderholm's assertion that Frank Bartleman had deliberately misled readers by claiming that William Seymour had not spoken in tongues before his arrival in Los Angeles.[26]

Several American theologians studied speaking in tongues during this same period,[27] but no major historical study of Pentecostalism would be published in English for half a century.[28] The most significant academic treatments of Pentecostalism during its first twenty-five years, then, came from these Swedish theologians and from the German theologian, Paul Fleisch, who set the stage in his 1912 history of the German *Gemeinschaftsbewegung*[29] for his later study of the *Pfingstbewegung* in Germany.[30] This makes the first English language, single-author history of the worldwide pentecostal movement Stanley Frodsham's *With Signs Following*, published in 1926.[31]

Like his American predecessors, Frodsham was not a trained historian, and his collection of vignettes firmly placed into his narrative follows somewhat the style of Lawrence and Holmgren, but it clearly reflects his own thinking as well. In this volume, Frodsham constructed a narrative of the "early days of the outpouring" using extensive quotations taken from a range of sources that were then woven together to form a cohesive story.[32] While he traced the growth of the movement around the world, he compiled more than a history book. Frodsham constructed the volume with an apologetic purpose, using the movement's success as evidence of his eschatologically driven restorationist motif that led to the final two chapters, "What Next?" and "The Glory Yet to Be Revealed." His 1941 revision saw significant editing and deletion of some material, with additional material on regions where revival had broken out more recently. Frodsham deleted the final two chapters that appeared in the 1926 edition, leaving his readers with a closing chapter that addressed the question, "Is This a Scriptural Revival?" and called his readers to repentance, urging them to seek the baptism in the Holy Spirit.

COMPETING NARRATIVES

In the early pentecostal sources, the restorationist motif, invoking themes such as "lost and restored" based on Joel 1:4–2:25[33] or "early and latter rain" rooted in Joel 2:23,[34] each representing discontinuity with the past, was dominant. The New Testament account of Pentecost (Acts 2) was viewed as the "early rain," providing the first chapter of the church's story. The pentecostal movement at the beginning of the twentieth century was viewed as the Latter Rain, signalling for many, the imminent end of the church age and the last chapter in its story.[35] Still, many Pentecostals were ambivalent regarding the role of the church through history and the place of Pentecostalism in it.

For instance, Frank Bartleman, a committed restorationist, authored an article in 1910 in which he suggested that the current outbreak of the Spirit was in keeping with the way God had always worked throughout church history.[36] Similarly, while the Assemblies of God published Lawrence's restorationist work, it also offered the complete set of Ante-Nicene Fathers for sale – at half price, no less – noting that their use would be an aid to its pastors.[37] Thus, from the beginning Pentecostals were sure that their movement was something new, but they were also sure that they were somehow related to the church through history, and in this way, they were also part of something ancient. Although the restorationist position dominated, lip service was still given to scattered movements and individuals throughout history who manifested what might be described as a "trail" of pentecostal phenomena.[38]

A second narrative present in many early accounts gives rise to another set of historiographical questions. In the United States, the earliest version favoured a 1900 Topeka, Kansas, origin, with Charles Parham playing the central role. As might be expected, Charles Parham and his followers championed this account,[39] which appeared in various secular and religious papers.[40] This was also the original narrative held and published by William J. Seymour from Los Angeles.[41] Charles Parham arrived in Los Angeles in late October 1906, having accepted the continuity of Seymour's work with his own, while Seymour viewed Parham as his "Father in this gospel of the Kingdom."[42] However, within days of his arrival, Parham rejected Seymour's work as both unseemly and fanatical, criticized Seymour for sending out untested workers,[43] and disparagingly labelled the mission "a cross between the Negro and Holy Roller form of worship."[44] Parham and his followers then took the position that Parham's work alone was the only *genuine* pentecostal work and Seymour's was a counterfeit, and Parham travelled the country denouncing Seymour's work.[45]

With Parham's rejection, the narrative published by Seymour and the Azusa Street Mission also shifted.[46] Seymour no longer mentioned Parham. He concentrated on getting out the story of the Azusa Street

Mission by publishing its newspaper, the *Apostolic Faith* (Los Angeles, CA), for growing lists of domestic and international subscribers and by commissioning and sending out a host of evangelists and missionaries. By this means and from his perspective, the "center" of the globally expanding revival became Los Angeles as these workers went forth. That message, not unlike Bartleman's, was carried by secular newspaper accounts, the *Apostolic Faith*, and the many Azusa workers who travelled the globe. No other center matched its global reach; it was unquestionably "the driving force behind the rapid spread of the movement."[47]

Once these competing narratives were in place, several factors worked against the Parham narrative, giving the Seymour account dominance. First, Parham commissioned and sent out comparatively few workers, especially missionaries, when contrasted with Seymour. Second, Parham seemed to have been undecided about which direction to go with his movement. On November 28, 1906, he resigned as the "projector" of the movement,[48] only to pick up that title again two months later.[49] Third, at the same time, Parham became embroiled in power struggles with Wilbur Voliva, the leader of Zion, Illinois, and with his own state director, W. F. Carothers, dissipating his energy.[50] Fourth, in August 1907, he was arrested and charged with sodomy.[51] In the end, the charges were dropped, but his reputation was ruined.[52] Finally, Parham's influence was strikingly regional, and his work was confined largely to Kansas, Missouri, Texas, and Zion, Illinois. Thus, his name was never widely known in the circles where the movement spread. G. F. Taylor,[53] A. J. Tomlinson,[54] even T. B. Barratt,[55] A. A. Boddy,[56] and Donald Gee[57] seem to have known only of the Azusa Street Mission and not of Charles Parham until much later. By that time, the Azusa Street narrative dominated.

The dominant story line throughout North America and much of Western Europe favoured the 1906 Azusa Street narrative with Pastor Seymour playing the central role. Seymour's communication network was much broader than Parham's. Although this narrative may have been popularized by Frank Bartleman, he was by no means its sole proponent. One could find it widely expressed in America's secular press,[58] and through the testimony of the Norwegian pastor Thomas Ball Barratt, who told of it long before he met Bartleman. While in New York in 1906, Barratt had read an issue of the *Apostolic Faith*, written the mission asking for guidance,[59] met Lucy Leatherman from the mission who prayed with him to receive his baptism in the Spirit, and having received it, travelled with a dozen Africa-bound Azusa Street missionaries from New York as far as Liverpool, England.[60] Even though Barratt appreciated what he had received by way of Azusa Street, he interpreted his experience of tongues as the "seal" of his baptism in the Spirit, and not the "evidence" of that baptism.[61] From Liverpool, he went on to Christiana (Oslo), Norway, where within days of his return, Barratt held a meeting that attracted widespread attention, including that of several future European pentecostal leaders.[62]

Barratt's 1907 meeting with Alexander Boddy from Sunderland, England, and the ongoing correspondence from George Studd to Alexander Boddy undoubtedly extended the influence of the Azusa Street narrative. Boddy publicized this narrative through his annual Sunderland Whitsunday conferences and his singular periodical, *Confidence*.[63] It would not be until 1926 that Parham's work gained traction in the United States and England. This narrative was adopted by Stanley Frodsham that year, although without mentioning Parham by name.[64] So thoroughly dominant was the Azusa narrative in Britain, that in his review of Frodsham the following year, Donald Gee noted that many would be surprised to read for the first time "of the first shower of the Latter Rain at Topeka, Kansas, in 1900."[65]

Only in Germany were questions raised early about the Los Angeles narrative. It came in the September 15, 1909, publication of "The Berlin Declaration" following a controversial summer revival that took place in Kassel, Germany, in 1907.[66] The Azusa narrative arrived in Kassel by way of two young Norwegian women, Dagmar Gregersen and Agnes Thelles, who were members of Barratt's congregation in Christiana, and they had been invited to share their testimonies in Kassel. The meeting in Kassel was quickly identified with fanaticism[67] and questions raised regarding these meetings led back to Los Angeles through Christiana. Drawing on complaints published in Los Angeles, detractors of the movement decided that the pentecostal movement associated with these and other places was not from the Holy Spirit above but "from below."[68] This led German Pentecostals to favour the Parham narrative over the Seymour narrative.

A third narrative that runs counter to both of these earlier narratives came in 1922, in a monthly publication edited by A. J. Tomlinson titled *The Faithful Standard*. While acknowledging the roles that Parham and Seymour had played, the unnamed author offered that in the end, leadership of the movement could not be ascribed to any particular individual, because "The Holy Ghost has Himself been the leader."[69] It was a theme very similar to that first mentioned in Los Angeles, when Seymour was asked about Parham's role,[70] and it has been echoed repeatedly by others. Carl Brumback, for instance, wrote an entire chapter to demonstrate why "Pentecost can 'call no man . . . father'. To find the 'Father of twentieth-century Pentecost,'" he contended, "one must look beyond the merely human to the divine. . . ."[71] This fact, he asserted, was something in which Pentecostals should "glory," for their movement was "in a definite sense, a 'child of the Holy Ghost,'"[72] governed by no single individual and no institution. Although this position appears again to champion the providential approach, it delivered those with apologetic interests from the need to acknowledge either someone charged with a sexual crime (Parham) or an African American (Seymour) as the founder of the movement and contributed to a revisionist account of history as well as to racial and ethnic bias.

WHAT OF PREVIOUS AND PARALLEL OUTPOURINGS?

As reports claiming that a great number of people had spoken with tongues in earlier years and in different places around the world began to spread more widely, one of the difficulties that confronted historians of the period was how to account for them in light of the Parham and Seymour narratives that privileged the United States as the fountainhead of the movement. Most contemporary historians are aware of the claims made regarding the presence (or absence) of charisms such as healing, miracles, speaking in tongues, and prophecy throughout the history of the church.[73] Many early pentecostal writers were also aware of other places where similar manifestations had taken place in the past or were taking place during the time that they wrote.[74] Even as the revival in Los Angeles spread, reports circulated widely from "revivals" and "outpourings" that had taken place in Wales (1904–05), in the Khassia Hills of northern India (1905), at Pandita Ramabai's mission in Mukti, India (1905–06), among pietistic Scandinavians in North Dakota and Minnesota (1906), at the Hebden Mission in Toronto (1906), in "The Korean Pentecost" of Pyungyang, Korea (1907), and among the Methodists in Valparaiso, Chile (1909). The historiographical question of the time was "How are these manifestations to be understood and interpreted?"

The most common approach was to label all prior incidents as preliminary showers to what would become the Latter Rain. They were related, but they did not fully represent everything that the movement now represented. As the author of the series in *The Faithful Standard* pointed out:

> There have been instances of people being baptized with the Holy Ghost and speaking with other tongues at intervals throughout history. But the first shower of the Latter Rain with the most distinct

evidences was at Topeka, Kansas, in 1900. . . . The first really great shower of the Latter Rain fell in Los Angeles, in 1905 [sic.], but before news could have reached them, a similar shower fell in a Mission School in India with the same wonderful signs.[75]

That such preliminary showers existed was taken for granted. However, what were they missing? Two important sites, one from Asia and the other from Latin America, illustrate the situation.

The author of the series continued, "We do not say that this was part of the Latter Rain outpouring, because those who received the Baptism did not realize what it was until after 1906, when they heard of the outpouring in Los Angeles. But looking back they realize it was the same thing, the same Spirit, the same power and the same manifestations."[76] These same claims were made regarding the revival in Mukti, India. According to Gary McGee, speaking in tongues did not occur there until after they had read about the revival in Los Angeles[77]; even so, those in Mukti such as Minnie Abrams took unknown tongues as a legitimate "sign" of baptism in the Spirit but refused to say that "no one is Spirit-baptized who has not received this sign."[78] The roots of the revival in Valparaiso, Chile, stemmed from 1902, but it clearly appeared as a pentecostal revival in 1909 when the group developed both a practice of speaking in tongues and a theology that included it. The story of this revival was serialized first in the denominational magazine, *Fuego de Pentecostés*, between 1928 and 1930 and was subsequently published as a book titled *Historia del Avivamiento pentecostal en Chile* in 1930.[79] However, the Pentecostals in Chile, like those in Mukti, understood the evidential nature of baptism in the Spirit to be drawn from a broader pallet of choices than most groups in the United States or even England were used to. From the beginning, Chilean Pentecostals have claimed "that dancing [in the Spirit], visions, prophesying, or other manifestations that conform to the Word of God" such as speaking in tongues are all valid evidences of baptism in the Holy Spirit.[80]

THEOLOGICAL DEBATES OVER THE ROLE OF TONGUES

The author of *The Faithful Standard* series was willing to acknowledge that the presence, power, miracles, healing, and even tongues-speaking among the Holiness folk occurred but claimed that they "thought of it only as a mighty manifestation of the power of God, and did not realize that it was dew drops of the Latter Rain."[81] In short, having a pentecostal experience was fine, but one was not a Pentecostal until he or she also had the theology of baptism in the Holy Spirit that explained or interpreted the meaning of that experience. The author viewed as wrong-headed what he called "holiness" explanations that explained these experiences as manifestations of "power" or saw "speaking in tongues" solely as a gift or a sign of the Spirit apart from the definitive eviden-tial explanation. It was necessary to have an explanation akin to that of Charles Parham's explanation, which had found its fullness of expres-sion at Azusa Street. This became the dominant explanation in North America, and it was spread to other nations by means of missionaries.[82] It also set up a competition between defining norms for the movement as a whole that continue to the present.

The debate over the appropriate evidence for recognizing bap-tism in the Spirit has important implications for the definition of Pentecostalism. Recent historians have cited the important role that shared materials and personalities played in the spread of the movement around the world, but seldom in the earliest years was this recognized or acknowledged. Perhaps more importantly, no one studied why there were competing narratives regarding the appropriate evidence(s) for bap-tism in the Spirit. In 1953, the missionary Bishop of the Church of South India, Lesslie Newbigin, posited, perhaps in keeping with the Mukti narrative, that the Pentecostal was an independent and vital stream of Christianity whose unique purpose was to enliven both Catholic (includ-ing Orthodox) and Protestant streams by bringing "the experienced power and presence of the Holy Spirit" to the whole Church.[83] What has been less studied is why Americans became so enamoured with the explanation first provided by Charles F. Parham. The answer may lie in the American context at the beginning of the twentieth century.

The latter half of the nineteenth century in the United States was dominated by several movements that seemed to coalesce as Parham began his pentecostal ministry. Among them were the continued influ-ence of (1) the Wesleyan-Holiness movement, (2) the growth of the modern missionary movement, (3) the rise of dispensational premillennialism that highlighted the imminent return of the Lord, and (4) "the Christian Evidences movement that relied on [5] Scottish Common Sense Realism for its method and expression." Parham's evidential formulation found fertile ground in this context.[84] In a more broadly fundamentalist-like religious culture searching for rational responses to the rising influence of Darwinian thought and the questions being raised by higher critical studies, to have a tangible evidence of the Holy Spirit's activity, indi-cating empowerment for international missionary work in light of the imminent end of the age, was only logical.

CONCLUSION: TWO HISTORIOGRAPHICAL STREAMS
AND THEIR LEGACIES

While many of these factors were also at work in Europe and in Asia, the distinctive testimony of American Pentecostalism was not readily embraced. More formative in the understanding of people such as T. B. Barratt in Norway, Minnie Abrams in India, and Willis C. Hoover in Chile were the Holiness and Keswick expectations that lifted up the place of sanctification, the role of baptism in the Spirit as the source of empowerment rather than a quest for a physical evidence of the Lord's dealings in Christians. Today, these two schools of thought still separate two types of Pentecostalism. In 1976, it was Kilian McDonnell, OSB, who defined as classical Pentecostals, "those groups of Pentecostals which grew out of the Holiness Movement at the beginning of the [twentieth] century."[85] Given this definition, both groups may be identified as classical Pentecostals. They share a common nursery that stems from the nineteenth-century holiness movement. The question remains, "Will their future be together?"

If these were the only two narratives with which students of Pentecostalism had to deal, differences might be relatively simple to resolve; however, they are not. As will be seen throughout this volume, especially in the chapters focused outside the United States, definitions of Pentecostalism differ widely. Although many of the churches described under the pentecostal rubric may become members in the Pentecostal World Fellowship, most would never fit, given the requirement that applicants affirm that they "believe in the baptism in the Holy Spirit with the evidence of speaking in other tongues as the Spirit gives utterance according to Acts 2:4."[86]

Notes

1   A. Cerillo, Jr. and G. Wacker, "Bibliography and Historiography of Pentecostalism in the United States," in Stanley M. Burgess and Eduard M. van der Maas, eds., *The New International Dictionary of Pentecostal and Charismatic Movements* (Grand Rapids, MI: Zondervan, 2002), 382–403.
2   Allan Anderson, *Spreading Fires: The Missionary Nature of Early Pentecostalism* (Maryknoll, NY: Orbis Books, 2007), 17–19.
3   D. D. Bundy, "Bibliography and Historiography of Pentecostalism outside North America," in Burgess and van der Maas, 403–17.
4   Anderson, *Spreading Fires*, 5–9.
5   Paul Tsuchido Shew, "History of the Early Pentecostal Movement in Japan: The Roots and Development of the Pre-War Pentecostal Movement in Japan (1907–1945)," unpublished PhD diss., Fuller Theological Seminary (2003), 17–22, 41–46.

6   Cornelis van der Laan, "What Good Can Come from Los Angeles? Changing Perceptions of the North American Origins in Early Western European Pentecostal Periodicals," in Harold D. Hunter and Cecil M. Robeck, Jr., eds., *The Azusa Street Revival and Its Legacy* (Eugene, OR: Wipf and Stock, 2006), 141–59.

7   Many examples may be found in papers such as *Apostolic Faith (Los Angeles, CA), Word and Work (Framingham, MA), Bridegroom's Messenger (Atlanta, GA), Pentecost (Indianapolis, IN), Triumphs of Faith (Oakland, CA), Church of God Evangel (Cleveland, TN), Confidence* (Sunderland, England), and to a lesser extent in *Spade Regen* (Amsterdam, Netherlands).

8   "Holy Jumpers Are Opening Missions," *Los Angeles Record* (November 20, 1906), 5; "Alleged Gift of Tongues," *St. Louis Palladium* (April 13, 1907), 3; "Woman Sticks to Bluks; Husband Asks Divorce," *Indianapolis News* (June 5, 1907), 4; "The 'Tangled Tongues' in Oregon," *Oregon Journal* (July 28, 1907), Magazine Section 3, page 5; "The Religious Realm," *Dallas Morning News* (August 4, 1907), 5.

9   Andrew D. Urshan's story was first preached at the Persian Mission in Chicago in July 1916. It was published in serial form in a column edited by B. F. Lawrence titled "The Works of God." Andrew D. Urshan, "Article XVII: Pentecost in Persia," *Weekly Evangel* 153 (August 19, 1916), 4–5. This serial ran through September 23, 1916.

10 Frank Bartleman's participatory accounts appeared in nearly twenty different Holiness and pentecostal periodicals in the United States, England, Norway, Sweden, and Japan, and in five of his books; Cf. *Witness to Pentecost: The Life of Frank Bartleman* (New York: Garland Publishing, 1985).

11 Minnie Abrams, *The Baptism in the Holy Ghost and Fire* (Kedgaon, India: Mukti Mission Press, 1906).

12 G. F. Taylor, *The Spirit and the Bride* (Dunn, NC: privately published, circa 1908), 90–99, reprinted in *Three Early Pentecostal Tracts* (New York: Garland Publishing, 1985).

13 F. Bartleman, *My Story: "The Latter Rain"* (Colombia, SC: John M. Pike, 1909), was followed by his more famous account, *How Pentecost Came to Los Angeles: As It Was in the Beginning* (Los Angeles: F. Bartleman, 1925). Similarly, T. B. Barratt, *In the Days of the Latter Rain* (London: Simpkin, Marshall, Hamilton, Kent & Co., 1909), was followed by *When the Fire Fell and an Outline of My Life* (Oslo: privately published, 1927).

14 A. J. Tomlinson, *The Last Great Conflict* (Cleveland, TN: Press of Walter D. Rodgers, 1913), 184–219.

15 Aimee Semple McPherson, *This Is That: Personal Experiences, Sermons and Writings* (Los Angeles: Bridal Call Publishing House, 1919). It was reissued in 1921 and 1923, each time with new material added.

16 Bernard F. Lawrence, *The Apostolic Faith Restored* (St. Louis: Gospel Publishing House, 1916), reprinted in *Three Early Pentecostal Tracts* (New York: Garland Publishing, 1985).

17 Lawrence, *The Apostolic Faith Restored*, 7.

18 Lawrence, *The Apostolic Faith Restored*, 12.

19 Cf. "The Apostolic Faith Restored," *Weekly Evangel* 138 (May 6, 1916), 16.

20 Andrew D. Urshan, *The Story of My Life* (St. Louis: Gospel Publishing House, *circa* 1917).

21 B. F. Lawrence, "To the Members of the Evangel Family, Greeting: -," *Weekly Evangel* 169 (December 16, 1916), 2

22 A. A. Holmgren, *Pingströrelsen och des Förkunnelse* (Minneapolis: S. V. Publishing House, 1919).

23 Holmgren, *Pingströrelsen och des Förkunnelse*, 4.

24 Efraim Briem, *Den moderna Pingströrelsen* (Stockholm: Svenska Kyrkans Diakonistyrelses Bokförlag, 1924), 29–31.

25 Emanuel Linderholm, *Pingströrelsen: Dess förutsättningar och uppkomst: Ekstas, under och apokalyptik i bibel och nytida Folkreligiositet* (Stockholm: Albert Bonniers Förlag, 1924).

26 G. E. Söderholm, *Den svenska pingstväckelsens Historia 1907–1927*, 2 vols. (Stockholm: Förlaget Filadelfia, 1927), 1:167n2.

27 George Barton Cutten, *The Psychological Phenomena of Christianity* (New York: Charles Scribner's Sons, 1912), 49–60; D. A. Hayes, *The Gift of Tongues* (New York: Eaton and Main, 1913); Alexander Mackie, *The Gift of Tongues: A Study in Pathological Aspects of Christianity* (New York: George H. Doran Company, 1921); George B Cutten, *Speaking with Tongues* (New Haven, CT: Yale University Press, 1927).

28 John Thomas Nichol, *Pentecostalism* (New York: Harper & Row, 1966).

29 Paul Fleisch, *Die moderne Gemeinschaftsbewegung in Deutschland* (Leipzig, Germany: H. G. Wellman, 1912; repr., New York: Garland Publishing, 1985), 585–89.

30 D. Paul Fleisch, *Die Pfingstbewegung in Deutschland: Ihr Wesen und ihr Geschichte in fünfzig Jahren* (Hanover, Germany: Feesche, 1957), reprinted as *Geshichte der Pfingstbewegung in Deutschland von 1900 bis 1950* (Marburg, Germany: Francke-Buchhandlung GmbH, 1983).

31 Stanley H. Frodsham, *"With Signs Following": The Story of the Latter Day Pentecostal Revival* (Springfield, MO: Gospel Publishing House, 1926).

32 Frodsham, *"With Signs Following"*, 5.

33 "The Pentecostal Baptism Restored," *Apostolic Faith* (Los Angeles, CA) 1:2 (October 1906), 1.1. Aimee Semple McPherson claimed that her often-preached and published sermon, "Lost and Restored" came to her in a vision while in London, England, in 1910.

34 Cf. Bartleman, *My Story: "The Latter Rain"*, T. B. Barratt, *In the Days of the Latter Rain*, and D. Wesley Myland, *The Latter Rain Covenant and Pentecostal Power* (Chicago: Evangel Publishing House, 1910).

35 William D. Faupel, *The Everlasting Gospel: The Significance of Eschatology in the Development of Pentecostal Thought* (Sheffield: Sheffield Academic Press, 1996).

36 Frank Bartleman, "God's Onward March through the Centuries," *Latter Rain Evangel* 2:10 (July 1910), 2–3; "The Wonderful History of the Latter Rain: Remarkable Repetition of the Acts of the Apostles," *Faithful Standard* 1.3 (June 1922), 3. It also appeared in journal titles such as the *Latter Rain Evangel (Chicago)* and *Spade Regen* (the Netherlands).

37 Cf. "Ante-Nicene Fathers," *Weekly Evangel* 143 (June 10, 1916), 7.

38 Lawrence, *The Apostolic Faith Restored*, 32–37.

39 W. F. C[arothers], "History of Movement," *Apostolic Faith (Houston, TX)*, special Reference Edition, 2.2 (1908) 1.3; Agnes N. O. LaBerge, *What God Hath Wrought* (Chicago: Herald Publishing Company, *circa* 1920).

40   In "Apostolic Faith to Go into Camp," *Houston Chronicle* (July 30, 1906), 5, Parham is the "leader of the movement." "Apostolic Faith," *Houston Daily Post* (August 2, 1906), 4, calls him the "projector of the movement," and "Apostolic Faith People Here Again," *Whittier Daily News* (December 13, 1906), 1, claims him as "founder of the faith." See also W. F. C. "History of Movement," 4.3–4, and Thomas Atteberry, "Zur Geschichte der Pfingstbewegung," *Pfingstgrusse* 1:1 (February 1909), 11–13.

41   "The Old-Time Pentecost," *Apostolic Faith (Los Angeles, CA)* 1.1 (September 1906), 1.2; "The Pentecostal Baptism Restored," *Apostolic Faith (Los Angeles, CA)* 1.2 (October 1906), 1.1.

42   K. Brower, "Origen [Sic.] of the Apostolic Faith Movement on the Pacific Coast," in the *Apostolic Faith (Goose Creek, TX)* (May 1921), 6.

43   Charles F. Parham, "Unity," *Apostolic Faith (Baxter Springs, KS)* 1.4 (June 1912), 9–10.

44   Untitled Item, *Apostolic Faith (Baxter Springs, KS)*, (January 1912), 6–7. While this quotation comes five years later than the rejection, it summarizes well Parham's earlier position.

45   "Apostolic Faith People Here Again," *Whittier Daily News* (December 14, 1906), 1; "Gift of Tongues without Babble," *Cleveland Plain Dealer* (January 11, 1907), 5.

46   "Pentecost with Signs Following," *Apostolic Faith (Los Angeles, CA)* 1.4 (November 1906), 1.1–2.

47   Anderson, *Spreading Fires*, 6.

48   "Voliva's Rival Quits Job," *Waukegan Daily Gazette* (November 30, 1906), 1.

49   Chas. F. Parham to Howard Goss (January 31, 1907), 2, copy at the Flower Heritage Center.

50   Parham to Goss, 2.

51   "Evangelist Is Arrested," *San Antonio Light* (July 19, 1907), 1.

52   "Notice about Parham," *Word and Work* 8:8 (October 20, 1912), 3.3.

53   Taylor, *The Spirit and the Bride*, 92, mentions Topeka, Kanas, in one line but does not mention Parham.

54   Tomlinson, *The Last Great Conflict*, 211, traces his reception of the baptism in the Spirit through G. B. Cashwell to Los Angeles but does not go back to Parham.

55   Barratt, *In the Days of the Latter Rain*, 142, mentions only Los Angeles.

56   Cees van der Laan, "What Good Can Come from Los Angeles?", 142, notes that *Confidence* does not carry a single reference to Parham but is in contact with Azusa Street from 1908 onward.

57   Donald Gee, "An Eagerly Awaited Book," *Redemption Tidings* 3:5 (May 1927), 5.

58   "Negro Bluk Kissed," *Indianapolis Morning Star* (June 3, 1907), 3; "The 'Tangled Tongues' in Oregon," *Oregon Journal* (July 28, 1907), Magazine Section 3, page 5; "Not 'Holy Rollers,' Says Leader," *Highland Park Herald* (August 3, 1907), 5.

59   David Bundy, "Spiritual Advice to a Seeker: Letters to T. B. Barratt from Azusa Street, 1906," *Pneuma: Journal of the Society for Pentecostal Studies* 14:2 (1992), 159–70.

60 "Speeding to Foreign Lands," *Apostolic Faith (Los Angeles, CA)* 1.5 (January 1907), 3.1; "Pentecost in New York," *Apostolic Faith (Los Angeles, CA)* 1.4 (December 1906), 4.5; Barratt, *When the Fire Fell*, 139.

61 T. B. Barratt, "The Seal of My Pentecost," *Living Truths* 6:12 (December 1906), 736–38.

62 David D. Bundy, *Visions of Apostolic Mission: Scandinavian Pentecostal Mission to 1935*, Studia Historico-Ecclesiastica Upsaliensia 45 (Uppsala, Sweden: Uppsala University, 2009), 176–79; [A. A. Boddy], "New Scandinavian Revival," *Apostolic Faith* (Los Angeles, CA) 1:6 (February-March 1906), 1.4.

63 W. Frodsham, "A Pentecostal Journey in Canada, British Columbia, and the Western States," *Confidence* 4:4 (June 1911), 141; A. A. Boddy, "At Los Angeles, California," *Confidence*, 5:10 (October 1912), 232–34. Boddy holds to the primacy of Azusa in Los Angeles and to the theory that throughout church history people spoke in tongues.

64 Frodsham, *"With Signs Following"*, 9.

65 Donald Gee, "An Eagerly Awaited Book," *Redemption Tidings* 3:5 (May 1927), 5.

66 The Berlin Declaration appears in Dieter Lange, *Eine Bewegung bricht sich Bahn* (Giessen, Germany: Brunnen Verlag, and Dillenburg: Gnadauer Verlag, 1958), 287–90.

67 "'Holy Rollers' Invade Germany," *Los Angeles Herald* (August 18, 1907), 6.

68 van der Laan, "What Good Can Come from Los Angeles?", 155–59, identifies Thomas Atteberry, "Zur Geschichte der Pfingstbewegung," *Pfingstgrusse* 1:1 (February 1909), 11–13, as the source of these claims. Atteberry, echoed some earlier claims of another Los Angeles pastor, Joseph Smale, "The Gift of Tongues," *Living Truths* 7:1 (January 1907), 32–43, but he clearly reflects the influence of Charles Parham.

69 "The Wonderful History of the Latter Rain," *Faithful Standard* 1:3 (June 1922), 7.

70 "Pentecost with Signs Following," *Apostolic Faith (Los Angeles, CA)* 1.4 (November 1906), 1.1–2. "We thought of having him for our leader. . . . But the Lord commenced settling us down, and we saw that the Lord should be our leader. So we honor Jesus as the great Shepherd of the sheep. He is our model."

71 Carl Brumback, *Suddenly . . . from Heaven* (Springfield, MO: Gospel Publishing House, 1961), 48.

72 Brumback, *Suddenly . . . from Heaven*, 63.

73 See, for example, Stanley M. Burgess's three volumes, *The Spirit and the Church: Antiquity* (Peabody, MA: Hendrickson Publishers, 1984); *The Holy Spirit: Eastern Christian Traditions* (1989); and *The Holy Spirit: Medieval Roman Catholic and Reformation Traditions* (1997), which provide a positive reading. Benjamin B. Warfield, *Miracles Yesterday and Today* (Grand Rapids, MI: Wm. B. Eerdmans Publishing Company 1918, repr. 1965), gives an alternate interpretation.

74 Bartleman, "God's Onward March through the Centuries," 2–3; Lawrence, *The Apostolic Faith Restored*, 34–39; "The Wonderful History of the Latter Rain," 6.

75 "The Wonderful History of the Latter Rain," 7.

76   "History of Pentecost," *Faithful Standard* 1.6 (September 1922), 5; Tomlinson, *The Last Great Conflict*, 211.
77   Gary B. McGee, "'Baptism of the Holy Ghost and Fire!' The Mission Legacy of Minnie Abrams," *Missiology: An International Review* 27:4 (2003), 518–19.
78   Minnie Abrams, "A Message from Mukti," *Confidence* 1:6 (September 15, 1908), 14.
79   The book was reprinted as *Historia del Avivamiento, Origen y desarrollo de la Iglesia evangelica pentecostal* (Santiago, Chile: Eben-Ezer Press, 1977), translated into English with additions by Mario G. Hoover as W. C. Hoover and Mario G. Hoover, *History of the Pentecostal Revival in Chile* (Santiago, Chile: Eben-Ezer Press, 2000).
80   C. Alvarez, P. Correa, M. Poblete, and P. Guell, *Historia de la Iglesia Pentecostal de Chile* (Santiago, Chile: Ediciones Rehue Ltda, n.d.), 54, includes the affirmation from the Declaration of Faith of *la Iglesia Pentecostal de Chile*, 10. "*CREEMOS: en el Espíritu Santo como una gracia y promesa para todos los creyentes en EL.* 11. *-Que: el hablar en otros lenguas, danzar, tener visiones, profetizar o cualquier manifestación conforme a la palabra de Dios, son una evidencia del bautismo del Espíritu Santo.*"
81   "History of Pentecost," *Faithful Standard* 1:7 (October 1922), 9.
82   Juan Sepúlveda, "Another Way of Being Pentecostal," in Calvin L. Smith, ed., *Pentecostal Power: Expressions, Impact and Faith of Latin American Pentecostalism* (Leiden, Netherlands: Brill, 2011), 46.
83   Lesslie Newbigen, *The Household of God* (London: SCM Press, 1953), 87.
84   Kenneth Richard Walters, Jr., "Why Tongues? The History and Philosophy behind the Initial Evidence Doctrine in North American Pentecostal Churches," unpublished PhD dissertation, Fuller Theological Seminary (2010), 223.
85   Kilian McDonnell, *Charismatic Renewal and the Churches* (New York: Seabury Press, 1976), 2.
86   See http://www.pentecostalworldfellowship.org.

Further Reading

Anderson, Allan, and Edmond Tang, eds. *Asian and Pentecostal: The Charismatic Face of Christianity in Asia*. Oxford: Regnum Books International, and Baguio, Philippines: APTS Press, 2005.

Haustein, Jörg. *Writing Religious History: The Historiography of Ethiopian Pentecostalism*, Studies in the History of Christianity in the Non-Western World 17. Wiesbaden, Germany: Harrassowitz Verlag, 2011.

Hollenweger, Walter J. *Pentecostalism: Origins and Developments Worldwide*. Peabody, MA: Hendrickson Publishers, Inc., 1997.

Irvin, Dale T. "Pentecostal Historiography and Global Christianity: Rethinking the Question of Origins." *Pneuma: Journal of the Society for Pentecostal Studies* 27:1 (2005), 35–50.

Van der Laan, Cornelis. "Historical Approaches," in Allan Anderson, Michael Bergunder, André Droogers, and Cornelis van der Laan (eds.), *Studying Global Pentecostalism: Theories and Methods*, 202–19, Berkeley, CA: University of California Press, 2010.

2 Charismatic Renewal and Neo-Pentecostalism: From North American Origins to Global Permutations

MICHAEL J. MCCLYMOND

From their early-twentieth century origins, Pentecostals sought newness. Breaking from existing traditions, they wanted a restoration of supernatural, apostolic Christianity. Citing a biblical text regarding the church's first Pentecost, they highlighted the interruptive, disruptive character of their own movement: "Suddenly there came a sound from heaven as of a rushing mighty wind" (Acts 2:2, AV). Unlike their evangelical and modernist contemporaries, early Pentecostals did not propose plans for the church's gradual amelioration. God would accomplish what no human beings could ever do. The Pentecostals wanted to replace Christendom, not reform it. This impetuous, impatient insistence on total change has never wholly left the global pentecostal movement.[1] Yet the Pentecostals from their earliest years confronted the existing Christian churches and their varied reactions of curiosity, antipathy, or sympathy. They faced what might be called "the prior existence of the church."[2] In responding to the reactions of others, they whipsawed between conflicting sectarian and ecumenical impulses. William Seymour went to preach in Los Angeles, only to find himself padlocked from a church building – a fitting symbol of the Pentecostals' identity as exiles. The sectarian perspective held that Pentecostals needed to maintain their message and not worry about who agreed with it. Other early Pentecostals – sharing the same supernaturalist vision – expected their movement to sweep through the existing churches, restoring apostolic faith and fervor to multitudes. Their ecumenical perspective held that the multiracial, multiethnic worship at Azusa Street in Los Angeles was prelude to a great reunification of nations and denominations. God was melting the denominational scrap metal in the fire of revival and preparing to remold it.

The present essay summarizes some ways in which the pentecostal message encountered the so-called historic churches – that is, those

already in place when the pentecostal movement began. The focus here
is on the post–World War II era. Whereas most American pentecostal congregations had formed themselves into denominations by this
point, there were signs in the 1950s of a crossing over of pentecostal-
type experiences and spiritual gifts to those outside the pentecostal
denominations. What became known in the early 1960s as the charismatic renewal was, in the words of David du Plessis, a "new Pentecost"
or "Pentecost outside Pentecost."[3] British pentecostal evangelist Smith
Wigglesworth is said to have prophesied in 1936 that the pentecostal
message would spread.[4] Yet when mainline Protestants began speaking
in tongues – followed soon after by Roman Catholics – this was both a
surprise and a shock to many denominational Pentecostals.[5] Some who
spoke in tongues continued in the historic churches. Whether welcomed
or merely tolerated, these mainline Charismatics formed themselves
into prayer or fellowship groups with like-minded brethren. In other
cases, especially in Latin America and Africa, entire congregations or
denominations were "Pentecostalized."

THE CHALLENGE OF TAXONOMY AND TERMINOLOGY

From a century's retrospect, the global pentecostal-charismatic movement shows a complex pattern, rendering it difficult to find an adequate
taxonomy and terminology.[6] Until recently, pentecostal-charismatic
historiography was based on North American history.[7] According to this
historiography, the century-long history fell into three phases, sometimes
described as three different "waves" of the Spirit: (1) a "Pentecostal"
era, beginning in 1901, expanding in the Azusa Street Revival in Los
Angeles (1906–09), and issuing in "classical Pentecostal" denominations
(Assemblies of God, Church of God in Christ, etc.); (2) a "Charismatic"
era, beginning around 1960 and affecting historic Protestant churches
(Episcopal, Lutheran, Presbyterian, Methodist, Baptist, etc.) and the
Roman Catholic Church, cresting in the 1970s and then declining; and
(3) a "neo-Pentecostal" or "Third Wave" era, beginning in the 1980s and
including evangelical Christians who became pentecostalized (e.g., the
Vineyard Churches), as well as independent groups practicing spiritual
gifts (e.g., the Word-Faith churches).

Even in the North American context, the notion of "three waves"
is debatable. This framework becomes less plausible in other global
regions. The American "first wave" is misunderstood when detached
from its international context. The years 1901–11 witnessed revivals in
many countries. To most contemporaries, the leading revival of the era

had taken place in Wales in 1904–05.[8] Nonetheless this revival did not involve such charismatic gifts as tongues-speaking, or at least not to the same degree as the revivals seen in India, Chile, and the United States. When believers outside of Wales prayed for a Welsh-type revival to come to them, something else often seemed to happen. The 1905 revival in India included tongues-speaking yet centered on repentance. The 1907 Korean revival stressed repentance but lacked tongues-speaking. The 1908 Chile revival featured visionary experiences.[9] Even the overtly charismatic revivals (India, the United States, Chile, etc.) showed local variations. The East African revival in Rwanda and Uganda (1930s–50s) permeated the Anglican Church, involved spiritual manifestations such as trembling, weeping, and visions, and yet did not highlight tongues-speaking nor split the church. In some respects, this African movement anticipated the "second wave" in renewing an historic church, although without an explicit teaching on Spirit baptism.[10] Twentieth-century revival history thus challenges any strict dichotomy between pentecostal and evangelical types of revival.

The first wave in Britain and Europe followed a different path than North America. Arguably, much of early Pentecostalism there was a charismatic renewal of historic churches. Many of European Pentecostalism's leading lights – such as the Anglican vicar Alexander Boddy in England and the French Reformed minister Louis Dalliere in France – never left their churches of origin.[11] Latin America also broke from the North American pattern. The pentecostal movement affected large numbers of Chilean Methodists, leading ultimately to schism and the formation of the Methodist Pentecostal Church. In Brazil, pentecostalized congregations describe themselves as *Presbiteriana Renovada* (renewed Presbyterians) and *Baptista Renovada* (renewed Baptists). In parts of Africa, there were indigenous churches (African Initiated Churches, or AICs) that experienced divine healing, dreams, and visions prior to the onset of non-African pentecostal influences. In Nigeria during the 1970s, the evangelical or "born-again" movement became substantially pentecostalized.[12] Since the 1980s, many Nigerian churches have highlighted spiritual warfare and the breaking of curses – considered a "third wave" emphasis in the North American context.[13] Ogbu Kalu underscored the essential continuity of Spirit-based movements in Africa. Pentecostal influences stimulated African initiatives to reclaim indigenous practices, often in combination with nonindigenous elements.[14]

The indigenous Chinese and Indian churches are also a challenge to taxonomic categories and terminological conventions. Grassroots, rural congregations in China show pentecostal characteristics, yet many have had little or no contact with Christianity outside of China. Academic specialists on China disagree as to whether such churches are aptly termed "Pentecostal."[15] Michael Bergunder had discussed this issue with regard to indigenous Indian churches.[16]

The evidence shows that the global movement does not fit any simple, synchronous sequence. In certain aspects (e.g., the early, near-total rejection of Pentecostals by historic churches), the North American history is anomalous rather than normative. It may be best, therefore, to think of North American Pentecostalism as a *regional exemplification* of the global Spirit-filled movement rather than as a *normative pattern* or a *diffusive center* for the whole. The complexity of the pentecostal-charismatic scene need not leave us devoid of heuristic categories. Allan Anderson suggests four: (1) classical Pentecostals; (2) charismatic renewalists; (3) neo-Charismatics (or neo-Pentecostals – the hardest to define); and (4) the indigenous Spirit churches (especially in Africa, practicing spiritual gifts prior to Pentecostalism). What brings these under a single category is that all are "concerned primarily with the *experience* of the working of the Holy Spirit and the *practice* of spiritual gifts."[17] Anderson's categories are workable and can function as a starting point, although one must be alert to data that might challenge any set of categories. Not only global diversity, but also rapid evolution, makes classification difficult. When the eighteenth-century scientist Carl Linnaeus produced his comprehensive classification of plants and animals, the species he examined were not changing as he studied them. If fish were morphing into reptiles within a decade's time, then we might have a fitting analogy for the taxonomic challenge at hand. Before one's research is complete, the Spirit-filled movement has already moved on.

CHARISMATIC RENEWAL IN THE MAINLINE CHURCHES

The charismatic renewal may have had roots not only in classical Pentecostalism but also in the 1940s Latter Rain Revival in Canada and Healing Revival in the United States.[18] In 1948, the Latter Rain Revival broke out in a pentecostal Bible college in Saskatchewan, Canada. George Hawtin and his students had prayed and fasted for weeks, inspired by Franklin Hall's *Atomic Power through Prayer and Fasting* (1946). With the leaders' laying on of hands, and accompanied by prophetic declarations, participants reported not only tongues-speaking but also manifestations of the "nine gifts" of the Spirit (1 Corinthians 12:8–10). What made the Latter Rain Revival controversial was its opposition to denominational patterns of church organization. It also affirmed contemporary "apostles and prophets" whose leadership was said to be essential to the unity and to the proper functioning of the church.[19] Although neglected in scholarly literature, the Latter Rain foreshadowed themes that emerged from the 1970s to the early 2000s, for example, personal prophecy, the "five-fold ministry" (apostles, prophets, evangelists, pastors, teachers), prolonged fasting, Christian unity, and contemporary worship. Latter Rain participants – ousted by the pentecostal denominations – became a diaspora of the Spirit. The 1950s–60s charismatic renewal, the 1970s Shepherding Movement, and the 1990s New Apostolic Reformation all owed something to the Latter Rain Revival.[20]

Another prelude to charismatic renewal was the Healing Revival, from 1947 to 1958. More than 100 healing-evangelists associated with the Voice of Healing network (and the periodical of the same name) crisscrossed the United States and Canada. Most notable were Oral Roberts, William Branham, and Kathryn Kuhlman T. L. Osborn took the Healing Revival overseas and stimulated missionary interest. Pentecostal leaders were generally ambivalent about the healing evangelists, who were largely independent of denominational oversight. Yet the publicity surrounding healing brought Pentecostalism to a wider audience. Another initiative was the founding of the Full Gospel Businessmen's Fellowship in Los Angeles in 1951 by Demos Shakarian, a former dairyman who wanted to give laymen from various denominations an opportunity to share personal testimonies. The fellowship grew to 3,000 chapters internationally before a split occurred in 1987. A sister organization – Full Gospel Women's Fellowship (later Women's Aglow, then Aglow International) – began in Seattle in 1967 and became larger than its counterpart.[21]

Prior to the late 1950s, only a few instances of pentecostal phenomena occurred outside of pentecostal denominations. By the early 1960s this trickle became a flood. The charismatic renewal brought tongues-speaking and Spirit baptism to growing numbers of Episcopalians, Presbyterians, Lutherans, and Methodists. Beginning almost simultaneously in 1967 in the United States and in Colombia, the renewal crossed over to Roman Catholics. The Catholic Primate of Belgium – Léon-Joseph Cardinal Suenens – helped secure Vatican sanction for the Catholic charismatic renewal. In 1975, a charismatic mass was held in St. Peter's Basilica in Rome. In 1977, the North American charismatic renewal climaxed in the Kansas City conference, drawing 45,000, with roughly equal numbers of Protestant and Catholics. By the 1990s even the Southern Baptists, who had long criticized Pentecostals, had growing numbers who privately spoke in tongues and/or accepted charismatic teachings.[22] Nonetheless, the ecumenical impulse so conspicuous in Kansas City in 1977 soon faded. Replacing lay leaders in the renewal with clerics, and reemphasizing devotion to Mary, many Catholic bishops wittingly or unwittingly severed Protestant from Catholic Charismatics. Moreover, the wider charismatic renewal in the United States and Canada began to decline in the 1980s, even as it expanded overseas.[23] Foreign-born citizens and residents in the United States have been an exception. About half of all U.S. Hispanic Catholics identify as charismatic.

The charismatic renewal differed theologically from Pentecostalism, because Charismatics held that the Holy Spirit was at work outside, as well as inside, the Spirit-filled communities. Some refused to say that they had "received" the Spirit in their experience of Spirit baptism, preferring to speak of the "release" of the Spirit, who had already been conferred in conversion (the evangelical Protestant model) or else in baptism (the Roman Catholic or High Church model).[24] Because many Charismatics doubted or de-emphasized the pentecostal doctrine of "initial evidence" (i.e., that tongues-speaking marks Spirit baptism), the boundaries distinguishing Charismatics from non-Charismatics became blurry. Some Charismatics formed "covenant" communities that worshipped, shared meals, and sometimes resided together. Catholics especially – with their history of religious orders – readily embraced the notion of a common life.

Early British and European Pentecostalism – more than North American – involved clergymen who remained in their churches of origin. The British-Norwegian Thomas B. Barratt was a Methodist-turned-Pentecostal who preached throughout Europe from 1906 until 1940. The French Reformed minister Louis Dalliere was also among the "old church" Pentecostals. His *Union de Prière* (estimated 1946) encouraged prayer for renewal. David du Plessis, whom some called "Mr. Pentecost," traveled in England, Holland, Switzerland, and elsewhere in the 1960s, spreading the charismatic message. Like du Plessis, the American Lutheran Harald Bredesen was a roving apostle of charismatic joy.[25] In Britain, Charismatics briefly cooperated with the Pentecostals, although they soon settled into more of a friendly coexistence. British evangelical leader John Stott opposed the charismatic renewal from 1964 until reaching rapprochement in 1977. Michael Harper, Stott's assistant at his London parish, himself experienced Spirit baptism and went on to lead the Fountain Trust, a service agency for British charismatic renewal from 1964 to 1980.[26] One success of the British Anglican Charismatics has been the Alpha Program – intended originally as a method for catechesis but later adapted for evangelistic use. As of 2014, fifteen million people globally are said to have attended an Alpha Program, including two and a half million in the United Kingdom alone.[27]

In the mid-1970s, the British house church or "restoration" movement espoused a more radical vision. Noel Stanton, of the New Creation Christian Community, commented that "we were enthused by the Spirit to follow the teachings of Jesus without attempting to dilute them in any way."[28] Sharing possessions, caring for the poor, and relating deeply were hallmarks. Some mainline Charismatics joined the house churches, frustrated by the sluggish pace of renewal in their churches. Built on the idea that the church needed to be restored to its primitive glory, one wing of the house church movement was exclusive and organized – with "apostles" who exercised strict rule – whereas another wing cooperated with outsiders and saw their leaders as enablers and servants to the community.[29]

In Germany the early renewal was associated with such Christian communities as the Jesus Brüderschaft. In Darmstadt, Germany, the Ecumenical (later Evangelical) Sisters of Mary under Sister Basilea Schlink manifested spiritual gifts as early as the 1940s. The French Catholic charismatic renewal began in 1972 and came to include 500,000 participants – the largest such movement in Europe. In Poland, a movement called Oasis (later called Life-Light) aided the renewal. The Hungarian Reformed Church generally resisted the renewal, as did almost all Orthodox churches. In the Soviet Union there were sporadic expressions among Orthodox, Lutheran, and Baptist Christians. Among Finnish Lutherans, some 49 percent of parishes showed charismatic influence by 1995. In Rome, the Catholic charismatic renewal began in 1971–73 in an English-language prayer group. Europe held the first major international charismatic gathering in Strasbourg in 1982, drawing 20,000 participants.

At the core of Catholic charismatic renewal in Latin America are the *grupos de oración* (prayer groups) that generally have approximately 25–35 people, meet weekly, and facilitate spiritual deepening. In Brazil today, an estimated 49 percent of all *active* Catholics are charismatic. During the 1990s alone, charismatic Catholics in Brazil quadrupled (from 2 million to 8 million) and met in 60,000 groups. The largest Catholic gatherings in Latin America are the charismatic rallies held in football stadiums on Pentecost Sunday, drawing up to 170,000 people. In Latin America generally, the ecumenical aspects of the renewal have not fared well. Fearful of losing their flock, and with little to gain from cooperation with Protestants, some Catholic bishops repudiated the movement. One Mexican bishop dubbed it "the smoke of Satan"; another forbade hand clapping in worship. Protestant-Catholic conflicts were evident in an infamous 1995 episode in which a Brazilian neo-pentecostal leader – from the Universal Church of the Kingdom of God – kicked a statue of the Virgin Mary during a nationally televised broadcast.[30]

During the 1980s and 1990s, Argentine Protestant Charismatics exerted global influence through the example of such revival preachers as Carlos Annacondia and Claudio Freidzon. Many Baptist churches in Argentina are charismatic (e.g., Central Baptist in Buenos Aires). The Argentines emphasize prayer, repentance, holiness, and unity.[31] John and Carol Arnott reported that their visit to Argentina helped launch the Toronto Blessing Revival in 1994. Throughout Latin America in the 1990s, the Protestant churches have been pentecostalized. Among them are the International Charismatic Mission in Bogota, Colombia, led by César and Claudia Castellanos (30,000 members), El Shaddai in Guatemala City, led by Harold Cabelleros (8,000 members), and Calacoya Christian Center in Mexico City (6,000 members). In Brazil, the Sana Nossa Terra (Heal Our Land) Movement includes 200 congregations and focuses on combating spiritism. In Cuba, the Methodist Church is predominantly charismatic, and so are many Baptists. César Castellanos introduced the "cell church" or G12 model (Groups of 12, or Government of 12) to aid church growth, with great effect in Latin America and also in Kensington Temple in London.

The charismatic renewal spread through the Catholic and Protestant mission churches of Africa, although more extensively in East and West Africa than Central Africa. The rapid spread of neo-Pentecostalism in Nigeria and Ghana caused some mainline churches to embrace the charismatic renewal. In Ethiopia, the Evangelical Mekane Yesu Church (Lutheran) and the Meserete Kristos Church (Mennonite) have experienced renewal. Tanzania has witnessed a strong renewal among Lutherans.[32] The German pentecostal revivalist Reinhard Bonnke has held mass rallies with up to 2 million people at one time in Nigeria and other nations. As of 2011, almost 70 million persons have signed decision cards at his campaigns.[33] Boundaries between historic and newer churches are blurry, because renewal movements arose in the context of interdenominational school and campus organizations. Methods for evangelism include door-to-door visitation, "cottage meetings" in homes, and preaching in buses, on street corners, and other public venues. African Pentecostal-Charismatics typically seek to establish a

Christian presence in the public sphere. Businesses bear names such as "To God be the Glory Computers," "Hands of God Beauty Salon," or "El Shaddai Fast Foods."[34]

Although Asia as a whole remains primarily non-Christian, some regions have seen waves of renewal. This includes South Korea, the Philippines, and China, as well as regions of India, Indonesia, and Malaysia. The rapid expansion of the Korean Church began with the 1907 Great Revival, centered in Pyongyang – in present-day North Korea – and continuing through the era of the Japanese occupation and Korean War. The 1970s–80s witnessed mass evangelistic campaigns, jointly hosted by many denominations. Subsequently, Korean revival took a more pentecostalized form, under the initiative of David Yonggi Cho and his 800,000-member Yoido Full Gospel Church, in Seoul, South Korea.[35] In China, perhaps half of the unregistered churches display pentecostal characteristics. Singapore has been a center for charismatic renewal, including the Anglican Church under the leadership (since 1982) of Bishop Moses Tay. In the Philippines, Mariano "Mike" Velarde founded the El Shaddai ministry for Catholic Charismatics, with some 300,000 registered members and up to 2 million attendees at Sunday gatherings (as of 2003). In India, the most visible expression of Catholic Renewal has been in Chalakudy, Kerala, where Father Mathew Naikomparambil holds weekly crusades and brings together up to 200,000 for conferences. From the 1970s onward, both Pentecostalism and charismatic renewal expanded in Malaysia. In Indonesia, the Timor revival (1965–68) – like the earlier "Great Repentance" Revival in Nias (1916–22) – included charismatic manifestations of tongues-speaking, prophecy, and divine healing.[36] In Australia, the mainline charismatic renewal weakened during the late 1990s, with many leaving the Uniting Church to join the new charismatic networks. Also during the 1990s the Toronto revival affected the historic churches in Australia, as in Britain. In New Zealand, renewal in the Anglican and Presbyterian churches was stronger than in Australia. Papua New Guinea experienced a spiritual outpouring in 1988–89 at the Lutheran Training Center.

TRENDS AND THEMES IN GLOBAL NEO-PENTECOSTALISM

The term "neo-Pentecostal" embraces various churches. In China alone, there are innumerable indigenous groups.[37] In the United States, the so-called Word-Faith (or prosperity) teaching was long associated with Kenneth Hagin, Sr., and his Rhema Bible Institute (Tulsa, Oklahoma).

Hagin – together with Kenneth Copeland, Frederick K. C. Price, and others – helped launch a global movement.[38] Rhema has more than 23,000 alumni, many of whom planted churches. Ray McCauley's Rhema Bible Church in Randburg, South Africa (16,000 members; with 270 affiliated congregations) is one example. Another is the 2,000-member Word of Life Church in Uppsala, Sweden.[39] In Brazil, an influential neo-pentecostal church is the Universal Church of the Kingdom of God (UCKG), founded in 1977 by Edir Macedo, a former lottery worker. The UCKG embraces the Word-Faith message and establishes new churches worldwide.[40] During the 1980s, the UCKG conducted a holy war against Brazilian spiritists, desecrating their temples and "tying up" their spirit beings through prayer.[41] Their prosperity message has become controversial.[42] Another controversial feature in neo-Pentecostalism is an allegedly authoritarian style, whereby leaders are regarded as God's "anointed" and not accountable to anyone else.[43] In Western Nigeria, two neo-pentecostal churches founded in the 1980s were William Kumuyi's Deeper Life Bible Church and David Oyedepo's Living Faith Church (renamed Winners' Chapel). Oyedepo claims that his main tabernacle – located near Lagos and seating more than 50,000 – is the world's largest church building. Mensa Otabil of Ghana is known for his Afrocentric teaching, stressing the global role of the black race.[44]

In surveying neo-Pentecostalism, a thematic approach may work best. Here we will consider a series of movements in rough, chronological sequence. *Healing ministry* – although never absent from Pentecostalism – was reemphasized in the late 1940s by independent, itinerant healing-evangelists (as noted earlier) and has continued since the 1970s (Benny Hinn, Randy Clark, Mahesh Chavda). In many global regions, healing rather than tongues-speaking is the most widely known charismatic manifestation. Moreover, healing stimulates church growth. Non-Christians who report divine healing later affiliate with pentecostal churches, often accompanied by family members. All around the world, popular religion is pragmatic. Because many of the sick are healed after receiving pentecostal prayers, people regard Pentecostalism as true. Of those in certain Chinese churches, 90 percent attribute their conversion to a healing experience.[45] Episcopal and Catholic Charismatics – catering to a more upscale clientele – practice "inner healing," redressing emotional wounds from traumatic experiences. Agnes Sanford and Drs. Frances and Judith MacNutt have been leaders in this area.

From their earliest days, pentecostal-charismatic Christians have been proponents of *media ministries* in their successive forms – radio, television, cassette tapes, CDs, DVDs, and the Internet. A recent development is the live streaming of worship and revival services. The International House of Prayer (IHOP) in Kansas City, Missouri, maintains twenty four hour prayer, now broadcast over the Internet. God.tv broadcasts services from various locations. Modern media makes it possible to penetrate new public and private spaces and thus goes hand in hand with a missionary impulse. African neo-Pentecostals believe that recorded scripture or preaching (on tapes, CDs, or DVDs) has curative powers.[46]

During the 1970s, the *Shepherding Movement* appealed to a notion of "five-fold ministry" to argue that every believer needed to submit to a higher authority. To critics, the movement looked like pyramid marketing, with its own leaders ("the Ft. Lauderdale Five") at the apex. There were reports that disciples had to consult with their authority figures over decisions regarding education, finances, and marriage. To proponents, the movement was a pastoral response to the rootless, undisciplined ethos of 1970s charismatic Christianity. When televangelist Pat Robertson branded it as heresy, things soon unraveled.

The 1980s witnessed a Pentecostalization of North American evangelicals, exemplified by John Wimber and his Vineyard Churches.[47] Wimber used the term "power evangelism" to refer to a phenomenon better known outside of the United States – namely, healing ministry as a means of witness to nonbelievers. Wimber's course on healing – co-taught at Fuller Seminary with C. Peter Wagner – provoked controversy over *signs and wonders* in Christian ministry.[48] In the 1980s neo-Pentecostals began to emphasize *prophetic gifts* and hold conferences at which self-described prophets delivered personalized messages to individuals seeking their spiritual guidance. This development – like the Shepherding Movement – raised issues of spiritual authority. Debate centered on the "Kansas City Prophets" (Paul Cain, Bob Jones, et al.), associated with Mike Bickle and his Metro Christian Vineyard Church. The failure of high-profile predictions – including Wimber's forecast of a Christian revival in England – led to greater caution. Prophetic statements had to pass tests before being promulgated; prophets too had to be tested.[49] Some written prophecies were less personal and more apocalyptic, predicting a harvest both of wickedness and of souls to be saved before Christ's return.[50]

The 1990s witnessed the rise of *strategic-level spiritual warfare*. C. Peter Wagner taught that demons could dominate not only individuals but also whole communities. "Warfare prayer" could break satanic "strongholds" and thus facilitate evangelism.[51] Such teachings fit well in an African context, where exorcism or deliverance ministry is understood as a part of conversion.[52] One step in the process was "spiritual mapping" – that is, locating sites of false religion, violence, or broken covenants that may have given demons a "legal right" to infest a territory. Another step was "identificational repentance," whereby believers verbally confess the sins of others, asking for God's forgiveness. For some neo-Pentecostals, overcoming evil requires action as well as prayer. In 1990, the New Zealand native John Dawson founded the International Reconciliation Coalition to redress historic crimes and injustices.[53] Some Pentecostals and neo-Pentecostals began to show greater interest in social change and social justice. Donald E. Miller's research – based on interviews at twenty-nine sites – revealed a shift toward social engagement among global Pentecostal-Charismatics.[54]

The 1990s witnessed major revivals in Toronto, Canada (from 1994), and Pensacola, Florida (from 1995).[55] Canadian Vineyard pastors, John and Carol Arnott, welcomed more than two million visitors to their congregation over several years. The revival's physical manifestations – laughing, weeping, shouting, trembling, and even "animal sounds" – disturbed many observers and led Wimber to cut ties of fellowship with this congregation. Despite opposition, Toronto became a neo-pentecostal pilgrimage site. Thousands of churches in North America, Britain, and East Asia were affected when their members returned from Toronto. Holy Trinity Brompton (a London suburb) embraced the Toronto movement (and launched the Alpha Program – as noted earlier). After migrating to London, the movement spread to Pensacola, Florida, where the *Brownsville Revival* broke out in 1995 in an Assemblies of God church. The Pensacola revival centered on repentance. The Toronto Movement, by contrast, offered a deep, refreshing experience of God's love, especially welcome to beleaguered pastors.

Worship is central for neo-Pentecostals. With roots in the California counterculture, and in the "Jesus rock" of Larry Norman and Keith Green, contemporary Christian music has mushroomed since the 1980s.[56] The Australian megachurch, Hillsong, is emblematic of this trend.[57] In what we might call the *manifestational approach to prayer*, worshippers do not petition God with specific requests but instead seek to "draw God's presence." Today's younger neo-Pentecostals see worship *as* evangelism, worship *as* healing. Sins, addictions, and burdens will be lifted – if only God's people worship.[58] *The 24/7 or house of prayer movement*, led by Mike Bickle and Lou Engle, and centered on the IHOP in Kansas City, encourages prolonged and intense prayer, often accompanied by fasting. The DVD of George Otis, Jr., *Transformations*

(1999), offered case studies to show that prayer changes entire cities and nations, preparing the way for church revival and even for economic revitalization. Global migration has produced *migrant/immigrant missionaries*, who see themselves as sent not to earn money but to effect spiritual revitalization. African Christians are generally more hopeful about Europe's religious future than are European Christians. They believe that God will save Europe from secularism.[59]

One overarching neo-pentecostal theme is *dominionism*. Beginning with the Latter Rain Revival, neo-Pentecostals began to reject the eschatological pessimism of premillenialism and to embrace postmillennialism and the vision of a restored or "glorious church."[60] Some have insisted that Christ's earthly reign will be exercised through an elite corps of disciples, led by super apostles whose authority will exceed that of the first-century apostles.[61] Others – such as C. Peter Wagner – offer less grandiose visions for the future and yet insist that the church must seek to influence all "seven mountains" of human life (business, government, media, arts and entertainment, education, the family, and religion).[62] This approach has appeal in Africa, where many Christians see no problem in public expressions of faith. Frederick Chiluba, president of Zambia from 1991 to 2001, declared on national television: "I submit the Government and the entire nation of Zambia to the Lordship of Jesus Christ." The preamble to Zambia's constitution declares the republic "a Christian nation."[63] The Nigerian-based Redeemed Christian Church of God (RCCG) seems a case study in dominionism. The RCCG plants not only churches around the world but also banks, supermarkets, bakeries, and other businesses thus challenging any division of spiritual and physical.[64]

A final theme is *Christian unity*. A French study traced a process of "denominational recomposition" bringing divided Christians back together.[65] Some speak of a "convergence movement," while others use the phrase "city church" to call Christians to become united with all other Christians in their locality.[66] The Protestant churches of Buenos Aires, Argentina, have begun such a process. Neo-Pentecostals favoring the "five-fold" ministry call for something like a renewed episcopacy, whereby one pastor will coordinate all ministries within a given region. This latest idea on church governance is also the oldest.

CONCLUDING THOUGHTS

There is little doubt about the scope of the charismatic renewal. In the United States, a 2006 poll indicated that 23 percent of all Christian believers identified themselves as renewalists, with 5 percent belonging to classical pentecostal denominations and 18 percent to other churches.[67] Globally speaking, Charismatics outnumber Pentecostals by a factor of some eight or nine to one.[68] The Roman Catholic Church claims that 120 million of its baptized members are Charismatic, or almost 1 of every 9 Catholics globally.

As the presentation has suggested, it is time to abandon what one might call the Big Bang theory of global Pentecostalism, namely, the notion that all the major elements of later pentecostal-charismatic theory and practice were already present in early twentieth-century American Pentecostalism. Instead of a Big Bang – where everything emanates from a single center – we should think of the twentieth century as a String-of-Firecrackers. Each new bang was separated from the others in time and space and represented a diffusive center for new pentecostal-charismatic ideas or practices. Such centers would include – southern California (for the Azusa Street Revival of 1906–09, the 1940s fasting revival in San Diego, the early charismatic renewal of the 1950s–60s, and the 1980s "Third Wave" movement); the south central United States (for the 1940s healing revival and the 1970s–80s emergence of prosperity theology); Saskatchewan, Canada (for the 1948 Latter Rain Revival); Kansas City, Missouri (for the 1980s prophetic movement and the more recent 24/7 prayer movement); England (for the 1980s house church or restorationist movement and the 1990s Alpha Program); Argentina and Nigeria (for concepts of spiritual warfare, since the 1980s); South Korea (for "prayer mountains" and other intensive prayer practices, and the "cell church" model, since the 1980s); Toronto, Canada, and Pensacola, Florida (for two mid-1990s revivals); Sydney, Australia (for Hillsong and its global influence on contemporary worship, since the 1990s); and Capetown, South Africa (for the Global Day of Prayer movement, since the 2000s).

Assessments of charismatic renewal and neo-Pentecostalism depend on one's academic discipline and/or personal stance. Social scientists show interest in the themes of innovation, growth, institutionalization, sect formation, and new religious practices. Anthropologists highlight indigenization – the ways in which emerging pentecostal-charismatic groups incorporate elements of local cultures. Christian believers will likely celebrate the movement's missionary successes. Yet believers themselves show differences of perspective. Classical Pentecostals generally see charismatic renewal as their legacy and evaluate it accordingly. Mainline Charismatics have often found early Pentecostalism to be rude and unsophisticated, and they interpret charismatic renewal as a necessary corrective. Ecumenical Christians have called the charismatic renewal a new opportunity for the church.[69]

For Spirit-filled Christians, the growing ranks of post-Charismatics and post-Pentecostals might be cause for concern.[70] According to classical pentecostal theology, de-Pentecostalization ought not happen. Spirit baptism is thought to be a once-for-all, permanent transition to a higher state of Christian experience. Likewise, the spiritual outpouring of the early 1900s was considered to be the final, definitive, end-times revival. What early Pentecostals did not expect was the gradual institutionalization and stagnation of their own "Spirit-filled" churches. Today, most native-born Assemblies of God United States congregations are not growing numerically and witness only occasional manifestations of charismatic gifts in their worship services.[71] Might we then refer to some congregations as well as some individuals as post-Pentecostal? Could an entire denomination become post-Pentecostal? The question is worth pondering. There are further questions: Can post-Pentecostal individuals, congregations, or denominations be re-pentecostalized? If so, in what way?

It has been the fate of every Christian renewal movement to lose momentum and focus over time. The list would include early Christian monasticism, the medieval religious orders, Catholic mysticism, Protestantism, Puritanism, Jansenism, Pietism, Methodism, and the Holiness Movement. The renewal itself has had to be renewed. From a century's retrospect, Pentecostalism may be less like a house wired with electricity and more like a battery that becomes depleted and needs recharging. On this basis, we might say that charismatic renewal is not an historical epoch, or a finished process, but an ongoing and indeed permanent challenge. To adapt an old Calvinist slogan, *ecclesia reformata semper reformanda* ("the reformed church is always being reformed"), we might say instead, *ecclesia renovata semper renovanda* ("the renewed church is always being renewed").

Notes

1   This impulse described here has been variously termed "restorationist," "apostolic," "radical," and "primitivist." Grant Wacker's *Heaven Below: Early Pentecostals and American Culture* (Cambridge, MA: Harvard University Press, 2001), opts for "primitivist," which he defines as "a determination to return to first things, original things, fundamental things," expressing itself in a "yearning to know God directly" (11–12).

2   Simon Chan, *Pentecostal Theology and the Christian Spiritual Tradition* (Sheffield, UK: Sheffield Academic Press, 2000), 97–104.

3   David du Plessis, *Pentecost Outside "Pentecost": The Astounding Move of God in the Denominational Churches* (n.p., 1960).

4   Russell P. Spittler, "David Johannes du Plessis," in Stanley M. Burgess and Eduard M. Van Der Maas, eds., *The New International Dictionary of Pentecostal and Charismatic Movements* (Grand Rapids, MI: Zondervan, 2003), 590.

5   Benjamin Wagner, "Pentecost Outside Pentecost: Classical Pentecostal Responses to the Charismatic Renewal Movement in the United States, 1960–82," unpublished PhD diss., Saint Louis University (2009).

6   See Allan Anderson, "Varieties, Taxonomies, Definitions," in Allan Anderson, Michael Bergunder, André Droogers, and Cornelis van der Laan, eds., *Studying Global Pentecostalism: Theories and Methods* (Berkeley: University of California Press, 2010), 13–29; Paul Freston, "'Neo-Pentecostalism' in Brazil: Problems of Definition and the Struggle for Hegemony," *Archives de sciences sociales des religions* 44 (1999), 145–62.

7   Prominent among those who challenge the North-American-centered narrative is Allan Anderson's *An Introduction to Pentecostalism: Global Charismatic Christianity* (Cambridge: Cambridge University Press, 2004).

8   For a Wales-centered view of the early 1900s revivals, see Noel Gibbard, *On the Wings of the Dove: The International Effects of the 1904–05 Revival* (Bridgend, Wales: Bryntirion Press, 2002).

9   Gary B. McGee, "'Latter Rain Falling in the East': Early-Twentieth-Century Pentecostalism in India and the Debate Over Speaking in Tongues," *Church History* 68 (1999), 648–65; Willis Collins Hoover, *History of the Pentecostal Revival in Chile*, trans. Mario G. Hoover (Santiago, Chile: Imprenta Eben-Ezer, 2000); Sung-Deuk Oak, ed., *Primary Sources of the Korean Great Revival, 1903–1908* (Seoul: Institute for Korean Church History, 2007).

10 Brian Stanley, "East African Revival: African Initiative within a European Tradition," *Churchman* 92 (1978), 6–22; Kevin Ward and Emma Wild-Wood, eds., *The East African Revival: History and Legacies* (Burlington, VT: Ashgate, 2012).

11 Walter J. Hollenweger, *Pentecostalism: Origins and Development Worldwide* (Peabody, MA: Hendrickson Publishing, 1997), 334–49.

12 Richard Burgess, *Nigeria's Christian Revolution: The Civil War Revival and Its Pentecostal Progeny (1976–2006)* (Carlisle, UK: Paternoster, 2008).

13 C. Peter Wagner and Joseph Thompson, *Out of Africa: How the Spiritual Explosion among Nigerians is Impacting the World* (Ventura, CA: Regal Books, 2004).

14 Ogbu Kalu, *African Pentecostalism: An Introduction* (New York: Oxford University Press, 2008). Paul Kollman offers an appreciation and critique of Kalu in "Classifying African Christianities: Past, Present, and Future: Part One," *Journal of Religion in Africa* 40 (2010), 3–32.

15 See Gotthard Oblau "Pentecostals by Default? Contemporary Christianity in China," and Edmond Tang, "'Yellers' and Healers: Pentecostalism and the Study of Grassroots Christianity in China," both in Allan Anderson and Edmond Tang, eds., *Asian and Pentecostal: The Charismatic Face of Christianity in Asia* (Oxford, UK: Regnum Books International, 2005), 411–36 and 467–86, respectively.

16 Michael Bergunder, "Constructing Indian Pentecostalism," in Anderson and Tang, eds., *Asian and Pentecostal*, 177–213.

17 Allan Anderson, "Varieties," 16–17; quoting Robert M. Anderson, *Vision of the Disinherited: The Making of American Pentecostalism* (Peabody, MA: Hendrickson, 1979), 4.

18 Information in this section is taken from Peter D. Hocken, "Charismatic Movement," in Stanley M. Burgess and Eduard M. Van Der Maas, eds., *The New International Dictionary of Pentecostal and Charismatic Movements*, 477–519; and Anderson, *An Introduction to Pentecostalism*, 144–65.

19 See Richard M. Riss, *Latter Rain* (Mississauga, Ontario, Canada: Honeycomb Visual Productions, 1987).

20 S. David Moore, *The Shepherding Movement: Controversy and Charismatic Ecclesiology* (London: T & T Clark, 2003); C. Peter Wagner, ed., *The New Apostolic Churches* (Ventura, CA: Regal Books 1998).

21 R. Marie Griffith, *God's Daughters: Evangelical Women and the Power of Submission* (Berkeley: University of California Press, 1997); Matthew William Tallman, *Demos Shakarian: The Life, Legacy, and Vision of a Full Gospel Business Man* (Lexington, KY: Emeth Press, 2010).

22 Albert Frederick Schenkel, "New Wine and Baptist Wineskins: American and Southern Baptist Denominational Responses to the Charismatic Renewal, 1960–1980," in Edith L. Blumhofer, et al., eds., *Pentecostal Currents in American Protestantism* (Urbana, IL: University of Illinois Press, 1999), 152–67.

23 David A. Reed, "Denominational Charismatics – Where Have They All Gone? A Canadian Anglican Case Study," in Michael Wilkinson, ed., *Canadian Pentecostalism: Transition and Transformation* (Montreal: McGill-Queen's University Press, 2009), 197–213.

24 Henry I. Lederle, *Treasures Old and New: Interpretations of "Spirit-Baptism" in the Charismatic Renewal Movement* (Peabody, MA: Hendrickson, 1988).

25 David J. du Plessis, *The Spirit Bade Me Go: The Astounding Move of God in the Denominational Churches* (Plainfield, NJ: Logos, 1970); Harald Bredesen, *Yes, Lord* (Plainfield, NJ: Logos, 1972).

26 Connie Ho Yan Au, *Grassroots Unity in the Charismatic Renewal* (Eugene, OR: Wipf and Stock, 2011).

27 Stephen Hunt, *The Alpha Enterprise: Evangelism in a Post-Christian Era* (Aldershot, UK: Ashgate, 2004).

28 William K. Kay and Anne E. Dyer, eds., *Pentecostal and Charismatic Studies: A Reader* (London: SCM Press, 2004), 286.

29 Andrew Walker, *Restoring the Kingdom.* 4th ed. (Guildford, UK: Eagle, 1998).

30 R. Andrew Chesnut, *Competitive Spirits: Latin America's New Religious Economy* (New York: Oxford University Press, 2003), 64–101, citing 71–2, 91–2.

31 C. Peter Wagner and Pablo Deiros, *The Rising Revival: Firsthand Accounts of the Incredible Argentine Revival* (Ventura, CA: Renew, 1998); Norberto Saracco, "Argentine Pentecostalism: Its History and Theology," unpublished PhD diss., University of Birmingham (UK), (1989).

32 Mika Vähävangas and Andrew A. Kyomo, eds., *Charismatic Renewal in Africa: A Challenge for African Christianity* (Nairobi, Kenya: Acton Publishers, 2003).

33 Paul Gifford, "'Africa Shall Be Saved': An Appraisal of Reinhard Bonnke's Pan-African Crusade," *Journal of Religion in Africa* 17 (1987), 63–92.

34 Anderson, *Introduction to Pentecostalism*, 160–61. On public religious display, see J. Kwabena Asamoah-Gyadu, "'Christ is the Answer: What is the Question?' A Ghana Airways Prayer Vigil and Its Implications for Religion, Evil and Public Space," *Journal of Religion in Africa* 35 (2005), 93–117.

35 Young-Hoon Lee, "The Korean Holy Spirit Movement in Relation to Pentecostalism," in Anderson and Tang, eds., *Asian and Pentecostal,* 509–26.

36 Lode Wostyn, "Catholic Charismatics in the Philippines," Tan Jin Huat, "Pentecostals and Charismatics in Malaysia and Singapore," and Gani Wiyono, "Pentecostalism in Indonesia," in Anderson and Tang, eds., *Asian and Pentecostal,* 363–83, 281–305, and 307–28; Katherine L. Wiegele, *Investing in Miracles: El Shaddai and the Transformation of Popular Catholicism in the Philippines* (Honolulu: University of Hawaii Press, 2005).

37 Deng Zhaoming, "Indigenous Chinese Pentecostal Denominations," in Anderson and Tang, eds., *Asian and Pentecostal,* 437–66; Lian Xi, *Redeemed By Fire: The Rise of Popular Christianity in Modern China* (New Haven, CT: Yale University Press, 2010).

38 For background and bibliography, see Pavel Hejzlar, *Two Paradigms for Divine Healing: Fred F. Bosworth, Kenneth E. Hagin, Agnes Sanford, and Francis MacNutt in Dialogue* (Leiden: Brill, 2010).

39 See Simon Coleman, *The Globalisation of Charismatic Christianity* (Cambridge: Cambridge University Press, 2000).

40 Paul Freston, "The Universal Church of the Kingdom of God: A Brazilian Church Finds Success in Southern Africa," *Journal of Religion in Africa* 35 (2005), 33–65.

41 Chesnut, *Competitive Spirits*, 16.

42 Andrew Perriman, *Faith, Health and Prosperity* (Carlisle, UK: Paternoster Press, 2003); Joe Maxwell and Isaac Phiri, "Gospel Riches," *Christianity Today* (July 2007), 22–29.

43 David J. Garrard, "Leadership versus the Congregation in the Pentecostal/ Charismatic Movement," *Journal of the European Pentecostal Theological Association* 29 (2009), 90–103.

44 A. Christian van Gorder, "Beyond the Rivers of Africa: The Afrocentric Pentecostalism of Mensa Otabil," *Pneuma* 30 (2008), 33–54.

45 Tang, "'Yellers' and Healers," 481.

46 Lovemore Togarasei, "Broadcasting the Word: Modern Pentecostal Churches' Use of Media Technology," *Journal of Theology for Southern Africa* 129 (2007), 70–81; J. Kwabena Asamoah-Gyadu, "'Get on the Internet! Says the Lord': Religion, Cyberspace and Christianity in Contemporary Africa," *Studies in World Christianity* 13 (2007), 225–42.

47 Bill Jackson, *The Quest for the Radical Middle: A History of the Vineyard* (Anaheim, CA: Vineyard, 1999).

48 James R. Coggins and Paul G. Hiebert, *Wonders and the Word* (Winnipeg, Canada: Kindred Press, 1989).

49 Mike Bickle, *Growing in the Prophetic* (Lake Mary, FL: Creation House, 1996); Jon K. Newton, "Holding Prophets Accountable," *Journal of the European Pentecostal Theological Association* 30 (2010), 63–79.

50 Rick Joyner, *The Harvest* (Pineville, NC: Morningstar Publications, 1989); Damian Thompson, *Waiting for Antichrist: Charisma and Apocalypse in a Pentecostal Church* (New York: Oxford University Press, 2005).

51 Erwin van der Meer, "Strategic Level Spiritual Warfare and Mission in Africa," *Evangelical Review of Mission* 34 (2010), 155–66; J. Kwabena Asamoah-Gyadu, "Pulling Down Strongholds: Evangelism, Principalities and Powers and the African Pentecostal Imagination," *International Review of Mission* 96 (2007), 306–17; and Samuel Hio-Kee Ooi, "A Study of Strategic-Level Spiritual Warfare from a Chinese Perspective," *Asian Journal of Pentecostal Studies* 9 (2006), 143–61.

52 Allan Anderson, "Exorcism and Conversion to African Pentecostalism," *Exchange* 35 (2006), 116–33.

53 John Dawson, *Taking Our Cities for God: How to Break Spiritual Strongholds* (Lake Mary, FL: Creation House, 1989), and *Healing America's Wounds* (Ventura, CA: Regal Books, 1994).

54 Donald E. Miller and Tetsanao Yamamori, *Global Pentecostalism: The New Face of Social Engagement* (Berkeley: University of California Press, 2007).

55 Steve Rabey, *Revival in Brownsville: Pensacola, Pentecostalism, and the Power of American Revivalism* (Nashville, TN: Thomas Nelson Publishers, 1998).

56 Don Cusic, ed., *Encyclopedia of Contemporary Christian Music: Pop, Rock, and Worship* (Santa Barbara, CA: Greenwood Press, 2010).

57 Cassandra Zichini, "Taking Revival to the World [Hillsong Church]," *Christianity Today* (Oct. 2007), 34–40.

58 Mark Jennings, "'Won't You Break Free?': An Ethnography of Music and the Divine–Human Encounter at an Australian Pentecostal Church," *Culture and Religion* 9 (2008), 161–74.

59 Claudia Währisch-Oblau, *The Missionary Self-Perception of Pentecostal-Charismatic Church Leaders from the Global South in Europe: Bringing Back the Gospel* (Leiden: Brill, 2009).

60 Peter Althouse and Robby Waddell, eds., *Perspectives in Pentecostal Eschatologies: World Without End* (Eugene, OR: Pickwick, 2010).

61 Paul Cain and other 1980s "Kansas City" prophets expressed such ideas, as recounted in Mike Bickle's audio memoir, *Encountering Jesus: IHOP-KC's Prophetic History* (2009).

62 C. Peter Wagner, *Dominion!: How Kingdom Action Can Change the World*, (Grand Rapids, MI: Chosen Books, 2008).

63 Henk von den Bosch, "A New Reformation in Africa? On the Impact of the Growth of Pentecostalism," *Religious Studies Review* 34 (2008), 63.

64 See Asonzeh F. K. Ukah, *A New Paradigm of Pentecostal Power: A Study of the Redeemed Christian Church of God in Nigeria* (Trenton, NJ: Africa World Press, 2008).

65   Sébastien Fath, "Evangelical Protestantism in France: An Example of Denominational Recomposition?", *Sociology of Religion* 66 (2005), 399–418.

66   Francis Frangipane, *House United: How Christ-Centered Unity Can End Church Divisions* (Grand Rapids, MI: Chosen Books, 2005).

67   Lynn Bridgers, "Emotion, Experience, and Enthusiasm: The Growing Divide in U.S. Religion," *Modern Believing* 50 (2009), 16.

68   David B. Barrett and Todd M. Johnson, *World Christian Trends, AD 30-AD 2200* (Pasadena, CA: William Carey Library, 2001), 284, lists 65 million classical Pentecostals and some 460 charismatic or neo-charismatic/neo-pentecostal renewalists (for the year 2000).

69   Arnold Bittlinger, ed., *The Church is Charismatic: The World Council of Churches and the Charismatic Renewal* (Geneva: World Council of Churches, 1981).

70   Barrett and Johnson, *World Christian Trends*, 287. "Postpentecostals," for Barrett and Johnson, are those who leave pentecostal denominations, while "Postcharismatics" are those who are "no longer regularly active" in the renewal.

71   Margaret M. Poloma, *The Assemblies of God at the Crossroads: Charisma and Institutional Dilemmas* (Knoxville: University of Tennessee Press, 1989). Poloma, with John C. Green, offers a sequel in *The Assemblies of God: Godly Love and the Revitalization of American Pentecostalism* (New York: New York University Press, 2010).

Further Reading

Bergunder, Michael. *The South Indian Pentecostal Movement in the Twentieth Century.* Grand Rapids, MI: Eerdmans, 2008.

Brown, Candy, ed. *Global Pentecostal and Charismatic Healing.* New York: Oxford University Press, 2011.

Cleary, Edward L. *The Rise of Charismatic Catholicism in Latin America.* Gainesville, FL: University Press of Florida, 2011.

Harrell, David Edwin, Jr. *All Things are Possible: The Healing and Charismatic Revivals in Modern America.* Bloomington, IN: Indiana University Press, 1975.

Hocken, Peter. *Streams of Renewal: The Origins and Early Development of the Charismatic Movement in Great Britain.* Exeter, UK: Paternoster, 1986.

Hunt, Stephen. *A History of the Charismatic Movement in Britain and the United States of America: The Pentecostal Transformation of Christianity.* Lewiston, NY: Edwin Mellen Press, 2009.

Kay, William K. *Apostolic Networks in Britain: New Ways of Being Church.* Waynesboro, GA: Paternoster, 2007.

McClymond, Michael J., ed. *Encyclopedia of Religious Revivals in America.* 2 vols. Westport, CT: Greenwood Press, 2007.

McDonnell, Kilian, ed. *Presence, Power, Praise: Documents on the Charismatic Renewal.* 3 vols. Collegeville, MN: The Liturgical Press, 1980.

Omenyo, Cephas N. *Pentecost Outside Pentecostalism: A Study of the Development of Charismatic Renewal in the Mainline Churches in Ghana.* Zoetermeer, the Netherlands: Boekencentrum, 2002.

Poloma, Margaret M. *Main Street Mystics: The Toronto Blessing and Reviving Pentecostalism.* Walnut Creek, CA: Altamira Press, 2003.

Synan, Vinson. *The Holiness-Pentecostal Tradition: Charismatic Movements in the Twentieth Century.* 2nd ed. Grand Rapids, MI: Eerdmans, 1997.

3 Then and Now: The Many Faces of Global Oneness Pentecostalism

DAVID A. REED

INTRODUCTION

Oneness Pentecostalism (OP) appeared unexpectedly in 1914, during the second decade of the Pentecostal Revival and within the newly formed Assemblies of God. The catalyst was a baptismal sermon during the 1913 Worldwide Pentecostal Camp Meeting near Los Angeles in which the preacher suggested that biblically, baptism could be administered in the name of the Lord Jesus Christ.[1] Evangelist Frank Ewart (1876–1947) was so captivated by the notion that one year later he launched a new movement. Known initially as the New Issue, it spread rapidly as countless believers accepted the new baptism. Disagreement over its rejection of the doctrine of the Trinity, however, resulted in schism in 1916, and the third stream of the Pentecostal Revival was born.[2]

Three beliefs and practices are fundamental to OP identity. First, the singular name "Jesus" is the revealed proper name by which God chooses to be known in the age of the New Covenant. Second, water baptism is to be administered in the name of Jesus as the central, uncompromising, and only valid name to be invoked in Christian baptism. This act constitutes *identification* with Christ (Rom 6:4) and, for the majority of OPs, an essential element in the *new birth* when accompanied by repentance and Spirit-baptism (Acts 2:38). Finally, OP teaches a non-Trinitarian, modalistic theology of God. As God's name is one, so is God's nature one without distinction.[3] Founding OP theologians were deeply influenced by William Durham's (1873–1912) Finished Work theology (1910–12), as well as early evangelical christocentric interpretations of the Old Testament names and titles of God.

We begin this essay with a brief review of early OP as a racially integrated movement in 1917 to the painful split in 1924 and formation of the white United Pentecostal Church in 1945. Second, we turn our attention globally, first to examine the appeal of OP within other cultures, then to offer an account of the three earliest OP revivals abroad, followed by a summary of the movement's current demographic profile. We conclude with brief cases of two of the largest Oneness groups and their journey to independence.

NORTH AMERICAN BEGINNING – RACIALLY HEROIC BUT TAINTED LEGACY

At a time when many Christian denominations in America had already succumbed to racism, the fledgling Oneness movement had within it the seeds of success or failure. When Garfield T. Haywood (1880–1931), prominent black leader from Indianapolis, cast his lot with OP, the racial demographics permanently distinguished OP from its excommunicating body, the Assemblies of God.

The organizational home of OP was a small ministerial fellowship, the Pentecostal Assemblies of the World (PAW).[4] Within a brief time large numbers of blacks joined its ranks until they soon constituted a majority in the Northern states. However, by 1921, cracks in the bond of racial unity were showing. Because of segregation policies in the South, racially integrated meetings were virtually impossible. With tensions mounting, the 1923 annual ministers meeting proposed a "division by color" by which two presbyters of each race would sign credentials for their respective groups. This pleased the whites but did little to assuage the dissatisfaction of the blacks. The General Conference of 1924 attempted further compromise but ultimately ended in schism. Many whites were relieved, claiming they could now evangelize in the South without racial restrictions. Blacks, on the other hand, considered the compromise policies offensive to the unity of the body.[5]

During the years from 1924 to 1931, the PAW grew slowly and the white constituency became fractious, resulting in the formation of two white organizations: the Pentecostal Ministerial Association (PMA) and the Apostolic Church of Jesus Christ (ACJC). However, restlessness for unity persisted and by 1931 leaders called a Unity Conference in Dayton, Ohio. While efforts to bring together the PMA and ACJC were unsuccessful, through a separate meeting between ACJC and PAW a merger was quickly finalized, and its name changed to the Pentecostal Assemblies of Jesus Christ (PAJC).

As a result of the swiftness of the merger, major decisions were made without due process, leading some blacks to suspect the motives of the whites. Quickly the original PAW charter was revived, and most blacks returned. The final blow occurred in 1937 when the white leadership of the PAJC announced that integrated accommodations were not available for the annual conference in Tulsa, Oklahoma. Most of the remaining blacks left and returned to the PAW.

In 1945 the PAJC and Pentecostal Church, Inc. (PCI, formerly PMA) secured a permanent union with the formation of the United Pentecostal Church, which is the largest Oneness organization in North America. However, with the spread of OP around the world, it is no longer just black, white, and North American. Its faces are many and its story is global.

A GLOBAL PENTECOSTAL MOVEMENT

The pentecostal movement spread rapidly in large part because of what scholar of Chinese Christianity Daniel Bays calls its "transnational" character. It has from the beginning embodied features that enable it to "transcend and cross national or cultural boundaries." The receptor culture, for its part, recognizes these "congenial explanatory belief systems" that provide the opportunity for incorporating and indigenizing those features.[6] Pentecostalism bears a similar supernatural world view and close affinity of spiritual experience with the body.

Understanding the Oneness Appeal

The pentecostal expansion should not be construed as moving in only one direction, from missionary to missionized. Global society is marked by a social network of interactions or "global flows," which, in Michael Wilkinson's words, "move back and forth, over and under, betwixt and between, the traditional borders of society." A culture does not passively receive ideas, rituals, and movements from outside, but engages, confronts, and restructures them, and sometimes precipitates "reverse flows." The result is a process called "glocalization" whereby the global and local interact to produce a new reality, a "hybrid." This new social phenomenon does not eradicate the local and global but transforms them. Anticipating the dizzying variety of global Pentecostals, Wilkinson concludes that Pentecostalism did not spread unilaterally from Azusa Street to the rest of the world, but produced a hybrid, "a social process that shapes and reshapes this type of Christianity."[7] One important way in which hybridity is manifest in global OP is the way in which its distinctive doctrine functions. In many regions of the world OP enjoys popularity and large followings for at least two reasons, both related to its shared Pentecostal identity.

First, unlike the creedal and confessional traditions, experience of the Spirit is central to pentecostal identity and practice. Pentecostal religion is holistic, wedding body and spirit. Doctrines are necessary, not solely as intellectual propositions of belief but as explications of the God Pentecostals know through their spiritual encounter and the corroborating teaching of Scripture. This means that when Pentecostal converts receive Spirit-baptism or other transformative spiritual experience, the doctrine they hear preached is the account that "makes sense" of that experience. The doctrine provides the metanarrative, an intellectual articulation of the meaning of the spiritual experience, for the group.

The second reason is related to the pentecostalization of the Name. The name of Jesus has a long tradition in devotion, from the Eastern Church's ascetical tradition to Protestant Pietism.[8] In early Pentecostalism, the Name had especially come to denote spiritual power. Finally, in OP the power of the Name became attached to its invocation in water baptism.

Roswith Gerloff, scholar on African Oneness (Apostolic) Pentecostal Diaspora, points to the dynamic spiritual energy and power resident in core OP theology. She recalls that the focus of the debate over OP at the beginning was not the question of the Trinity but "in whose power, or name, or authority, or presence do we preach, teach, heal, baptize, and build the church?" The answer is, "in the name of Jesus only." Black Oneness believers in particular embraced the name of Jesus as a "liberating force."[9] This dynamic power is embedded in the holistic incorporation of belief, ritual, and experience envisioned in Acts 2:38. As a global experiential faith, OP doctrine functions neither autonomously nor superfluously; it is the necessary dimension of a claimed life-altering spiritual experience.

Then – Earliest Global Beginnings

The impact of the New Issue in North America was felt almost immediately on the global scene. Missionaries and magazines played their part in carrying the message of an ever-unfolding restoration of pure apostolic Christianity. It was unpredictable that the New Issue would be taking root on foreign soil at precisely the same time it was winning the allegiance of its second and prominent theologian G. T. Haywood. Although details of the Oneness doctrine of God were absent or sketchy, the act of baptism in the name of Jesus appears to have been the central feature, replete with apostolic power. As best we can determine, Mexico and China were the first recipients of the new message, remarkably as early as late 1914 and early 1915, with Russia following in the spring of 1916.

The *Mexican* story begins with an immigrant woman. Romana Valenzuela arrived with her husband in Los Angeles in 1912, fleeing civil war in their home country. Although reared Catholic, they soon joined a small Spanish Pentecostal house church, which, according to Oneness scholar Kenneth Gill, was likely under the oversight of the early PAW.[10] Homesick for her family and desiring their conversion, Romana returned to Mexico in 1914. Gill believes that when she returned to convert her family, "it was the Jesus' Name Pentecostal message she brought." Her family was initially critical on account of her leaving the Catholic faith, but she gained the trust of a respected nephew, Miguel García. At a house gathering on the evening of November 1, 1914, all twelve members present, including Miguel, experienced Spirit baptism.[11]

Romana was already a believer in "Jesus' Name" baptism and insisted that an ordained minister must perform the ritual. She persuaded a local Methodist minister, Rúben Ortega, of the necessity of the pentecostal experience and baptism in the name of Jesus. After he received Spirit baptism, they traveled together to El Paso, Texas, where a black minister, probably affiliated with the PAW, baptized Ortega. On their return to Villa de Aldama he baptized all twelve members and became their pastor. However, because of persecution from other Protestants and apparently unstable leadership, Ortega resigned two years later. The movement expanded into other cities but grew slowly until 1918. During that period the group was known as Iglesia Cristiana Espiritual. In 1918 Romana rejoined her husband in Los Angeles but became ill and died a month later.[12] With immigrants moving back and forth across the border, many small congregations appeared across northern Mexico. However, weak leadership and extremes led to instability and schisms. Still associated with the American-based PAW, the first convention was held in 1925. As a result of language difference, the Mexican group formed its own indigenous organization in March 1930, called Asamblea Apostolica de la Fe en Cristo Jesús (AAFCJ). The name was changed in 1946 to Iglesia Apostólica de la Fe en Cristo Jesús (ACFCJ), because by that time the Mexican-American Oneness group had taken the same name as its sister organization in Mexico.[13]

The ACFCJ is the oldest indigenous Oneness church in Mexico. By 1999 it had grown to more than 1,200 churches, 3,500 cell groups, and approximately 250,000 constituents.[14] One early convert, Eusebio Joaquín, left in 1926 to form his own group, La Luz del Mundo (The Light of the World). This highly exclusive prophet-oriented Oneness group is centered in Guadalajara, and with an estimated 1.5 million global adherents, may be the largest Oneness church in Central and South America.[15] The American-based United Pentecostal Church International (UPCI) has grown significantly from 2,000 followers in 1991 to more than 109,000 in 1911. A leadership dispute in 2012 resulted in a split between the newly formed United Pentecostal Church of Mexico and the UPCI, with the former securing about 71,000 adherents.[16]

The *China* story begins with an American Pentecostal missionary and a magazine. F. S. Ramsey and his wife from Batavia, New York, accompanied by Elizabeth Steiglitz of Iowa, arrived in Shanghai in June 1910, eventually settling in Ta Tung Fu, Shanxi Province in North China. For eighteen months they did little else except learn Chinese, pray, and (unsuccessfully) attempt to make pentecostal converts of other missionaries who were together residing at the Swedish Holiness Mission. In 1912 Alma Hult from Denver, Colorado, joined the team. An early missionary letter from Ramsey appears in the April 1911 issue of *Trust*, the official paper of Elim Faith Work and Bible Training School in Rochester, New York. In it he writes about a general "cleaning up" and confessions among the Christians but makes no reference to conversions or baptisms.[17]

Certainly no later than the winter months of 1914–1915 Ramsey and his team received a copy of Ewart's paper, *Meat in Due Season* (*MDS*). Their response was immediate: "We perceived it at once and began to preach and practice Acts 2:38." Conversions quickened but baptisms were postponed until spring. The first baptism included the team and thirteen Chinese converts, except Ramsey himself who chose to wait until another missionary could perform the ceremony. The revival quickly spread into a local mountain village through the Swedish mission station. During the next two years (1915–1917) "over 600 Chinese converts had received the baptism of the Holy Spirit in that province."[18] One significant feature of Ramsey's missionary strategy – boldly punctuated in Hult's report – was his policy on native independence. Hult writes, "From the time of its beginning, this Assembly, which is called Pentecostal, has been entirely native and independent of any American or European influence .... These assemblies support themselves, their own missionary work, and have their own native pastors, elders, deacons and teachers.[19] They even held occasional clergy conferences and some churches started schools for children, all within a span of two years.

The Ta Tung Fu Revival had a far-reaching effect on the future of Oneness Pentecostalism in China. More than three decades later it survived the religious suppression of the new communist regime begun in

1949 and the Cultural Revolution (1966–76). French estimates that the current (1999) numerical strength of OPs is conservatively one million, although this figure is difficult to verify.[20]

The second legacy of OP expansion in China was its influence on the large indigenous and exclusive True Jesus Church (TJC), established in Beijing in 1917. Paul Wei, one of the three founding TJC workers, came in contact in 1916 with Bernt Berntsen, a Norwegian American missionary. Although Berntsen had come to China in 1904, he embraced the pentecostal experience at Azusa Street in 1906. By 1910 he had established his primary mission in Zhengding, a city southwest of Beijing, before moving to Beijing in 1917.[21] From 1912 through 1916 he published a Chinese language paper called *Popular Gospel Truth (PGT)*.[22]

The first mention of Berntsen's embrace of the Oneness belief appears in *PGT* as early as 1915, and by 1916 he was expounding on Oneness doctrine.[23] His name appears for the last time on the ministerial roster of the Assemblies of God in 1915 and reappears in 1919 as a minister with the PAW.[24] It turns out that all three founding leaders of the TJC – Paul Wei, Zhang Ling-Shen, and Banabas Zhang – had met Berntsen early on. He ordained Zhang Ling-Shen in Beijing in 1917. Berntsen reported the testimony of Banabas Zhang's Spirit-baptism in a 1912 issue of *PGT*. Wei and Berntsen became friends until some of Wei's teachings and a disagreement over a loan by Berntsen for Wei's fabric business resulted in a breach of fellowship.[25] However, they were reconciled in 1919 as Wei lay dying. Berntsen's Oneness legacy in China is that his teaching became a fundamental doctrine of the TJC. In 1949, the TJC was the largest of the three major independent churches, with an estimated strength of more than 100,000.[26] Today the numerical strength of the TJC in China may be 500,000, with more than 100,000 outside. The TJC suggests the numbers could be as high as one million.[27]

The *Russia* story emerges from the crucible of persecution. Andrew Urshan (1884–1967), a Persian immigrant, arrived in Chicago in 1901. Son of a Presbyterian pastor, he eventually received pentecostal Spirit-baptism at Durham's North Avenue Mission in 1908.[28] Urshan returned to Persia as a missionary in 1914 but within a year fled to Russia because of the Ottoman conflict. He stopped in Tabriz (Tehran) and Tiflis (Tbilisi), Georgia, preaching and ministering among Persian immigrants. Restrictions against foreigners preaching forced him to proceed to Armavir, Russia, where he ministered successfully among refugees.[29]

Urshan's Oneness legacy in Russia would not have occurred had it not been that he lost his passport and citizenship papers in Persia.

He was issued a temporary passport to return home through Russia. When he arrived in Petrograd (St. Petersburg) and was invited to preach at the Free Protestant Mission, numbers swelled within weeks. It was during the spring months of 1916 that Urshan made the decision to baptize exclusively in the name of Jesus Christ.[30] Following his own rebaptism, he baptized about seventy-five converts including one Nikolai P. Smorodin who would soon become pastor of this fledgling group and a prominent leader of the Russian movement. His leadership of the church in Petrograd was eventually shared with Alexander Ivanov.[31] The church – and the movement – were called Evangelical Christians in the Spirit of the Apostles, although they were often labeled Urshanites or Smorodintsy.[32] By 1920 they had grown to eighty congregations.[33] In 1924 Urshan reported more than 1,000 followers, including about 50 in Estonia, who were "an offspring of the Petrograd revival."[34]

Today the strength of the Oneness movement in Russia and neighboring republics is approximately 31,000, according to French. It is currently divided into two main groups. The smaller and most conservative is affiliated with the UPCI. The larger, more open group holds membership in the broader Union of Christians of Faith, Evangelical-Pentecostal.[35] The overseer is Dimitri Shatrov, currently pastor of the largest pentecostal church in St. Petersburg. The primary doctrinal difference between the two Oneness groups is that Shatrov believes like other Evangelicals that salvation is achieved by faith alone and does not view rebaptism as necessary to be born again. Although he holds to the Oneness view of God, neither that doctrine nor water baptism is a church-dividing issue. Reciprocally, the wider association accepts Shatrov and his churches without questioning their orthodoxy. The UPCI lists nine affiliated churches in the conservative group. According to Mart Vahi, Estonian Oneness leader, the group associated with Shatrov consists of nine churches in St. Petersburg and eight in other areas.[36]

Early Russian OP is distinctive in its emphasis on the spiritual significance of persecution. No other early Oneness writer gives such attention to persecution as a lived dimension of the Name as does Urshan. Its importance in his theology is undoubtedly related to the persecution and death threats he endured in Persia, as well as his painful expulsion from the Assemblies of God in 1919.[37] This persecution theme is picked up by Smorodin, who was imprisoned three times and died in prison in 1953. In one of his letters, he reminds his readers that every Christian should experience three baptisms: "water baptism, the baptism of the Holy Spirit and the baptism of fire .... Baptism of Fire is trial and suffering, and everyone should be ready to go through them, and be ready even to die for their faith in Jesus Christ."[38]

Now – A Global Glance

Church-related statistics are notoriously imprecise, depending on methodology and who counts. French has conducted the most comprehensive study to date, identifying organizations, constituents, and churches. French casts the net wide, including groups that practice baptizing in the name of Jesus Christ, but hold varying views on the Godhead, christology, soteriology, or ecclesiology. Some are Oneness in doctrine and practice but exclusive in ecclesiology. They may baptize believers or infants, handle snakes, keep the Seventh Day Sabbath, and sacramentally teach spiritual communion or transubstantiation.[39]

French estimates that global OPs approach 20 million, with 5 million located in the United States. He lists 180 global organizations.[40] The two largest American Oneness organizations are the UPCI and PAW, the original Oneness organization. In 2011, the UPCI claimed 600,000 constituents in the United States and Canada and a total global strength of 3 million.[41] The interracial but predominantly black PAW reported in 2006 a global constituency of 1.5 million.[42] An umbrella association, Apostolic World Christian Fellowship (AWCF), was formed in 1970 to express and cultivate unity among the Oneness organizations, providing a venue for regional, national and global fellowship, and coordinating ministries.[43] AWCF currently lists 191 organizations, 60 percent of which are outside North America. In total, AWCF represents 5.5 million Apostolics worldwide, excluding UPCI figures.[44]

Case One: Colombia, South America

The Oneness movement began in Colombia in 1936 with the arrival of Swedish Canadian missionary Verner Larsen. He was joined in 1949 by a fellow Canadian, William ("Bill") Drost, both serving under the auspices of the UPC.[45] Their ministry was remarkably successful even under violent persecution, with growth outstripping by many times all other Protestant missions combined.[46] The rapid growth was largely a result of Drost's unconventional evangelistic methods. Being a theologically untrained but evangelistically zealous lay missionary at the time, his strategy was to encourage all new converts to evangelize.[47] This contravened the traditional "colonial" pattern of requiring basic instruction in the faith before nationals were permitted to evangelize on their own. However, Drost's approach was highly effective. Beginning with services in his home, within the first year the work had grown to several congregations and more than 500 baptized converts. By 1959, there were more than twenty churches and preaching points. One observer summed up Drost's approach as "immediate spontaneous evangelization by new believers."[48]

Drost was likewise committed to treating the Colombians as equals in all matters of church leadership, including administration. He and Larsen encouraged independence, self-sufficiency, and national ownership as quickly as possible. In 1967 the UPC voted to nationalize and form the United Pentecostal Church of Colombia. Only 5 percent remained with the American-based UPC, including its American missionaries. The Colombian organization is now the largest Protestant church in Colombia, claiming over one million constituents with churches throughout Latin America, North America, and Europe.[49]

Case Two: Apostolic Church of Ethiopia

The story of the Apostolic Church of Ethiopia (ACE) is inseparable from the spiritual and theological biography of its leader Teklemariam Gezahagne. This is evident in Nona Freeman's account of the Ethiopian (Oneness) Revival, which she narrated through the lens of Teklemariam's life story and leadership of the largest Oneness church in the world.[50] It is also the story of a church born in persecution at the hands of ecclesiastical and government authorities alike through three regimes, enduring numerous imprisonments and the death of Teklemariam's infant son from a brutal mob attack.[51]

Teklemariam was reared a Coptic Christian in the Tigray region of northeastern Ethiopia. However, his spiritual devotion and craving for education from an early age led him into studies at Lutheran Bible College and short programs sponsored by the Seventh Day Adventists and Mennonite Bible Academy. He was introduced to the pentecostal movement during the widespread revival of the sixties among university students. In 1964 he attended a Finnish Pentecostal Mission where he received the pentecostal experience of Holy Spirit baptism.[52]

It did not take long before Teklemariam emerged as a leading pentecostal evangelist, preaching wherever he was given permission. Although he often preached for the pentecostal organization Full Gospel Believers Church (FGBC), he remained nondenominational and claims to have never affiliated with FGBC or any Christian group until he became Oneness.[53]

The account of Teklemariam's conversion to Oneness Pentecostalism begins with Bobbye and Kenneth Wendell, missionaries with the UPC, who arrived in Addis Ababa in the early 1960s. Through developing a trusting relationship and a tract, "Baptism in Jesus' Name," Teklemariam was finally convinced and baptized, along with his wife Erkenesh, by Kenneth Wendell in 1969.[54] During the early years, the Ethiopian work was simply known as the United Pentecostal Church of Ethiopia. However, in 1972 all missionaries were required to leave the country, at which point the church registered with the government under the name Apostolic Church of Ethiopia.[55] The government of Emperor Haile Selassie fell to a Communist revolution in 1974, which required the ACE to reaffirm its status as a legally constituted religious body. Interestingly, although the new government, the Derg, persecuted other Christian groups and forced Trinitarian Pentecostals underground, it was surprisingly lenient toward two heterodox groups: ACE and Jehovah's Witnesses.[56]

The expulsion of all missionaries – unwittingly at the time – became the first step toward the ACE's independence. The ACE was now fully registered and legally recognized by the government, although it continued to function under the administration of the Foreign Missions Department of the UPC. Two events illustrate the continuing oversight of the UPC. The first was a power struggle for leadership that arose between 1972 and 1975, requiring intervention by the UPC. A small split occurred, but Teklemariam finally succeeded in gaining sufficient support to become its national leader. The second occasion was the building of the mother church in Addis Ababa. Funds were provided by the UPC District of Louisiana, and local members built the church with volunteer labor.[57] The funds were freely given but undoubtedly with the understanding that the UPC was supporting one of its own.

The ACE continued to grow rapidly in numbers from 1975 onwards, while still functioning under the administration of the UPC. Teklemariam made his first visit to the UPC General Conference in 1984. However, the ACE demonstrated an independence that was evident in its bold evangelistic programs and fundraising initiatives. In the 1990s it instituted a number of programs that have been effective, most popularly the Annual International Apostolic Church Crusade held in the southern region. Numbers in attendance have increased each year since 1991 until the ACE estimates its current attendance at 500,000. A yearly national conference attracts 100,000 adherents. Three organizations currently raise funds beyond tithes and offerings for evangelism, leadership training, building new churches, and service to widows and orphans. By 2000 the ACE constituency had grown to approximately 1.5 million.[58]

The next demonstration of its independence was a theological one. In 1999, Teklemarian published a major book on biblical theology, which placed in print a distinctive Christology that he had been teaching since the inception of the ACE.[59] In it he set forth a distinctive christology that was simultaneously at odds with the traditional teaching of the UPCI and triggered resonances with the ancient Coptic doctrine of the "one nature" of Christ.[60] In brief, the premise with which Teklemariam's christology begins is one common to other Oneness theologians, including some fundamentalists and traditional Trinitarians – namely, the belief that the sin of Adam is inherited through biological transmission. The virgin birth of Christ is necessary, therefore, to bypass the corrupted Adamic family tree to produce a pure, undefiled human being, an "unblemished Lamb" capable of being the perfect sacrifice for the sins of the world. More narrowly, some fundamentalists and Pentecostals, including OPs, believe that because Scripture teaches that "the life of the flesh is in the blood" (Lev 17:11, KJV) and "without shedding of blood is no remission of sins" (Heb 9:22, KJV), the salvific agency in the atonement is the physical, literal blood of Jesus. Extending the virgin birth and blood efficacy argument, some conclude further that biologically the blood of Jesus must be incorruptible – divine blood or both human and divine.[61]

Teklemariam extends this logic of divine blood even further and in another direction. First, he agrees with the others that only flesh and blood died on the cross, which was all that the atonement demanded: "His physical death on the cross is sufficient for our salvation."[62] However, he adds the qualification that like Jesus' blood, his flesh also must be divine. It matters not that God "will not mingle His holy, divine nature with sinful humanity," because God by nature is ontologically incarnational. God is *potentially* "flesh, blood and bones" as well as Spirit, therefore inherently capable of producing an undefiled human being. That is, God is both Word and Spirit: "Whenever God acts, He breathes Spirit and emanates Word." The incarnation was not merely a remedial act by God to fix a broken world but was in the mind of God as Word from all eternity and was simply manifest in history at the appointed time. Because God the Father ontologically has flesh, blood, and bones, "these three are inseparable for eternity."[63]

Teklemariam's language of Christ's divine flesh is offensive to the Nestorian-leaning OPs.[64] However, it resonates with the "divine flesh" rhetoric of the ancient Alexandrian school in which the hypostatic union of the two natures in the incarnation is so indissoluble that one can speak of divine flesh without denying the reality of Jesus' full humanity.[65] Teklemariam's controversial views reverberated throughout the UPCI leadership and finally led to his expulsion at its 2003 General Conference. The ACE promptly embraced the "divine flesh" teaching of its leader as part of its official doctrine.[66] That decision also secured the separation of the ACE from the UPCI.

Teklemariam's theology invites two initial questions for exploration. The first relates to the nature of the divine flesh. Can it be accepted as an affirmation of the full humanity of Christ? That is, if God is potentially incarnational (with the capacity to *be* human), is the flesh that becomes Jesus less than fully human because Mary made no contribution to it, or is it fully human but incorruptible (as in Adam's original state)? The second question relates to the UPCI. Although belief in the divine blood is not part of its official doctrine, it does consider the blood of Jesus to be the salvific agency for atonement without requiring a hypostatic union of the Second Person of the Trinity in Chalcedonian terms. More interesting is that many UPCI preachers have for years taught that the blood of Jesus was different from ours. This point was observed by Bishop Degu, who was quick to point to the inconsistency of permitting "divine blood" teaching while excommunicating a leader, and with him the ACE, on the basis of "divine flesh" theology.[67]

Although the controversy is theological, the journey of the ACE to unaffiliated independence is surely a larger story. Teklemariam is a humble but forceful independent thinker. His divine flesh doctrine resonates deeply with the ancient Coptic doctrine of the "one nature." The ACE has grown to 3.3 million constituents, with more than 5,700 churches and 6,700 ordained pastors – arguably by far the largest Oneness church in the world.[68] The ACE may have outgrown its affiliated status. Although the expulsion of missionaries and seminal adaptation of a near-century-old Oneness theology were not intentional acts of dissociation, the destination may have been inevitable.

PROSPECTIVE

As OP approaches its centenary, it has produced thriving communities of faith throughout the world. However, almost universally they do so in isolation from the wider Christian community and sometimes from each other, often with little regret from within or without. OPs are organizationally numerous and independent of one another. Some are exclusive and do not recognize other OPs. However, as they grow in numbers, as they surely will, an urgent need is for greater mutual understanding, trust, and hopefully cooperation.

Doctrinal difference is a deep fault line between OPs and Trinitarians. We offer these suggestions. First, because academic societies are neutral spaces for dialogue without requiring ecclesiastical participation, they can be encouraged to welcome qualified Oneness persons to present papers and participate in research projects. Second, although continued study and dialogue will focus on Oneness distinctives, soteriology and ecclesiology should be given attention as they often dictate policies regarding fellowship with non-OPs. Finally, we encourage further exploration into the nature of contextual theology and how global expressions of embodied Oneness theology may prove to be more ecumenically fruitful than western speculative approaches.

Notes

1   See Frank Ewart, *The Phenomenon of Pentecost: "A History of the Latter Rain"* (St. Louis, MO: Pentecostal Publishing House, 1947), 76–77; see chapter 6 in David A. Reed, *"In Jesus' Name": The History and Beliefs of Oneness Pentecostals* (Dorset, UK: Deo Publishing, 2008), 136–46.

2   Early Oneness leaders had been part of the first schism, the Finished Work of Calvary teaching, which occurred during the years 1910–12 under the leadership of William Durham, a Chicago-based evangelist.

3   For select writings by founding Oneness theologians, Frank Ewart, Garfield T. Haywood, and Andrew D. Urshan, see Donald W. Dayton, ed., *Seven "Jesus Only" Tracts* (New York: Garland, 1985); for recent theological writings, see David K. Bernard, *The Oneness of God* (1983), *The New Birth* (1984), and *The Oneness View of Jesus Christ* (1994), all published by United Pentecostal Church International (Hazelwood, MO: Word Aflame Press).

4   For an in-depth study of the history and development of the Pentecostal Assemblies of the World, see Talmadge L. French, *Early Interracial Oneness Pentecostalism: G. T. Haywood and the Pentecostal Assemblies of the World (1901–31)* (Eugene, OR: Pickwick Publications, 2013).

5   See chapter 10 in Reed, *"In Jesus' Name"*; see also Arthur L. Clanton, *United We Stand – A History of Oneness Organizations* (Hazelwood, MO: Pentecostal Publishing House, 1970), 33.

6   "The Protestant Missionary Establishment and the Pentecostal Movement," in Edith Blumhofer, Russell P. Spittler, and Grant Wacker, eds., *Pentecostal Currents in American Protestantism* (Urbana: University of Illinois Press, 1999), 50–67.

7   Michael Wilkinson, "Religion and Global Flows," in Peter Beyer and Lori Beaman, eds., *Globalization, Religion and Culture* (Leiden: Brill Academic Books, 2007), 377, 380–81, 387. Similar globalization theory is applied particularly to the "world-making" vision of global Pentecostals by Birgit Meyer, "Pentecostalism and Globalization," in Allan Anderson, et al., eds., *Studying Global Pentecostalism: Theories and Methods* (Berkeley: University of California Press, 2010), 113–30.

8   Kallistos Ware, "Ways of Prayer and Contemplation – I. Eastern," in Bernard McGinn, John Meyendorff, and Jean Leclercq, eds., *Christian Spirituality: Origins to the Twelfth Century* (New York: Crossroad Publishing, 1988), 402–10. For the Jesus-piety of early Evangelicalism, see Reed, chapters 2 and 3 in *"In Jesus' Name"*.

9   Roswith I. H. Gerloff, *A Plea for British Black Theologies: The Black Church Movement in Britain in its Transatlantic Cultural and Theological Interaction*, 2 vols. (New York: Peter Lang, 1992), I.90–95.

10 Oneness historian Talmadge French points out that the Pentecostal Assemblies of the World was initially organized as a loose association in 1906, but from 1914 to 1918 included early Oneness ministers. It did not become exclusively Oneness until 1918; see French, chapters 3 and 4 in *Early Interracial Oneness Pentecostalism*.

11 Kenneth D. Gill, *Toward a Contextualized Theology for the Third World: The Emergence and Development of Jesus' Name Pentecostalism in Mexico*, Studies in the Intercultural History of Christianity 90 (New York: Peter Lang, 1994), 43–44.

12 Gill, *Toward a Contextualized Theology*, 45–46, 49. According to Mexican Oneness leader Manuel J. Gaxiola-Gaxiola, growth within the Mexican community in both Mexico and the United States would also have included many who had been involved in the Azusa Street Revival: "Later, most of these Mexicans became part of the Oneness movement"; see "Latin American Pentecostalism: A Mosaic within a Mosaic," *Pneuma* 13:1 (Fall 1991), 115.

13 A history of the *Iglesia Apostólica de la Fe en Cristo Jesús* was published by one of its prominent bishops Manuel Gaxiola-Gaxiola, *La Serpiente y La Paloma: Historia, Teología y Análisis De la Iglesia Apostólica De la Fe in Cristo Jesús (1914–1994)* (Mexico City: Libros PYROS, 1970, 1994). For a brief overview of ACFCJ, see Talmadge French, *Our God Is One: The Story of the Oneness Pentecostals* (Indianapolis, IN: Voice and Vision Publications, 1999), 133–36.

14 French, *Our God Is One*, 134, n17.

15 See French, *Our God Is One*, 135. The approximate constituent strength is stated by David Bundy, "Light of the World Church," in Stanley M. Burgess, et al., ed., *New International Dictionary of Pentecostal and Charismatic Movements*, rev. ed. (Grand Rapids, MI: Zondervan, 2002), 840–41.

16 E-mail open correspondence from T. Wynn Drost, Mexico City, November 26, 2012.

17 See "Missionary letters," *Trust* X:2 (April 1911), 17. Ramsey was not listed as a supported missionary but apparently welcome to send reports. Elim supported only "faith" missionaries who trusted God for their support; see *Trust* X:4/5 (June and July 1911), 23.

18 Alma Hult wrote a lengthy report of the revival for the September 1917 issue of *MDS*, "Pentecost in China." The account was reprinted in Ewart's *The Name and the Book* (Chicago: Daniel Ryerson, 1936), 42–48.

19 Ewart, *The Name and the Book*, 47. Ramsey was committed to the indigenous principle that national believers should become independent as soon as possible.

20 French, *Our God Is One*, 149, n65.

21 See *Popular Gospel Truth* 15 (1917),1; cited in Iap Sain-Chin, "Bernt Berntsen – A Prominent Oneness Pentecostal Pioneer to North China" (paper presented at the 41st Annual Meeting of the Society for Pentecostal Studies, Virginia Beach, VA, March 1–3, 2012), 6. His name appears in 1910 as a missionary under William Durham's North Avenue Mission in Chicago.

22 For a brief summary of Berntsen's work as an Apostolic Faith missionary, see Cecil M. Robeck, Jr., *The Azusa Street Mission and Revival: The Birth of the Global Pentecostal Movement* (Nashville, TN: Thomas Nelson, 2006), 259–62.

23 *PGT* 8 (1915), 1–3, and *PGT* 13 (1916), 1; cited in Iap Sain-Chin, "Berntsen," 18–19.

24 *Minutes of the General Council of the Assemblies of God in the United States of America, Canada and Foreign Lands held at Turner Hall, St. Louis, MO. October 1–10, 1915* (printed by organization, n.d.), 9–16; *Minute Book and Ministerial Record of the General Assembly of the Pentecostal Assemblies of the World, Minute Book 1919 (1907–1919 – Pentecostal Assemblies of the World)* (printed by organization, n.d.).

25 For a brief overview of these relationships, see Iap Sain-Chin, "Berntsen," 12–15.

26 Daniel H. Bays, "China," in *New International Dictionary*, 63. Two other prominent independent groups founded in the 1920s are the Pentecostal-type Jesus Family and Watchman Nee's Little Flock.

27 TJC leadership provided this estimate during my research. Although hard data for the figure of one million was not given, the following factors should be considered. First, in China many men are absent from regular worship because they work away from home in areas where there is no TJC congregation. Further, because the TJC practices infant baptism, these children are considered members. Finally, like other Christian groups, there is usually not a systematic culling of records when a person dies or ceases to participate. A rough estimate of regular TJC attenders in China is between 250,000 and 300,000. French's estimate of 3 million is unrealistic; see French, *Our God Is One*, 152.

28 See Urshan's own account in chapter 9, Andrew Bar David Urshan, *The Life Story of Andrew Bar David Urshan: An Autobiography of the Author's First Forty Years*, 5th ed. (Stockton, CA: W. A. B. C. Press, 1967), 104–11. For a comprehensive study of the life, ministry, and theology of Urshan, see Daniel Segraves, "Andrew D. Urshan: A Theological Biography," PhD dissertation, Regent University (2010).

29 See Urshan, chapter 15, *Life Story*; and Segraves, "Andrew Urshan," 207–15.

30 Pentecostal historian Cecil M. Robeck, Jr., reconstructed Urshan's journey, concluding that he likely ministered in St. Petersburg during April–May, 1916, before returning to New York in June. See Robeck, "A Pentecostal Witness in an Eastern Context," Prague '97: "Building Bridges, Breaking Barriers," *Prague, Czech Republic* (September 12, 1997).

31 Urshan, *Life Story*, 234–38; Segraves, "Andrew Urshan," 209–15.

32 French, *Our God Is One*, 145.

33   Roman Lunkin, "Traditional Pentecostals in Russia," *East-West Church and Ministry Report* 12:3 (Summer 2004), http://www.eastwestreport.org/articles/ew12302.html (accessed December 17, 2012).

34   Urshan, "Missionary Supplement," *Christian Outlook* 7:12 (January 1924), 3.

35   Lunkin, "Traditional Pentecostals." Lunkin categorizes Pentecostals who are part of the Union of Christians of Faith, Evangelical-Pentecostal as "moderates," whereas the more exclusive groups are "Traditional Pentecostals."

36   Phone interview with Mart Vahi, Estonia, January 4, 2013.

37   See Reed, *"In Jesus' Name"*, 334–35.

38   See http://www.acts29.ru/biography/?id=2 (accessed December 17, 2012).

39   French, *Our God Is One.*

40   French categorizes organizations by numbers, churches, continent and nation.

41   Official UPCI statistics posted on its website: http://www.upci.org/about-us/about-us (accessed June 11, 2013).

42   Report by the Association of Religion Data Archives, http://www.thearda.com/Denoms/D_985.asp (accessed June 11, 2013).

43   See http://awcf.org/content/view/35/65/ (accessed January 10, 2013).

44   Phone interview with the chairman of AWCF, Bishop Samuel Smith, January 9, 2013. From the beginning, the UPCI refused to join AWCF on grounds that G. B. Rowe, father of its first chairman, had been expelled from the UPCI in the 1950s over a teaching regarding the nature of Christ that deviated substantially from orthodox Oneness doctrine. The UPCI claimed that the son, Worthy Rowe, never denounced his father's teaching.

45   The original name did not include "International."

46   The story of revival and persecution in Colombia is well chronicled by Cornelia Butler Flora, *Pentecostalism in Colombia: Baptism by Fire and Spirit* (Cranbury, NJ: Associated University Presses, 1976).

47   Drost was later ordained; e-mail correspondence with Drost's son, Verner Drost, June 7, 2013.

48   Donald C. Palmer, *Explosion of People Evangelism* (Chicago: Moody Press, 1974), 60.

49   French, *Our God Is One,* 138–39.

50   Nona Freeman, herself a veteran missionary, was drawn into the Ethiopian story in part through her husband's appointment as Superintendent of Ethiopia with the UPC when the fledgling movement was still under its oversight. She tells the story of the early missionary years, conversion of Bishop Teklemariam, and subsequent revival in *Unseen Hands: The Story of Revival in Ethiopia* (Hazelwood, MO: Word Aflame Press, 1987).

51   For the account of his son's death, see Freeman, *Unseen Hands*, 142.

52   The first Pentecostal missionaries arrived in 1951, sponsored by the Free Finnish Foreign Mission; in 1956 they moved their ministry base to Addis Ababa; see Jörg Haustein, "Brief History of Pentecostalism in Ethiopia," *GloPent*, http://www.glopent.net/Members/jhaustein/ethiopia/brief-history-of-pentecostalism-in-ethiopia (accessed December 13, 2012). In 1967 the Full Gospel Believers Church (FGBC) was formed from student gatherings spawned by the revival on university campuses; see Jörg Haustein, *Writing Religious*

History: The Historiography of Ethiopian Pentecostalism, Studies in the History of Christianity in the Non-Western World 17 (Weisbaden: Harrassowitz Verlag, 2011), 14. Freeman reports that by 1967 more than 40,000 young people had experienced pentecostal Spirit baptism (*Unseen Hands*, 42).

53 Freeman, *Unseen Hands*, 42.

54 The tract was written by Michael Trapasso; cited in Freeman, *Unseen Hands*, 80.

55 The name was suggested by Teklemariam. The word Pentecostal (or Pente) was deliberately removed because it had become a term of derision and often attracted unnecessary hostility and persecution; see Freeman, *Unseen Hands*, 145.

56 Haustein, *Writing Religious History*, 218.

57 Support from the District of Louisiana was provided through the initiative of T. F. Tenney, who was at that time district superintendent. His acquaintance with the ACE began during his tenure as national director of foreign missions (1970–75), when as the UPC representative he was called on to moderate the ACE dispute. The first service in the mother church was held on Christmas Day 1980.

58 Interview with Bishop Degu Kebede, national bishop of the ACE, May 10, 2011, Addis Ababa, Ethiopia.

59 Teklemariam Gezahagne, *Bible Writers' Theology*, rev. ed. (Hazelwood, MO: Apostolic Experience Publishing, 1999; rev. 2007).

60 Teklemariam indicates that his motivation for writing the book was in response to the publication of Gregory A. Boyd's critique of Oneness theology, *Oneness Pentecostalism and the Trinity* (Grand Rapids, MI: Baker Book House, 1992). He also acknowledges there are "similarities" between his Christology and Coptic doctrine but also differences. Interview, Awassa, Ethiopia, March 11, 2012.

61 For an overview of this tradition with reference to the blood of Christ in Fundamentalism and Oneness atonement theology, see David Reed, "'There's Power in the Blood' – Hidden Evangelical Heresy in Oneness Blood Atonement Theology?" (paper presented at 42nd Annual Meeting of the Society for Pentecostal Studies, Seattle, March 21–23, 2013). A slightly revised version is published as chapter 21 in Rob Clements and Dennis Ngien, eds., *Between the Lectern and the Pulpit: Essays in Honour of Victor A. Shepherd* (Vancouver: Regent College Publishing, 2014), 309–20.

62 Teklemariam, *Bible Writers' Theology*, 182.

63 Teklemariam, *Bible Writers' Theology*, 128, 129.

64 For an overview of Oneness Christology, see chapter 13 in Reed, *"In Jesus' Name"*.

65 The difference between the ancient Alexandrian and Teklemariam's doctrine of the "divine flesh" is that for the former one can speak of the "one nature" only after the incarnation, whereas Teklemariam teaches that, although God is Spirit, the incarnation was potentially within God's nature in the form of Word from all eternity. His view appears to be a form of supralapsarianism.

66 See Article 3, "The Son of God," in *The Articles of Faith of the Apostolic Church International* (Addis Ababa, Ethiopia: privately published, n.d.), 10–16.

67   Degu, interview. I have been told by numerous Oneness leaders that the "divine blood" teaching is not uncommon in their circles and never challenged. It is simply not official UPCI doctrine.
68   Degu, interview.

Further Reading

Butler, Daniel L. *Oneness Pentecostalism: A History of the Jesus Name Movement.* Bellflower, CA: International Pentecostal Church, 2004.

Fudge, Thomas. *Christianity without the Cross: A History of Salvation in Oneness Pentecostalism.* Parkland, FL: Universal Publishers, 2003.

Norris, David S. *I Am: A Oneness Pentecostal Christology.* Hazelwood, MO: Word Aflame Press Academic, 2009.

Richardson, James C., Jr. *With Water and Spirit: A History of Black Apostolic Denominations in the U.S.* Washington, DC: Spirit Press, 1980.

Teklemariam Gezahagne. *The Identity of Jesus Christ*, rev. ed. Addis Ababa: Privately published, 2010.

Wegner, Linda. *Streams of Grace: A History of the Apostolic Church of Pentecost of Canada.* Edmonton, AB: New Leaf Works, 2006.

Part 11

Regional Studies

4 North American Pentecostalism

DAVID D. DANIELS III

INTRODUCING NORTH AMERICAN PENTECOSTALISM

Conservative Protestantism shaped the context in which North American Pentecostalism emerged at the dawn of the twentieth century. In a world populated with Baptists, Methodists, Presbyterians, Lutherans, and the Disciples of Christ, conservative Protestantism controlled the major Protestant denominations and their network of academic institutions and missionary societies during the emergence of Pentecostalism. North American Pentecostalism rose from the margins of conservative Protestantism; it was constructed out of the religious currents that most conservative Protestants had dismissed or deemphasized by the advent of the twentieth century: holiness, restorationism, bible prophecy, and healing. Attracting segments from the margins of conservative Protestantism known for demonstrative worship such holy rollers, holy jumpers, and holy kickers along with segments accused of using hypnotism further distanced the nascent Pentecostalism from the center of conservative Protestantism; glossolalia (speaking in an unrecognizable or unlearned language) became a minor distinction. The North American pentecostal propensity for interracial and multiracial gatherings, an embrace of recent European immigrants as leaders, and the presence of women clergy reinforced its outsider status within conservative Protestantism. It was too different; it transgressed too many recognized religious and social boundaries. North American Pentecostalism initially found itself in tension with the mainstream of conservative Protestantism.[1]

As a twentieth-century movement, North American Pentecostalism was constructed by segments of various nineteenth-century Protestant movements: the radical wing of the (white) Wesleyan holiness movement, the African-American holiness movement (Baptist and Methodist), Restorationists, the Keswick movement, and the (white and African American) sabbatarian movement. The differing and conflicting theological perspectives of these movements created the climate in which North

American Pentecostalism was constructed as a polycentric movement of myriad currents. The polycentric genesis of Pentecostalism carved within this emerging movement competing, and even contradictory, polities, worship forms, theologies, ethics, and sabbaths. The antidenominational impulse with its opposition to regulations and hierarchical control created a climate in which this diversity would flourish.[2]

In North America, most Protestant ecclesial traditions were basically mono-racial during the early twentieth century. Pentecostalism, however, emerged as a multiracial Protestant ecclesial tradition with a racial diversity akin to the Baptist, Methodist, and Holiness family of churches. As a multiracial ecclesial tradition, early Pentecostalism differed from its particular multiracial Protestant ecclesial counterparts in that it possessed a sector of interracial and multiracial congregations as well as interracial and multiracial denominations during the height of racial segregation in the United States. Additionally, as a multiracial ecclesial tradition, Pentecostalism differed from its multiracial Protestant ecclesial counterparts in that these counterparts possessed denominations solely founded by whites or African Americans, whereas Pentecostalism included denominations founded and governed by Latinos and Asian Americans, respectively, in addition to African Americans and whites. Emerging as a multiracial ecclesial tradition consisting of interracial and multiracial congregations and denominations as well as denominations founded and governed by African Americans, Latinos, and Asians, Pentecostalism generated new forms of Protestant organizational life and fashioned a new Christian witness. Consequently, Pentecostalism inaugurated a new moment within the history of Christianity in North America.[3]

A distinction should be made between the pentecostal tradition being multiracial in terms of its racial composition and types of racial organizations, as opposed to the movement being constituted overwhelmingly as racially inclusive organizations. In the midst of the multiraciality of the pentecostal tradition were major sectors within the movement that reproduced the dominant Protestant racial form of segregation, thus adopting the racial hierarchy model of denominational organization designed by the Baptists and Methodists during the nineteenth century.[4]

HISTORY AND PENTECOSTAL BELIEF

The Azusa Street Revival, the center for the emergence of Pentecostalism in North America as well as on other continents, erupted out of a congregation associated with the Black Holiness Movement. In 1906 a small black holiness congregation, headed by Julia Hutchins, hoped to sponsor a revival led by William J. Seymour. It did not work out as she had hoped, although Seymour soon led a revival in Los Angeles in which the black holiness began to participate in the construction of Pentecostalism.[5]

Seymour's meeting on Bonnie Brae Street attracted the attention of local whites and blacks. At the Apostolic Faith Mission on Azusa Street, the meetings drew large numbers of blacks, whites, Latinos, and Asians, especially those involved in the holiness community. Soon afterwards representatives of local and regional holiness groups throughout North America converged on Azusa Street to examine the new teaching.[6]

Within twelve months, the Azusa Street Revival spawned an international movement and published a monthly newspaper, the *Apostolic Faith*. From 1906 through 1908, Seymour, the Apostolic Faith Mission, and the *Apostolic Faith* gave the movement a major center and crucial early leadership. Like its holiness counterpart, the pentecostal movement was basically local and regional with varied leadership headed by women and men. In various places Pentecostalism absorbed entire holiness congregations and fellowships. The Azusa Street Revival defined Pentecostalism in North America, shaping it theologically and multiracially.[7] Even so, although multiracial congregations have existed from the beginning of the movement, they have always formed a small percentage of the whole.

Seymour was introduced to the pentecostal interpretation of the holiness message by Charles Parham. Parham popularized the linking of *xenolalia* (speaking in a recognized language) with the biblical pentecost event of Acts 2 and described this experience as the postsanctification experience of baptism of the Holy Spirit. He began preaching this new doctrine in 1901 within holiness circles in the midwestern United States. In 1905, William J. Seymour "enrolled" in Parham's school in Houston, although Parham's enforcement of segregation prevented him from sitting with the students. In 1906, Seymour took this new message to Los Angeles. By 1908, Seymour and others had redefined the baptism of the Holy Spirit in terms of glossolalia, deeming a sanctified life as a prerequisite for this baptism.[8]

Broadly defined, Wesleyan and Reformed Christianity, two major conservative Protestant theological traditions, dominated early Pentecostalism in North America. These traditions also informed a theological controversy that engulfed early Pentecostalism related to the theology of God. Additionally, minor theological currents flowed from sabbatarianism into some sectors of Pentecostalism.

Reflecting the Wesleyan perspective, the Church of God in Christ and the Pentecostal Holiness Church teach the doctrine of entire sanctification, whereas the Pentecostal Assemblies of the World, the Pentecostal Assemblies of Canada, and the Assemblies of God, reflecting the Reformed perspective, teach the doctrine of progressive sanctification. The Reformed perspective was often espoused in terms of "the Finished Work of Christ" and classified as Baptistic. William Durham, the key theological architect of this latter position, highlighted the atonement of Christ, with justification, as including the beginning of a lifelong process of sanctification and the experience of baptism in the Holy Spirit. At least for William Seymour and Charles Harrison Mason the Wesleyan doctrine of sanctification as the second work of grace was integral to the doctrine of the baptism of the Holy Spirit because it made ethics central to pentecostal teaching rather than glossolalia as initial evidence.[9]

During the 1910s, another theological controversy evolved around the biblical baptismal formula and the theology of God. Two baptismal formulas were promoted by Pentecostals: The Trinitarian formula (*in the name of the Father, Son, and Holy Spirit;* Matt. 28:19) and a Christocentric formula (*in the name of Jesus Christ;* Acts 2:38). By 1913, the Reformed pentecostal stream split theologically over the interpretation of the doctrine of God into two camps: one of them Trinitarian and the other, Oneness. The Oneness doctrine was introduced by the Australian American Frank Ewart. Although the vast majority of Pentecostals remained classical Trinitarians, a significant number of Pentecostals embraced the Oneness doctrine. Oneness theologians contend that the classical Trinitarian statement with its "three persons" does not adequately recognize the monotheistic commitment of Christian faith but devolves into a form of tritheism. Appealing to a modalist explanation of God, these theologians recognized Jesus as the "Name" of the God who at different times manifested God's self in the form (mode) of Father, Son, or Holy Spirit. The Trinitarians confessed the Nicene-Constantinopolitan doctrine of the Trinity.[10]

Sabbatarianism also shaped a trajectory within Pentecostalism in various ways. Central to sabbatarianism was recognizing Saturday as the Christian sabbath rather than Sunday. Sabbath-day observers included the Church of God, Saints of Christ among African-American Pentecostals; the Soldiers of the Cross of Christ and the Evangelical International Church among Latino Pentecostals; and the predominately white Seventh Day Church of God, which had a pentecostal constituency with occasional white leaders such as Milton Grotz and

African-American leaders such as R. A. R. Johnson and Wentworth A. Matthews. Other theological beliefs such as deeming Christmas, Lent, and Easter as unbiblical and unworthy of being celebrated by Christians, or avoiding certain foods such as pork, could be found among some Pentecostals.[11]

RACE, GENDER, AND PENTECOSTALISM

While theological differences defined early Pentecostals, pentecostal debates about the role that race and gender would play in the construction of early Pentecostalism also defined the movement. The centrality of Los Angeles in the advancement of Pentecostalism in North America and the Apostolic Faith Mission at 312 Azusa Street as a multiracial and egalitarian community offers a vision of the church that counters the racial and gender inequality practiced within conservative Protestantism by most white Christians. Key to understanding the debate is the reconstruction of the early pentecostal community, determining how distant or close it approximated the racial and gender arrangements of conservative Protestantism.

The historian Cecil M. Robeck has tracked Seymour's ministry from a small all-African-American revival in February 1906 to a predominately African-American revival with a few whites by April of the same year to a majority white event with 300 whites and about 25 African Americans by September 1906. He has contended that William J. Seymour, the pastor of the Apostolic Faith Mission, envisioned a racially inclusive congregation and practiced gender equality. Seymour and others who embraced this vision infused the early pentecostal movement with this impulse.[12]

Countering the conservative Protestant racial norm, the interracial and multiracial character of the Azusa Street Revival found expression in North American Pentecostalism in many ways, albeit limited. Multiracial and interracial congregations were scattered throughout the United States. In some places, the interracial pattern was whites participating in black pentecostal congregations. In Portland, Oregon, for instance, Florence Crawford assumed the leadership from an African-American couple who had led a Holiness mission. In New York City, groups of whites along with black missionaries worshipped at a black Union Holiness congregation pastored by Jonas Sturdevant. In Memphis, Tennessee, Glenn Cook, A. J. Tomlinson, and others preached at Mason's black congregation. In New England during the late 1910s and the 1920s, there existed an interracial pentecostal fellowship of Afro-Caribbeans, especially Barbadian Americans, and whites. Vinson Synan noted that the practice of biracial worship among poor whites and African Americans also existed in parts of the South.[13]

The racial climate of the United States should not be underestimated in its effect of undermining the interracial and multiracial impulse within early North American Pentecostalism and pressuring Pentecostals to conform to the patterns of racial and gender equality practiced in conservative Protestantism. As racial segregation became more entrenched throughout United States during the early twentieth century, Pentecostals who had embraced the interracial and multiracial impulse increasingly encountered opposition from religious and secular leaders. In 1908, African Americans withdrew from the Fire-Baptized Holiness Church, now the International Pentecostal Holiness Church. In 1913, the Pentecostal Holiness Church dismissed its remaining black congregations. In 1911, Florence Crawford led the withdrawal of many white congregations from Seymour's Pacific Apostolic Faith Movement, although her mission in Portland remained interracial for several years. In 1914, a large white group withdrew from the Church of God in Christ. In 1923, Francisco Olazábal withdrew from the Assemblies of God to organize the Latin American Council of Christian Churches; the Assemblies of God had sponsored its first Mexican-American convention in 1918. In 1924, the majority of whites, who held a slight majority in the Pentecostal Assemblies of the World, withdrew from the denomination, which was nearly 50 percent African American. In 1925 Antonio C. Nava and others had held a national convention for twenty-five Mexican and Mexican-American pastors within the Pentecostal Assemblies of the World; then, in 1930, Nava led a group of Latino congregations out of the then predominately black Pentecostal Assemblies of the World, forming the Apostolic Assembly of Faith in Christ Jesus.[14] In 1933, some Filipino Americans withdrew from the Assemblies of God, organizing the First Born Church.

Countering the racial pattern of conservative Pentecostalism that increasingly defined early Pentecostalism, there were Pentecostals who resisted this trend; this included whites and Latinos who joined black-led denominations. Between 1909 and 1924, four groups of white clergy and churches joined the black-led Church of God in Christ. The African-American leadership of the denomination tried three different ecclesial experiments to sustain interracialism. From 1909 to 1914, the Church of God in Christ functioned as a federation of three clergy networks: the original religious body led by Charles Harrison Mason, the nearly all-white religious body led by Howard Goss and E. N. Bell, and a nearly all-white religious body with a few Latinos led by Leonard P. Adams. As mentioned earlier, in 1914 the Goss-Bell network left and joined other white groups of clergy and churches to organize the Assemblies of God. However, the Adam's group would be joined by a small white group of clergy who left the newly formed Assemblies of God in 1916. This group was led by William Holt. Holt was instrumental in the second and third interracial experiment. In the second experiment (1916–24), Holt, Adams, and other whites would integrate the leadership of the original body led by Mason, with Adams being recognized as a member of the bishopric (called the board of overseers) and Holt becoming the first general secretary. During the second phase at least four Latino congregations also joined the denomination.

In the third phase (1924–32), the Church of God in Christ adopted a Protestant model of establishing a minority conference, specifically a white conference, to unite the white congregations across the United States that belonged to the predominately black denomination. This development was in response to the clergy who questioned the anomaly of white congregations in a black denomination as being a racial minority within the larger system and sought to maximize their presence by uniting them under a common administrative unit. The conference existed until 1932 when the predominately black leadership abolished the conference, accusing the white leadership of attempting to form a denomination with white members of the Church of God in Christ. For the remainder of the early pentecostal era, the Church of God in Christ would continue to attract some white clergy and laity as members.[15]

Another trajectory was the formation of a predominately white interracial denomination whose clergy membership increased rapidly over a five-year period from approximately 5 percent to nearly 50 percent African American. The Pentecostal Assemblies of the World was a small Protestant organization established in 1907 that was predominately white until the 1920s when its 1,054 ministers were nearly evenly split between white and black. In late 1924, the convention voted down a resolution to divide the clergy into two governing bodies: white and African American. The defeat of the resolution and the plan to maintain an interracial organization in governance led to the exodus of a large group of white clergy. By 1925, the Pentecostal Assemblies of the World became a predominately African-American, albeit interracial, denomination.

By 1931, the bishopric of the Pentecostal Assemblies of the World was interracial with four African Americans and three white Americans. The denomination sponsored interracial national conventions in northern cities including white delegates from the South. After the death of presiding Bishop G. T. Haywood in 1931, some of the African Americans merged with a white group of clergy and churches in 1932, leaving the Pentecostal Assemblies of the World an even smaller religious body. Although the predominately black denomination possessed fewer churches overall with even fewer white churches, it remained interracial and initiated the practice of consecrating a white clergyman every time an African-American clergyman was elevated to the bishopric to preserve its ideal of interracial leadership. In 1937 almost all the African Americans who left in 1932 returned.[16]

In eastern Canada during 1918, a group of Pentecostals had planned to join the Pentecostal Assemblies of the World. Instead, in 1919 they secured a charter from the Canadian government, establishing the Pentecostal Assemblies of Canada (PAOC). In western Canada, a group of Pentecostals joined the Assemblies of God in 1919. Between 1920 and 1925, the PAOC joined the General Council of the Assemblies of God. Similar to the United States, Canada also had a history of racial segregation in churches, with the existence of black Baptist and Methodist denominations. With Toronto, Ontario as its epicenter, Canadian Pentecostalism had emerged during late 1906 from the East End Mission led by Jim and Ellen Hebden. During the mid-1920s, however, Clarence Leslie Morton, an Afro-Canadian, began evangelizing in Ontario. By 1926, he had established Church of God in Christ congregations in Windsor and Harrow. Early Pentecostalism in Canada also included the Apostolic Church of Pentecost, the Canadian Assemblies of God (originally the Italian Pentecostal Church of God), and the Pentecostal Assemblies of Newfoundland and Labrador.[17]

A Native American pentecostal denomination did not emerge until 1945 with the establishment of the American Indian Evangelical Church. Among Native Americans, missions to Native Americans in the Shasta Lakes region of Northern California had begun during the late 1910s, and later in Nevada. By the 1930s, there were Native American missions in Washington State and Oklahoma as well as among the Navajos and Apaches. By the 1940s, missions to Native Americans had begun in Idaho, Montana, Minnesota, Wisconsin, North Dakota, and British Columbia. Although most of these missions were led by missionaries associated with the Assemblies of God and the Pentecostal Assemblies of Canada, a couple of missions were led by ministers associated with black-led denominations like the Church of God in Christ. By the 1940s, Native American pentecostal leaders associated with the Assemblies of God included George Effman, a Klamath; Charlie Lee, a Navajo; John McPherson, a mixed-blood Cherokee; and Andrew Maracle and Rodger Cree, both Mohawks.[18]

Following the dominant racial pattern within conservative Protestantism, today African-American and white American Pentecostals in United States are typically members of denominations in which their respective races are the majority of the members and the leadership; this is less the case for Latinos, Asian Americans, and Native Americans. Latinos, Asian Americans, and Native Americans have tended to belong to white-led pentecostal denominations and to be assigned to language or ethnic-specific districts within these denominations. Minor currents within these Latino, Asian American, and Native American communities are minority-led denominations of each respective race or ethnicity: the Apostolic Assemblies of Faith in Christ Jesus and the Church of God Pentecostal, International Movement, are predominately Latino; the Korean Full Gospel Church and the Filipino Assemblies of the First Born are predominately Korean and Filipino, respectively; the American Evangelical Church is predominately Native American. In Canada, however, all races tend to be represented in the majority white and white-led pentecostal denominations such as the Pentecostal Assemblies of Canada, which includes eighty-five First Nations congregations, for instance.[19] Although denominations such as the Church of God in Christ have existed in Canada since 1929, the majority of Afro-Canadians have refrained from following the U.S. model of white-black denominational configuration.

During the first generation of Pentecostalism, Pentecostals began increasingly to conform to the conservative Protestant norm of gender inequality – the role of gender in North American pentecostal ministry follows a trajectory akin to the white-black racial model. As early Pentecostalism became institutionalized the social space for women's leadership became more constricted, especially within white Pentecostalism, as its members sought respectability and identified with Evangelicalism. Differences must be noted, however, between pentecostal denominations and their Protestant counterparts, which mostly refrained from supporting women's ordination during the first half of the twentieth century, except in some Holiness and Methodist denominations. From its beginning, some North American pentecostal groups have ordained women: the United Holy Church, the Assemblies of God, the International Church of the Foursquare Gospel, and the Pentecostal Assemblies of the World. The cultural upheaval throughout American society during the 1920s produced varied responses against women's ordination within other parts of American Pentecostalism. Women pastors came under attack from some quarters for "usurping authority over men." Other male-led denominations always limited clerical authority to men. Some denominations such as the Church of God in Christ, the Church of Our Lord Jesus Christ, and the Church of God (Cleveland, Tennessee) have denied women ordination following their earlier Baptist or Methodist proscriptions of women. Although ordination was denied to women in the Church of God in Christ, the denomination argued that women could be evangelists and "teaching" missionaries or "women in ministry." This female classification was coupled with a "dual-sex system" of male-female leadership in which male leadership roles had parallel female leadership counterparts in the design, but women's roles possessed less authority.[20]

An outcome of the debate on women's ordination within North American Pentecostalism has been that more African-American pentecostal women than pentecostal women of other races have adopted the model of female-led denominations in which full male-female equality in the church is promoted. Consequently, the majority of female-led denominations was founded by African-American pentecostal women. Among the first female-led pentecostal denomination was the Church of the Living God, Pillar and Ground of the Truth founded by Magdalena Tate in 1903, which became pentecostal in 1908. Others include Holy Nazarene Tabernacle Church of the Apostolic Faith, Kings Apostle Holiness Church of God, Mt. Sinai Holy Church, All Nations Pentecostal Church, African Universal Church, and Mt Calvary Pentecostal Faith Church. Female-led denominations were founded by whites such as Florence Crawford and Aimee Semple McPherson and Pacific/Asian-American women leaders such as Rose H. Kwan, founder of the Lamb of God denomination in Hawaii. The major denominations founded by white women such as Apostolic Faith Church (Portland, Oregon) and International Church of the Foursquare Gospel became male-dominated within a generation. More women-led denominations possibly existed in African-American Pentecostalism because African-American Pentecostalism was less aligned within white Evangelicalism and its brand of patriarchy than white Pentecostalism, creating theological and ecclesial space for African-American pentecostal women to adopt the model of female-led leadership.

PENTECOSTALS IN THE CIVIC AND ECCLESIAL ARENAS

Pentecostals and the Labor Movement and the Military

Certain sectors within North American Pentecostalism were involved in the civic arena that spawned a trajectory supporting the labor union movement, pacifism, patriotism, and the civil rights movement. Often these sectors represented racial and/or class differences. Standing against the many Pentecostals who were opposed to labor unions, deeming them secret societies because of their secret oaths and passwords, leaders and laity of the Church of God Mountain Assembly and the Church of God of the Union Assembly supported unions from the beginning of the pentecostal movement. Church of God in Christ congregations in places such as Kansas City and Memphis hosted Brotherhood of Pullman Porter meetings and events. The Church of God (Cleveland, Tennessee) and Assemblies of God during its first generation allowed their laypeople to join unions.[21]

Both white and African-American pentecostal denomination espoused pacifism during World War I and to a lesser degree during World War II. During World War II, the Latino-led Apostolic Assembly of Faith in Christ Jesus adopted a pacifist stance, limiting military service to noncombatant status for its members. During World War II, some pentecostal leaders such as Lillian Brooks Coffey of the Church of God in Christ supported the double victory campaigns: democracy in Europe and Asia along with racial equality in the United States. Campaigns for civil rights also found other advocates in addition to Coffey.[22]

Pentecostals and Civil Rights

The Civil Rights movement polarized U.S. Pentecostals. William Roberts, a Church of God in Christ bishop, was a member of the delegation from the Fraternal Council of Negro Churches, which went to Washington, DC, in 1941 to demand jobs for African Americans. Robert Lawson, the bishop of Church of Our Lord Jesus Christ, joined Adam Clayton Powell, Jr., and other Harlem (New York City) clergy in campaigns for black jobs.

White pentecostal congregations such as the First Assembly of God in Memphis, Tennessee, attracted national attention when it barred African Americans from even attending a worship service, reflecting the racial stance of many southern pentecostal congregations during the 1950s. As a denomination, the Assemblies of God chose to conform "to American law and society"[23] in 1945 but, in 1957, tried to remain neutral on racial integration as a denomination, while allowing local and regional differences of opinion.[24]

Within black Pentecostalism there were clergy and laypeople who were involved in local civil rights campaigns during the 1950s and 1960s in their respective cities: Arthur Brazier and Louis Henry Ford in Chicago; Herbert Daughtry, Frederick Douglass Washington, Frank Clemmons, and Ithiel Clemmons in New York City; Smallwood Williams in

Washington, DC; Arenia C. Mallory in Lexington (Mississippi); Victoria Way DeLee in Dorchester County (South Carolina); J. O. Patterson, Sr., in Memphis (Tennessee); and Jasper Roby in Birmingham (Alabama). A few white Pentecostals such as Earl Paulk in Atlanta were also involved in local civil rights campaigns. Among Latinos, J. R. Rodriguez was involved in politics in Puerto Rico during the 1950s and 1960s related to constitutional status of Puerto Rico. Additionally, meetings for the Latino-run United Farm Workers were held in a congregation affiliated with the Apostolic Assembly of Faith in Christ Jesus.[25]

Pentecostals and Other Churches

By 1930, conservative Protestantism had lost its place as the center of American Protestantism and was fractured into confessional streams of smaller denominations, various theological camps within mainline denominations, major revivalistic denominations such as the Southern Baptists, and newer fundamentalist organizations along with Wesleyans, Pietists, and Pentecostals. Although the World's Christian Fundamentals Association formally rejected Pentecostalism in 1928, white and Latino Pentecostals still found openness to building coalitions with some fundamentalist sectors, especially Gerald Winrod and his Defenders of Christian Faith as well as J. Elwin Wright's New England Fellowship. These conservative ecumenical alliances were pivotal to the development of Pentecostalism as it delineated the epicenter of the movement during the mid-twentieth century that distanced itself from Oneness Pentecostalism, sabbatarianism, and Christmas/Lent/Easter as pagan. Amid the vast array of competing and contradictory perspectives within the emerging pentecostal tradition, the epicenter would lay claim to pentecostal identity and become representative of the majority of pentecostal people.

Gerald Winrod joined various Pentecostals in political causes and evangelistic campaigns. He worked with Aimee Semple McPherson and Jonathan Elsworth Perkins in California along with Juan Francisco Rodriguez-Rivera in Puerto Rico. During the 1930s, Winrod and McPherson joined together in fundamentalist-oriented youth rallies. McPherson's magazines (*Bridal Call* and *Crusader*) reprinted Winrod's articles on Bible prophecy and contemporary events until late 1938. Perkins, a cousin of Winrod, pastored a pentecostal congregation in Los Angeles that promoted some of Winrod's causes. Winrod led an evangelistic crusade in 1931 after which his host, Juan Francisco Rodriguez-Rivera, became the leader of a group of pentecostal churches that resulted from the crusade. This group became the Puerto Rican nucleus of the

Defenders of the Faith and the vast majority of the churches within the Defender of Christian Faith organization.[26]

Francisco Olazábal found non-pentecostal conservative Protestant support for his evangelistic crusades from the *Sunday School Times*. His 1934 crusade in Puerto Rico attracted Baptist clergy such as Daniel Eschevarria and Presbyterian clergy such as Carlos Sepulveda. Olazábal's 1934 crusade in Puerto Rico resulted from his invitation by the Puerto Rico's Defenders of the Faith.

During the 1930s, the black Pentecostals embraced black ecumenism. Black pentecostal denominations, according to historian Mary Sawyer, slowly joined the Fraternal Council of Negro Churches. The council, founded in 1934, was the first major ecumenical thrust of black Protestant denominations and leaders in white-led mainline denominations in the twentieth century. Among the black pentecostal denominations that joined were the Church of God in Christ, Church of Our Lord Jesus Christ of Apostolic Faith, Bible Way Church of Our Lord Jesus Christ Worldwide, and the Pentecostal Church.[27]

In New England during the mid-1920s and early 1930s, the New England Fellowship grew out of the conservative ecumenical vision of the pentecostal-run First Fruit Harvesters led by J. Elwin Wright. Fundamentalists such as William Bell Riley spoke at his conferences in New Hampshire. In 1931, Wright renamed the Harvesters the New England Fellowship. According to Joel Carpenter, "by 1935 the Fellowship was sponsoring fifty-two evangelistic campaigns, over seven hundred special services and short conferences, four summer conferences and a Bible study circuit that held 240 services in 35 cities and towns" along with youth summer camps, youth and young adult ministry, a businessmen's ministry, and radio broadcast.[28] The fellowship attracted a cross section of conservative Protestants, ranging from Congregationalists to Presbyterian, Baptists, Methodists, Nazarenes, Evangelical Covenanters, the Salvation Army, Christian Reformed Church, and the Assemblies of God.

In 1942 white conservative Christians from various movements promoted by Wright's ecumenical vision and Dr. Harold John Ockenga's leadership formed the National Association of Evangelicals (NAE) to provide a distinct voice for conservative Christians that could be differentiated from the separatist or militant stance of fundamentalists. The NAE also granted white Pentecostalism respectability and acceptance. The alliance between white Pentecostals and their evangelical counterparts eventually offered white Pentecostalism new conservative partners and access to a larger institutional network such as the flagship institutions of Fuller Theological Seminary and Gordon-Conwell Theological Seminary, religious publications such as *Christianity Today*, parachurch organizations such as Inter-Varsity and Campus Crusade, and institutions for the most part identified with the fundamentalist trajectory that reformed large parts of Fundamentalism into Evangelicalism. An extension of white conservative ecumenism was the formation of the Pentecostal Fellowship of North America in 1948, a pentecostal ecumenical body that denied membership to African-American pentecostal denominations. During the mid-1960s, Canadian Pentecostalism joined the Evangelical Fellowship of Canada and made shifts similar to those of their white American counterparts.[29]

By the 1960s, white Pentecostals assumed prominent roles within white-led conservative ecumenism through the NAE, marked by the presidency of Thomas Zimmerman and decades later Donald Argue, both of the Assemblies of God. African-American Pentecostals assumed prominent roles as cofounders and leaders of the National Black Evangelical Association, founded in 1963; these leaders included William Bentley and George McKinney. African-American Pentecostals were also cofounders and leaders of the Congress of National Black Churches; these leaders included Roy Winbush, a president of the Congress.[30]

Following the fundamentalist model of alternative mainline Protestant institutions, North American Pentecostalism has become undergirded by an array of institutions beyond the denominational and congregational structures that buttress the movement. These institutions range from Bible institutes and colleges, magazines and journals, to radio, television, and Internet broadcast as well as channels. White-led Pentecostalism has the largest network of institutions with more than twenty educational institutions, including seminaries and universities. Major charismatic educational institutions such as Oral Roberts University and Regent University widen this institutional orbit. These institutions serve as major employers of white pentecostal (and charismatic) educators, creating a class of pentecostal theologians and other intellectuals as well as educating generations of Pentecostals. Supporting the educational effort are the denominational publishing companies such as Pathway Publishing and Gospel Publishing House as well as independent publishers such as Creation House. Two major journals publishing scholarship by and about Pentecostals are *Pneuma: The Journal of the Society for Pentecostal Studies* and the *Journal of Pentecostal Theology*. Two major cable television networks dominated by Pentecostals are the Christian Broadcasting Network and Trinity Broadcasting Network.[31]

HEALING, DELIVERANCE, AND CHARISMATIC CURRENTS

As conservative ecumenical alliances reoriented the pentecostal movement away from sectarianism and assisted in delineating the epicenter
of the movement as a moderate form of Pentecostalism, there arose a
competing vision of Pentecostalism that emphasized the gifts of healing, prophecy, and deliverance. With an accent on the miraculous and
exorcism, these healing evangelists challenged the new pentecostal epicenter. In 1946, William Marion Branham, a white healing evangelist,
began to bring his focus on healing and prophecy to revival tents. This
new accent soon found expression in a 1948 Canadian revival in North
Battleford, Saskatchewan. The revival followed a Branham crusade in
Vancouver, British Columbia, during the fall of 1947. Branham's cou-
pling of the gift of healing with the word of knowledge – in this instance
revealing specific illnesses – impressed the faculty of the Sharon Bible
School in North Battleford, who conducted a revival on their return from
Vancouver. This revival spawned a movement called the New Order of
the Latter Rain.[32]

By the 1950s, Oral Roberts and Kathryn Kuhlman would headline
the healing evangelistic movement and A. A. Allen would headline
the deliverance movements. Among African-American Pentecostals,
Arturo Skinner emerged as a key figure who expanded the traditional
black pentecostal emphasis on prayer and healing to include demonology, exorcisms, and a heightened stress on miracles. During the 1960s,
other African-American deliverance ministries would be led by E. E.
Cleveland, Benjamin Smith, and Richard Henton. The healing and deliverance movements were the first major interracial experiment among U.S.
Pentecostals during the 1950s since the interracial experiment of early
Pentecostalism essentially ended in the 1930s. During the 1950s these
healing and deliverance evangelists challenged the segregationist ethic
of white Pentecostals and other U.S. Christians by rejecting segregated
seating in their evangelistic crusades, forging a new alliance between
black and white Pentecostals against the racial norm of segregation.[33]

Supporting the healing and deliverance movements was a group of
pentecostal businessmen that founded the Full Gospel Business Men's
Fellowship International and held their meetings in restaurants and
hotel conference halls rather than in revival tents. While their speakers
included Branham and Roberts from the sawdust trail, they also welcomed speakers from mainline denominations who had received the
baptism of the Holy Spirit.

During the late 1940s, Kathryn Kuhlman began to pivot toward the pentecostal epicenter and beyond it toward an inclusion of mainline Protestants, holding her healing services in Pittsburgh (Pennsylvania) at Carnegie Hall and First Presbyterian Church. During the 1950s, Oral Roberts also began to pivot toward the pentecostal epicenter and beyond it, including not only mainline Protestants but also lay Catholics. He began broadcasting on television in 1954 and renamed his magazine *Abundant Life*, known first as *Healing Waters*. In 1965, he established the Oral Roberts University in Tulsa, Oklahoma. Joining Roberts in producing Christian television shows with cross-appeal were Kuhlman, Rex Humbard, and Marion G. (Pat) Robertson.[34]

SUMMARY

Although U.S. Pentecostals have limited involvement with those who occupy the traditional ecumenical circles treated in Chapter 14, the largest sector of pentecostal ecumenism intersects with conservative Protestantism, especially the contemporary evangelical movement for whites, Black Church ecumenism for African Americans, and Latino Church ecumenism for Latinos. For white Pentecostals, the National Association of Evangelicals, Moral Majority, and Christian Coalition were prime organizations during the late twentieth century as Evangelicals became a major force in the electoral politics and culture wars of the United States. African-American Pentecostals supported the Congress of National Black Churches along with the civil rights agenda of the Rainbow/PUSH – a merger of two organizations: the National Rainbow Coalition and Operation PUSH (People United to Save Humanity) – and other progressive agencies. Latino Pentecostals engaged the civic arena through new organizations such as La Raza.[35]

Although North American Pentecostalism has spawned literally hundreds of denominations within Canada and the United States, it is as much a history of consolidation as fragmentation. North American Pentecostalism basically mushroomed in numerical growth as autonomous missions or small fellowships. However, very early there were trajectories that promoted mergers, especially the Church of God in Christ and the Assemblies of God. Interestingly the outcome has been that almost 90 percent of Pentecostals in Canada belong to two denominations: the Pentecostal Assemblies of Canada and the Pentecostal Assemblies of Newfoundland. Likewise, almost 90 percent of Pentecostals in the United States belong to four denominations: the Assemblies of God, the Church of God in Christ, the Church of God

(Cleveland, Tennessee), and the Pentecostal Assemblies of the World. Thus, the proliferation of North American pentecostal denominations indicates little about the organizational configuration of Pentecostalism in North America and more about religious liberty on the continent. The majority of Pentecostals in North America are organized in these few denominations, exhibiting a high degree of unity, indicating that movement in North America has grown and developed more by unity and less by schism.

North American Pentecostalism arrived at the dawn of the twenty-first century as a vital expression of a resurgent conservative Protestantism. Having migrated from the periphery to the center, Pentecostalism marginalizes its Oneness Pentecostal, sabbatarianism, and anti-Christmas/Lent/Easter constituency and promoted its commonalities with more mainstream forms of conservative Protestantism. Its white sector engages the larger white evangelical movement; its African-American sector partners with the larger Black Church; its Latino sector allies itself with Latino Protestantism; and its Asian Americans side with Asian American Protestantism. Consequently, the epicenter of Pentecostalism that encompasses the majority of Pentecostals can be plotted within the center of conservative Protestantism in North America, illustrating the loss of multiracial vision that marked early Pentecostalism.

Notes

1   See H. Richard Niebuhr, *Social Sources of Denominationalism* (New York: World Publishing Company, 1972 [1929]); C. Eric Lincoln, *Race, Religion, and the Continuing American Dilemma* (New York: Hill and Wang, 1984).

2   R. G. Robins, *Pentecostalism in America* (Santa Barbara, CA: Praeger, 2010); Vinson Synan, *The Holiness-Pentecostal Tradition: Charismatic Movements in the Twentieth Century* (Grand Rapids: William B. Eerdmans Publishing Company, 1997).

3   David D. Daniels, "'Everybody Bids You Welcome': A Multicultural Approach to North American Pentecostalism," in Murray W. Dempster, Byron D. Klaus, and Douglas Petersen, eds., *The Globalization of Pentecostalism: A Religion Made to Travel* (Oxford, UK: Regnum Books International, 1999), 227–31. The black-led "interracial" pentecostal denominations in United States include the Church of God in Christ, Pentecostal Assemblies of the World, the United Pentecostal Council of the Assemblies of God, the Holy Nazarene Church of the Apostolic Faith, and All Nations Pentecostal Assembly.

4   James S. Thomas, *Methodism's Racial Dilemma: The Story of the Central Jurisdiction* (Nashville, TN: Abingdon Press, 1992).

5   Cecil M. Robeck, Jr., *The Azusa Street Mission and Revival: The Birth of the Global Pentecostal Movement* (Nashville: Nelson Reference & Electronic, 2006), 69–86.

6   Robeck, *Azusa Street Mission and Revival*, 186–234.

7   Cecil M. Robeck, Jr., "William J. Seymour and 'Bible Evidence,'" in Gary B. McGee, ed., *Initial Evidence: Historical and Biblical Perspectives on the Pentecostal Doctrine of Spirit Baptism* (Peabody, MA: Hendrickson Publishers, 1991), 81.

8   Synan, *Holiness-Pentecostal Tradition*, 89, 92–94; Douglas Nelson, "For Such A Time As This: The Story of Bishop William J. Seymour and the Azusa Street Revival," PhD diss., University of Birmingham, United Kingdom (1981).

9   Donald W. Dayton, *The Theological Roots of Pentecostalism* (Grand Rapids, MI: Zondervan, 1987).

10 Douglas Jacobsen, *Thinking in the Spirit: Theologies of the Early Pentecostal Movement* (Bloomington, IN: Indiana University Press, 2003), 194–95.

11 Deidre Crumbley, *Saved and Sanctified: The Rise of a Storefront Church in Great Migration Philadelphia* (Gainesville, FL: University of Florida Press, 2012), 37, 125; Jacob Dorman, *Chosen People: The Rise of American Black Israelite Religion* (New York: Oxford University Press, 2013), 115, 153–55.

12 Robeck, *Azusa Street Mission and Revival*, 88.

13 Among the early multiracial congregations in the southwest were the Apostolic Faith Mission and Saints Home Church of God in Christ in Los Angeles and the Pilgrim Mission, predecessor to the first Church of God in Christ congregation in Phoenix, Arizona. The majority of African-American congregations with white members included Holy Nazarene Tabernacle and All Nations Pentecostal Church in Chicago, Christ Temple Pentecostal Assemblies of the World in Indianapolis, the Church of God in Christ in Detroit, Mt. Calvary Pentecostal Faith Church in New York City, First Church of God in Christ in Brooklyn, New York, and Holy Temple Church of God in Christ in Springfield, Massachusetts. The majority of white congregations with black members included the Stone Church in Chicago, Glad Tidings Tabernacle in New York City, and Hopkinsville, Kentucky, Church of God in Christ.

14 See Gaston Espinosa, "Francisco Olazábal: Charisma, Power, and Faith Healing in the Borderlands," and Daniel Ramirez, "Antonio Castaneda Nava: Charisma, Culture, and *Caudillismo*," in James R. Goff, Jr., and Grant Wacker, eds., *Portraits of a Generation: Early Pentecostal Leaders* (Fayetteville, AR: University of Arkansas Press, 2002), 183–84, 299–300, and Morris E. Golder, *History of the Pentecostal Assemblies of the World* (1973; reprint, Birmingham, AL: Faith Apostolic Church, 1993), 58–59, 70–72; cf. Talmadge French, "Early Oneness Pentecostalism, Garfield T. Haywood, and the Interracial Pentecostal Assemblies of the World, 1901–1931," PhD diss., University of Birmingham (2011).

15 David D. Daniels, "Charles Harrison Mason: The Interracial Impulse of Early Pentecostalism," in James R. Goff, Jr., and Grant Wacker, eds., *Portraits of a Generation: Early Pentecostal Leaders* (Fayetteville, AR: University of Arkansas Press, 2002), 264–69.

16 Golder, *History of the Pentecostal Assemblies of the World*, 76–86.

17 Michael Di Giacomo, "Pentecostal and Charismatic Christianity in Canada: Its Origins, Developments, and Distinct Culture," in Michael Wilkinson, ed., *Canadian Pentecostalism: Transition and Transformation* (Montreal: McGill-Queen's University Press, 2009), 18–19, 21–23; Dorothy Shadd Shreve, *The AfriCanadian Church: A Stabilizer* (Jordan Station, Ontario: Paideia Press, 1983), 91–96.

18 Robert K. Burkinshaw, "Native Pentecostalism in British Columbia," in Michael Wilkinson, ed., *Canadian Pentecostalism: Transition and Transformation* (Montreal: McGill-Queen's University Press, 2009), 142–70; Angela Tarango, "Choosing the Jesus Way: The Assemblies of God's Home Missions to American Indians and the Development of an Indian-Pentecostal Identity." PhD diss., Duke University (2009).

19 Eileen W. Lindner, ed., *Yearbook of American and Canadian Churches 2012* (Nashville: Abingdon Press, 2012), 187, 194–95, 205–06.

20 Estrelda Alexander, "The Future of Women in Ministry," in Vinson Synan, ed., *Spirit-Empowered Christianity in the 21ˢᵗ Century* (Lake Mary, FL: Charisma House, 2011), 375–400; Anthea Butler, *Women in the Church of God in Christ: Making a Sanctified World* (Chapel Hill, NC: University of North Carolina Press, 2007), 45–48.

21 David D. Daniels III, "Doing All the Good We Can: The Political Witness of African American Holiness and Pentecostal Churches During the Post-Civil Rights Era," in Maryann N. Weidt and R. Drew Smith, eds., *New Day Begun: African American Churches and Civic Culture in the Post-Civil Rights America* (Durham, NC: Duke University Press, 2003), 168–69.

22 Paul Alexander, *Peace to War: Shifting Allegiances in the Assemblies of God* (Telford, PA: Cascadia Publishing House, 2009); Theodore Kornweibel, Jr., "Bishop C. H. Mason and the Church of God in Christ during World War I: The Perils of Conscientious Objection," *Southern Studies: An Interdisciplinary Journal of the South* 26:4 (Winter 1987), 261–81.

23 *Minutes of the Twentieth General Council of the Assemblies of God Convened in Springfield, Missouri, September 13–18, 1945* (Springfield, MO: Gospel Publishing House, 1945), 35.

24 "Segregation Versus Integration," a paper adopted by the General Presbytery of the Assemblies of God, now available at the Flower Heritage Center in Springfield, Missouri.

25 Daniels, "Doing All the Good We Can," 168–69; Smallwood E. Williams, *This is My Story: A Significant Life Struggle: Autobiography of Smallwood Edmonds Williams* (Washington, DC: Wm. Willoughby Publishers, 1981); Arthur Brazier, *Black Self-Determination: The Story of the Woodlawn Organization* (Grand Rapids: William B. Eerdmans Publishing Company, 1969). On Victoria Way DeLee, see Rosetta Ross, *Witnessing and Testifying: Black Women, Religion, and Civil Rights* (Minneapolis: Augsburg Fortress Press, 2003), 117–37.

26 Matthew Avery Sutton, *Aimee Semple McPherson and the Resurrection of Christian America* (Cambridge, MA: Harvard University Press, 2007), 251; Geraldine Winrod Korell, *Rodriguez of Puerto Rico* (Wichita, KS: Defenders of the Christian Faith, 1950). Winrod's organization was called Defenders

of the Christian Faith; Rodriguez's became known as the Defenders of the Faith.

27 Mary Sawyer, "The Fraternal Council of Negro Churches, 1934–1964," *Church History* 59 (March 1990), 51–64.

28 Joel A. Carpenter, *Revive Us Again: The Reawakening of American Fundamentalism* (New York: Oxford University Press, 1997), 143.

29 Carpenter, *Revive Us Again*, 143–60; George M. Marsden, *Reforming Fundamentalism: Fuller Seminary and the New Evangelicalism* (Grand Rapids, MI: William B. Eerdmans, 1987), 47–50.

30 Robins, *Pentecostalism in America*, 78; Cheryl J. Sanders, *Saints in Exile: The Holiness-Pentecostal Experience in African American Religion and Culture* (New York: Oxford University Press, 1996), 99.

31 Robins, *Pentecostalism in America*, 86–90.

32 Robins, *Pentecostalism in America*, 79–80; C. Douglas Weaver, *The Healer-Prophet: William Marion Branham, a Study in the Prophetic in American Pentecostalism* (Macon, GA: Mercer University Press, 2000).

33 Robins, *Pentecostalism in America*, 80–91; Arturo Skinner, *Deliverance* (Newark, NJ: Deliverance Evangelistic Centers, 1969).

34 Robins, *Pentecostalism in America*, 86–90.

35 Robins, *Pentecostalism in America*, 112–19.

Further Reading

Alexander, Estrelda Y. *Black Fire: One Hundred years of African American Pentecostalism*, Downers Grove, IL: IVP Academic, 2011.

Blumhofer, Edith. *Restoring the Faith: The Assemblies of God, Pentecostalism, and American Culture*, Urbana: University of Illinois Press, 1993.

Sanchez-Walsh, Arlene. *Latino Pentecostal Identity: Evangelical Faith, Self, and Society*, New York: Columbia University Press, 2003.

Wacker, Grant. *Heaven Below: Early Pentecostals and American Culture*, Cambridge: Harvard University Press, 2001.

Wilkinson, Michael, and Peter Althouse, eds. *Winds from the North: Canadian Contributions to the Pentecostal Movement*. Leiden: Brill, 2010.

5 Pentecostalism in Europe and the Former Soviet Union

JEAN-DANIEL PLÜSS

CATALYSTS

The traditional narrative about the beginning of the pentecostal movement in Europe begins with Thomas Ball Barratt (1862–1940), an English-born minister of the Methodist Episcopal Church of Norway. Barratt had been an energetic evangelist, pastor, social worker, and presiding elder in Oslo. In spite of his achievements, he struggled to find funding for his City Mission project and hoped that the American Methodists would provide for his financial needs. Consequently, he travelled to the United States in October 1905. After an unsuccessful fundraising campaign, he was getting ready to return to Norway when he came in contact with writings of the Azusa Street Revival at A. B. Simpson's Missionary Home in New York City.[1] It was in the fall of 1906 that he experienced spiritual renewal that was later followed with the experience of glossolalia. This proved to be a transforming and energizing experience. Barratt returned to Norway in December and held the first meeting sharing the pentecostal message on December 23, 1906.

A revival ensued and soon spread to England, Germany, the Netherlands, Switzerland, the Baltic area as well as other parts of Europe. By the end of 1907 the pentecostal message had caught fire among many Christians longing for renewal in their churches. Not only were religious periodicals reporting about well attended meetings, but also there was a lot of reflection as to the nature of Christian spirituality, the urgency of mission, and a return to an apostolic (original) understanding of the church. This intense interest was not created in a vacuum. There were a number of catalysts preparing the ground for this receptive attitude toward what would eventually be termed a pentecostal revival.

One catalyst was certainly a renewed fervency in pietistic circles, especially in countries where the Lutheran Church was strong. Scandinavia had been experiencing popular revivals in the eighteenth and nineteenth century that had translated into religious conversions, a deep interest in the message of the Bible, and a concern for interior spirituality. In Finland, folk revivals had definite charismatic expressions, and it would be groups that had been nourished by this religious memory that would invite T. B. Barratt to Helsinki to minister to them in 1911.[2] In the Baltic region similar revivals were happening among Baptists.[3] In Germany the Lutheran Pietists gathered under the umbrella of the *Gemeinschaftsbewegung* and organized as *Gnadauer Verband*. They held evangelistic tent meetings in different parts of Germany and gathered in Silesia for yearly conferences in Brieg (now Brzeg, Poland) and Breslau (now Wroclaw, Poland) and were dedicated to the revitalization of their churches.[4] Pietism in the southern part of Germany had been influenced by Johann Christoph Blumhardt (1805–80) and his conviction that one could be victorious in Christ, especially when facing dark forces and sickness. He and his son Christoph Friedrich Blumhardt (1842–1919) brought a tangible dimension to the Kingdom of God by emphasizing the healing of the sick and the liberation of the poor.[5] The pietistic tradition played a major role in preparing the ground for the pentecostal revival because it encouraged concrete devotion as well as emphasized a physical dimension of God's Kingdom in the coming.

Another catalyst was the Methodist holiness movement, especially in its Keswick expression. It influenced many Protestant and Free Church leaders throughout Europe toward the end of the nineteenth century. Sermons by Charles G. Finney (1792–1875), Reuben A. Torrey (1856–1928), and others not only brought a focus on conversion and personal sanctification but also provided a rationale for spiritual renewal by speaking about "enduement with power from on high" and the need for a "baptism with the Holy Ghost."[6] In 1874 a Holiness Conference took place in Oxford, England, organized by Robert Pearsall Smith (1827–98), an American businessman who had been influenced by the holiness movement's emphasis on living a "Higher Christian Life," a deep commitment to the Scriptures, and a teaching that stressed living in purity and close communion with the risen Christ. During that time there was a growing understanding that the forgiveness of sins, the sanctification of the believer, and the restoration to health were all part of Christ's work on the cross and that there was effectiveness to prayer.[7] The approximately 3,000 participants left the Oxford Holiness Conference with enthusiasm, convinced that God had started doing great things to rebuild his church. Another author and conference speaker who had a great influence, especially in German speaking Holiness circles, was the Swiss pastor Markus Hauser (1849–1900), who focused on the baptism of the Holy Spirit and the second coming of Jesus. With regard to receiving the baptism of the Holy Spirit he emphasized especially one's attitude and an upright faith in requesting this blessing from God. The emphasis on the second coming of Jesus implied a need for setting things right before God and an urgency for mission.[8] The holiness movement then had prepared major themes that would be important for the pentecostal movement in Europe: a deep respect for the Bible, God's provision through the power of the Holy Spirit, the belief that sanctification as well as physical healing were God given possibilities, and the conviction that the work of the Holy Spirit would be especially relevant as the second coming of Christ was imminent.

A third catalyst for the outbreak of the pentecostal movement in Europe was the Welsh Revival, especially the period between 1904 and 1905. The prayer meetings and church services led to many conversions, resulted in radical transformations of the new believers, and included highly emotional phenomena. The secular and religious press regularly reported on the events in Wales, so that no church leader was unaware of the revival that touched more than 32,000 people. Quite a number of future pentecostal leaders in Great Britain had visited the revival and were affected by it. This was certainly the case with Alexander A. Boddy (1854–1930), Anglican vicar of All Saints Church, Monkwearmouth, Sunderland in the Northeast of England, who would become a leading pentecostal figure. After studying the Welsh revival Boddy travelled to Oslo in 1907 to acquaint himself with the pentecostal revival. He met T. B. Barratt, who later that year visited Boddy in Sunderland, where many experienced the baptism of the Holy Spirit.

To bring it to a point, it can be said that Pentecostalism in Europe was not just an import from the United States. At the beginning of the twentieth century the religious soil in Protestant Europe was ready for spiritual renewal. Many conservative Christians were seeking what increasingly was referred to as baptism of the Holy Spirit.

FEATURES

When talking about Pentecostalism many mention particular features that they associate with this movement. Either it is the practice of "speaking in tongues" or the importance given to praying for healing, the preoccupation with prophetic speech, or the belief in demonic powers. These are obviously visible phenomena that may or may not meet the characterization of current pentecostal churches in Europe, but there are also other features that are significant, especially if they are considered over a longer time span.

One such feature is the international network that existed among many pastors at the dawn of Pentecostalism. In an age of high mobility and electronic communication, networking is even more significant in the present. However, it is remarkable that at the beginning of the twentieth century, when air travel was not yet an option, so much travelling was being undertaken by church leaders. We heard about Alexander Boddy who visited the Welsh revival and then visited T. B. Barratt in Oslo. Lewi Pethrus (1884–1974), a Baptist minister in Stockholm, visited Barratt in January 1907. Jonathan Paul (1853–1931), a Lutheran pastor in Germany, also went to visit the Pentecostals in Oslo in the spring of that year.[9]

T. B. Barratt himself answered invitations from England, Germany, Switzerland, and Finland (then partly occupied by Russia) during the first few years of the revival. When Gerrit Polman (1868–1932), a Dutch minister with the Salvation Army, wanted to learn about the new movement, he travelled in October 1907 with his wife to Zurich, Switzerland, and visited a group that had experienced their Pentecost. As Polman went to a conference in Hamburg, Germany, in December 1908, he met leaders from more than a half dozen European countries.[10]

An even more significant role in developing the European pentecostal network is attributed to the yearly Sunderland Conventions that took place between 1908 and 1914.[11] Not only were these meetings visited by many European pentecostal pastors, evangelists, and missionaries, but also the messages and deliberations were reported in many religious papers and pentecostal periodicals began to be published all over the continent.[12] By 1913 not only did the Sunderland Conventions attract people from three continents, but also events were reported by the *Daily Mirror* and the *New York Times*.[13] This international networking would be abruptly terminated during World War I but found another climax shortly before World War II, when a large pentecostal conference took place in June 1939 in Stockholm. Delegates from twenty-one European countries met for worship and discussions in matters of pentecostal faith and practice.[14] Such meetings not only contributed significantly to the spread of Pentecostalism and its theological vision but also have remained an important feature of this international and multicultural movement.

A second important feature of European Pentecostalism is its theological plurality and ecumenical attitude. It is common to put Pentecostals into the evangelical fold because they have high respect for the Bible as the Word of God and because they consider a personal conversion essential to Christian life. However, it is easily forgotten that the European Pentecostals of the first hour came from a variety of theological and ecclesial traditions.[15] Whereas T. B. Barratt of Norway was a Methodist, A. A. Boddy was an Anglican vicar and remained such for the rest of his life. Lewi Pethrus of Sweden was a Baptist, Jonathan Paul in Germany was a Lutheran pastor, and Gerrit Polman in the Netherlands was a Salvationist. Pentecostals in Switzerland and France had ties to the Reformed church.[16] The famous English evangelist Smith Wigglesworth (1859–1947) became instrumental for the growth of the pentecostal movement in England, France, and Switzerland, but he never became a member of a pentecostal denomination. Instead he maintained his ties with the Brethren, the church affiliation of his young adult life.[17] Wigglesworth also became posthumously famous for his prophecy to David du Plessis (1905–87), a South African pentecostal minister, telling him that God would send him to all churches, bringing them a pentecostal message of renewal. This happened when David du Plessis began his involvement with the World Council of Churches and the Roman Catholic Church for which he also became an important liaison and advisor at the beginning of the charismatic movement.[18] When the pentecostal movement started, it seemed clear to its followers that the Holy Spirit was to be "poured out on all flesh" to invigorate all churches. That was the reason why many preferred a strictly congregational polity and were at the beginning apprehensive about creating a pentecostal denomination in their country.[19] This open original vision was also apparent in the writings of Donald Gee (1891–1966) in England, the initiation of the First World Pentecostal Conference in Zurich with the help of the Swiss pentecostal Leonhard Steiner (1903–92), and the sociopolitical activities of Lewi Pethrus in Stockhom, Sweden.[20]

As a result, European Pentecostals were theologically in agreement with fundamental tenants of faith – such as justification by faith through grace, the need of personal conversion, the authority of the Bible, the work of the Holy Spirit, and the second coming of Christ – but were more flexible in terms of ecclesial structure or the role and function of sacraments. For instance, Alexander Boddy continued to practice infant baptism, the Apostolic Church in Great Britain considered the Lord's Supper to be a sacrament not just an ordinance, and the first pentecostal denomination in Germany, the *Christlicher Gemeinschafts Verband GmbH Mülhein-Ruhr*, that had emerged from the Lutheran church, left it to the conscience of the parents whether they would want to baptize their child or wait until the child could request baptism on the basis of personal convictions.[21]

Similarly some European Pentecostals joined their American colleagues in teaching that glossolalia was the initial sign of Spirit-Baptism, whereas others did not.[22] Many Pentecostals in Russia practiced foot washing, whereas their Western brothers and sisters did so only in some groups.

Furthermore, as far as theological diversity is concerned, it is interesting to note that Andrew Urshan, Nikolai Smorodin, and Alexander Ivanov, who were instrumental in spreading the pentecostal message in Russia during the period of World War I, were Oneness Pentecostals.[23] They did not baptize with a Trinitarian formula but chose to follow a pattern from the Book of Acts and baptize in the name of Jesus Christ. In the early 1920s most Pentecostals in Russia were part of this "Jesus Only" or "Oneness" movement counting about eighty churches.[24] In the years following, Trinitarian Pentecostals under the leadership of former Baptist Ivan Voronaev and Gerogi Schmidt, both Trinitarians, made big gains in many parts of the former Soviet Union. By the end of that decade there were probably as many as 35,000 Trinitarian Pentecostals meeting in 850 churches.[25] It seems that the common experience of persecution during the communist repression between 1929 and the Brezhnev Era (1964–82) somewhat united Oneness and Trinitarian Pentecostals in spite of their different interpretations on the nature of God. In the 1990s the two groups had again a common agenda when they pushed for less emotional forms of worship and spoke out against the "prosperity" teaching that was flooding the many new charismatic and neo-pentecostal churches.[26] In spite of an influx of many Western pentecostal missionaries since the collapse of the Soviet Union there seems to be little influence by the classical Oneness pentecostal organizations from the United States and Latin America,[27] although the globalization of Pentecostalism has created many migrant churches in the large urban centers in Russia. Just how far Oneness Pentecostalism has influenced some of these groups deserves further study.

Another feature of European Pentecostalism is that specific ethnic groups played a major role in the spread of the movement. During the early days, for instance, it made considerable gains among German-speaking Europeans. The German minorities in Poland, the Baltic region, the Ukraine, and Transylvania (Romania) soon were visited by missionaries. Regular reports from these communities were published in various pentecostal journals up to World War II. After the fall of the Iron Curtain a stream of immigrants from the East returned to Germany because of their ethnic roots, and a good number of them were Pentecostal.

Another ethnic group that had a considerable influence on European Pentecostalism are the Roma (Gypsies). The Roma seem to have embraced the pentecostal message ever since Clément le Cossec started preaching to and praying with them in the early 1950s. The beginning of the pentecostal revival among Gypsies in Europe has been attributed to a healing miracle near Lisieux in France, when a mother brought her son, who had been given up by the doctors, to a church service and asked for prayer. The child was instantly restored to health and the whole family was converted.[28] Today the Roma in Romania, France, southern Spain as well as parts of Serbia and Bulgaria make up a significant segment of the pentecostal constituency.[29]

Another feature of ethnicity that is important to European Pentecostalism is the growing influence of migrant communities. The influx of Caribbean and African migrants to Great Britain after World War II led to the creation of new churches that for the most part were Pentecostal in character. The spiritual needs of migrants were practically ignored by the established Protestant churches, and the labourers from abroad did not feel welcome in the white dominated congregations. It was the achievement of Dr. Roswith Gerloff and Prof. Walter J. Hollenweger that these communities were first given attention in the 1970s. This involvement led to the creation of the Centre of Black and White Christian Partnership at Selly Oak Colleges in Birmingham.[30] Although the original intent was theological in nature, this project revealed that there were countless numbers of migrant churches that the historic churches had no knowledge of, and a good number of dialogues and projects were initiated helping many pentecostal churches to assert themselves in their social context and to empower their own initiatives. Similar actions began in the 1990s when various continental European churches began to realize that there were culturally diverse Christians in their country who had not only needs but also something to offer.[31] Although many of these migrant churches may not label themselves as Pentecostal, they share to an important extent a pentecostal spirituality. Migrants from Latin America, Africa, and Asia are now also joining classical pentecostal churches, sharing their vibrant faith and significantly increasing the number of Pentecostals, especially in urban centers. Furthermore, some pastors who came to Europe as missionaries from the global South have established large churches that cater not only to their ethnic constituencies but also to the indigenous population. Perhaps the most noticeable example is the congregation known as the Embassy of the Blessed Kingdom of God for all Nations, in Kiev, Ukraine. Its senior pastor, Nigerian-born Sunday Adelaja, is now responsible for a congregation that counts more than 20,000 members and serves the people of Kiev as well as its satellite communities.[32]

Also significant for Pentecostalism is its commitment to missions. Its root is found in taking seriously biblical passages such as the Great Commission in Mt. 28:19–20, the longer ending of Mark 16:15–18, and the call to evangelism in Acts 1:8 combined with the expectancy of the second coming of Christ. This commitment not only was significant for the spread of the pentecostal faith across the globe during the initial years of its inception but also is considered a major factor contributing to the surprising growth of the movement from the second half of the twentieth century onward. The European pentecostal mission activity can be seen on different levels. In January 1909 the first pentecostal missionary agency was founded in England. The Pentecostal Missionary Union sent missionaries and coordinated their field of action, often in cooperation with other mission societies. It set up training homes and took care of raising financial support. By 1915 the Pentecostal Missionary Union had six missionaries in India, eighteen in China, and one in the Belgian Congo.[33]

The Scandinavian pentecostal churches, on the other hand, have kept to a strictly congregational polity. It could be argued that they carried it to an extreme. "It was unthinkable that any central decision-making body should be permitted to have authority over the individual local churches."[34] Avoiding the formation of organizations, every individual church felt the need to provide to the missions mandate by their own means and missionaries. In Finland there is about one missionary to every 140 church members; in Sweden there are currently about 400 active missionaries in more than 50 countries.[35] These figures are directly related to the congregational emphasis in these countries. However, because of the need to coordinate missionary efforts, not in the least because of governmental funding for social projects, these countries began to set up statewide mission organizations.[36]

Another example of the centrality of missions in the pentecostal mind-set can be seen in the Swiss Pentecostal Mission, the largest pentecostal denomination in Switzerland. It was first a mission society founded in 1921, and the affiliated churches became a denomination only in 1935.[37] That their self-understanding as a missionary church is still significant can be seen in the fact that it is still customary in these congregations to raise at least one monthly offering for their missions and social development projects.

The history of the European pentecostal movement can be seen from two angles. The first would look at the revivalist background that permeated many of the historical and free churches at the beginning of the twentieth century and chronicle the development from there. This has been done at the beginning of this chapter. Little, however, has been said about Pentecostalism in southern Europe. This is where a historiographic approach is helpful that follows pentecostal missionary endeavours in Europe. France and Italy, for instance, had pockets of pentecostal believers early on, but the pentecostal message was brought to these countries by overseas missionaries, especially since the 1920s and 1930s. Probably because of the fact that these countries have been traditionally Roman Catholic, there was no indigenous movement ready to receive the revival. Instead, a classical missionary approach bore fruit – calling people to a living faith in Christ and praying as well as providing for their needs. Prayer for physical healing has been an especially important aspect of proclaiming the Good News by Pentecostals. The English preachers Smith Wigglesworth in the 1920s and Douglas Scott and George Jeffreys in the 1930s had successful ministries in French-speaking Europe; praying for the sick was frequently practiced. Italy was introduced to Pentecost through the Chicago-based Italian migrant church Assemblea Christiana that sent missionaries to their homeland.[38] Another evidence of dedicated missionary work can be seen in the fact that the relatively large pentecostal denominations in France and Italy carry the names of their North American siblings, for example, the Assemblies of God and the Church of God. Similar contexts can be found in Portugal, Spain, Greece, and eastern Europe.

TRENDS

As briefly mentioned, early European Pentecostals had no interest in leaving their own churches to form new denominations. They considered the presence of God they experienced to be a blessing meant for all churches and all nations. The newly created periodical *Confidence* reported about the first Sunderland convention: "We were Anglicans, Methodists, Friends, Salvationists, Congregationalists, Mission Members, etc., but 'Denomination' was forgotten. All one in Christ Jesus was true. Then we were English folk, Scottish folk, Welsh folk, Irish folk, Norwegian folk, Danish and Dutch, yet all one in Christ."[39]

However, with time denominations were formed, be it because some Pentecostals were ousted from their mother church as in Germany, be it because the government required a union or denominational entity as in the former Soviet Union, or be it because of practical necessity as in Switzerland. Furthermore, overseas missionaries of already established denominations founded new churches in Europe as part of the home organization. Now at the beginning of the twenty-first century there is a trend for certain congregations breaking away and forming independent entities. This may have been facilitated by the Neo-Pentecostal House Church movement in the 1980s and the rise of megachurches. The leaders in these groups argue that the New Testament does not endorse organizations but focuses on the Holy Spirit's dynamic role in the local Body of Christ through the God-given charisms of its leaders (Eph. 4:11). They also believe that the established churches, including pentecostal ones, are too slow and cumbersome to respond to the mandate of the day.[40]

Another trend that began in the 1990s is the transformation of churches into cell-based communities. The rationale is that a large congregation cannot be properly nourished by simply attending a Sunday worship service. The likelihood of an individual believer drifting into spiritual anonymity is to be reckoned with, especially in a postmodern world. For this reason small groups have been established that meet during the week, where believers can be encouraged to grow in faith and be personally approached and with whom others can pray. As these cells usually meet in private homes, they also facilitate the introduction of newcomers to a pentecostal church in an informal way. Small group leaders are being trained to ascertain a basic level of theological and leadership competency. If challenges arise that call for pastoral assistance, church staff is contacted. Cell-group-based churches can now be found all over Europe. In 2003 Kensington Temple in the center of London had a membership of about 11,000 and counted approximately 1,800 cells.[41]

A quite visible and audible trend has been the charismatization of other churches. Whereas Pentecostals were looked on with a certain amount of disdain in the middle of the twentieth century, their style of worship is now frequently being emulated with regard to contemporary worship songs, the raising of hands in praise, and the occasional service with prayer for those who have a physical or spiritual need. This has created new avenues for dialogue among the churches, but it also begs the question about the essence of Pentecostalism; Does such consist in the practice of charisms like speaking in tongues, the gift of prophetic speech, or the ministry of prayer for healing? Is it the style of worship or is there a theological dimension that can be called Pentecostal? New ecumenical challenges await Pentecostals, especially in Europe with its rich Christian heritage, as well as in view of the secularization and individualization of its societies.

Maybe the most significant trend relates to the globalization of Pentecostalism. European Pentecostals have frequently taken cues from their North American partner churches. However, now there is an awareness of impulses from the global South. It began with the participation of Latinos, Africans, and Asians in Sunday worship services. Their way of sharing their vibrant faith has invigorated many a congregation. Now as new migrant churches are mushrooming in Europe's urban centers, there arises the need for more ministers coming from their ranks. The candidates need training and join established pentecostal Bible colleges and theological seminaries. As they bring their stories and points of views into the class rooms, they challenge the theological status quo. They also share their enthusiasm and passion that can rekindle the fire among the third and fourth generation Pentecostals in the West, who in many cases have become less passionate in their faith convictions.

A look at statistics provided by the Federation of Pentecostal Churches in Germany illustrates the influence from the global South.[42] In 1992 the Federation counted 391 churches of which 13 were of foreign ethnic and/or linguistic background, and in the year 2000 it counted 493 member churches of which 72 were of foreign ethnic/linguistic back ground – an increase from 3.3–14.6 percent from the global South. In the year 2009 the trend had snowballed to 46.7 percent – that is, the federation had 498 member churches of which 233 were of other ethnic/linguistic origin. This trend could be easily complemented with figures from other areas in Europe[43] and certainly poses some challenging questions.

CHALLENGES

The pentecostal churches in Europe have a long history of facing all kinds of challenges. One that had a deep impact on Pentecostals in German-speaking areas of Europe was the *Berliner Erklärung*, a declaration drafted and signed in Berlin on September 15, 1909, by fifty-six conservative evangelical Protestant leaders condemning the new pentecostal movement as having demonic origins.[44] The reason for this reaction was provided by a number of chaotic worship services held in Kassel in the summer of 1907. Although the Pentecostals replied with their own declaration one month later,[45] explaining the context and their theological position, colossal damage had been done and would be propagated until the 1980s. The Berlin Declaration had a devastating influence on conservative Protestant Christianity in Central Europe and stigmatized Pentecostals as sectarian. Cooperation with other free churches and evangelical alliances was difficult if not outright impossible. Ecumenical encounters were few and rather private in nature. Only on June 18, 1996, did representatives of the Pietists and Evangelicals as well as Pentecostals and charismatic representatives meet for official reconciliation. They published a common statement, the *Kasseler Erklärung*.[46] That this conflict threw waves beyond Germany was also evident in the need for mutual public reconciliation ceremonies between Protestants and Pentecostals in the Netherlands in September and November 2007.[47]

The rule of communism in eastern Europe until the breakdown of the Iron Curtain in 1989 has also presented a formidable challenge to Pentecostals, especially those who would refuse to register officially for fear that they would compromise their faith if they were dealing with an atheist government. Harassment, imprisonment, deportation to labour camps, torture, and even death were the fate of many Pentecostals during a large part of the twentieth century. In places such as Bulgaria and the Soviet Union it was understandable if people argued that a true Pentecostal was one who had suffered.[48] Now there is a new challenge of course: How do new generations of Pentecostals define themselves?[49] Their spiritual identity is no longer established against the actions of an oppressive regime, but in view of Western liberties. The division between good and evil, the sacred and the profane is no longer easily drawn – unless one focuses on moral taboos and cultural mores. That the division between good and evil may be easier to establish in moral categories than in contextual ones may also be illustrated by the odd coincidence that while communism was the cause for much suffering in Eastern Europe, Italian Pentecostals found supporters in the 1950s among the ranks of the Italian Communist Party: lawyers who championed the rights of Pentecostals to assemble freely and defended them in an appeal to the Council of State declaring the persecution of Pentecostals illegal and revoking laws that had been established through decrees in 1939 and 1940.[50]

It has been mentioned that World War I put an end to the travelling activities of the early pentecostal leaders. It also put a strain on their theological understanding, because if the Spirit of God was infusing his church with "power from on high" (Luke 24:49), and the believers were encouraged to "make every effort to keep the unity of the Spirit through the bond of peace" (Eph.4:3), how could it then be that brothers in the faith could go to war against each other? Many early Pentecostals were therefore pacifist or conscientious objectors,[51] or they actively engaged in international bridge-building activities.[52] World War II also led to a collapse of many churches. Pastors were conscripted to military service and had to leave their congregations in the hands of lay leadership. The financial income to the churches (tithing) was severely hampered as many people no longer had a steady income. Work among the youth was in many cases given up. The young men had left for the army, and young women had to do the work of those who had left home. Support for foreign mission projects was made impossible as international financial transactions were no longer possible. The negative impact of World War II can only be guessed when reading statements such as "WW II also had an adverse effect on the growth of the pentecostal movement in Germany. It is estimated that 412 preachers, 11 female workers, and 7,000 members lost their lives during the war."[53]

Demography poses a further challenge. The historic churches in Europe have witnessed a steady decline in membership since the 1960s. This was upset to some degree by rising membership figures among evangelical free churches. A recent finding suggests that many of these free churches in Western Europe are now stagnating and that it is only the pentecostal and charismatic/neo-pentecostal churches that are still growing.[54] The question is, of course, whether such continued growth will be sustainable. Part of the answer lies in how pentecostal identity is being perceived and in how far Pentecostals can remain relevant partners in society. With regard to identity one may ask, how do Pentecostals define themselves? Is it through external markers such as speaking in tongues or a certain worship style? Is it through a particular spirituality that can be called Pentecostal? And if so, is this spirituality sufficiently strong to affect the newcomers? With regard to relevance the question is, can a dynamic faith be transmitted to a young generation of Pentecostals and can they be kept in the churches because this faith offers satisfying answers to the issues of society in a personal as well as global context? Will Pentecostals have a voice in a postmodern, individualist, and increasingly materialist world? Or will increasing prosperity in Europe tempt Pentecostals to consider their faith as little more than an attractive fundamental option? The answer to these questions may reside in the rediscovery of a prophetic challenge that European Pentecostals could be willing to maintain or make their own. It would be a prophetic and countercultural challenge to keep sharing the Good News until Christ returns, because people are increasingly lured to a self-centered lifestyle that is not satisfying in the long run. It would be a prophetic challenge to be responsible stewards of God's creation. It would be a prophetic challenge to remain a caring community, where people are not only fed intellectually but also ministered to physically and relationally. And last but not least, the Pentecostals of Europe, now that they are no longer marginalized and persecuted, may be challenged to work with a consciously ecumenical attitude, sharing their stories of how God has brought them together to keep the unity of the Spirit in the bond of peace and minister in the power of the Holy Spirit to edify the Church as the global Body of Christ.

Notes

1. A detailed account of T. B. Barratt's ministry prior to his pentecostal experience is given in David Bundy, "Thomas Ball Barratt: From Methodist to Pentecostal," *EPTA Bulletin* 13 (1994), 19–49.

2. Jouko Ruohomàki, "The Call of Charisma: Charismatic Phenomena during the 18th and 19th Centuries in Finland," *Journal of the European Pentecostal Theological Association* 29:1 (2009), 26–41.

3. Valdis Terlaukalns, "Origins of Pentecostalism in Latvia," *Cyberjournal for Pentecostal-Charismatic Research* 6 (1999), http://www.pctii.org/cyberj/cyber6.html (accessed February 3, 2012).

4. Chr. Krust, *50 Jahre Deutsche Pfingstbewegüng: Mülheimer Richtung* (Altdorf bei Nürnburg: Missionsbuchhandlung und Verlag, 1958), 33–39.

5. Frank D. Macchia, *Spirituality and Social Liberation: The Message of the Blumhardts in the Light of Wuerttenberg Pietism* (Metuchen, NJ: Scarecrow Press, 1993), 160.

6. Donald W. Dayton, *Theological Roots of Pentecostalism* (Grand Rapids, MI: Francis Asbury Press, 1987), 102; Jost Müller-Bohn, *Entscheidende Jahrhundertwende 1895–1905* (Reutlingen: Evangelische Film-, Buch- und Traktatmission, 1972), 308–18.

7. R. P. Smith was influenced by the theology of W. E. Broadman, who saw a connection between forgiveness and healing. Overall nineteenth century Pietism and the holiness movement brought about an openness to prayer for healing (Dayton, *Theological Roots*, 115–30).

8. Walter Hollenweger, *Handbuch der Pfingstbewegung*. Vol. II Part 5 (University of Zurich, 1965), 2036–39; Markus Hauser, *Komme bald Herr Jesus! Aus Schriften von Markus Hauser zusammengestellt und bearbeitet von Albert Jung* (Zurich: Verlag Hoffnungsstrahlen, 1902).

9. Krust, *50 Jahre Deutsche Pfingstbewegung*, 46.

10. People who would play a significant role in the fledgling pentecostal movement in Europe were already present, such as Alexander A. Boddy and Cecil Polhill (England); T. B. Barratt (Norway); Jonathan Paul, Eugen Edel, and Emil Humburg (Germany); E. and T. S. Cooke-Collis (Switzerland); G. R. Polman and P. Oltmann (the Netherlands); Andrew Johnson (Sweden); and Eleanor Patrick and Baroness M. Von Brasch, women who would play a vital role in bringing the pentecostal message to the Baltic states and Central Russia (cf. Krust, *50 Jahre Deutsche Pfingstbewegung*, 59–65).

11. Cornelis Van der Laan "The Proceedings of the Leaders' Meetings (1908–1911) and of the International Pentecostal Council (1912–1914)," *PNEUMA: The Journal of the Society for Pentecostal Studies* 10:1 (1988), 36–49.

12 In spring 1908 A. A. Boddy began with the publication of *Confidence*, just before *Spade Regen* was printed for the first time in Amsterdam. In 1909 Germany saw the first issue of *Pfingstgrüsse*, and in the same year Swiss Pentecostals started their periodical *Verheissung des Vaters*. Other papers such as T. B. Barratt's *Byposten* simply turned into pentecostal publications.

13 Cf. "A Pictorial History of the Sunderland Convention 1908–1914," in Tony Cauchi, ed., *The Works of Alexander A. Boddy 1854–1930* (Bishop's Waltham: Revival Library, 2010).

14 *Europeiska Pingstkonferensen I Stockholm den 5–12 juni 1939: Tal, samtal och predikningar* (Stockholm, Sweden: Förlaget Filadelfia, 1939), 436. Cf. also the report by Donald Gee in the *Gospel Call*, made accessible in http://webjournals.alphacrucis.edu.au/journals/AEGTM/1939-october/the-great-european-pentecostal-conference/ (accessed February 3, 2012).

15 Walter J. Hollenweger, *Pentecostalism: Origins and Developments Worldwide* (Peabody, MA: Hendrickson Publishers, 1997), 334–49.

16 Robert Willenegger was ordained by the Reformed Church of Bern, Switzerland, and Fritz de Rougemont was pastor of a Reformed church in Neuchatel, Switzerland; see Andreas Roessel, ed., *Erinnerungen an die Zukunft: Das Buch zum 80. Geburtstag der BewegungPlus* (Bern: Berchthold Haller Verlag, 2007). Louis Dallière, pastor of the French Reformed Church was an important advocate for the pentecostal movement in Belgium and France; see David Bundy, "Louis Dallière: Apologist for Pentecostalism in France and Belgium 1932–1939," *PNEUMA: The Journal of the Society for Pentecostal Studies* 10:2 (1988), 85–115.

17 http://en.wikipedia.org/wiki/Smith_Wigglesworth (accessed August 18, 2011).

18 Walter Hollenweger, *The Pentecostals* (London: SCM Press, 1972), 346.

19 This was the case in many European countries during the first generation of Pentecostals, especially in Scandinavia.

20 David Bundy, "The Ecumenical Quest of Pentecostalism," *Cyberjournal for Pentecostal-Charismatic Research* 5 (1999), http://www.pctii.org/cyberj/cyber5.html accessed February 12, 2012.

21 James E. Worsfold, *The Origins of the Apostolic Church in Great Britain* (Wellington: Julian Literature Trust, 1991), 31, 98f.; Chr. Krust, *Was wir glauben, lehren und bekennen*, 2nd ed. (Altdorf: Missionsbuchhandlung und Verlag, 1980), 135–41.

22 Jonathan Paul argued that speaking in tongues could not be a "shibboleth" by which Christians could be ranked (*Pfingstgrüsse* 1:1, February 1909, 1+2). Leonhard Steiner considered glossolalia as a common, but not exclusive, sign of Spirit-Baptism (*Mit folgenden Zeichen*, 174–78.) The German Pentecostals of the Mülheim-Ruhr stated that Spirit-Baptism is just another way of referring to conversion or coming to a living faith (Chr. Krust, *Heilszeugnisse*, 1:1, February 1967, 135, and *Was wir glauben, lehren und bekennen*, 107). Keith Warrington argues that George Jeffreys and T. B. Barratt did not believe that tongues was the (exclusive) sign of Spirit-Baptism, Keith Warrington, *Pentecostal Theology: A Theology of Encounter*, (London: T & T Clark, 2008), 121. Varying views were often tolerated within the same denomination.

23 Up to the end of the twentieth century Russian pentecostal historiography –
e.g., the article on Russia by Steve Durasoff in Stanley M. Burgess and
Eduard M. Van der Maas, eds., *New International Dictionary of Pentecostal
and Charismatic Movements* [hereafter *NIDPCM*] (Grand Rapids, MI:
Zondervan, 2003), 217–19 – assumed that the pentecostal movement started
in Russia shortly after the Bolshevik Revolution in 1917. Recent research
has, however, revealed earlier beginnings. See, for instance, J. L. Hall, "Early
Pentecostals in Russia," *Pentecostal Herald* (December 1991), 3–5. Albert
W. Wardin, Jr., "Pentecostal Beginnings among the Russians in Finland and
Northern Russia (1911–1921)," *Fides et Historia* 16:2 (1994), 50–61.

24 Roman Lunkin, "Traditional Pentecostals in Russia," *East-West Church
and Ministry Report* 12:3 (2004), 4–7.

25 Roman Lunkin, "Traditional Pentecostals," 5. Other sources claim that by
1927 the Union of Christians of Evangelical Faith, a union of Pentecostal
churches, had already 85,000 members. Cf. http://www.russian-assemblies.
org/index.php?option=com_content&view=article&id=53&Itemid=28&lan
g=en (accessed August 23, 2011).

26 Roman Lunkin "The Charismatic Movement in Russia," *East-West Church
and Ministry Report* 13:1 (2005), 1–3.

27 The United Pentecostal Church International (http://www.upci.org) has
its focus on Spain, Britain, and France. The Pentecostal Assemblies of the
World (http://www.pawinc.org) have two European districts, but its influence is limited to ministering to Afro-American and Caribbean migrants
in Europe. The Apostolic Assembly of Faith in Jesus Christ (http://www.
apostolicassembly.org) focuses its ministry to Spanish-speaking people.

28 S. L. Thomas "Gypsies," *NIDPCM*, 683–86.

29 Miroslav A. Atanasov, *Gypsy Pentecostals, The Growth of the Pentecostal
Movement among the Roma in Bulgaria and Its Revitalization of Its
Communities* (Lexington, KY: Emeth Press, 2010).

30 Hollenweger, *Pentecostalism*, 106–16. Roswith I. H. Gerloff, *A Plea for
British Black Theologies: The Black Church Movement in Britain in Its
Transatlantic Cultural and Theological Interaction with Special Reference
to the Pentecostal (Oneness) and Sabbatarian Movements*, 2 vols. (Frankfurt
am Main: Peter Lang, 1992).

31 Germany, the Netherlands, Switzerland, Sweden, and other countries now
have a variety of projects engaging with migrant churches. See, for instance,
Claudia Währisch-Oblau, *The Missionary Self-Perception of Pentecostal/
Charismatic Church Leaders from the Global South in Europe: Bringing Back
the Gospel* (Leiden: Brill, 2009). Afe Adogame, "Transnational Migration and
Pentecostalism in Europe," *PentecoStudies: An Interdisciplinary Journal
for Research on the Pentecostal and Charismatic Movements* 9:1 (2010),
56–73. Michael Bergunder and Jörg Haustein, eds., *Migration und Identität:
Pfingstlich-charismatische Migrationsgemeinden in Deutschland* (Frankfurt
am Main, Germany: Otto Lembeck, 2006), 206. Bernice Martin "The Global
Context of Transnational Pentecostalism in Europe," *PentecoStudies: An
Interdisciplinary Journal for Research on the Pentecostal and Charismatic
Movements* 9:1 (2010), 35–55.

32 See http://www.godembassy.com, accessed August 19, 2011.

33 P. D. Hocken "Pentecostal Missionary Union," *NIDPCM*, 971. The Pentecostal Missionary Union lasted until 1925 when its activities were merged with the newly formed Assemblies of God in Great Britain and Ireland. Peter Hocken "Cecil H. Polhill-Pentecostal Layman," *PNEUMA: The Journal of the Society for Pentecostal Studies* 10:2 (1988), 116–40.

34 Alf Lindberg, "The Swedish Pentecostal Movement: Some Ideological Features," *EPTA Bulletin* 6:2 (1987), 40.

35 Arto Hämmäläinen, "The Journey of the Finnish Pentecostal Mission," *Journal of the European Pentecostal Theological Association* 30:2 (2010), 51; L. Ahonen and J. E. Johannesson, "Sweden," in *NIDPCM*, 257f.

36 The protracted difficulties involved in establishing the Swedish Free Mission as an official representative between the individual churches and the governments are illustrated in Bertil Carlsson, *Organizations and Decision Procedures within the Swedish Pentecostal Movements* (Mariefred: published by author, 1974), 63–75. Finland began to seriously organize their mission activities in the 1970s; Arto Hämmäläinen, "The Journey," 60–64.

37 http://www.pfingstmission.ch/sets/geschi.html (accessed August 19, 2011).

38 G. Traettino, "Italy," in *NIDPCM*, 134f.

39 *Confidence* no. 3 (June 1908), 9f.

40 Michael Harper, *Beauty or Ashes?* in William K. Kay and Anne E. Dyer, eds., *Pentecostal and Charismatic Studies* (London: SCM Press, 2004), 252.

41 Colin Dye, *Kensington Temple: London City*, in Kay and Dyer, eds., *Pentecostal and Charismatic Studies*, 292. Figures from the *Christliches Centrum Buchegg* in Zurich seem to indicate a similar ratio of about 9 to 1 in terms of membership and small groups.

42 The "Bund Freikirchlicher Pfingstgemeinden" is the major umbrella organization of German Pentecostals, http://www.bfp.de/pages/wir-ueber-uns/statistik-zahlen.php (accessed August 23, 2011).

43 For similar figures, see for instance the 2005 English Church census indicating that non-white church attendance has significantly increased and that London, with 44% black and 14% other non-white church goers, has the highest amount of non-white church participation in the country, http://www.eauk.org/resources/info/statistics/2005englishchurchcensus.cfm#findings (accessed August, 23, 2011). For the growing influence of new independent charismatic churches in Russia, see http://www.eastwestreport.org/articles/ew13101.html (accessed August 23, 2011).

44 The accusation of demonic origin, literally *von unten*, clearly reflected a racial bias by the leaders of the Gnadauer Verband. It was not much help that the German Pentecostals stopped referring to the Azusa Street Revival, which had demonstrated an interracial character, and instead claimed that the pentecostal movement started in Topeka, Kansas, through the leadership of Charles Fox Parham, a white evangelist. See Cornelis van der Laan, "What Good Can Come from Los Angeles?" in Harold D. Hunter and Cecil M. Robeck, Jr., eds., *The Azusa Street Revival and Its Legacy* (Cleveland, TN: Pathway Press, 2006), 141–59. The text of the Berlin Declaration is available at http://de.wikipedia.org/wiki/Berliner_erklärung_(Religion) (accessed August 23, 2011).

45 For the text of the *Mühlheimer Erklärung*, see Ernst Giese, *Jonathan Paul, ein Knecht Jesus Christi – Leben und Werk* (Altdorf: Missionsbuchhandlung und Verlag, 1965), 165–69.

46 The text of the 1996 Kassel Declaration is available at http://novus-m.com/christusportal/christusportal/upload/P06_Praxishilfen_ben/Jahrhundert-Konflikt/die_Konflikt-Wende/Befreiende_Wende.pdf (accessed August 23, 2011).

47 Corrie Sleebos's "In vuur en vlam voor God en mensen," *Parakleet: Kaderbald voor geestelijk werkers* 27:104 (Fall 2007), 3–4, provides the account of events on September 15 at the Olympic Stadium in Amsterdam. For the speech delivered by Peter Sleebos to the Synod of the Protestant Church in the Netherlands, see 'Reactie Pinkesterbeweging op toespraak Dr. B. Plaisier tijdens Synode PKN," at http://www.vpe.nl/index.php?option=com_content&task=view&id=530&Itemid=78, accessed August 23, 2011.

48 Ivan Voronaev and other ministers began to preach about a "baptism of suffering" that Christians had to endure as state repression and hostility began to increase in 1928. Roman Lunkin, "Traditional Pentecostals," 5.

49 Charismatic and neo-pentecostal groups have had a considerable influence on traditional Pentecostals in the former Soviet Union. In the 1970s the Baptist Charismatic St. Olav's Church (Oleviste kirik) in Tallinn deeply affected other Christian groups way beyond the confines of Estonia, introducing new styles of church music and new approaches to evangelism. Whereas more traditional groups, such as the New Generation Church Movement led by Alexey Ledyaev (Riga, Latvia), whose writings are widely read, prefer to focus on conservative religious and political values. See William Yoder, "Penicillin or Cyanide?," *Baptist Relations News* (July 25, 2011), http://www.baptistrelations.org/page1.html (accessed August 30, 2011).

50 Hollenweger, *The Pentecostals*, 252.

51 Jay Beaman, *Pentecostal Pacifism* (Hillsboro, KA: Center for Mennonite Brethren Studies, 1989), 32ff., 60–65, 101.

52 Gerrit Polman, the founder of Pentecostalism in the Netherlands, ministered to imprisoned German soldiers in England and English prisoners of war in Germany. A. A. Boddy and A. Urshan were also crossing war zones. See Beaman, *Pentecostal Pacifism*, 87–95.

53 A. Adogame, "Germany," *NIDPCM*, 110.

54 Matthias Herren, "Mitgliederzahlen der Freikirchen stagniert. Nur pfingstlerische Gemeinden konnten in den letzten Jahren zulegen," *Neue Zürcher Zeitung* (July 25, 2011), 8. The Federation of Pentecostal Churches in Germany reports a 32% increase in church attendance between 1996 and January 1, 2009 (from 48,500 to 64,100) and an increase in membership from 28,000 to 44,100 (from 57.7% to 68.8% of total attendance) in that same time period, http://www.bfp.de/pages/wir-ueber-uns/statistik-zahlen.php (accessed August 23, 2011).

Further Reading

Beckford, Robert. *Dread and Pentecostal: A Political Theology for the Black Church in Britain.* London: Society for Promoting Christian Knowledge, 2000.

Coleman, Simon. *The Globalisation of Charismatic Christianity: Spreading the Gospel of Prosperity.* Cambridge Studies in Ideology and Religion 12. Cambridge, UK: Cambridge University Press, 2000.

Eisenlöffel, Ludwig David. *Freikirchliche Pfingstbewegung in Deutschland.* Göttingen: V&R Unipress, 2006.

Fletcher, William C. *Soviet Charismatics: The Pentecostals in the USSR.* Frankfurt am Main: Peter Lang Publishing, 1985.

Hocken, Peter. *Streams of Renewal: Origins and Early Development of the Charismatic Movement in Great Britain.* 2nd ed. Milton Keynes, UK: Paternoster Press, 1997.

Jansen, Mechteld, and Hijme Stoffels, eds. *A Moving God: Immigrant Churches in the Netherlands.* Zürich: LIT Verlag, 2008.

Kay, William K. *Pentecostals in Britain.* Milton Keynes, UK: Paternoster Press, 2002.

Kay, William K., and Anne E. Dyer, eds. *European Pentecostalism.* Leiden: Brill, 2011.

Murphy, Liam D. *Believing in Belfast: Charismatic Christianity after the Troubles.* Durham, NC: Carolina Academic Press, 2010.

Robinson, James. *Pentecostal Origins: Early Pentecostalism in Ireland in the Context of the British Isles.* Carlisle, UK: Paternoster Press, 2005.

Ugbe, Abel. *Shades of Belonging: African Pentecostals in Twenty-First Century Ireland.* Trenton, NJ: Africa World Press, 2008.

van der Laan, Cornelis. *Sectarian against His Will: Gerrit Roelof Polman and the Birth of Pentecostalism in the Netherlands.* Metuchen, NJ: Scarecrow Press, 1991.

Versteeg, Peter G. A. *The Ethnography of a Dutch Pentecostal Church: Vineyard Utrecht and the International Charismatic Movement.* Lewiston, NY: Edwin Mellen Press, 2011.

Wakefield, Gavin. *Alexander Boddy: Pentecostal Anglican Pioneer.* Carlisle, UK: Paternoster Press, 2007.

Wanner, Catherine. *Communities of the Converted: Ukrainians and Global Evangelism.* Ithaca, NY: Cornell University Press, 2007.

6 Pentecostalism in Latin America

DANIEL RAMIREZ

INTRODUCTION

The flood of pentecostal revivalism in the Spanish and Portuguese-speaking Americas in the last quarter of the twentieth and first decade of the twenty-first centuries captured the attention of social scientists. Andrew Chesnut explored Pentecostalism's thaumaturgic charms and later applied rational choice theory to explain the movement's success.[1] David Martin opined about its democratic political potential.[2] Such sanguine assessments glossed over historical sociologist Jean-Pierre Bastian's earlier lament over the mutation of historic Protestantism's critical liberalism into a hybrid religious magical system that replicated the strongman features (*caudillismo*) and clientelism of Latin American populism.[3] For others, pneumatic revivalism threatened to dim liberation theology's flame (in tandem with the Vatican's suppression). Threaded throughout the analyses was a shared recognition of impressive growth. Many of the templates and patterns emerging out of the contemporary data, however, can also be observed in the movement's early decades. This chapter assays an interdisciplinary discussion of Latin American and Latino Pentecostalism from the vantage point of history. It also seeks to engage the cultural insights proffered by pentecostal scholars from the region, where pentecostal history stands in need of a careful nuancing (so, too, do the received typologies and rubrics). This thematic approach necessarily sacrifices a comprehensive chronology. For a more specific, country-by-country discussion, readers are encouraged to consult the valuable survey by Everett Wilson as well as the bibliographic references.[4]

CAVEATS

A recognition of the longer history of *evangelicalismo* in Iberia and in Hispanic and Lusophone America helps guard against the notion of

Pentecostalism as a *tabula rasa*. Projects of religious dissent date back to proto-*evangélico* antecedents such as the Waldensians in twelfth-century northern Italy (their Protestantized progeny appear in the important nineteenth-century migrations to the southern cone); sixteenth-century Bible translators Juan Enzinas, Casiodoro de Reina, and Cipriano de Valera (their corpus endured to seed the *evangelicalismo* of the nineteenth century); and nineteenth-century Masons, and Liberals, including priests (their hard-won, albeit uneven, separation of church and state opened crevices of dissent into which flowed Bibles and Protestant missions).[5] An urge for autonomy, however, was evident from *evangelicalismo*'s earliest days. Mexico's nationalistic Iglesia de Jesús (formed by dissident priests) waged a bitter debate with Methodists over the former's claim to an organic genealogy (akin to sixteenth-century Anglicanism) and the latter's subordination to U.S. bishops. Other proto-*evangélico* scissions in Mexico, the southwest United States, and Chile discarded confessional labels altogether (e.g., the Iglesia Evangélica Independiente). The often clumsy unilateral implementation of comity agreements (e.g., the 1914 Cincinnati Plan divvying up Protestant work in Mexico), the growing tensions between liberal and fundamentalist camps in U.S. denominations and missionary agencies, the drastic interruption of war (e.g., the Mexican Revolution of 1910–17), and protracted church-state conflicts made for uneven maturation and even resentment.[6] As *evangelicalismo* entered into adolescence, the catalyst for future growth arrived, borne in the burning hearts of pentecostal migrants and missionaries. The infusion would trigger the already fissiparous *evangélico* DNA into a perennial and intensifying process of metastasis. This confessional ambivalence and mobility correct a view of early Pentecostals as parasitic opportunists. They also should give pause to contemporary leaders and students of Pentecostalism, who insist on fixed loyalties and identities.

It is also worth noting here a difference between the Anglo-American and the Latino/Latin American pentecostal experience. Although Methodist, Presbyterian, and Holiness orbits pulsed, as did their North American counterparts, with revival expectations and yearnings for a "higher life," these impulses – save for the experiences of some missionaries – did not reflect generally an exasperation with an institutionalizing Protestantism. With some notable exceptions, there were simply too few *evangélico* institutions to renew or "come out of." Rather, *pentecostalismo* arrived as a younger sibling religiosity and buttressed *evangelicalismo*'s viability in the Catholic-dominated ecologies of Latin America. Early *pentecostales* gathered up and energized scattered nuclei of proto-*evangélico* believers and reached deeply into the proletarian and peasant niches missed by historic Protestantism. The subsoil of popular Catholic religiosity (with its expectation of the miraculous and battle with the demonic) and popular culture (with its corporeality and festive musicality) provided the elements for a distinct hybrid. The reaction of detractors is telling, especially the epithet of choice they coined early on to hurl at this particularly noisy brand of *evangélico*: *Aleluya*. The term denoted the transgressive sonic and aesthetic features of the upstart movement. In Chile, early Pentecostals were tagged as *canutos*, a derisive allusion to a precursor: Juan Canut de Bon (1846–96), a combative street preacher-tailor of Spanish-Catalán extraction (and former lay Jesuit) who flitted between Presbyterian and Methodist identities. Both epithets signaled a downscale evangelism and were appropriated later as badges of pride in pentecostal hymnody and folklore.

EARLY *PENTECOSTALES*

The movement's periodical record documents Mexicans' early participation in the Los Angeles Azusa Street Revival (1906–09). Notably, the revival's heavenly cacophony included the speech acts of a "poor," "rough" Indian from central Mexico, who, on hearing the testimony of a German-speaking woman, was moved to lay hands on an English-speaking woman suffering from consumption and then to testify at some length in his indigenous language. Unfortunately, the editors' linguistic captivity led to the severe redaction of this intriguing discursive unit in the *Apostolic Faith*. They only reported the words that were intelligible to them: "Jesus Christ" and "Hallelujah."[7] Thus, we are left bereft of more information about one of Azusa's original languages (whether Otomí, Purepecha, Totonaco, Nahuatl, Mixteco, or other language of Mesoamerica) – an ironic omission given the revival's xenolalic thrust. We also lack any traces of the indigenous migrant's later trajectory and possible return to deep Mexico. By contrast, the editors published the bilingual testimony of "Spanish" evangelists Abundio and Rosa López, replicating, as a result, the racialized social hierarchies of New Spain and Mexico. The historical problem is compounded further by the exit of some Mexican participants from the Azusa Street Mission in 1909 (others stayed). Thereafter the movement's record privileged accounts of missionary strategy and action, as well as sites of origin and conflict in North America (e.g., Topeka, Houston, Azusa Street, Chicago, Arroyo Seco, Hot Springs). The experiences and beliefs of Latinos and Latin Americans – especially indigenous ones – were often treated as derivative and rarely constitutive of early Pentecostalism.

The available record generally points to an expansion of the movement via migration throughout the long borderlands swath from the Pacific Ocean to the Gulf of Mexico and to deeper incursion into north central Mexico by 1914. A parallel expansion followed the contours of the new Puerto Rican labor diaspora that stretched from that newly acquired Caribbean territory to northern California and Hawaii. The epistolary record also points to parallel revival streams flowing out of Wales and South India. The latter site and its ties to global Methodist circuits proved catalytic, for example, to the pneumaticization of *evangelicalismo* in the Southern Cone.

PERIODIZATION

In broad strokes, then, the periodization of Latin American Pentecostalism can begin with the capture of a renewalist sector of Methodist, Presbyterian, and Christian Missionary Alliance churches in Chile in 1909, the arrival of Swedish and Italian migrant preachers to Argentina and Brazil in 1910, the return of a migrant woman to Chihuahua in 1914, and the arrival of a Puerto Rican labor migrant-turned-evangelist to the Caribbean in 1916. Concurrently, the decade of the 1910s saw the arrival of pioneer missionaries – of several nationalities and ethnic extractions – to Venezuela, Peru, and Central America. In the case of Mexico, weakened Congregationalist and Methodist connections (the revolutionary tumult had pushed most missionary forces out of the country) facilitated the arrival of Pentecostalism. In El Salvador, the first conversions were, in fact, spirit baptisms among Baptist and Central American Mission *evangélicos*.

The following period saw the full-fledged entrance of young U.S. denominations (Assemblies of God, Church of God, Foursquare Church), the splintering of native ones, the spillover into contiguous republics (e.g., from Venezuela to Colombia, and from El Salvador to Nicaragua), and the onset of persecution. Latin American scholars have set off this "missionary" period from the earlier one. The different periods and points of genesis prompted Manuel Gaxiola (Mexico) and Juan Sepulveda (Chile) to argue for an autochthonous *criollo* (native) Pentecostalism that predates and stands apart from a missionary one.[8] Missiologist Douglas Peterson noted, however, that the thin geographical coverage by veteran and novice U.S. missionaries allowed the growing and vast number of native preachers and laypersons to fashion an effectively *criollo* Pentecostalism as well. For Peterson, the ties linking national leaders of Assemblies of God denominations represent more a consensual confederation than a U.S.-dominated hemispheric franchise.[9] Nevertheless, the perennial assertion of autonomy, evident in schisms, hints at some measure of discontent. Catholic antagonism also spread and strengthened the movement. Colombia's civil war (1947–63) between Conservatives and Liberals pushed Oneness believers, whose origins in that country dated to the 1930s, into Venezuela (1955) and Ecuador (1957). In Mexico, Archbishop Luis Martínez's "Cruzada en Defensa de la Fe Católica," launched as part of the golden anniversary of the coronation of the Virgen de Guadalupe as Patroness of the Americas (1944–45), culminated a series of bishops' pastoral letters warning about foreign beliefs that were "stealing from Mexicans their dearest treasure, the Catholic faith, which the Very Holy Virgin of Guadalupe brought us four centuries ago."[10] The discursive attacks, together with violent ones across the country prompted David Ruesgas and other leaders (including Masons) to form the Comité Nacional Evangélico de Defensa in 1948. The 1958–59 Cuban Revolution represented another development that threatened to impinge on pentecostals' longevity. The exit of foreign missionaries, however, allowed Pentecostals on the island to "Cubanize" their churches over time.

The next major periodization put forth by scholars generally reflects the emergence of the charismatic movement in historic Protestant churches (with continued schisms among pentecostal denominations and the appearance of new ones such as Manoel de Mello's Brasil para Cristo and its spinoff Deus é Amor) and, more importantly, the emergence of a potent renewal movement in the Catholic Church in the 1960s. At the lay level, denominational loyalties were constantly superseded by the fluid proclivities inherited from earlier proto-*evangélicos*. Pneumatic Christians continued to flit easily between denominational rubrics. Leaders discovered, to their chagrin, that the same opportunistic tendencies that allowed their movement to thrive at the expense of historical Protestant churches, also later facilitated the growth of charismatic and neo-pentecostal movements. Thus, the several iterations of pneumatic revivalism – Classic, Charismatic and neo-Pentecostal – should not be viewed as discrete phenomena but rather as organically linked and overlapping. In the case of the charismatic movement, precursor evangelists such as William Branham and Eugene Garrett found great receptivity on the ground for their faith healing and "Latter Rain" messages in the late 1940s. They also modeled ways of convening different groups around healing and evangelistic campaigns. This primed and reinforced Pentecostals' readiness to engage in broader initiatives, such as a Billy Graham tour in 1957 and the Evangelism-In-Depth program started by the Latin America Mission in Central America in 1960. Later faith-healing evangelists, such as Oral Roberts, similarly inspired broad cooperation and parallel careers, including that of José Joaquín "Yiye" Avila of Puerto Rico, perhaps the most ubiquitous faith-healing evangelist of the following decades. Several U.S.-based charismatic groups followed the missionary patterns of their classic predecessors. The Eureka, California-based Gospel Outreach attracted veteran Guatemalan general Efraín Rios Montt to its Iglesia del Verbo; his installation as president of Guatemala through a military coup in 1982 enjoyed the church's blessing. His short-lived regime represented a controversial first for *evangélico* politics.[11] Events of the period also widened fissures between ecumenical liberationists and conservatives. The latter group received vigorous support from U.S. quarters, including the Billy Graham Evangelistic Association and Church Growth exponents wielding data drawn from pentecostal case studies. Similar tensions threatened to pull Nicaraguan pentecostal churches apart after the Sandinista Revolution triumphed in 1979. Believers' sympathies ran the gamut, as the denominations found themselves at ground zero of the Cold War.[12] The armed conflict also sparked a substantial migration of young church members fleeing the military draft. The *nica* influx left a deep imprint on *tico* (Costa Rican) Pentecostalism.

The 1980s saw the emergence of the most innovative version of pneumatic Christianity. Neo- or Third Wave Pentecostalism pressed the boundaries of sociological definition, as old rubrics began to dissolve. Groups such as Amistad Cristiana, led by missionary scion Marcos Witt, relaxed denominational distinctives and intensified the embrace of technology and pop culture, especially in the sphere of music and worship. Brazil's Igreja Universal do Reino de Deus (IURD), founded by Edir Macedo and Romildo Soares in 1977, went even further, jettisoning most elements of the traditional *evangélico* service in favor of a thaumaturgic program that featured (and scheduled) exorcism, healing, and prosperity. Equally as important, the IURD acquired that country's second largest television network. Within a decade, the platform catapulted the church into national prominence as a competitor to the Globo television network and the Catholic Church and as an object of intense journalistic scrutiny. The IURD and the Soares-led spinoff, Internacional da Graça de Deus, have also attracted a veritable cottage industry of social scientific inquiry.[13] The same period also witnessed the most successful *evangélico* incursion into politics up to that date: the election of a *bancada evangélica* consisting of thirty-two deputies in the postdictatorship Constituent Assembly of 1986. While the Asambleias de Deus and Convenção Batista

Brasileira led the initial foray, the IURD gradually increased its numbers, placing sixteen deputies in the Congress elected in 1999 (compared to ten each for the Asambleias and Convenção Batista). Disillusionment with the governing party (and scandals involving *evangélico* congressmen) led to a broader approach to partisan representation, including important alliances with the leftist Workers' Party. One notable measure of expanded strength can be seen in the protests by Afro-Brazilian religious groups against neo-pentecostal hostility and harassment.[14]

Darío López has traced a similar transition from pilgrims to power brokers among Peruvian Pentecostals. Their flirtation with confessional parties and support of Alberto Fujimori during his 1990 election ended in feelings of betrayal.[15] The failed experiments in confessional parties can be attributed, in part, to the electoral ambivalence of pentecostal laity. The several experiences with political engagement – from endorsement of military coups and juntas (Chile and Guatemala) to *evangélico* political parties and legislative caucuses (Peru, Argentina, Colombia, and Brazil) – have left a mixed record.[16] In many countries, leaders' power of convocation remains limited to evangelistic campaigns and to defense of legal status.

The matter of *evangélico* juridical identity was largely settled by the end of the twentieth century, thereby robbing Protestants of one of their major motivations for interdenominational cooperation. Lacking this raison d'etre, some denominational prerogatives have yielded to currents of political theology and spiritual mapping introduced by the New Apostolic Reformation (NAR). Comprised of several components, the NAR has retained the anthropological methods of church growth missiology and intensified the cosmic and apocalyptic features of signs and wonders practice.[17] In a sense, the NAR's eschewal of denominational structures confirms Jean-Pierre Bastian's prescient lament. Intensified globalization and neoliberal arrangements must also share part of the blame for the atomization of the *evangélico* religious field. Older pentecostal churches are challenged to discern the chaff from the wheat in neo-Pentecostalism. Although many denominations have hewed resolutely to established practices and identities, the religious actors best positioned to maximize opportunities in an intensely globalizing era may be those institutions with hemispheric visions (e.g., the Catholic Church) and/or niche specialties (e.g., Brazil's Igreja Universal, Mexico's Luz del Mundo, Colombia's Misión Carismática Internacional-G12) and actors adept at consumer marketing and at ease with new digital technologies (e.g., music empresarios). In short, the future of *evangelicalismo*, although probably a pneumatic one, remains up for grabs.

HISTORIOGRAPHICAL PROBLEMS

Like the case of the anonymous Indian at Azusa, the extreme mobility of migrants, missionaries, and symbolic goods obscures our view of pentecostal origins in many regions of Latin America. Early denominational narratives skewed the story in institutional (and coherent) directions; however, these largely triumphalistic accounts told only half of the story. They obscured the constitutive agency of many Latin American and Latino pioneers, especially migrating preachers and laypersons (and, for that matter, lapsed believers). The following discussion scours the cartography of early Pentecostalism in search of missed contours and missing pilgrims.

The work and spiritual progeny of independent missionaries such as Canadian Federico Mebius in El Salvador and Nicaragua presented nascent missionary agencies with a challenge: incoherence, dissipation, and heterodoxy. To counter these, the Assemblies of God implemented a strong program of supervision and ministerial training. The southwestern United States provided the first laboratory for this, especially in the face of an upstart Oneness movement (Francisco Llorente, Antonio Nava, and Felipe Rivas) and in the wake of significant defections over questions of autonomy in the United States (Francisco Olazábal) and Mexico (David Ruesgas). Assemblies strategists such as Methodist-trained H. C. Ball, Anglican-trained Alice Luce, and Melvin Hodges forged a durable but flexible template of organizational structure and Bible institutes that gradually placed native leaders at the helm of national denominations tied to regional cooperative bodies. Other U.S. denominations replicated this approach to varying degrees. Its ultimate success depended, of course, on the strength, sensibilities, and condition of the criollo Pentecostalism already on the ground.

In moments of disarray or need, North American succor could seem attractive indeed. Even while still chafing over the Assemblies' paternalism, Olazábal variously flirted with merging his new Concilio Mexicano (later Latinoamericano) de Iglesias Cristianas (CLADIC) with Aimee Semple McPherson's Foursquare Church and A. J. Tomlinson's Church of God of Prophecy. The latter move was never consummated, owing to the unexpected demise in 1936 of Latino Pentecostalism's most successful evangelist. Juan Lugo's Iglesia de Dios Pentecostal, Puerto Rico's largest group, similarly cultivated and then abandoned affiliation with the Assemblies of God. Over the course of a decade, David Ruesgas invoked the harsh anticlerical articles of the 1917 Constitution, provisions originally aimed against foreign Catholic clergy, to extricate the Iglesia de Dios en la República Mexicana first from the embrace of the Assemblies of God and later from the Church of God. Further south, the Iglesia Metodista Pentecostal (IMP) of Chile, assuming pride of place and origin, viewed itself as a flagship church, needful of neither U.S. connections nor even its own American founder. Forced out of the IMP by Manuel Umaña in 1933 over charges of immorality and autocratic administration, Willis C. Hoover formed the Iglesia Evangélica Pentecostal (IEP) and considered merging it with the Assemblies of God. In the wake of his death at this vulnerable juncture, however, Chile's second twin flagship opted, ultimately, for continued autonomy.

The penchant for autonomy militated against internal unity as much as it did external dependency. By 1952, the criollo pentecostal movement in Chile consisted of at least twenty-one groups. After Francisco Olazábal's death in 1937, regional and interethnic tensions (between Puerto Ricans and Mexicans) split CLADIC into an array of denominations. (Historian Gastón Espinosa has traced the Olazábal spiritual lineage of at least fourteen concilios.[18]) Further south, the Oneness variant in northern and western Mexico entered its second decade divided among three institutional streams: the Iglesia Apostólica (tied to the Apostolic Assembly in the United States), the Consejo (later Iglesia) Evangélico Espiritual Mexicano, and the Luz del Mundo. Their shared genesis notwithstanding, each group claimed a separate progenitor. The assertion of autonomy, then, can be seen in the recovery and celebration of origins as well as in the exercise of ecclesial control.

INTERDISCIPLINARY OPTICS

While doctrinal and polity debates help explain many schisms – studied from the vantage points of theology, sociology, history, and political science – we also cannot discount the centrifugal push of culture and, frankly, testosterone, hence, the value of anthropology and gender studies. The latter field also can illumine the still understudied contributions of important middle-class matriarchs and cultural brokers such as Romana Valenzuela, María Atkinson, and Chonita Howard (the latter two, Mexicans married to Anglos, pioneered Pentecostalism along the U.S.-Mexico border), the gradual constraining of female agency within institutionalizing movements, the power dynamics at play in the conflictive relationship between Anglo-American female missionaries and restive male native leaders and in the disciplining of charismata. Elaine Laidlaw's conflict with Methodist authorities in Santiago, after all, carried a higher cost than missionary Willis Hoover's. He was merely excommunicated. She was jailed (see below).[19]

In a similar vein, students of indigenous Latin America must engage historians over the long history of ethnic Pentecostalism – from the Mesoamerican Indian at Azusa to the Seri of Sonora and the Totonaco of Hidalgo to the Chakchiqel Maya of Guatemala to the Toba of Argentina to the Aymara of Bolivia to the Mapuche of Chile. Unfortunately, much of the current social scientific literature on the question of religious change in Latin America keeps the nation state as the unit of analysis; however, the much-touted *evangélico* growth is often a subnational, regional phenomenon overlaid with important ethnic features (in the case of Mexico, states in the indigenous south register *evangélico* populations double to five times the national rate). Put simply, the indigenous Americas are slipping out of the control of the Roman Catholic Church. Finally, we still await a comparative survey of histories and resonances of Pentecostalism within the Afro-Americas to place in conversation with, say, the observations of anthropologist John Burdick in Brazil.[20] The lacuna is striking, especially given the much larger Afro-derived populations of Latin America and the Caribbean and the role of race in early U.S. pentecostal history.

MIGRATION AND GLOBALIZATION

The burgeoning fields of migration and globalization studies also offer new paradigms for the early pentecostal story. For example, the robust early growth of the Assembleias de Deus in Brazil – against the background of prior Baptist work – occurred while the church remained loosely tethered, through its founding missionaries Gunnar Vingren and Daniel Berg to Lewis Pethrus' Filadelfia Church in Stockholm, Sweden. Thus, the Assembleias' later cooperation with the U.S. Assemblies of God represented more a meeting of equals than a case of dependency. The ethnic and religious roots of the Congregação Cristã kept Brazil's second flagship denomination within the orbit of the pentecostalized Italian diaspora headed by Luigi Francescon and Giacomo Lombardi and others. The story of this stream of Southern Cone Pentecostalism could just as profitably be rendered in terms of the Italian labor migratory diaspora that stretched over the turn of the twentieth century from Italy to Brazil to Argentina to the United States and Australia. Like Vingren and Berg, Francescon and Lombardi experienced spirit baptism in the North Avenue Mission pastored by William Durham, hence, the salience of Chicago (and Los Angeles) in the story of Brazilian pentecostal origins.

Nevertheless, the separate circuits in which they traveled – especially the migratory one for Francescon and Lomardi – and the distinct religious diasporic cartographies that informed their decisions suggest a ratchetting down of Chicago's primacy in the narrative and a foregrounding of, say, Waldensian and Presbyterian networks. (The denomination later had to transition to reach broader Brazilian populations.)

The story of early Caribbean and Mexican Pentecostalism likewise could be rendered in terms of labor migration. Indeed, the history of the latter movement throughout the whole of the twentieth century could be framed episodically, following the capricious course of U.S. immigration policy: from the favored welcome of agricultural and railroad labor during the 1920s to the massive repatriation of Mexicans (one out of every three) in the 1930s to the official Bracero guest worker program of 1942–64 to perennial xenophobic measures such as Operation Wetback (1952, the precursor of several similar initiatives in the 1990s) to the several immigration law reforms (1965, 1986, 1996). Ironically, U.S. xenophobia not only at first unwittingly tripled Pentecostalism's geographic expanse in Mexico in the 1930s but also primed its targets to maximize opportunities for future migration-driven growth. These many instances of "reverse missions," of course, predate contemporary case studies of global South Christianities missionizing the global North.

PENTECOSTAL CONTRIBUTIONS TO MISSIOLOGY

Pentecostal success with bracero and indigenous evangelism did not escape critical and scholarly notice. Some observers decried the abandonment of propriety as *evangélicos* were drawn to what missiologist J. Merle Davis characterized in a 1940 study of Mexico as "irresponsible Protestant sects."[21] The cacophony of pentecostal worship services and the percussive intensity of clapping and jerking bodies, especially female and indigenous bodies, also provided a ready straw man for Catholic antagonists. Mexican Jesuit scholar Pedro Rivera, writing two decades after Merle, tweaked leading Protestant apologists, such as John Mackay, Alberto Rembao, and Gonzalo Baez-Camargo, with his description of a "pseudocharismatic Christianity," whose "mystical rapture and sensual rhythms do not reflect precisely the evangelical purity of which the Protestants boast so much." (Rivera also contrasted pentecostal self-sufficiency with the inequitable arrangements of mainline missionary-native worker structures: "the one lives as lord and the other as servant").[22] Viewing matters differently, Donald McGavran observed that "America-returned" braceros, who had proven responsive to "churches of the common man," were leavening Evangelical growth in Mexico.[23] Such observations helped the veteran India missionary and others flesh out an incipient theory of church growth. McGavran's co-authored *Church Growth in Mexico* anchored a series of anthropological studies of "people group" evangelism in Brazil (1965) and Latin America (1969), leading up to McGavran's major opus, *Understanding Church Growth* (1970).[24] Thus, migrant-driven and initiated evangelism provided some of the building blocks for the conceptual apparatus developed by McGavran, Alan Tippett and, importantly, Peter Wagner (like McGavran, a returned missionary). Wagner's *Look Out! The Pentecostals Are Coming!* (1973) signaled a turn in evangelical missions strategy.[25] Importantly, like McGavran, Wagner benefitted from the experience and insights of Latin American Pentecostals (e.g., Manuel Gaxiola), who brought their grounded experience to their studies at Fuller Seminary's School of World Mission. In other words, Latin American Pentecostalism provided not only the raw material but also the labor for one of the major missiological innovations of the mid-to-late twentieth century. The value-added product, church growth theory, was then marketed back to the region from whence the original elements were extracted. The finished product also strengthened Wagner's hand against Latin American theologians seeking to engage *evangélico* thought and practice with liberationist currents coursing through the hemisphere. This history renders intelligible Wagner's later foundational protagonism in the New Apostolic Reformation. The spiritual mapping and other strategies and techniques deployed by theorists and practitioners of the NAR represent, in part, borrowed elements from Latin American pentecostal practice as well as circular processes of extraction, processing, marketing, and consumption. The Toronto Blessing and Brownsville (Pensacola) Revival must also be viewed in light of this circularity. Although some scholars have credited (or discredited) the originary contributions to the NAR by Argentine evangelists such as Carlos Annacondia, Claudio Freidzon, and Omar Cabrera (and Korean leader Paul Yonggi Cho), few have taken into account Annacondia's own tribute of spiritual paternity to Panamanian evangelist Manuel Ruiz.[26] Annacondia's own call, and Ruiz's ministry and techniques, like those of Puerto Rican evangelist Yiye Avila, predate and overlap the received chronology of NAR origins. In other words, a century after the multisited emergence of pneumatic Christianity, it remains problematic and anachronistic to view developments in neo-Pentecostalism or Third Wave Pentecostalism as simple unilinear processes of expansion from singular points of origin.

CULTURE

Early *pentecostales* left thin archival and textual records; thus, historians must borrow from other disciplinary toolkits. Scholars must concern themselves not only with the retrieval of submerged histories but also with their meanings. For example, the severely redacted testimony of the anonymous Indian from central Mexico, together with the many other discursive components of Azusa's polyglot mix, now can be viewed through semiotics lens, to arrive at a fuller understanding of the stakes at play in the representation of modern pentecostal origins. Such an approach also can help untangle the binary (black-white) knot of racialized historiography that has tied up the guild in North America and hampered its relations with non-U.S. ones. In part, that conundrum has been weighted down by linguistic limitations. U.S. and British scholars' reliance on surveys and summaries of research filters out much of the primary material and scholarship available in the languages of Latin America. Thankfully, the long overlooked early periodical record has begun to render considerable fruit in pentecostal cultural studies. Miguel Mansillas and Luis Orellana, in particular, have explored deeply the emotive contours of pentecostal life on the Chilean street, the *canuto* identity disdained by Catholic society and elegized in pentecostal music and memory.[27] Mansillas has probed the affective and lyrical dimensions of subaltern life to understand how *canuto* culture faced and interpreted disease, death, and persecution. This more fully fleshed out picture of early Pentecostalism casts the later period studied by Swiss sociologist Lalive d'Epinay (and even later ones) in a different light.[28] The transitions in Chilean Pentecostalism from despised *canutos* to prized citizens (courted eagerly by political elites) are rendered much more sharply with Mansillas' clearer composite as the starting point.

As in *canuto* culture, the guitar emerged early on as a marker of a new subaltern musical aesthetic throughout the Spirit-swept *Américas*. In contrast to mainline missionaries' (and their progeny's) disdain for the instrument, owing to its evocative shape and profane use, Pentecostals found it the ideal companion for travel and public evangelism around the farm worker campfire and on the street corner. The performance field within church settings made possible the inclusion of other popular instruments, especially percussive ones. Popular instrumentation led inevitably to popular musical framing. As a result, even standards from the Anglo-American repertoire could be rendered *chileno, peruano, colombiano, caribeño,* or *mexicano* in performance. In situ performance also layered on additional valences missing from the original composition. In 1909, as Santiago police authorities led Elaine Laidlaw away from the Methodist temple and to jail, her sympathizers followed and broke out in musical protest: "Cuando Dios a los huestes de Israel/Las mandó al desierto a vagar" (When God sent the hosts of Israel to wander in the wilderness). C. Austin Miles' 1904 composition, "The Cloud and Fire," loosely translated by Azusa Street pioneer Abundio López, provided a symbolic resource to deploy against both ecclesial (Methodist) and civil authorities. Other martial anthems acquired iconic status through public use. "Cristo Es Nuestro Jefe" (Christ is Our Chieftain) and "Firmes y Adelante" (Spanish Anglican bishop Juan Cabrera's translation of "Onward Christian Soldiers"), in particular, firmed up believers' resolve in the face of social opprobrium, anticlerical antipathies, and even internal schism.[29] Periodical accounts from *cristero*-dominated regions of Mexico often included descriptions of instances of this hymnodic tradition in temple dedication marches. This oppositional valence would have been absent, of course, in the more tolerant setting of the United States or England.

Ultimately, however, Pentecostals demanded a more adequate repertoire. Take, for example, F. M. Lehman's 1909 "The Royal Telephone," a catchy tune in which the Holiness composer inserted the metaphor for prayer in every stanza. The clever metaphor disappeared a decade later at the hands of Calexico, California, composer Elvira Herrera. Given the novel appliance's absence in most homes in the Imperial and Mexicali Valleys, the Methodist-turned-pentecostal borderlander opted instead for images more readily accessible to her community – a celestial throne, fervent supplication, and so on – as well as for a clear emphasis on Christocentric versus Marian intercession. Rendered thus more functional, "Es la Oración" traveled widely soon thereafter, reaching Puerto Rico and Andean countries within a decade, before phone service became widely accessible there. Such poetic license can be seen also in the first wave of original Spanish-language compositions. Composers such as Marcial de la Cruz and other *repatriados* (United States and Mexico), Juan Concepción (Puerto Rico and New York), and Genaro Ríos (Chile) appropriated the several popular musical genres of their time, sanctifying, thereby, such transgressive styles as the polka, ranchera, and bolero (the latter is particularly notable, given the genre's Afro-Cuban derivation and its transmission via early radio). The introduction by Ríos and his brothers of circus music (their former vocation) widened the rift between the Iglesia Metodista Pentecostal and the Iglesia Evangélica Pentecostal. The aesthetic outcomes bear noting. Willis Hoover solidified Methodism's choral tradition within the IEP, while Manuel Umaña's IMP grew a unique mandolin-based orchestral one. Ríos ultimately left the IMP to found the Ejército Evangélico de Chile and develop a robust band tradition akin to that of the Salvation Army. The still unwritten critical biographies of pioneer evangelist-troubadours and later ones, such as Guatemalan Alfredo Colom (the composer of "Pero Queda Cristo" [But Christ Remains] and "América Será para Cristo" [America Will Be for Christ]); Mexican American brothers Román, Rosario, and Juan Alvarado (Los Hermanos Alvarado); and Mexicans Juan Romero (the composer of "Visión Pastoral," a bolero version of the lost sheep parable) and Manuel Bonilla, promise new understandings of aesthetics, poesis, and performance – in short, of pentecostal cultures and networks. The long overdue ethnomusicological study of early original Spanish-language pentecostal musics can help circumvent the tone deafness of much historical scholarship and allow us to bore into the emotional core of revivalist Christianity. An examination of the sonic, lyrical, corporeal, and migratory dimensions of early pentecostal musics can help us understand the broader global movement's still considerable proselytizing charms. The analysis of media, distribution circuits, and consumption patterns can also shed comparative light on the processes of artistic production and consumption in today's globalized marketplace of Christian worship music. Ironically, the digital era has made possible the retrieval of older musics, including contemporary tributes to many of the earlier mentioned singers on YouTube. Thus, ironically, the new media have facilitated the circulation of nostalgia-laced artistry (along with vanguard musics such as reggaeton, rock *en español*, and hip-hop) to the migrant diaspora. They also have enabled, of course, the flattening out of heterogeneous regional musical cultures under the marketing genius of savvy music empresarios such as Marcos Witt.

ROMAN CATHOLIC CHARISMATIC RENEWAL

Pentecostal expansion in the hemisphere tested the resiliency of Catholicism's previous ability to contain Protestant incursions. Ironically, however, Pentecostalism's success in accessing a common substratum of religiosity shared with popular Catholicism (belief in miracles, popular music, trance, ecstasy, corporeality, etc.) also facilitated Catholic appropriation of pentecostal practices and affects. This is important when seeking genealogies that link Catholic charismatic groups in Latin America to points of origin in U.S. Catholic universities. Edward Cleary has argued for multiple and overlapping origins, for example, among

Brazilian Baptists in the late 1950s and among liberationist priests in Bolivia in the mid-1960s.[30] Scant attention has been paid, however, to the broader impact of regular, quotidian contact over decades between Catholics and their *aleluya* relatives and neighbors. Most Pentecostals, after all, do not inhabit sectarian enclaves. The ubiquity of decades-old pentecostal *coritos* in the musical repertoire of Catholics – of all stripes – hints strongly at long-standing permeation across confessional boundaries, a permeation finally legitimized by the liturgical innovations legislated at Vatican II. With the passage of time, such standards as "Alabaré a Mi Señor" (I will Praise My Lord), "No Hay Dios tan Grande como Tú" (There is No God As Great as You), and "Yo Tengo Un Amigo que Me Ama" (I Have a Friend Who Loves Me) acquired a Catholic identity. In the case of the third *corito*, Catholics proved adept innovators, switching easily between "amigo" and "amiga." (The intensified Marian devotion has confounded Pentecostals' expectations that an encounter with the Holy Spirit would lead away from the cult of saints.) In any case, charismatic revivalism certainly helped flip the switch from a defensive to an offensive position, as the church promoted deeper Bible literacy and enculturation. In Cleary's view, the renewal empowered laity, buttressed a faltering Catholicism, and eclipsed a withering liberation project. The unprecedented number of Spirit-empowered catechists also provided the foot soldiers to help address the numerical imbalance between Catholic and pentecostal clergy. (Cleary argued that the theological and pastoral training of catechists even matched that of most pentecostal preachers; although a counter argument would weigh comparatively the sheer man hours in the pastoral trenches over many decades.) Like its pentecostal precursor, the Catholic Charismatic Renewal has taken deep root in Latin American soil. In 2003, historian Gastón Espinosa estimated that one out of three Latino and Latin American Christians (Protestant and Catholic) was of one pneumatic variety or another.[31] Thanks to the disciplining prowess of the Catholic Church, the future of the Charismatic Renewal probably will hew closely to that of the institution.

ECUMENISM

Ironically, the world region where the Catholic Charismatic Renewal has evidenced strong staying power is also where Catholic-Pentecostal relations remain the most conflicted. In part, this is owing to old predilections: Catholics for social power and Pentecostals for spiritual pugilism, especially "Marianicide". As a result, the nearly four decades of the International Catholic-Pentecostal Dialogue have unfolded without the participation of flagship denominations from Latin America. Although individual Pentecostals and smaller denominations have participated in significant ecumenical initiatives such as the Consejo Latinoamericano de Iglesias (CLAI) and World Council of Church-sponsored meetings, the problem of absence in the Dialogue persists. This should not surprise us. The several parallel dialogues among the Vatican and Protestant bodies and confessional families emerged in the global North after a long process of accommodation between relatively equal ecclesial institutions embedded in secular nation states in late modernity and comprised of increasingly indistinguishable flocks. Latin America presents a different starting point and, hence, a different trajectory. If Catholicism represents the binding mortar of Latin American identity and unity (to paraphrase Pope Benedict XVI's charge to the bishops gathered in the 2007 Consejo Episcopal Latinoamericano [CELAM] conclave in Aparecida, Brazil, in 2007), then its corrosion under the influence of moral relativism, hypersecular laicism, and opportunistic sects truly threatens the social structure. It may be asking too much of the Catholic reconstruction project to expect it to move beyond a history of cultural and political hegemony.

In the United States, the Catholic-Evangelical-Pentecostal convergence also often has flowed around shared ideologies, idealized histories, patriotism, and moralizing political projects. The conflictive legacy of church-state relations continues to haunt Latin American societies, however; thus, rhetoric invoking a virtuous past in the pursuit of political mobilization carries little cross-denominational appeal. Perhaps the most striking general difference from the United States is the asymmetry between Catholicism and Pentecostalism, especially in terms of institutional prerogatives and access to levers of power and influence. Put simply, there are higher stakes – political, social, economic – at play in Latin America. Both sides are playing for keeps. Catholic hegemons are seeking to keep and recover power, and Pentecostals are keeping no prisoners while flanking the public square. An older iconoclastic discourse (evidenced in an old cumbia-rhythm *corito* that would be unthinkable in English-speaking settings, "Los Idolos No Tienen Poder" [The Idols Have No Power]) has been overtaken by a spiritual mapping strategy that seeks to identify and bind spiritual forces too long tolerated by a syncretistic Catholicism.

To be sure, the contours and dynamics of ecumenism in Latin America reflect national and diocesan particularities. The Brazilian hierarchy's openness, for example, contrasts sharply with the actions of their Colombian and Mexican counterparts. Finally, inasmuch as Latin America continues to bleed over into the United States, the Latino community presents a unique opportunity for ecumenism: Latino Christianity represents a hybrid specimen that reflects both the more open ecology of the United States and the less tolerant niches of Latin America. Among Mexicans and Central Americans, the common experiences of border-crossing, sojourn (often illegal), and xenophobic persecution can shape a shared existential view of Jesus as the "Divine Companion of the Road" (as expressed in the well-traveled ranchera hymn of that title).[32]

To conclude, Latin America's *evangélicos* entered the twenty-first century in much greater absolute and relative numbers than they reported in the mid-twentieth century, but the very impulses that drove religious dissent before that midpoint (and the patterns of mobility and cultural expression of earlier periods) continue to pull in the direction of atomized incoherence. In other words, even if ecumenically minded Catholic leaders were to seek them out, it would be extremely difficult to find pentecostal partners. They will find, however, plenty of *pentecostales* willing to share their stories and songs.

Notes

1   R. Andrew Chesnut, *Born Again in Brazil: The Pentecostal Boom and the Pathogens of Poverty* (New Brunswick: Rutgers University Press, 1997); *Competitive Spirits: Latin America's New Religious Economy* (Oxford: Oxford University Press, 2003).

2   David Martin, *Pentecostalism: The World Their Parish* (Oxford: Blackwell, 2002).

3   Jean-Pierre Bastian, *La mutación religiosa de América Latina. Para una sociología del cambio social en la modernidad periférica* (México, DF: Fondo de Cultura Económica, 1997).

4   See the several contributions by Everett Wilson to Stanley Burgess and Ed Van der Maas, eds., *New International Dictionary of Pentecostal and Charismatic Movements* (Grand Rapids: Eerdmans, 2003).

5   Charles Hale, *Mexican Liberalism in the Age of Mora, 1821–1853* (New Haven: Yale University Press, 1968); Arnoldo Canclini, *Diego Thomson: Apóstol de la enseñanza y distribución de la Biblia en América Latina y España* (Buenos Aires: Asociación Sociedad Bíblica Argentina, 1987); Juan Martínez, "The Bible in *Neomejicano* Protestant Folklore during the 19th Century," *Apuntes* 17:1 (1997), 21–26.

6   Jean-Pierre Bastian, *Los disidentes: Sociedades protestantes y revolución en México, 1872–1911* (México, DF: El Colegio de México, 1989).

7   *The Apostolic Faith* (Los Angeles, CA) (September 1906), 2–3.

8   Manuel J. Gaxiola Gaxiola, "Latin American Pentecostalism: A Mosaic within a Mosaic," *PNEUMA* 13:1 (1991), 107; Juan Sepúlveda G., *De peregrinos a ciudadanos. Breve historia del cristianismo evangélico en Chile* (Santiago: Facultad Evangélica de Teología, 1999).

9 Douglas Peterson, "The Formation of Popular, National, Autonomous Pentecostal Churches in Central America," *PNEUMA* 16:1 (1994), 23–48.

10 Deyssi Jael de la Luz García, *El movimiento pentecostal en México: La Iglesia de Dios, 1926–1948* (México, DF: Editorial Letra Ausente, 2010), 191–222.

11 Virginia Garrard-Burnett, *Protestantism in Guatemala: Living in the New Jerusalem* (Austin: University of Texas Press, 1998), 138–71.

12 Carlos Aguirre Salinas y Alberto Araica, *Pentecostalismo en transición y globalización en Nicaragua. Influencia de la nuevas corrientes religiosas en la praxis social y política de las iglesias pentecostales* (Managua: Casa Giordano Bruno, 2010), 235–68.

13 See Leonildo Silveira Campos, *Teatro, temple e mercado: Organização e marketing de um empreendimento neopentecostal*, 2a ed. (Sao Paolo: Universidad Metodista de São Paulo, 1999).

14 Vagner Gonçalves da Silva (org.), *Intolerancia religiosa: Impactos do neo-pentecostalismo no campo religioso afro-brasileiro* (São Paulo: Universidade de São Paulo, 2007).

15 Darío R. López, *La seducción del poder. Los evangélicos y la política en el Perú de los noventa* (Lima: Instituto de Ciencias Políticas, Investigacion y Promoción del Desarrollo Nueva Humanidad, 2004).

16 Alvaro Cepeda van Houten, *Clientelismo y fe: dinámicas políticas del pentecostalismo en Colombia* (Bogotá: Editorial Bonaventuriana, 2007); Kevin Lewis O'Neill, *City of God: Christian Citizenship in Postwar Guatemala* (Berkeley: University of California Press, 2010).

17 René Holvast, *Spiritual Mapping in the United States and Argentina, 1989–2005: A Geography of Fear* (Leiden: Brill, 2009).

18 Gastón Espinosa, "Francisco Olazábal: Charisma, Power, and Faith Healing in the Borderlands," in James R. Goff, Jr., and Grant Wacker, eds., *Portraits of a Generation: Early Pentecostal Leaders* (Fayetteville: University of Arkansas Press, 2002), 192–93.

19 Luis Orellana U., *El fuego y la nieve. Historia del movimiento pentecostal en Chile, 1909–1932*, tomo I (Concepción: Centro Evangélico de Estudios Pentecostales, 2008), 27–37.

20 John Burdick, *Blessed Anastacia: Women, Race and Popular Christianity in Brazil* (New York: Routledge, 1998).

21 J. Merle Davis, *The Economic Basis of the Evangelical Church in Mexico: A Study Made by the Department of Social and Economic Research of the International Missionary Council* (London: International Missionary Council, 1940), 31–32.

22 Roberto Rivera R., *Instituciones protestantes en México* (México, DF: Editorial Jus, 1962), 97, 114, 125.

23 Donald McGavran, John Huegel, and Jack Taylor, *Church Growth in Mexico* (Grand Rapids: Wm. B. Eerdmans, 1963), 58.

24 William Read, *New Patterns of Church Growth in Brazil* (Grand Rapids: Wm. B. Eerdmans, 1965); William Read, Victor Monterroso, and Harmon Johnson, *Latin American Church Growth* (Grand Rapids: Wm. B. Eerdmans, 1969); Donald McGavran, *Understanding Church Growth* (Grand Rapids: Wm. B. Eerdmans, 1970).

25 C. Peter Wagner, *Look Out! The Pentecostals Are Coming!* (Carol Stream: Creation House, 1973).

26 Holvast, *Spiritual Mapping*, 41–66.

27 Miguel Angel Mansilla, *La cruz y la esperanza. La cultura del pentecostalismo chileno en la primera mitad del siglo XX* (Santiago: Editorial Universidad Bolivariana, 2009); Orellana, *El fuego y la nieve*.

28 Christian Lalive d'Epinay, *Haven of the Masses: A Study of the Pentecostal Movement in Chile* (London: Lutterworth, 1969).

29 Orellana, *El fuego y la nieve*, 96–100.

30 Edward L. Cleary, *The Rise of Charismatic Catholicism in Latin America* (Gainesville: University Press of Florida, 2011).

31 Gastón Espinosa, "The Pentecostalization of Latin American and U.S. Latino Christianity," *PNEUMA* 26:2 (2004), 262–92.

32 Sammy G. Alfaro, *Divino Compañero: Toward a Hispanic Pentecostal Christology* (Eugene: Wipf and Stock, 2010).

Further Reading

Boudewijnse, Barbara, André Droogers, and Frans Kamsteeg, eds. *More than Opium: An Anthropological Approach to Latin American and Caribbean Pentecostal Praxis*. Lanham: Scarecrow Press, 1998.

Chiquete, Daniel, and Luis Orellana, eds. *Voces del pentecostalismo latinoamericano III. Identidad, teología historia*. Hualpén, Chile: Red Latinoamericano de Estudios Pentecostales, 2009.

Corten, André, et André Mary, eds. *Imaginaires politiques et pentecôtismes. Afrique/Amérique Latine*. Paris: Éditions Karthala, 2000.

De Melo, José Marques, Maria C. Gobbi, and Ana Claudia Braun Endo, eds. *Mídia e religião na sociedade do espetáculo*. São Paulo: Universidade Metodista de São Paulo, 2007.

Freston, Paul, ed. *Evangelical Christianity and Democracy in Latin America*. Oxford: Oxford University Press, 2008.

Garma Navarro, Carlos. *Buscando el espíritu: Pentecostalismo en Iztapalapa y la Ciudad de Mexico*. México, DF: Universidad Autónoma Metropolitana, Iztapalapa, 2004.

Gutierrez, Benjamin F., and Dennis A. Smith, eds. *In the Power of the Spirit: The Pentecostal Challenge to Historic Churches in Latin America*. Louisville: Presbyterian Church (US), Worldwide Ministries Division, 1996.

López, Darío. *Pentecostalismo y transformación social*. Buenos Aires: Kairos, 2000.

Shaull, Richard, and Waldo Cesar. *Pentecostalism and the Future of the Christian Churches: Promises, Limitations, Challenges*. Grand Rapids: Eerdmans, 2000.

7 African Pentecostalism

CEPHAS N. OMENYO

INTRODUCTION

The growth of Pentecostalism in sub-Saharan Africa since the turn of the twentieth century cannot be overlooked by any serious student of African Christianity. Pentecostalism had been established in most of sub-Saharan Africa by the 1920s, but steady expansion gathered massive momentum in the 1960s and 1970s. Although contestable, available estimates indicate Pentecostals constitute 11 percent of the population of the entire African continent in 2000, while their numbers range from 10 to 50 percent of the national population in Zimbabwe, Kenya, Nigeria, Ghana, Zambia, the Democratic Republic of Congo (DRC), and South Africa.[1]

The impact of Pentecostalism in Africa is felt in all spheres of life, particularly in politics, educational institutions, communities, public institutions, and even the older/mainline western founded churches that were formerly opposed to the movement.[2] Most African churches founded by western missionaries in the nineteenth century are fast becoming pentecostalized. Consequently, the pentecostal genre of Christianity is becoming the dominant form of Christianity in contemporary Africa.[3]

This chapter attempts a definition of the terminology "Pentecostalism" and briefly outlines the typology of the phenomenon in Africa. It discusses the African prophets, precursors of African Pentecostalism, and the churches that emerged as a result of their activities as well as the emergence of other strands of Pentecostalism in Africa. Some specific features of African Pentecostalism – its view of salvation, its role in the public square, and its emphases on mission – are discussed, before concluding with some attention on the Africanness of African Pentecostalism.

Terminology and Typology

Modern Pentecostalism takes its name from the Day of Pentecost narrative in Acts 2. Essentially, the movement puts emphasis on the power and presence of the Holy Spirit and believes that the gifts of the Spirit are meant to equip believers to proclaim that Jesus Christ is Lord, to God's glory. Manifestations of pneumatic phenomena such as speaking in tongues, prophecies, visions, healing, miracles, and signs and wonders are expected. Thus Pentecostalism is a label for that genre of Christianity that claims to be distinctive as a result of its stress on the experience of repentance, personal salvation, and a changed life because of the power of the Holy Spirit.

The label "Charismatic" is often used synonymously with "Pentecostal" and they are conterminous in the African context. Although not all Pentecostals and Charismatics share all the features as described, what binds them together is their belief that the gifts of the Spirit are available in the contemporary church and that contemporary Christians ought to seek the power of the Holy Spirit.

The variety and diversity of African Pentecostalism is palpable. It is sometimes suggested that we should speak of "African Pentecostalisms" rather than "African Pentecostalism" because of the existing complexities of categorizations.[4] This makes typologizing African Pentecostalism extremely difficult. Omenyo and Atiemo have used a typology of African Pentecostalism that takes into consideration historical and theological categories.[5] They are outlined as follows:

1. The African Initiated Churches (AICs) or Aladura Churches, the oldest type established at the turn of the twentieth century as the result of the ministries of the African Prophets.[6]
2. The classical pentecostal movements, some of which have roots in William Seymour's Azusa Street revivals of North America that began in 1906 while others started through African initiatives. Examples are the Assemblies of God, the Apostolic Faith Mission, the Full Gospel Church of God, the Church of Pentecost, and the Deeper Christian Life Ministry.[7]
3. Trans-denominational fellowships, for example, Full Gospel Business Men's Fellowship International (FGBMFI), Women Aglow Fellowship International, and Intercessors for Africa.[8]
4. Charismatic renewal groups in the mainline churches.[9]
5. The Independent Neo-Pentecostal/Charismatic Churches and Ministries, which were started as a result of local initiatives, such as the International Central Gospel Church led by Mensa Otabil in Ghana and Andrew Wutawanashe's Family of God in Zimbabwe.[10]

6.   Neo-Prophetism, the latest form of pentecostal movements, which is an amalgamation of forms of ministries of the AICs and neo-pentecostal churches.[11]

Generally, the AICs comprising the first category listed are declining, particularly in West Africa. A major exception is the case of the Zionist churches in Southern Africa where positive growth is being recorded. There is no gainsaying that the AICs are the earliest form of authentic expression of Christianity in the African milieu. Their emphasis on the pneumatic, particularly in rituals such as healing and exorcism/ deliverance, lively and Africanized forms of worship, and fellowship (*koinonia*), challenged the western founded mainline churches to critically examine their ministries to keep their members. Contemporary African Pentecostalism has largely been built on major AIC emphases and styles of ministry. These streams of pentecostal-type churches have much in common with one another.

This chapter adopts an inclusive definition of African Pentecostalism as referring also to charismatic churches or movements that stress the experience of the Spirit and the practice of spiritual gifts. We adopt a broad terminology used to describe the entire spectrum of pentecostal churches in Africa. Although Pentecostalism shares common features and values across cultures and boundaries, in this chapter we will highlight the African colorations in their beliefs and practices. The following pays more attention to the independent neo-pentecostal churches/ ministries, while drawing examples from the classical Pentecostals when the need arises.

THE AFRICAN PROPHETIC MOVEMENTS AND THE AFRICAN INITIATED CHURCHES

The early decades of the twentieth century witnessed the emergence of prophetic figures who were converts of western missionary endeavors throughout Africa. These prophetic figures are generally known as the precursors of African Pentecostalism. Some examples are prophets William Wadé Harris and Sampson Oppong of the Gold Coast (Ghana), Garrick Sokari Braide and Joseph Babalola of Nigeria, Simon Kimbangu of the Belgian Congo, Alice Lenshina of Zambia, John Chilembwe of Central Africa, and Isaiah Shembe of South Africa. These indigenous prophets operated from the African perspective and endeavored to make Christianity comprehensible and relevant to Africans. Their era ushered in a paradigm shift in the history of Christianity in Africa that emphasized African agency.[12]

The need met by these prophets had to do with the fact that large sectors of African converts were dissatisfied with the tendency by western mission-founded churches to explain away the charismatic and life-giving experiences found in the Bible, including God's countering the reality of evil. In the experience of the African converts, western mission Christianity lifted up abstract prayers to an unseen God that yielded no visible results, left diseases and afflictions uncured, and did little to allay the widespread fear of unseen malevolent forces and witchcraft. As a result, African converts saw a yawning gap between their old faith and the newfound faith mediated by western missionaries and their African agents. Many of these converts desired to bridge the gap by using the newfound faith to achieve the old aspirations. The prophetic figures of the early twentieth century launched a process that in some ways enhanced the importance of traditional religion for the consolidation of the Christian faith.

Yet a clear pattern of emphases in the ministries of the African prophets was also the teaching on complete trust in Jesus as the all-sufficient Lord and God, who is able to provide all needs and to heal all afflictions. Their ministries seemed to produce quick and visible results. Whereas the western mission churches produced converts in trickles, the African prophets produced converts in torrents. The ministries of the African prophets led to the healing of diseases at a rate greater than that of traditional African religions or European medical science. Consequently, many of the African prophets gathered a following from the converts of western missionaries.

Students of African Christianity have argued that western missionary preaching produced the spread of Christianity in Africa horizontally and often superficially over wide areas. Thus African Christianity as transmitted by western missionaries has been variously described as a "thin veneer or shallow," "alien or superficial,"[13] and "unable to sympathize with and relate to the spiritual realities of the African spiritual outlook."[14] In the West African Ghanaian context, one observer wrote, "it also failed to meet the Akan in his personally experienced religious need."[15]

Activities of the African prophets invoked negative attitudes from the leadership of the western mission-founded churches and the mainline churches. Although the African prophets themselves initially did not aspire to found their own churches, because of the attitude of the mainline churches, their successors established their own churches that were variously called African Instituted Churches, African Initiated Churches, African Independent Churches, or African Indigenous

Churches, all referred to as AICs.[16] These are generally reckoned as the first stream of African Pentecostals.

The spiritually gifted African men and women who started the AICS claimed that they were called by God through visions and prophetic utterances to begin a spiritual movement. They emphasized the efficacy and sufficiency of prayers alone as a panacea for all human needs and as a solution to life's problems. In addition to the use of the Bible, they borrow heavily from African religious idioms and cultural elements, especially those that deeply hold symbolic meanings. Prayers, songs, sermons, and the use of time and space media and metaphors reflect deep African spirituality.

An important feature of this group of spiritual leaders is their preoccupation with holiness. To maintain purity of body and soul, which is considered a precondition for the efficacy of their prayers and supplications, a number of prohibitions and taboos are maintained in places of worship, prayers, and healing rituals. In some cases, local streams are reserved for ritual cleansing for their members and those who seek assistance for healing. For these practitioners fervent prayers have the capacity to compel God to act in response. During prayers, the use of tangible elements such as water and candles gives church members extra confidence that their prayers will be answered.[17]

As a further mark of their holiness, a number of these church leaders require their members to wear white robes in worship, which they consider the cloth of the Holy Spirit as distinct from ordinary clothes of the body. Such attire distinguishes them from those outside the sacred canopy of their churches.

These churches also show marks of discontinuity with their indigenous traditions, as they maintain an ambivalent relationship with African religion and culture. Some of these churches explicitly reject African beliefs and religious practices, labeling them as pagan, although they surreptitiously employ cultural symbols from the very traditions they condemn. Some of their adherents set fires to traditional religious shrines during moments of evangelical fervor as an act of condemnation. Finally, some forms of pentecostal spirituality manifested in dreams, visions, spirit possession, and prophetic experiences are closely related to African indigenous religion. The AICs blazed a path that others have followed even in contemporary times. Their significance lies in the fact that "they have pointed to the direction in which broad sections of African Christianity were moving, and so they testified to the existence of some generalized trends in the African response to the Christian faith in African terms."[18]

CLASSICAL PENTECOSTALISM AND INDEPENDENT
NEO-PENTECOSTAL CHURCHES/MINISTRIES IN AFRICA

Cecil M. Robeck, Jr., who has studied the history of Azusa Street Revival extensively, devotes some space to the Azusa Street Mission in Africa, noting that "by far the largest number of the first-time missionaries who went out in 1906 from the Azusa Street Mission went to Africa."[19] He traces the history of some Azusa Street pentecostal missionaries in Africa, particularly in Liberia, Congo, and South Africa. These missionary endeavors, particularly those in Liberia and Congo, did not produce any known mission/church. Azusa Street missionaries to South Africa founded the Apostolic Faith Mission and contributed to many pentecostal-type traditions that "trace their roots directly to the earlier work of ... Apostolic Faith missionaries" of the Azusa Street Revival.[20] Nevertheless, the most enduring fruit of the Azusa Street Revival in Africa is the establishment of the Assemblies of God Church, a major classical pentecostal church.[21] Most classical pentecostal churches in Africa were started since the 1920s by indigenous leaders.

The next major strand of pentecostal churches in Africa, the Independent Neo-Pentecostal Churches, emerged on the African religious scene in the 1970s. In East Africa, it started with the Fellowship of Christian Unions (FOCUS), which linked a number of national student Christian Unions and facilitated the spread of charismatic renewal across borders. Kenyans were to play a major role in disseminating this renewal in East Africa. Paul Gifford has noted that in Uganda these churches are "mushrooming in luxuriant fashion."[22] The renewal arose in Ghana in the late 1970s when some members of transnational evangelical movements such as the Scripture Union and the University Christian Union/Fellowship came into contact with pentecostal literature and with other members who had pentecostal experiences in their churches. In addition, there were contacts with and influence from members of such pentecostal churches as the Church of Pentecost, the Apostolic Church, and a number of pentecostal prayer groups.[23]

In Nigeria, the Universities of Ibadan and Ife were the major centers of the charismatic revival in the early 1970s.[24] However, by the mid-1970s the charismatic revival in Nigeria had gained strength and spread beyond the university campuses into the wider society, and most Charismatics in that country are still educated elites who are generally fluent in English. The beginning of charismatic renewal in various francophone countries may be traced to the efforts of some Nigerian students who did their one-year language study in Benin,

La Côte D'Ivoire, Guinea, and elsewhere. On the whole, however, French-speaking West Africa did not witness the charismatic renewal until the mid-1980s.

A rising tide of evangelistic activities and promotion of pentecostal doctrine and experience characterized the renewal in its early years, and this doctrinal emphasis eased its rapid geographical spread. By the 1980s the movement had assumed a high social profile owing partly not only to the attention given to it by the media but also to multitudes of new churches and "ministries" that were emerging and erecting signboards all over the major cities in Africa.

The African charismatic movement seems to be an urban phenomenon, and most of the evangelistic programs and healing and miracle services of this group of ministries are targeted at urban dwellers, particularly upwardly mobile youth. The patronage of charismatic organizations in urban areas is a result in part to their utilization of the mass media to publicize their presence and their activities. It is also because of their focus on contemporary problems of urban areas such as joblessness, underemployment, loneliness, and inadequate health care.

Healing by faith in Jesus, through Bible reading and prayer, constitutes a significant aspect of the influence of the charismatic movement in contemporary Africa.[25] Through their application of healing to almost every area of life, the Charismatics have tried to meet the aspirations and needs of their members. Here again there are similarities with the Independent Churches. They have appropriated their traditional cultural backgrounds and have defined healing to include freedom from demonic attacks and oppression. The healing process is termed "deliverance," and it involves getting rid of the source of a problem or illness, which is always attributed to satanic manipulations.

The independent neo-Pentecostals denounce the AICs by demonizing them and calling them "white garment churches" or people covenanted to familiar (evil) spirits.[26] They criticize the AICs for their use of prayer items such as "holy water," "anointing oil," and "holy handkerchiefs," although interestingly, in recent times neo-Pentecostals also use such prayer items. Like the AICs, Independent Neo-Pentecostal Churches reject indigenous African religions, which they construe as harbingers of demons and evil spirits. The liturgical practice and worship mode of the charismatics are major identity markers. Their worship services are characterized by loud shouts to God in praise. Christian lyrics and songs, with instrumental accompaniment provided by accordions, brass bands, guitars, and trumpets, are used in most churches.

AFRICAN PENTECOSTAL MEDIATION OF SALVATION

African Pentecostalism is a very experiential religion, and a major reason why it is popular today is related to its adoption of the traditional African world view of mystical causalities. African Pentecostals open up access to the sacred and formulate interventionist rituals that help their clients cope with the fears and insecurities of life.[27]

The African understanding that religion should serve very practical ends, coupled with Pentecostalism's capacity to take on different local forms, promotes the appeal of pentecostal spirituality in contemporary Africa. Pentecostals have developed religious rituals that serve as a survival strategy to economically and socially disadvantaged Africans. The ability of African Pentecostalism to adapt to and fulfill religious aspirations continues to be its main strength. An African style of worship and liturgy and a holistic Christianity that offers tangible help in this world as well as in the next together constitute a uniquely African contextualization of Christianity.

The discourse on the existence of demons and evil spirits in the society is dominant among the Pentecostals. African Pentecostals have successfully managed to pit the Holy Spirit against local demons. Demons are believed to be the cause of illnesses, misfortunes such as childlessness, a bad harvest, political oppression, personal and communal crises, a late or failed marriage, joblessness, and poverty. As a consequence of this belief in demons, substantial time and space are devoted to exorcising these disturbing spirits. Casting out demons is normally the climax of revival meetings, open-air services, and private prayer meetings. Drawing from the traditional African concern for wholeness and the quest to maintain equilibrium, Pentecostals hold that there are varying degrees of demonic operation. In some cases demons take full possession of human beings, whereas in other cases the demons manifest themselves from time to time. It is believed that demonic attacks and oppression can only be resolved through a process called deliverance.

Divine healing is at the core of pentecostal and charismatic ministries. Pentecostals offer "Christian" variations of indigenous etiologies of illness, and these are overcome by their practice of divine healing. Most churches emphasize a holistic attitude toward healing – one that encompasses spiritual, physical, and emotional dimensions. Their understanding of healing is quite broad and so are the programs of action put in place to carry it out. They will normally cite copious scriptural references about healing, insisting that good health is the will of God for every believer and that believers who are not in good health are not benefiting from God's blessing. Despite this teaching, Pentecostals and Charismatics do fall and remain ill.[28] To account for such illness, the pentecostal understanding of the causation of illness is supported with biblical references that attribute every illness to Satan or to sin or to both. It is apparent that the present inaccessibility of health services in most African countries gives impetus to charismatic healing. In this regard it can be argued that Pentecostals and Charismatics are addressing themselves to the prevalent situations in Africa by promising and offering healing of all kinds of diseases at no cost to their patients.

In the 1980s another form of healing developed under the theme of "prosperity and success."[29] A careful examination of this teaching reveals that it has two dimensions. The first is the prosperity of the soul, and the second is material prosperity. According to some pentecostal leaders, people are poor either because they lack knowledge and are unaware of the divine will of God for their prosperity or because there is sin hindering the fulfillment of God's will. Therefore, the recipe for prosperity includes spending more time in God's Word, and above all, giving to God or sowing seed by giving money to the church concerned. Many have advocated that the more one gives to God, the more one receives in return. The antidote to failure, hardship in life, or difficulties of any kind is to appropriate God's promises in the scripture for oneself, respond in obedience, and then receive a life of sufficiency and abundance.

The prosperity message flowed into Africa from many places besides the United States. Preachers from Southeast Asia, the West Indies, and the United Kingdom also generated versions of the teaching.[30] Each offered his own variation on the theme to an avid consumer's market. It bears emphasizing that the popularity of the message was buttressed by its resonance with African indigenous concepts of salvation, abundant life, and the very practical African understanding of the goal of worship. In African traditional religion, salvation manifests itself in the transformation of material, physical, and psychic well-being. Every religious ritual seeks to preserve, enhance, and protect life. Abundant life to the African means peace with God, the gods, ancestors, fellow human beings, and the natural world. When a person is at peace with these agents, the natural forces cooperate by increasing their fruits.

However, many African communities share the understanding that prosperity and wealth are not material, but reflect inner peace, satisfaction, contentment, and the maintenance of social networks.[31] The Akan of Ghana use the concept of *nkwa* to denote abundant life. *Nkwa* includes the enjoyment of *ahonyade*, possessions, prosperity, and riches, as well as children. It also includes *asomdwei*, a life of peace and tranquility, especially peace with God, the ancestral spirits, kinsfolk, and neighbors. These are the content of indigenous liturgies and concerns expressed in libations.

Within this world view, there are forces that could thwart a person's *nkwa*. Such forces could be external and supernatural (witches, sorcerers, charmers, and wicked medicine men and women). They could also emanate from internal, moral faults or from polluting the land through criminal acts, misdemeanors, and the flouting of prohibitions. Offenses against spiritual forces have consequences that manifest themselves as hardship and afflictions in the physical realm. People consult traditional religious functionaries[32] who will diagnose the cause of suffering and offer the proper processes for ritual cleansing, propitiation, and restoration. The traditional religious functionaries acknowledge that they act on behalf of the one who saves, protects, and preserves life. This is the kind of Christology that is adopted by African Pentecostals and Charismatics. Jesus is presented not only as the eschatological savior but also as the healer, the deliverer from malevolent spirits, and the great provider of every good thing.

What sustains this quest for material resources is partly the present deteriorating economic situations in Africa. People have used various means to acquire wealth, but for Pentecostals and Charismatics, such means lie in their access to spiritual knowledge.[33] To then alleviate poverty, Pentecostals and Charismatics incorporate rituals that achieve the stabilization of relationships between the human, the divine, and the natural world. Restorations of the moral order ensure that human activities succeed and that evil is warded off. While human beings work hard to alleviate suffering, they need the ability to deal with negative moral forces through fasting and prayer. This has led the innovative pentecostal leaders to advocate different types of prayer: prayers of faith, prayers of agreement, intercessory prayers, prayers of dedications, and seed sowing. Pentecostalism has also introduced various forms of anointing services, particularly at the beginning of the calendar year, including anointing for favor, breakthrough, protection, productivity, healing and deliverance, promotion, prosperity, and open doors. These anointing services are advertised in handbills, wall posts, street banners, radio announcements, and television clips with dramatic scenes of the Holy Spirit in action. Anointing services are special occasions during which olive oil is applied to various parts of the body, or even sometimes taken orally, to effect healing, reverse misfortunes, or to empower people for successful living. For the prayers to be efficacious, they must be appropriate and offered at the right time, in the right place, and for the right purpose. Because of this, prayer services are held by various Pentecostals and Charismatics throughout the week. These are walk-in services to which people can come and pray, get themselves anointed with oil, and return to their daily lives with the assurance that God is in control.

The use of anointing oil during healing services transcends denominational barriers.[34] The overreliance on olive oil among the Pentecostals and charismatic renewal movements in the mainline churches resembles the use of "perfumed water"[35] among the older AICs. These substances are believed to be therapeutic and are becoming virtual fetishes in the hands of members. Their widespread use mirrors the African traditional religions' adoption of material elements in their healing practices. During anointing services, people make invocations, incantations, and declarations concerning their life's destiny. With the belief that words have performative effects, many engage in the exercise by stamping their feet and moving about renouncing curses and evil powers that are perceived to be holding them back. Typically pentecostal and charismatic leaders pour the oil on the ground, as if they are pouring libation, while making their decrees. All in all, African Pentecostals operate with a holistic understanding of salvation that takes in "a sense of well-being evidenced in freedom from sickness, poverty and misfortune as well as in deliverance from sin and evil."[36]

THE ROLE OF AFRICAN PENTECOSTALISM IN PUBLIC LIFE

One of the appeals of the pentecostal-charismatic movement is its ability to respond to the existential and pragmatic needs faced by modern urban congregations, including domestic and socioeconomic problems. Their emergence in most parts of Africa occurred under conditions of economic, political, and social hardship, which are accompanied by economic reforms, low wages and quality of life, the absence of social services, and the withdrawal of the welfare frontiers of the state. Many associations, including pentecostal and charismatic organizations, are increasingly replacing the state in the provision of supplies and resources to fulfill basic needs. In his major work on Pentecostalism in the southern African country of Zimbabwe, David Maxwell notes Pentecostalism's public role "seemed to appeal to those on the move, both physically and socially. Pentecostalism spoke to those experiencing the imposition or intensification of colonial rule."[37]

Pentecostals and Charismatics focus on contemporary challenges in Africa. They are quick in offering adherents biblical tools to engage with life-threatening situations. Pentecostal and charismatic churches have come to constitute a major factor in Africa's social, economic, and political landscape. The engagement with everyday issues was further reinforced by the advent of civilian administrations. Many African leaders saw their roles in government and their victories at the polls in the light of the biblical messiah. In many African countries, pentecostal and charismatic leaders adopted these self-styled messiahs as symbols of Christian control over the political sphere, believing that they were answers to their prayers and the fulfillment of their prophecies. Some went further to expect the ending of oppression and inept governance. State-organized Christian services were prominent in this context, with regular observances of morning devotions at the state houses. With this development, it became obvious that the churches' earlier attitude of detachment from politics gradually declined and there was a corresponding rise in their engagement with urban-based political affairs.[38]

At the community levels, these churches engaged in building businesses and establishing institutions that supplemented or replaced the weak public infrastructure, especially in the area of education. In Ghana today there is an emerging number of faith-based private universities that have strong pentecostal and charismatic orientation. They also have played an increasingly visible role in public debate concerning good leadership, corruption, public accountability, and religious conflicts.

At the family levels, the expected "social uplift" associated with pentecostal-charismatic teachings brought the men back home. Formerly men found expression for their masculine self-image in drinking, drugs, gambling, and womanizing. Without these social evils, they now enjoy competitive economic advantage over their neighbors and have the means to finance capital projects or invest in business enterprise. Many are encouraged to develop their entrepreneurial talents, for this in turn will mean generous financial support and donation to their churches. Also, with the social network encouraged in a church, many Pentecostals and Charismatics contribute to the individual social welfare of their members. People not only help each other when in need but also patronize each other's businesses and loan one another money for the pursuit of business opportunities.[39]

Another potential social impact of the Pentecostals and Charismatics is in the area of human rights. Everyone is made in the image of God, and all people have equal value in God's sight. At its root, the pentecostal and charismatic movement is a religion of the people; all believers have the right to interpret scripture for themselves. Believers have direct access to God, not needing a mediator, and everyone has a role in the church regardless of social class, race, ethnicity, or family lineage.

Some Pentecostals and Charismatics have undertaken civic education to enlighten Christians about their potential influence in national life. Through publications the churches have spoken on almost every political issue and in many cases have submitted memoranda to governments. A good example is the case of the Christian Students Social Movement (CSSM) of Nigeria.[40] It was established in May 1977 by leaders of Christian union groups in the universities and colleges. They set their aim as awakening Christians, mostly college students and graduates, to their social and political responsibilities.

AFRICAN PENTECOSTAL TRANSNATIONAL MISSIONS

A major trend in contemporary African Christianity is its exploits in offering chaplaincy to African migrants in other countries, particularly Europe and the Americas. Initially, this mission endeavor was targeted at people of the same nationality as the chaplains. With the passage of time, the trend changed to include other African nationals in the diaspora.[41] In one of the earliest scholarly studies of African migrant churches in Europe, Gerrie ter Haar observes that one of the major features of African immigrant churches is that "they are mostly black."[42] This point notwithstanding, the trend is changing. African-led immigrant churches have started reaching out to their hosts. A classic example is the church of the Embassy of Blessed Kingdom of God for All Nations in Kiev, Ukraine, led by a Nigerian-born pastor Sunday Adelaja.[43] The church has more than 20,000 adult members in the Ukraine, of whom more than 90 percent are indigenous Europeans.

The chaplaincy/mission initiative cuts across denominational barriers. Roman Catholics, Presbyterians, Methodist, AICs, Pentecostals, and Charismatics are all involved. Nevertheless, Pentecostals and Charismatics dominate in this chaplaincy/mission enterprise. A typical example is the Ghanaian Church of Pentecost, which has branches in 84 different countries, with 3,477 churches and an overall overseas membership of 292,450.[44] This trend constitutes a major paradigmatic change in the Christian mission, popularly labeled a "reverse mission." African Pentecostals are convinced that God's mandate to them is to reach out to the entire world. This conviction is captured by their including words such as "global," "international," and "world" in their nomenclatures.[45]

The Church of Pentecost, for instance, has explicitly stated that its vision is, "[p]lanting and nurturing healthy churches globally."[46] In pursuit of this goal African Pentecostals are making inroads into world mission and making the presence of a distinctive African Christianity felt around the world.[47] This transnational African Christian mission spearheaded by African pentecostal-type Christianity thus gives credence to the notion that African Pentecostalism is potentially a key player in the reshaping of global Christianity, particularly in Europe and the Americas in the twenty-first century.

THE AFRICANNESS OF AFRICAN PENTECOSTALISM

Pentecostalism is a worldwide movement with common characteristics. There are cases of African pentecostal churches that were founded by western pentecostal movements, but indigenous Africans quickly received the Pentecostals' powerful idioms and gave them local legitimacy. What are the specifically African features of Pentecostalism?

The upsurge of Pentecostalism in Africa has deepened awareness regarding Satan, demons, and evil in popular African Christianity. African cosmology clearly reckons with the devil and evil spirit beings or malevolent spirits believed to be at work on a daily basis. Max Assimeng, a Ghanaian sociologist concludes: "I believe that the central focus of religious activity in African traditional societies seems to be the warding off of what the Akan call *honhom fi* (evil spirit) from the affairs of man. This preoccupation of the traditional believer appears to me to be the central basis of traditional religiousness."[48] In her study of the Ewe of Ghana, Birgit Meyer corroborates Assimeng's position that, without this belief, the faith of the people "would be devoid of any basis."[49] This conviction has led African Christians to believe that life is a power encounter and a spiritual battle, requiring certain rituals or covenants to consolidate relationships with saints, angels, Jesus Christ, and the Holy Spirit. The primal world view of African religiosity encourages beliefs in libations, sacrificial objects, and incantations. Individuals and communities covenant themselves to spirits in the sky, land, water, and the ancestral world. These covenants are legally binding; the obligations can be inherited, deliberately entered into, unknowingly covenanted into, and transmitted to progeny. In this world view, the things that are seen are made of things that are not seen. Circumstances of life are determined in the spiritual realm. The African Pentecostals take this African map of the universe very seriously and make the spirits real, just as Christ is real.[50] Thus for African Pentecostals, a more realistic way of helping Christians deal with their deep-seated concerns is to reckon with the reality of both Satan and demons and to rank Jesus Christ as higher in status and power. The consequence is the prominence of healing and deliverance from evil. Numerous prophetic healing crusades and healing/deliverance prayer camps have sprung up to give Africans succor. This posture does not necessarily negate personal responsibility but rather enjoins a more alert, engaged, and honest life.

The belief is that anointing oils, prophetic prayers, and seed sowing of money or material things in the lives of pastors, their families, and churches, complements if not alleviates the practical responsibility of working hard to achieve the desired prosperity in life. In Africans' world view, the way to wealth is not just working hard but also, more importantly, getting the favor of the gods. Everybody struggles hard to obtain this favor. When this favor comes, it is believed that even water can flow out of the rock for such persons. Uncommon things become common in the gods' hands.

African Pentecostals teach that there is a strong connection between a nation's prosperity and Christian leadership. God, it is believed, blesses a nation only if the political leadership acknowledges His sovereignty, and such Christian leaders come to power only when Christians pray. This understanding informs pentecostal and charismatic outlooks and activities. In the African world, there are strong relationships between the Ruler and the Chief Priest or Diviner. It is this world view that has been transplanted into African Pentecostals' and Charismatics' consciousness.

African society is pervasively religious. There is a strong belief among African Pentecostals that God does break into human life. The sacred and the secular are inextricably bound together in all spheres of life. Therefore, Pentecostals expect miracles and the unexpected when they spend time in prayer, because the power of the living God is expected to move in spectacular ways.

Africans received the Gospel literally in the vernacular as God's message for their particular situation. The vernacular Bible is one of the major reasons for the fast growth of the AICs in Africa.[51] Justin Ukpong thinks most Africans obey the scripture without much questioning because in the world view of the traditional African society authority, especially religious authority, is accepted without question.[52] "Arising from the fact that Africans attach great potency to the spoken Word, the Bible is regarded as very 'powerful,' being the Word of God."[53] African Pentecostals believe that when well applied, the Bible is capable of helping them come to terms with all their struggles. As a result, African

Pentecostals have demonstrated a lively and concrete response to the gospel.

African Pentecostals continue to embrace an African primal cosmology involving spirit beings that is thought to be similar to that portrayed in the Bible. They contend that Jesus believed in the same. Hence, there is a high degree of unanimity in their emphasis on spiritual warfare, deliverance ministry, and the miraculous healing power of Christ.

CONCLUSION

African Pentecostalism is perceived as making a good attempt at establishing the root of African Christianity deep into African culture and life. African Pentecostalism is often identified by its dynamic and participatory worship and mission commitments. African Pentecostals draw on African traditional religiosity, and they pattern their religious practices to reflect their Africanness.

The growth of African Pentecostalism is both rapid and visible, to the extent that it cannot elude the casual observer. It is perceived by Africans as a relevant religion in that it is scratching where the African is itching most, because it takes the African world view seriously by responding to the issues that emerge from the African scene, a feat that western theology has not been able to accomplish adequately. On the whole, the posture adopted by African Pentecostalism has led to a process of "pentecostalization" that does not recognize denominational barriers in Africa. African Pentecostalism is increasingly the fastest growing sector of Christianity in Africa, permeating all facets of life and changing the face of African societies. Furthermore, its growth has led to its exportation to other parts of the world, where African migrants are found. African Pentecostalism is now making inroads into predominantly non-African societies. Indeed, it is reshaping global Christianity.

Notes

1   Patrick Johnstone and J. Mandryk, *Operation World: 21st Century Edition* (Carlisle, UK: Paternoster, 2001), 21.

2   Cephas Omenyo, *Pentecost Outside Pentecostalism: A Study of the Development of Charismatic Renewal in the Mainline Churches in Ghana* (Zoetermeer: Boekencentrum, 2002).

3   Robert M. Anderson, "Pentecostal and Charismatic Christianity," in Mircea Eliade, ed., *Encyclopedia of Religion*, vol. XI (New York: Collier Macmillan, 1987), 234.

4   Ogbu Kalu, *Africa Pentecostalism: An Introduction* (Oxford: Oxford University Press, 2008), 5.

5   Cephas Omenyo and Abamfo Atiemo, "Claiming Religious Space: The Case of Neo-Prophetism in Ghana," *Ghana Bulletin of Theology*, New Series 1:1 (2006), 55–68, at 58.

6   E.g., C. B. Baëta, *Prophetism in Ghana: A Study of Some 'Spiritual' Churches* (London: SCM Press, 1962); B. G. M. Sunkler, *Zulu Zion and Some Zwazi Zionists* (Oxford: Oxford University Press, 1976); M. L. Daneel, *Quest for Belonging: An Introduction to a Study of African Independent Churches* (Gweru: Mambo Press, 1987); G. C. Oosthizen, *The Healer-Prophet in Afro-Christian Churches* (Leiden: Brill, 1992); J. S. Pobee and Gariel Ositule II, *African Initiatives in Christianity: The Growth, Gifts and Diversities of Indigenous African Churches* (Geneva: WCC, 1998); and Allan Anderson, *Zion and Pentecost: The Spirituality and Experience of Pentecostal and Zionist/Apostolic Churches in South Africa* (Pretoria: University of South Africa Press, 2000).

7   Emmanuel Kingsley Larbi, *Pentecostalism: The Eddies of Ghnaian Christianity* (Accra: Center for Pentecostal and Charismatic Studies, 2001).

8   Samuel B. Aduboffour, "Evangelical Para-church Movements in Ghanaian Christianity: C. 1550 to early 1990s," PhD thesis, University of Edinburgh (1994).

9   See Omenyo, *Pentecost Outside Pentecostalism*.

10 J. Kwabena Asamoah-Gyadu, *African Charismatics: Current Developments within Independent Indigenous Pentecostalism in Ghana* (Leiden: Brill, 2005).

11 Paul Gifford, *Ghana's New Christianity: Pentecostalism in a Globalizing African Economy* (London: Hurst & Co., 2004).

12 See Kwame Bediako, *Christianity in Africa: The Renewal of a Non-Western Religion* (Maryknoll: Orbis, 1995), 63–66.

13 K. A. Busia, "Has the Christian Faith Been Adequately Represented?" *International Review of Mission* 50 (1963), 86–89.

14 S. G. Williamson, *Akan Religion and the Christian Faith* (Accra: Ghana Universities Press, 1965), 175.

15 Bediako, *Christianity in Africa*, 69.

16 Most of the well-established AICs work under the umbrella of the Organization of African Instituted Churches (OAIC), with its headquarters in Nairobi, Kenya; see http://www.oaic.org/.

17 J. K. Olupona, "Africa, West," in Stanley Burgess and Edward M. Van Der Maas, eds., *New International Dictionary of Pentecostal and Charismatic Movement* (rev. and expanded ed.; Grand Rapids: Zondervan, 2002), 14.

18 Bediako, *Christianity in Africa*, 66.

19 Cecil M. Robeck, Jr., *The Azusa Street Mission and Revival: The Birth of the Global Pentecostal Movement* (Nashville: Thomas Nelson Inc., 2006), 266.

20 Robeck, *The Azusa Street Mission and Revival*, 280.

21 See Cephas N. Omenyo, "William Seymour and African Pentecostal Historiography: The Case of Ghana," *Asian Journal of Pentecostal Studies* 9:2 (2008), 247–53, and C. M. Robeck, Jr., "Azusa Street Revival," in Stanley M. Burgess and Eduardo van der Maas, eds., *New International Dictionary of Pentecostal and Charismatic Movements* (Grand Rapids: Zondervan, 2002), 33.

22 Paul Gifford, *African Christianity: Its Public Role* (London: Hurst and Co., 1998), 157.

23 See Matthews A. Ojo, *The End-Time Army: Charismatic Movements in Nigeria* (Trenton, NJ: Africa World Press, 2007).

24 Kalu, *African Pentecostalism*, 90.

25 See Cephas N. Omenyo, "New Wine in an Old Wine Bottle? Charismatic Healing in the Mainline Churches in Ghana," in Candy Gunther Brown, ed., *Global Pentecostal and Charismatic Healing* (Oxford: Oxford University Press, 2011), 236–38.

26 J. Kwabena Asamoah-Gyadu, "'Born of Water and the Spirit': Pentecostal/Charismatic Christianity in Africa," in Ogbu U. Kalu, ed., *African Christianity: An African Story* (Trenton: Africa World Press, 2007), 348.

27 See J. Kwabena Asamoah-Gyadu, "'Unction to Function': Reinventing the Oil of Influence in African Pentecostalism," *Journal of Pentecostal Theology* 13 (2005), 231–56.

28 Matthews Ojo, "Charismatic Movement in Africa," in Christopher Fyfe and Andrew Walls, eds., *Christianity in Africa in the 1990s* (Edinburgh: Center for African Studies, 1996), 92–110.

29 Nimi Wariboko, "Pentecostal Paradigms of National Economic Prosperity in Africa," in Katherine Attanasi and Amos Yong, eds., *Pentecostalism and Prosperity: The Socio-Economics of the Global Charismatic Movement* (New York: Palgrave Macmillan, 2012), 35–60.

30 Kalu, *African Pentecostalism*, 276.

31 Kalu, *African Pentecostalism*, 278.

32 These functionaries are generally ritual agents such as traditional priests, traditional linguists, and evil medicine practitioners (formerly called witch doctors).

33 E.g., Asonzeh F. K. Ukah, *A New Paradigm of Pentecostal Power: A Study of the Redeemed Christian Church of God in Nigeria* (Trenton, NJ: Africa World Press, 2008), chs. 5–7.

34 Asamoah-Gyadu, "Unction to Function," 237.

35 Perfumed water is specially prepared water mixed with strong perfume and oil believed to ward off evil spirits.

36 Allan Anderson, "Global Pentecostalism in the New Millennium," in Allan Anderson and Walter Hollenweger, eds., *Pentecostals after a Century: Global Perspectives on a Movement in Transition* (Sheffield: Sheffield Academic Press, 1999), 215.

37 David Maxwell, *African Gifts of the Spirit: Pentecostalism and the Rise of a Zimbabwean Transnational Religious Movement* (Oxford: James Currey, 2006), 56–57.

38 See Amos Yong, *In the Days of Caesar: Pentecostalism and Political Theology* (Grand Rapids: Eerdmans, 2010), 9–11; also, Ruth Marshall, *Political Spiritualities: The Pentecostal Revolution in Nigeria* (Chicago: University of Chicago Press, 2009).

39 See the Centre for Development and Enterprise, South Africa, "Under the Radar: Pentecostalism in South Africa and Its Potential Social and Economic Role," in Attanasi and Yong, *Pentecostalism and Prosperity*, 63–86.

40 Matthews Ojo, "The Contextual Significance of the Charismatic Movement in Independent Nigeria," *Journal of Africa* 58:2 (1988), 135–56.

41 See Jacob K. Olupona, "Globalization and African Immigrant Religious Communities," in Jennifer I. M. Reid, ed., *Religion and Global Culture* (Lanham, MD: Lexington Books, 2003), 83–96.

42 Gerrie ter Haar, *Halfway to Paradise: African Christians in Europe* (Cardiff, Wales: Cardiff Academic Press, 1998), iv, 1–2, 6.

43 See J. Kwabena Asamoah Gyadu, "An African Pentecostal on Mission in Eastern Europe: The Church of the 'Embassy of God' in the Ukraine," *Pneuma: The Journal of the Society for Pentcecostal Studies* 27 (2005), 297–321.

44 See http://thecophq.org/ (accessed September 1, 2012).

45 Examples are Ghanaian International Central Gospel Church, Global Revival Church, and World Christian Outreach.

46 Vision Statement of COP, http://thecophq.org/ (accessed on September 1, 2012).

47 See the special theme issue devoted to "Open Space: The African Christian Diaspora in Europe and the Quest for Human Community," *International Review of Mission* 89 (July 2000).

48 Max Assimeng, *Religion and Social Change in Africa* (Accra: Ghana Universities Press, 1989), 60.

49 Birgit Meyer, "'If You Are a Devil, You Are a Witch, and If You Are a Witch, You Are a Devil': The Integration of 'Pagan' Ideas into the Conceptual Universe of Ewe Christians in South Eastern Ghana," *Journal of Religion in Africa* 23 (1992), 108.

50 Birgit Meyer, "Make a Complete Break with the Past: Memory and Post-colonial Modernity in Ghanaian Pentecostalist Discourse," *Journal of Religion in Africa* 28:3 (1998), 318.

51 Bediako, *Christianity in Africa*, 63–73; see also Lamin O. Sanneh, *Translating the Message: The Missionary Impact on Culture* (Maryknoll: Orbis, 1989), and Philip Jenkins, *The New Faces of Christianity: Believing the Bible in the Global South* (Oxford: Oxford University Press, 2008).

52 Justin Ukpong, "Popular Reading of the Bible in Africa and Implication for Academic Readings," in Gerald O. West and Musa W. Dube, eds., *The Bible in Africa: Transaction, Trajectories and Trends* (Leiden: Brill, 2000), 588.

53 Andrew OluIgenoza, "Contextual Balance of Scripture with Scripture: Scripture Union in Nigeria and Ghana," in West and Dube, eds., *The Bible in Africa*, 294.

Further Reading

Akoko, Robert Mbe. *'Ask and You Shall Be Given': Pentecostalism and the Economic Crisis in Cameroon.* Leiden: African Studies Centre, 2007.

Anderson, Allan. *African Reformation.* Trenton, NJ: African World Press, 2002.

Burgess, Richard. *Nigeria's Christian Revolution: The Civil War Revival and Its Pentecostal Progeny (1967–2006).* Milton Keynes, UK: Regnum, 2008.

Corten, André, and Ruth Marshall-Fratani, eds. *Between Babel and Pentecost: Transnational Pentecostalism in Africa and Latin America.* Bloomington: Indiana University Press, 2001.

Frahm-Arp, Maria. *Professional Women in South African Pentecostal Charismatic Churches*. Leiden: Brill, 2010.

Gifford, Paul. *Christianity, Politics and Public Life in Kenya*. New York: Columbia University Press, 2009.

Soothill, Jane. *Gender, Social Change and Spiritual Power: Charismatic Christianity in Ghana*. Leiden: Brill, 2007.

8 Asian Pentecostalism in Context: A Challenging Portrait

WONSUK MA

Asia is the home of five major world religions and myriads of regional, national and local ones. Asia, the largest continent, with almost two-thirds of the world's population, also has the widest array of cultures, histories, languages, and sociopolitical experiences. The complexity of the region makes any encounter with the host context exceptionally rich, creative, and complicated. Understandably, global Pentecostalism, estimated to have reached 612 million in the middle of 2011,[1] finds a wide range of forms and features in Asia.

The question of who Pentecostals are, especially in the Asian context, therefore, is a challenging inquiry. The pentecostal movement is shaped through the continual, dynamic interaction between the people of the pentecostal faith, regardless of their consciousness of being labeled as such, and their sociocultural environments. They often come from, but also unconsciously with, other religious orientations, holding a strong belief in and having a dynamic, often supernatural experience of the person and work of the Holy Spirit in their daily lives and worship. Thus, how this collective phenomenon of dynamic spirituality is categorized is only a secondary question. "Pentecostalism" here is used as an umbrella term to encompass classical, neo-, and others, including indigenous Pentecostals, and may be interchangeably used with charismatic Christianity.[2]

By the conclusion of this study, I wish to challenge the notion that Pentecostalism in Asia is a transplanted version of the pentecostal religion "made in the U.S.A." Clear historical links are difficult to establish for some cases. Also, I want to demonstrate that Pentecostalism interacts so dynamically with cultures, religions, and social issues that the end result of this encounter varies greatly from one context to another. This study will first present a picture of Asian Pentecostalism by sampling case studies of pentecostal-charismatic groups from three countries. Although the samples do not include South Asia, the survey is intended to provide a reasonable sense of the pentecostal landscape in

Asia. The second part is an analysis of Asian Pentecostalism intended to draw a set of traits observed not only in the samples but also in all charismatic Christianity in Asia. Therefore, I have not begun with any standard definition of Pentecostalism in Asia, against which Asian Pentecostalism is measured. Rather I hope to develop from this study an understanding of Asian Pentecostalism and the commonalities its local expressions share. The study ends with a brief reflection for the future.

FIVE PENTECOSTAL GROUPS IN THREE COUNTRIES

The cases have been selected to provide a fair spectrum of charismatic Christianity in Asia. For Korea, a well-known Prayer Mountain and a strongly charismatic Presbyterian network are chosen to illustrate the expression of indigenous Korean Pentecostalism and its spirituality in two very different social contexts and periods of the nation. For the Philippines, the focus is on a huge, controversial Catholic charismatic network, paying particular attention to their creative and controversial responses to the contemporary socio-religio-economic challenges. For China, two very different networks are chosen, one from the pre-1949 era and the other from the post-Cultural Revolution era. They again illustrate the responses of charismatic Christianity to different sociopolitical challenges.

KOREA

Although the first western pentecostal missionary to Korea, Mary Rumsey, began her missionary work in 1928, many scholars claim the 1907 Pyongyang Revival as the beginning of the Korean pentecostal movement. Therefore, from the beginning, the "Holy Spirit Movement" as it is popularly known among Korean Christians was never a denominational movement, until the arrival of pentecostal missionaries.[3] For this reason, this study will look at the indigenous stream of Pentecostalism that has played an important role in the shaping of Korean Pentecostalism as it is today. This may partly explain why pentecostal spirituality and worship have been widely spread across denominations, although their entry into common Christian life came through the "back door." It is also noticeable that indigenous forms of religiosity have been incorporated into pentecostal practices.

Yongmoon Prayer Mountain

The first back door of pentecostal spirituality is through Prayer Mountains. The origin of the Korean Prayer Mountain movement is unclear, but it proliferated after the independence of the country (1945). During the heights of Japanese oppression on Christianity when many churches were closed and leaders imprisoned, records reveal that Christians found mountains as handy places to spend days and nights in prayer.[4] Buddhists and Shamanists have also traditionally ascribed religious value to them.

The leader of the Prayer Mountain movement was Woon-mong Ra (1914–2009), a lay Methodist leader who was trained in Chinese classics.[5] He established not only Yongmoon-san Prayer Mountain in 1945 but also a Protestant monastery and a convent, as well as Bible schools and a weekly Christian newspaper. During its heyday, about 10,000 Christians attended a week-long summer revival camp in this remote place. This was a true pentecostal event in which topics such as healing, prophecy, miracles, and hearing God's voice were all freely taught, prayed for, and experienced.

Prayer Mountains were a seedbed of pentecostal Christianity particularly in the 1950s and 1960s. It is important to note that these topics were not openly discussed in most churches, especially among Presbyterian churches where supernatural manifestations were believed to have ceased at the close of the apostolic period. Some participants returned to their churches and "disrupted" normal church life by advocating charismatic gifts, such as those experienced at Prayer Mountains.

Later, Prayer Mountains appeared throughout the country and near urban centers, often led by students of Ra, drawing Christians with special needs, both physical (e.g., illness) and spiritual (seeking the Spirit's filling). Yeol-soo Eim estimates that by 1994, there were more than 500 of them.[6] Ra remained extremely influential, although sometimes controversial, until large churches began to incorporate pentecostal messages and practices from the early 1970s. Most of them also began to open their own Prayer Mountains, such as the Choi Jashil Memorial International Fasting Prayer Mountain of the Yoido Full Gospel Church in 1973.

Although Ra's place had been reduced to several institutions, as fewer visitors were attracted and doctrinal controversies around his theology continued, the role of the independent Prayer Mountains cannot be underestimated in spreading pentecostal spirituality throughout Korea.

Onnuri Community Church

Since the 1970s, the Holy Spirit movement has found its main stage in local churches. This is also the period when a significant growth of

Christianity has taken place, with the emergence of megachurches.[7] The second back door of pentecostal spirituality, however, has persisted in local church settings through annual revival meetings. Following the pattern of the Pyongyang revival, this week-long, three-meetings-a-day event has included intense spiritual experiences. The two main emphases are Bible study and prayer. Testimonies of healings, miracles, speaking in tongues, and the like abound. Large churches, often led by well-known preachers, have incorporated pentecostal aspects into their messages and worship, regardless of their denominational orientation. A study of megachurches in Korea, undertaken a decade ago, identified ten of fifteen as Pentecostal/Charismatic in their worship and preaching.[8]

The Onnuri Church, established in 1985 by Rev. Yongjo Ha (1946–2011), is a case in point. Although a part of the Presbyterian Church of Korea, the congregation has exercised a powerful influence through innovative worship and mission programs. Although never explicated, some programs of the church may trace their theological influence to Pentecostalism. For example, its highly successful Praise and Worship program is a brilliant incorporation of the pentecostal worship tradition that is celebratory and participatory. Also congruent with pentecostal traditions is the church's mobilization of the whole church for mission. Ha envisions mobilizing 1,000 missionaries and 20,000 Christian workers.

One historical link with Pentecostalism is Ha's earlier involvement with Youth with a Mission, a large movement mobilizing youth for mission, with a clear pentecostal link through the founder. The core value of the church's ministry is encapsulated in "Acts 29." Because the Book of Acts consists of only twenty-eight chapters, this ministry asserts that "the book has not been completed and is still being written."[9] The ideal of the church, according to the church's publication, is to be "led by the Holy Spirit, with actively mobilized laity, with a deep sense of calling."[10]

Until his recent death, Ha led numerous missionary campaigns in Japan and elsewhere. It is reported that the congregation has 9 campuses with 75,000 members. In addition, about twenty-five network churches are in operation in Korea, with more outside the country.

Thanks to indigenous Holy Spirit movement's spirituality, this widespread influence of pentecostal spirituality in Korea makes it difficult to know exactly how many pentecostal/charismatic believers are there in Korea. *Operation World* puts the number at 3.5 million for 2010[11]; *World Christian Encyclopedia* estimates 7.6 million for the mid-2000s.[12] Considering the deep-rooted pentecostal spirituality that has permeated church life for more than a century, and the various shapes and forms it takes to express itself, the larger figure appears to be more likely.

The Philippines, an island nation, has a very different historical and cultural orientation than that of Korea and China. The more than three-century-long colonial rule by Spaniards (1566–1898) not only shaped diverse people groups into a nation but also made the country the only dominantly Christian nation in Asia. Protestant Christianity was introduced, mainly by American denominations, only with the defeat of the Spanish fleet by the Americans in 1898. The establishment of various pentecostal denominations took place in the 1940s, although the first North American pentecostal missionaries arrived as early as in 1926, followed by a group of Filipino-American Pentecostals in the 1930s.[13] Classical Pentecostalism experienced waves of revival and the denominations are now well established. Many of them are members of the Philippine Council of Evangelical Churches.

Our discussion will focus on the emergence of charismatic Christianity in the early 1980s,[14] although the Catholic charismatic movement was introduced as early as 1969. The proliferation of Catholic prayer meetings and home fellowships is attributed to the social unrest under the Marcos dictatorship. It was the urban middle and upper classes that sought their spiritual haven in mushrooming new charismatic groups. When the Roman Catholic Church issued a directive in 1983 to keep the "Born Again" (Protestant) influence away from Catholics,[15] many groups eventually broke off and became independent "fellowships" and "family worship centers" in restaurants and hotel ball rooms.[16] However, here is one group that grew so large that the Catholic Church has to make a special provision.

El Shaddai

Mariano "Mike" Z. Velarde (or "Brother Mike," 1939–), a realtor and businessman, acquired a radio station as part of his business dealings and began a Christian radio program in 1982. As its popularity grew, he began a monthly prayer meeting that was soon to become a weekly meeting. *El Shaddai*, the title of the radio program, also refers to his large Catholic charismatic network today claiming 8 million followers.[17] Its explosive growth is frequently attributed to his radical claim for healing and material blessings as an "entitlement" for committed Christians.

The group's sheer size made it a formidable challenge to locate suitable meeting places large enough to hold the still growing crowd, until the fellowship finally built its own multimillion dollar facility called El Shaddai International House of Prayer. On any given Sunday in most major Asian cities such as Hong Kong, there is always a huge crowd of Filipino El Shaddai members (mostly women) in a large downtown park celebrating their weekly mass. Because of its size, the Catholic Church's *Guidelines*, published decades ago, proved to be inadequate for the El Shaddai; today, two Catholic bishops provide oversight over Velarde and his group.[18]

The El Shaddai movement deserves a close examination for its size and impact. Currently, there are only one scholarly monograph[19] and a handful of shorter articles available on them. The most prominent point in the group's theology is God's material blessings. In the beginning, the context provided the strongest justification for this preaching, as his followers were mostly the urban poor, struggling to survive each day. Nonetheless, in addition to the general problems associated with the so-called prosperity gospel, Velarde's flamboyant celebrity-like lifestyle betrays the daily context of his average members. Furthermore, this teaching can suggest that God can be manipulated by giving, consequently reducing his form of Christianity into just another folk religion. Velarde's presentation of divine healing can easily slip into the folk religious mode, as now he blesses objects such as handkerchiefs and tea leaves to become instruments of healing. In this way we can see similarities between the folk practices of many Pentecostals and those of many Catholics.

Equally controversial is Velarde's political involvement. His endorsement of the morally corrupt presidential candidate Joseph Estrada in the 1998 election was a scandal, as the president was impeached and ousted from his office in 2001. Velarde also translated his religious following into political machinery by creating a political party, Buhay Hayaan Yumabong. From the 2004 congressional election, the party has maintained at least two congressional seats including that of Velarde's son. Velarde's bid for a seat was unsuccessful in the 2010 election. The party's profile carries Catholic beliefs including the sanctity of unborn babies.[20]

The figure for pentecostal-charismatic Christians presented by *Operation World* for 2010 in the Philippines is 22.7 million,[21] while the *World Christian Encyclopedia* estimates 20 million for the middle of the 2000s (i.e., 2005). This figure can be further broken down to 0.8 million Pentecostals, 11.7 million Charismatics, and 7.6 million neo-Charismatics.[22]

CHINA

Many details of Chinese Christianity are difficult to ascertain, but the resurgence of Christianity after the Cultural Revolution (1966–76) has been consistently affirmed. Also widely agreed is the presence of a number of pentecostal elements among many, especially independent, church groups. With relatively younger and newer "uncles" and "aunts" with vague connections with the pre-1949 patriarchs,[23] today's Chinese Christianity may serve as a rare "laboratory" for the rise of indigenous Christianity with little external (e.g., missionary) interference. One then has to suspect that the various shapes of Chinese Christianity, their understanding of being Christian and a church, and Christian response to the immediate sociopolitical context have been determined by their reading of Scripture within their context. Although some groups with varying historical connections with pre-1949 western pentecostal Christianity have reappeared, the type of Christianity that was slowly introduced to the outside world throughout the 1980s and 1990s has mostly resembled the indigenous forms of Christianity, with varying expressions of deep spiritual experiences and pentecostal elements.[24] We will look at one group each from the pre- and the post-Cultural Revolution eras.

The Jesus Family

The Jesus Family was established in 1927 in north China, in Mazhuang, Taian County of Shandong Province, by Jiang Dianying (1890–1957). Jiang, a businessman, became Pentecostal in the 1920s through the influence of the American Assemblies of God mission in Xian. He later developed the idea of Christian community life, on the basis of the teachings of Jesus to the rich young ruler (Matt 19:16), in response to successive natural disasters in the vast area of north and central China where people were forced to look for any way to survive. He founded the Jesus Family by reorganizing and renaming the Christian silk-making cooperative he had earlier organized.

Jiang laid out rules for a self-sufficient Christian communal life. Members were to give up their properties for communal use, and at least in the early years of the movement, families were separated into male and female dormitories. Everyone was to work on farms or in light industries within the community. However, the members were to spend a considerable amount of time in worship and prayer each day.

Their theology was centered on three major emphases: regeneration (e.g., born again), being "filled with the Holy Spirit," and millennial eschatology. They practiced prayer for healing, speaking in tongues, prophecy, and other spiritual gifts.[25] Here, the influence of the western pentecostal belief in the baptism in the Spirit is apparent. In addition, prominent among the Jesus Family members was "dancing in the Spirit" and "testimony." One could be taken into the heavenly presence of the Lord through vision or trance, receive a direct revelation from Him, and convey it to the rest of the community in "testimony." Like many independent Christian groups, the Jesus Family also maintained an expectation of the immediate return of the Lord. Its egalitarian and socially secluded communal life had a strong appeal to the masses marginalized by chronic poverty,[26] although ironically the leadership of Jiang and local family heads whom he appointed were authoritarian. It is estimated that the movement grew to more than 100 communities throughout north and central China by 1949 with 10,000 members. The movement was disbanded in 1953, and today it survives only in Taiwan.

Born Again Fellowship

The Born Again Fellowship, or as it is sometimes called Full Scope Church of 'Weepers',[27] or the Word of Life Church[28] of Henan Province,[29] is one of the largest networks in China. This group was started in the early 1980s by Xu Yongze (Peter) (1940–). Being an effective evangelist, through his loosely networked congregations he deployed teams of young evangelists within Henan and nearby provinces. The group grew steadily, in spite of the repeated imprisonments of Xu and his leaders. Membership estimates differ vastly from 3 to 5 million adherents, but since Xu left China, the church has become fragmented.

The Born Again movement shares many characteristics with other independent churches, which, in turn, have adopted varying degrees of charismatic influence. First, Xu, being the pastor and co-worker of the famous Brother Yun, endorsed Yun's testimony of suffering and many cases of healings and miracles as authentic.[30] The network's "Statement of Faith" also includes a section on the Holy Spirit including the following points: "The Holy Spirit gives all kinds of power and manifests the mighty acts of God through signs and miracles"; "Christians can experience the outpouring and the filling of the Holy Spirit"; and "We do not forbid speaking in tongues nor do we insist that everyone must speak in tongues."[31] Prayers and claims for healing are a regular part of their worship. In fact, the prominence of healing is widespread among Chinese Christianity,[32] as it is also argued that healing is a common feature of most Chinese religions including Taoism, and Christianity offers a functional substitute.[33]

Second, common among the new independent Christian groups is egalitarianism in ministry. As rightly observed by Fielder, the new charismatically oriented congregations, especially in rural areas, adopted a simple church structure that allows anyone to lead a congregation.[34] Women quickly rose into active leadership roles, an astonishing development in view of the established Christian tradition as well as Chinese cultural norms. This radical promotion of lay and women leadership is often considered to be a major contribution toward the church's unprecedented growth.

The third is the affective and emotional dimension of Christian spirituality and worship, as Tang views the outbursts of emotion as one of the four main characteristics of the new Christian groups.[35] However, the Born Again Fellowship, as its nickname "Weepers" suggests, is often known for weeping as a sign of genuine repentance. Although leaders deny this as a requirement for its members, to common minds weeping has attained a theological significance.[36] It is possible that this "seemingly hysterical" emotional excess,[37] among others, caused the Born Again Fellowship to be charged as a cult in the mid-1990s by the Chinese authorities and the official Three-Self leadership.

Figures for Christianity in China as a whole are already challenging: 105.4 million according to *Operation World*[38] and 115 million according to the *Atlas of Global Christianity*[39] are viewed as overestimates, but many seem to agree that as many as one-half of all Chinese Christians are "renewalists," found both among un-registered as well as registered churches.

WHAT WE OBSERVE

Several important characteristics have emerged from these five cases, and four can be singled out as defining characteristics of Asian Pentecostalism: flourishing in adverse situations, indigenous expressions, charismatic leadership, and megasize movements.

FLOURISHING IN ADVERSE CIRCUMSTANCES

Except in the case of Onnuri Church, all five groups were born and continue to operate in harsh sociopolitical and economic contexts. Their spirituality was shaped in their attempts to provide spiritual, community, and practical ways to cope with contextual challenges. In fact, conservative Christianity, including Pentecostalism, tends to record significant growth under adverse and harsh circumstances. Pentecostal Christianity often counters sociopolitical and economic pressure by creating an alternative world, by redirecting the church's priority attention to something else. In the first several decades of the twentieth century, Chinese Christianity, still fresh with the memory of the Boxer Rebellion and two wars, turned out to become completely apolitical. The Jesus Family provided a practical alternative society, incorporating a strong spiritual component. It grew significantly through the war years, even though its founder had already died. Peter Xu interprets the destructive Cultural Revolution as God's tool "to destroy the old structure of the Chinese church so that he could rebuild it according to his purposes."[40]

In Korea, the Prayer Mountain movement was born shortly after the independence of the nation, which was quickly engulfed in the destruction of the Korean War. An escape to a remote mountain, away from daily routines, supplemented with otherworldly concentration with powerful spiritual experiences, provides a perfect spiritual haven. Almost predictably, Pentecostals and evangelical Christians were either silent or even supportive of military rulers in the 1970s and 1980s and achieved record church growth. In a sense, with intense attention to spiritual experiences, Pentecostalism created an alternative universe to draw strength for daily life and beyond. The independent charismatic churches in the Philippines are another case of pentecostal response to political oppression of the Marcos dictatorship. Social unrest was the soil where the powerful charismatic movement was born, especially among urban professionals. The new form of spirituality not only provided a new meaning to life in the specific context but also redirected restless minds to spiritual satisfaction.

When such a harsh political system no longer exists and society moves beyond poverty, however, there comes a real challenge to the movement. This has been observed in the West, and also in places such as Korea. Pentecostalism struggles without something to struggle with. At least two examples are observed in our cases. One is the pentecostal interest in politics: forming political parties and/or running for elected positions, including presidential seats. The motivation for this is not clear – whether this is an outcome of a deep theological and missional reflection, a desire for recognition, or the simple realization of political potential in sheer numbers. This trend, however, is slowly spreading among pentecostal leaders in the Philippines, Indonesia, and Korea. What turns Pentecostals, who are traditionally otherworldly and millenarian, toward politics is a question worth pondering.

The other is pentecostal response to economic hardship that is divided into two expressions. In earlier days, it was more a denial with a good dose of millennial eschatology and a strong emphasis on mission. The Jesus Family took a further practical step, countering the chronic hardship by establishing Christian communities. The Prayer Mountain is a spiritual haven satisfying an escapist impulse for an "out-of-world" experience for a week or so. It is important to note, however, that Ra originally began as a Christian activist among poor farmers, and his original idea for the Prayer Mountain was a Christian community.

The second is the development of theology of blessing. In Korea, the forerunner was David Yonggi Cho, whose theology was shaped in response to the dire poverty of the postwar Korean society in the 1950s. This focus was later reinforced by faith preachers such as Robert Schuler and Oral Roberts in the early 1970s. The El Shaddai group is the clearest demonstration of the prosperity gospel found in Asia. As discussed, material prosperity and divine healings occupy a prominent place in Velarde's message. Material abundance often serves as a tangible sign of God's blessing, especially for those whose daily survival is an urgent need.[41]

In both political and economic areas, Pentecostals have exhibited radically different responses, depending on their contexts. This, I believe, proves the ingenuity of the pentecostal ability to interact with and respond to both its religio-cultural and sociopolitical context. This unusual pentecostal capability to contextualize has been well documented in missionary settings.[42] This further explains why charismatic Christianity continues to evolve in different forms, expressions, and shapes in various contexts. It not only adapts to its setting but also appropriates traditional religious and cultural beliefs and symbols as well as modern communication technologies.

INDIGENOUS EXPRESSIONS AND ENGAGEMENT WITH THE WIDER WORLD

As noted, from the outset, almost all the groups studied have limited or no outside support. They were established through the vision and efforts of national Christian leaders. Some of them, such as the Jesus Family and Yongmoon Prayer Mountain, exhibit forms and ethos that are close to indigenous religiosity and culture. The reading of Scripture in their own contexts, informed by their own experiences, must have given birth to their unique understanding of Christianity and its mission. The Filipino charismatic groups also exhibit ingenuity in responding to their contemporary challenges with openness to their indigenous religious resources.

This, however, does not completely rule out outside influences. Often represented by missionaries, the influence of western Christianity can be broadly traced. For example, the Xu family had an abiding influence from Marie Monsen, a Norwegian woman missionary (1872–1962), which was transmitted through generations of the Xu family, including Peter and his sister Deborah. It is also fascinating to observe that the influence was preserved and relayed by women members of the extended family.[43] Generally speaking, at the turn of the twentieth century, all three countries were heavily influenced by American Evangelicalism through its missionaries. As Mark Noll argues convincingly, it may be the forms and ethos of Christianity practiced in the United States that had a heavy influence on the development of global Evangelicalism including these groups.[44] In all cases, including the Catholic charismatic El Shaddai, the form of charismatic Christianity observed resembles American Evangelicalism with its Bible-oriented, individualistic, voluntary, and pragmatic characteristics.[45] Even El Shaddai appears to be more American with Velarde's prosperity preaching than liturgy-based Roman. Ha's exposure to the missionary and pentecostal ethos of Youth with a Mission is also clear.

In spite of these traces of external influences, none of these groups had any significant missionary involvement in leadership or even a consulting influence. The closest is Denbow's role in the shaping of the Filipino charismatic movement in the early 1980s; however, his influence was, at best, indirect. Missionary influences, as observed in the case of the Xu family, are more in the area of spiritual formation. Even Monsen's heavy emphasis on repentance and the presence of the Holy Spirit took an indigenous external form of deep emotion.[46]

Secondly, all the groups exhibit their primary concern for the immediate contextual challenges as Christians. Both the Jesus Family and Yongmoon Prayer Mountain responded to extremely challenging economic and political difficulties by proposing the idea of Christian communities. Even the more modernist Onnuri Church network has effectively responded to the social and spiritual needs of an urban middle-class educated population. Ha's early exposure to an American pentecostal missionary group has been successfully incorporated into his own organizational and theological framework, resulting in the mobilization of a significant number of laity for missionary service.

Thirdly, the form and content of their spirituality were not a western import, but were more indigenously sourced. One of the last ambitions of Ha before his death in 2011 was to impact Japan with the gospel. His approach, often dubbed the "Korean Wave," was to harness the potent of cultural forces effectively. The "Love Sonata," Ha's successful gospel presentation in a well-staged cultural form designed for the Japanese population, unmistakably reminds one of the popular Korean drama *Winter Sonata*, which captivated Japanese viewers in 2002. However, not all indigenous forms are without problems. The Jesus Family's community movement lived out the egalitarian Christian principle in daily living, but its authoritarian leadership betrayed this very principle, which was in accordance with sociocultural traditions. When two forces, Christian and indigenous values, clash, how one negotiates a healthy and balanced tension is a critical role of any leader. The political efforts of two Filipino charismatic leaders may also be seen as an attempt to formulate a Christian response to contemporary challenges, which also stirred up much controversy both within and outside Christian circles. Almost all groups studied have appropriated and incorporated local sociocultural and even religious traits into their forms of Christian spirituality and life.

CHARISMATIC LEADERSHIP

In all the groups mentioned, the vision, dedication, and influence of the leaders are paramount to their network. Often it is their spiritual experience that has led to a radical vision of their network. One characteristic of charismatic Christianity, especially in the non-Western world, may be the presence and role of charismatic leaders. Often the path, which a pentecostal network takes, as observed, is almost always determined by the leader's understanding of self-identity, interpretation of the time, sense of calling, and vision for the group.

Often the leaders' charismatic authority comes from their encounter with God, frequently in crisis experiences. Miraculous healing is a common experience as seen in Velarde, Ha, Yonggi Cho, and many others, and their healing ministry seems to have been rooted in their firm faith in the authority of the Bible reinforced by their own experiences. Also, such personal encounters impact their theology and spiritual life, and the theology of their networks mirrors their leaders' orientation. The emphasis of the Jesus Family on the "testimony" can be traced to its roots in Jiang's experience-oriented spirituality, including the personal encounter and revelation he claimed to have received from the Lord. Xu's evangelistic experience in the beginning together with his repeated imprisonment built his spiritual resilience, and this is also seen in the militant deployment of young evangelists throughout Henan Province and beyond.

Their strong leadership is also seen in the development of their theology. Ha's total commitment to the mobilization of his church for mission is traced to his exposure to the pentecostal value encapsulated in a "Prophethood of All Believers,"[47] whereas the professional career of Vilanueva has led his church to be far more holistic in their missionary scope. El Shaddai's ministry includes community development, the caring for the urban poor and children, the providing of medical services and education, advocacies including antipornography campaigns, and many others in addition to evangelism and church planting.[48] Of course, Jiang's business experience and his leadership in the formation of a cooperative led him to the establishment of Christian communities.

Ra began as a scholar in Chinese classics, and this had at least two expressions. The first were his attempts to incorporate his learning into the Christian message. Some of his theological positions created severe controversy: he considered Buddha and Confucius as prophets of God. The second was his commitment to literature. He began a well-known Christian weekly newspaper, which regularly carried his interpretation of current world events in the light of Scripture. The charge that Velarde runs his ministry like a business is not without support, considering his business background and entrepreneurial thinking. For example, the new facilities have been built on twenty acres of land he owns. The church pays for the land in installments.

The mobilization of laity for ministry, an idea drawn from the classical pentecostal tradition, is common throughout these cases, except for the Jesus Family, which embodies a community-oriented lifestyle. The Born Again group epitomizes the massive mobilization of laity for evangelistic and pastoral ministries with a minimal amount of in-house training. The Onnuri Church has formalized this process with a series of training programs and an administrative structure to deploy a large number of missionary candidates drawn from the church's vast network, both in Korea and overseas. Ha's systematic evangelistic campaigns in Japan, for example, were accompanied by a large number of his members providing prayer, ministry, and administrative assistance. The Prayer Mountain movement with its general emphasis on experiences with the Holy Spirit served as a breeding ground for lay workers for ministry. The charismatic groups in the Philippines regularly draw their ministerial resources, including pastoral staff, from their members. To them, the sense of calling is more important than theological training, as is often observed throughout various forms of pentecostal churches.

The almost unquestioned authority of charismatic leadership is also witnessed in Africa and Latin America, where cultures tend to move such leaders beyond the common social sphere. Their religious orientation distances them further toward a sort of "holy" or "other-world," where their behaviors are often blindly approved by their followers, even when they are against common ethical norms.[49] Often the "independent" nature of their ministries places the leaders outside of normal accountability structures. This is not to imply that most megachurch leaders have a questionable moral standard, but rather to suggest that they are extremely vulnerable to the trap of moral and financial lures.

MEGASIZES

Evident in our survey is the growth and spread of most groups, giving birth to the megachurch movement. This global phenomenon has also been a characteristic of the pentecostal movement, partly encouraged and fueled by the popular church growth movement observed first by Donald McGavran and later by C. Peter Wagner. This North-American movement quickly discovered that Asia was leading the race, once claiming that more than half of the ten largest churches were in Korea. Soon such large congregations with more than 10 thousand members also rose in other large cities in Asia and throughout the world. These megachurches or networks are almost always pentecostal in spirituality, worship, and theology.

The five groups in this chapter include at least two groups that are not typically viewed as "churches": the Jesus Family and the Yong-moon Prayer Mountain. The former was a membership-based community, thus, its limited growth is understandable. Even then they demonstrate some aspects of this trend of popularity. Ra's Prayer Mountain, once one of the most renowned annual phenomena drawing tens of thousands to this remote mountain facility, was a remarkable scene. These were the days during which David Yonggi Cho's megachurch was building its large auditorium in Seoul. In fact, many believe that this Prayer Mountain laid a spiritual foundation by bringing traditional indigenous pentecostal practices into the center of Christian spirituality – that is, making it a part of the "normal part" of local congregational life. Interestingly, megachurches were born as the independent Prayer Mountain movement began to decline.

Some observers believe that the megachurch phenomenon is part of rapid urbanization. In Korea, for example, this correlation is almost certain, as the rise of large churches through the 1970s and 1980s coincides with rapid urbanization and industrialization under military dictatorship. The rise of the charismatic movement with independent networks was also an urban movement with a steady urbanization taking place. However, the independent church movement in China following the Cultural Revolution has been predominantly a rural movement with increasing urban congregations that tend to be large. We may see, along with a strong urbanization in China, the rise of large urban congregations both in the house church and the church networks. However, the urban culture of Chinese Christian spirituality with its rising education, economic, and even social standards will transform expressions of their spirituality and religious conviction. We may then see a new era of megachurch movement in China in coming days.

FOR THE FUTURE. . .

The radical shift of global Christianity now places the Asian church, especially pentecostal-charismatic Christianity, in a crucial position. Among the three major southern continents that now claim about two-thirds of the world's Christians, Asia is the least Christianized.[50] If world Christianity is going to grow beyond the one-third level of its population for the first time in history,[51] it has much to do with how Asian Christianity fares in the next decades with the largest population in the world. As about 50 percent of Asian Christians are Pentecostals, this form of Christianity then holds the key to this historic possibility. Judging from the trajectory of growth, both of Asian Christianity and pentecostal varieties, the twenty-first century may well be the century of Asia for world Christianity. This is a unique opportunity for Asian Pentecostalism to propel Asian, and consequently global, Christianity to an unprecedented level and sustain the expansion. This, of course, is on the basis of the assumption that the rest of the world maintains the current level of Christians, particularly in the West. Any further growth will certainly accelerate the global growth rate.

To bring this exciting possibility into a reality, challenges will be enormous, as we have already observed from its incredible variety in theology and practice. One priority area that Asian pentecostal communities need to explore seriously is their mission engagement. Most likely Asia will remain a religiously pluralistic continent for good reasons.[52] If so, Pentecostals, while continuing their committed evangelistic activities, need to learn to live with other religions. This means that they need to add "living peacefully in the same society" to their mission theology, further requiring them to develop a good theology of religions. Serious reflection on contextualization will be in order too, as the movement has already proven the "creativity of the Spirit" in extremely challenging social environments. A critical examination of its attempts will reveal that not everyone is admirable, as seen in the excesses of the prosperity gospel, for example. Equally challenging will be the pentecostal construction of its identity and mission in a free and even affluent environment. Ra's Prayer Mountain today no longer attracts a throng of visitors, signaling the dire need to move one step ahead of social change. This is what Chinese Christianity is about to face, as it may move from an inclement environment to a relatively freer and affluent context. The future of Chinese Christianity will significantly depend on how well it responds to the changing social context in the next decades. A similar challenge is also observed: the characteristic signs and wonders are no longer witnessed in the more "established" pentecostal circles. On the other hand, Ha's impact on urban middle-class Christians shows a good possibility for Pentecostalism to exercise its extraordinary contextual flexibility. However, this very flexibility and creativity can lead some communities into "more pentecostal but less Christian" paths, when the context overwhelms the theological construct. Also the pentecostal formulation of a theological foundation for the church-state relationship will not be uniform and requires a careful negotiation between pentecostal reading of the scriptures and the appropriation of contemporary contexts into theological dialogue. All of these will require theologically reflective minds that are well connected with real life settings. In this theologization process, we will be well advised to remember that by nature pentecostal theologies will venture into edgy areas, thus, the job will be rather messy.[53] Lastly, if Asian Pentecostalism holds an important key to the future of global Christianity, its communities need to develop a global perspective in their local engagement. Are these too much to expect from such a diverse movement? That is where the Spirit's empowerment is expected, I challenge, but with a good amount of human sweat.

Notes

1   Unless otherwise indicated, the figures in this study are taken from Todd M. Johnson, David B. Barrett, Peter F. Crossing, "Status of Global Mission, 2011, in Context of 20th and 21st Centuries," *International Bulletin of Missionary Research* 35:1 (Jan. 2011), 29.

2   This generic use of the term may be expressed using the small *p*, "pentecostal."

3   See Young-hoon Lee, *The Holy Spirit Movement in Korea* (Oxford: Regnum Books, 2009); also Boo-woong Yoo, *Korean Pentecostalism: Its History and Theology* (Frankfurt: Peter Lang, 1988), and Allan Anderson, *An Introduction to Pentecostalism* (Cambridge: Cambridge University Press, 2004), 136–41.

4 For example, Rev. Yong-do Lee, a controversial Methodist revivalist, experienced the work of the Holy Spirit in Geumgang Mountain during a ten-day fast and prayer; Lee, *The Holy Spirit Movement in Korea,* 51. Woon-mong Ra's first visit to Yongmoon Mountain in 1940 was similarly motivated; see Yeol-soo Eim, "South Korea," in Stanley M. Burgess, et al., eds., *New International Dictionary of Pentecostal and Charismatic Movements* (Grand Rapids: Zondervan, 2003), 241. The dictionary is henceforth referred to as *NIDPCM*.

5 For his life and ministry, see Chang-soo Kang, "The Analytical Study of the Life of Woon-mong Na, Indigenous Korean Pentecostal," ThM thesis, Asia Pacific Theological Seminary, Philippines (2002).

6 Eim, "South Korea," 241.

7 Young-gi Hong, "The Backgrounds and Characteristics of the Charismatic Mega-Churches in Korea," *Asian Journal of Pentecostal Studies* 3:1 (January 2000), 100n4, defines a megachurch as a congregation with a minimum of 10,000 adult members participating in Sunday worship.

8 Hong, "Charismatic Mega-Churches in Korea," 105–06.

9 "Onnuri Vision: Acts29," http://www.onnuri.org/about-onnuri/church-introduction/onnuris-vision/ (accessed August 16, 2011).

10 "The Ideal Church for Onnuri," http://www.onnuri.or.kr/sub.asp?gubun=2102 (accessed August 16, 2011).

11 Jason Mandryk, *Operation World: The Definitive Prayer Guide to Every Nation,* 7th ed. (Colorado Springs: Biblica, 2010), 510.

12 David B. Barrett, George T. Kurian, and Todd M. Johnson, eds., *World Christian Encyclopedia: A Comparative Survey of Churches and Religions in the Modern World,* vol. 1, 2nd ed. (Oxford: Oxford University Press, 2001), 682.

13 See Wonsuk Ma, "Doing Theology in the Philippines," *Asian Journal of Pentecostal Studies* 8:2 (2005), 217–18; also, "Philippines," in *NIDPCM,* 201–07. For the Philippines Assemblies of God, see Trinidad E. Seleky, "Six Filipinos and One American: Pioneers of the Assemblies of God in the Philippines," *Asian Journal of Pentecostal Studies* 4:1 (2001), 119–29.

14 See Ma, "Doing Theology in the Philippines," 204–06.

15 The Archdiocesan Office of Manila produced a booklet entitled "Guidelines for Prayer Groups" (1983) to regulate Bible study and prayer groups among Catholics.

16 In 1981, ten 5-star hotels in Manila regularly hosted at least one charismatic service; Dynnice Rosanny D. Engcoy, "A Reflection of a Missionary to the Philippines: Gary A. Denbow Interview," *Asian Journal of Pentecostal Studies* 8:2 (2005), 307–26, 319.

17 Even today, the original radio program is remembered by its name, *El Shaddai DWXI Prayer Partners Fellowship International.*

18 Archdiocesan Office of Manila, "Guidelines for Prayer Groups."

19 Katharine L. Wiegele, *Investing in Miracles: El Shaddai and the Transformation of Popular Catholicism in the Philippines* (Honolulu: University of Hawaii Press, 2006).

20 Buhay Party-list, "Party Profile," http://www.buhaypartylist.com.ph/about-us/ (accessed December 27, 2011).

21   Mandryk, *Operation World*, 638.

22   Barrett et al., *World Christian Encyclopedia*, I, 594.

23   David Aikman, *Jesus in Beijing: How Christianity Is Transforming China and Changing the Global Balance of Power* (Washington, DC: Regnery, 2003), uses these terms.

24   Edmond Tang, "The Changing Landscape of Chinese Christianity," *China Study Journal* 23 (Spring/Summer 2008), 37, and "'Yellers' and Healers: Pentecostalism and the Study of Grassroots Christianity in China," in Allan Anderson and Edmond Tang, eds., *Asian and Pentecostal: The Charismatic Face of Christianity in Asia*, 2nd ed. (Oxford: Regnum Books, 2011), 379–94.

25   Luke Wesley, *The Church in China: Persecuted, Pentecostal, and Powerful* (Baguio, Philippines: AJPS Books, 2004), 51.

26   At least three "families" existed near large cities: Shanghai, Wuhan, and Nanjing.

27   Aikman, *Jesus in Beijing*, 279.

28   Wesley, *The Church in China*, 35.

29   Often called the "Pentecostal capital of China"; Tang, "The Changing Landscape," 37.

30   Xu Yongze, "Preface" in Brother Yun and Paul Gattaway, *The Heavenly Man* (Peabody, MA: Hendrickson, 2002), viii.

31   "Chinese House Church Confession of Faith," quoted in Yalin Xin, *Inside China's House Church Network: The Word of Life Movement and Its Renewing Dynamic* (Lexington, KY: Emeth Press, 2009), 146.

32   Claudia Wahrisch-Oblau, "Church Growth in Anhui," *China Study Journal* 9 (August 1994), 2; also Caroline Fielder, "The Growth of the Protestant Church in Rural China," *China Study Journal* 23 (Spring/Summer 2008), 49, argues that in Anhui, more than 50% of rural believers are reported to have been attracted by healing experiences.

33   Fielder, "Growth of the Protestant Church in Rural China," 49.

34   Fielder, "Growth of the Protestant Church in Rural China," 45.

35   Tang, "The Changing Landscape," 38.

36   Aikman, *Jesus in Beijing*, 88–89.

37   Aikman, *Jesus in Beijing*, 279.

38   Mandryk, *Operation World*, 215.

39   Joshua Bhakiaraj, "Christianity in Eastern Asia, 1910–2010," in Todd M. Johnson and Kenneth R. Ross, eds., *Atlas of Global Christianity* (Edinburgh: Edinburgh University Press, 2009), 140.

40   Xu, "Preface" in *The Heavenly Man*, viii.

41   Wiegele, *Investing in Miracles*, 6–8, 17–27.

42   Andrew M. Lord, "The Holy Spirit and Contextualization," *Asian Journal of Pentecostal Studies* 4:2 (2001), 201–03.

43   Yalin Xin, "Deborah Xu: The Story of a Catalytic Leadership in the Chinese House Church Movement," in Beth Snodderly and A. Scott Moreau, eds., *Evangelical and Frontier Mission: Perspectives on the Global Progress of the Gospel* (Oxford: Regnum Books, 2011), 138–42.

44   Mark A. Noll, *The New Shape of World Christianity: How American Experience Reflects Global Faith* (Downers Grove: IVP Academic, 2009), 11–12.

45   Noll, *New Shape of World Christianity*, 120–25.
46   Xin, "Deborah Xu," 138–39.
47   Roger Stronstad, *The Prophethood of All Believers: A Study in Luke's Charismatic Theology* (Sheffield, UK: Sheffield Academic Press, 1999).
48   Wiegele, *Investing in Miracles*, 33–35.
49   Wiegele, *Investing in Miracles*, 37–39.
50   For comparison, Latin America is 92.5% Christian and African Christianity is 47.9%, whereas a mere 8.5% is Christian in Asia today (Johnson and Ross, *Atlas of Global Christianity*, 57).
51   Except around 1910 which recorded 34.5%, but consistently receded to 32.7% in the middle of year 2000, but reaches 33% in the middle of 2011, but a 1/3 yet; Johnson, et al., "Status of Global Mission, 2011," 29.
52   Daniel H. Bays, *A New History of Christianity in China* (Malden, MA: Wiley-Blackwell, 2011), 92–95, contested the American idea of Christian China at the turn of the twentieth century.
53   Bays, *New History of Christianity in China*, 207.

Further Reading

Bergunder, Michael. *The South Indian Pentecostal Movement in the Twentieth Century* (Grand Rapids: Eerdmans, 2008).

Cao, Nanlai. *Constructing China's Jerusalem: Christians, Power, and Place in Contemporary Wenzhou* (Stanford: Stanford University Press, 2010).

Kim, Ig-Jin. *History and Theology of Korean Pentecostalism: Sunbogeum (Pure Gospel) Pentecostalism* (Zoetermeer: Utigeverij Boekencentrum, 2003).

Part III

Disciplinary Perspectives/Contributions –
The Status Quaestiones

9 The Politics and Economics of Pentecostalism: A Global Survey

CALVIN L. SMITH

Are Pentecostals inherently political and materialist? The established wisdom until fairly recently was that they were neither. With notable exceptions such as stances on moral issues (for example, sanctity of life, sexuality), the occasional televangelist expressing politically conservative views, and intriguingly a long tradition of pacifism,[1] Pentecostals were largely apolitical and otherworldly. They often felt uncomfortable relating to wider society or engaging in worldly issues such as politics,[2] while their pietism, eschatology, and evangelism contributed to Pentecostalism's political quiescence.[3]

However, since the late 1970s an explosion of Pentecostalism, particularly in Latin America but also in Africa and Asia, has attracted considerable scholarly interest in its social impact and potential as a determinant of political behavior.[4] The ensuing (and substantial) body of interdisciplinary research yields a social, political, and economic picture of global Pentecostalism that strongly challenges the apolitical narrative. Thus, Harvard Divinity School's Harvey Cox describes how, some years ago while listening to the Pentecostal Benedita da Silva (Brazil's first black woman elected to congress) speaking in a church, a sinking feeling came over him: "I realized that nearly all my preconceptions about pentecostalism and politics, race and women, would now have to be junked."[5]

Examples of well-known American politicians coming from a Pentecostal background include former U.S. Attorney General John Ashcroft and Sarah Palin. However, this chapter is not concerned with identifying and discussing individual Pentecostal politicians (space simply does not permit). Rather, its aim is to provide readers with a global snapshot and brief synthesis of some of the literature detailing pentecostal engagement with the political and economic realms. The essay consists of two parts: the first offering a narrative of Pentecostal politics and economics followed by a brief discussion of several issues arising out of the global picture. Throughout I employ the term "Pentecostal" to refer to the wider movement (classical Pentecostalism and neo-Pentecostalism combined), but when specifying one or the other, I make this clear in the text.

PENTECOSTALS, POLITICS, AND MONEY

Several countries especially stand out as examples of Pentecostals capturing the dizziest heights of political power. Guatemala has produced not one, but two Pentecostal presidents. In 1982, military officer and former presidential candidate Efraín Ríos Montt came to power through a *coup d'état* instigated by junior military officers. A member of Guatemala City's neo-pentecostal El Verbo megachurch (headquartered in California), Ríos Montt received backing from his church elders who also advised him while in office. One observer explains how Ríos Montt and El Verbo melded church and state, seeking a moral reformation of Guatemala along biblical lines from the top down. Challenging Catholic mores, liberation theology, and Marxism, their aim was to transform Guatemala into a "spiritual stronghold," an "Israel of the Americas," and a beacon of light testifying to the power of the gospel to other nations.[6] The Pentecostal president famously preached to the nation weekly, to the consternation of the military, the Catholic Church (which he openly excoriated), and indeed some Guatemalan Evangelicals uncomfortable with his moralizing as military atrocities were carried out in the Mayan highlands. A little over a year after coming to power the general was deposed in another military-led coup.

Ríos Montt's activities attracted unwelcome attention by the authorities into the affairs of Guatemala's Protestants after his departure, leading to considerable evangelical criticism of El Verbo.[7] However, with Guatemala having one of the largest proportions of Pentecostals in the world, it was not long before another believer, Jorge Serrano Elías of the neo-pentecostal Elim Church and former colleague of Ríos Montt, sought the presidency. In 1985 he polled third, but in 1990, with Ríos Montt seeking a political comeback being constitutionally barred from standing, Serrano won the election in the second round, becoming Latin America's first elected Protestant president. However, just two years later, facing claims of corruption and economic maladministration, Serrano suspended the constitution in an unsuccessful "self-coup," forcing him to flee the country. Despite both setbacks some Guatemalan neo-pentecostals retain a thirst for political power with considerable activity since Serrano's departure in 1993.[8]

In Zambia, too, a Pentecostal secured the presidency in 1991. Frederick Chiluba, a trade unionist who was born again while in prison and later received the gift of tongues at an evangelist Reinhard Bonnke crusade, easily defeated Kenneth Kaunda (Zambia's president since independence in 1964) in the country's first multiparty elections since independence, sending shockwaves throughout dictatorship-controlled Africa. Chiluba's Movement for Multi-Party Democracy enjoyed strong support from Zambia's Pentecostal leaders, and Christians later claimed five born-again ministers in the government. Chiluba famously went on to declare Zambia a "Christian nation," inviting pentecostal televangelists Ernest Angley (with whom he had a long connection) and Benny Hinn to hold crusades in the country. Hinn visited Zambia in 1994 and 1995 and pledged money for Chiluba's reelection.[9]

Although Chiluba's "Christian nation" declaration was widely supported by Zambia's Pentecostals, some believed it did not go far enough. Thus, prominent Pentecostal televangelist Nevers Mumba (sometimes guest of Pat Robertson's *700 Club*) contested the 2001 elections, while former Chiluba colleague Godfrey Miyanda, the Pentecostal architect of the "Christian nation" declaration, also ran. Both stood on a Christian Zambia platform but fared poorly in an election regarded internationally as flawed.[10] Zambia's "Christian" status has been challenged by other religious communities and soured relations between the Christian majority and Muslim minority,[11] which is noteworthy in a region where growing Islamism and Pentecostal-Muslim tensions have sometimes spilled over into violence.

It is perhaps in postmilitary regime Brazil where Pentecostals most consistently enjoy electoral success. Bishop Edir Macedo's Universal Church of the Kingdom of God (UCKG) has proved particularly adept in winning elections and organizing itself into a powerful and effective parliamentary bloc. In 1998 it overtook the Assemblies of God to secure fifteen federal deputies, twenty-six state deputies, and 1.25 million votes in the congress elections, and in the process achieved Protestant political hegemony in Brazil.[12] Pentecostalism's continued rapid growth in a country where arguably it is at its strongest is matched by its strength as an electoral force, with secular politicians openly courting the Pentecostal vote. In the 2010 presidential elections the world's media reported at length on how Pentecostals forced a second round runoff between President Lula's chosen successor Dilma Rousseff and Jose Serra because they were suspicious Rousseff would liberalize abortion. Instead they switched support to the Green candidate Marina Silva (herself a Pentecostal), forcing a second round of voting. The picture is somewhat more complicated than these reports suggest (e.g., Edir Macedo supported Rousseff, clashing publicly with a former Assemblies of God leader backing Serra),[13] yet what is clear is how Brazil's Pentecostals have become important players in electoral politics.

In South Korea Protestants, particularly Evangelicals, have contributed substantially to the democratization of the country since the end of military authoritarianism in 1987.[14] Not only is Pentecostalism strong in Korea, but also its influence extends beyond its borders by "pentecostalizing" Protestantism in that country.[15] South Korea, of course, is the home of Yoido Full Gospel Church, led by David Yonggi Cho. With as many as a million members and its own daily newspaper, the church wields considerable clout in the public sphere. The 1992 elections saw Protestants winning a third of the seats in Congress and extended these gains in 2000, with Yoido members winning seats in each election, having received backing from Yonggi-Cho.[16]

Other examples of Pentecostal electoral success include the African Christian Democratic Party (ACDP) in South Africa, led by neo-pentecostal pastor Kenneth Meshoe, with links to Reinhard Bonnke. Newer neo-pentecostal churches and parliamentarians dominate the ACDP, which retains a strong charismatic worship culture. The ACDP, which campaigns on a Christian platform, has challenged the potential for African National Congress (ANC) abuse of power toward Christians, leading President Mbeki to accuse the party of a "mean, vengeful, soulless and retributive theology"; a leading Pentecostal in Mbeki's administration, Frank Chikane, similarly denounced the ACDP.[17] South Africa has also witnessed the rise of other Christian parties with a Pentecostal presence go on to win regional and national seats in elections.[18]

Pentecostals have also secured parliamentary representation, for example, in Australia,[19] Colombia,[20] Nicaragua,[21] and Peru,[22] and have helped form Christian political parties that have won parliamentary seats. A noteworthy case is Sweden's Christian Democrat Party, not only because it is in a continent where Pentecostals have struggled to make political headway but also because its Pentecostal founder, Lewi Pethrus, who challenged secularization by creating institutions to foster a Christian counterculture, was active at a time when Pentecostals in Sweden or the United States shunned politics.[23] Paul Freston's global survey of Protestant political parties details other Christian parties in which Pentecostals have been involved – some politically successful, others small and electorally insignificant.

Aside from forming Christian parties and standing in elections Pentecostals sometimes represent a powerful (although at times divided) force at the ballot box. Brazil has already been mentioned, and Chile's center-left coalition appears to have enjoyed substantial Pentecostal support over many years.[24] It is possible Nicaragua's Pentecostals, many of whom experienced repression under the Sandinistas, helped ditch the revolutionary government in the landmark 1990 elections.[25] Meanwhile, in the European media North American born-again believers are often portrayed as a powerful bloc that politicians, particularly within the Republican Party, ignore at their peril (although such an analysis tends to ignore the existence of both an Evangelical Left and Evangelical Right.)

Aside from the ballot box Pentecostal political power is also expressed through extolling (or denouncing) secular politicians and policies, although their ability to mobilize the corporate vote is sometimes overplayed by the media. Thus, Protestant endorsement of politicians plays an important aspect of Filipino politics[26]; indeed for this reason the neo-pentecostal El Shaddai is named in a U.S. embassy cable later published by WikiLeaks.[27] For their part, politicians have not been slow to seize on Pentecostal support where it is considered strategically valuable. Kenya's President Moi expertly played the religious card, attending revivalist churches and making public statements that Pentecostals wanted to hear. At one crusade he attended, Korea's Yonggi Cho declared Kenya was blessed to have a God-fearing leader such as President Moi, and after the meeting, people queued to join Moi's Kenya African National Union (KANU) party.[28]

Another example of courting the Pentecostal vote is in Venezuela, where after his release from prison for a failed coup attempt, Hugo Chavez sought a political base, successfully wooing lower-class Pentecostal support.[29] Many Pentecostals have continued to support and vote for Chavez over the years, although his demonization of Israel has caused problems. Dispensationalism, which strongly influences classical Pentecostalism in the twentieth century, maintains the establishment of Israel is a fulfillment of biblical prophecy. Hence, Zambia's Chiluba reestablished links with Israel and severed relations with Iraq and Iran.[30] In the 1989 elections Fernando Collor was supported by Brazil's Pentecostals in part because they believed he would be a friend of Israel.[31] In Guatemala some neo-pentecostal leaders are convinced God will one day bless the country for casting the deciding UN vote that created Israel.[32] As dispensational influence over classical Pentecostalism wanes, one would expect Pentecostal support for Israel to diminish. However, this is clearly not the case, even among autochthonous Pentecostals (although neo-Pentecostals are notably less

Zionist), suggesting either Pentecostal theology lends itself to Zionism in some other way, or else autochthonous Pentecostalism owes more to the Azusa cradle than it cares to admit.[33]

Of course, "doing politics" is not limited to formal institutions and processes such as voting, campaigning, elections, or forming political parties. Thus Amos Yong identifies a "prophetic politics" manifest in "counter-cultural and counter-conventional communities shaped by Pentecostal spirituality and piety," which function as an alternative *civitas* and *polis*.[34] From earliest times Pentecostals have been keen to ameliorate their societies.[35] Thus much of the current literature explores Pentecostal work with the poor, homeless, orphans and widows, and also alcoholics and drug addicts. In Colombia Pentecostal churches have taken a stand against the powerful drug cartels, creating strong church structures to support and protect converts, with effective results (attracting unwelcome attention from the drug barons in the process).[36] In the 1990s Doug Petersen mapped out considerable Pentecostal social involvement in Central America, together with a political theology of social concern, which captured significant scholarly attention.[37]

More recently Donald Miller and Tetsunao Yamamori explore this self-help and social aspect, which they call "progressive Pentecostalism."[38] Such Pentecostals emphasize a holistic gospel that addresses *both* people's spiritual and material needs – that one cannot separate the two. Rather than reforming existing social structures or government policies, progressive Pentecostals provide an alternative social reality from the ground up. Thus the authors detail how during their research they travelled the globe visiting impressive Pentecostal social programs, including prison work, emergency relief, pregnancy counseling, drug rehabilitation and education programs, HIV/AIDS prevention and medical care, support for families, domestic abuse programs, services to the elderly and handicapped, ministries providing housing, medical and dental care, and more.

Others highlight the social and economic impact of conversion and the Pentecostal life on family, community, workplace, gender, and the disinherited in the developing world.[39] Pentecostalism offers a strong sense of community to the uprooted, providing welcome sanctuary and material assistance to peasants migrating to the cities.[40] Pentecostalism equips drug addicts to overcome their addiction.[41] In El Salvador and the United States Pentecostalism has helped domesticate youth gang members.[42] Although not a feminist movement, Pentecostalism empowers women by emphasizing self-worth and autonomy, for example, in a Latin American culture of *machismo*,[43] although in a traditionally male-dominated society such as Korea the majority of Yoido Full Gospel Church's pastors are women.[44] In India, meanwhile, Pentecostalism has proved attractive to the *Dalits* (untouchable castes), giving them a sense of hope and worth.[45]

The literature also details economic benefits, mostly among marginalized Pentecostals trying to eke out an existence in the developing world where life can be grim. Thus conversion shifts wages from alcohol, gambling, and prostitution to the family. Greater disposable income, together with a new world view, positive outlook on life, and work ethic, can contribute to social upward mobility, a theme Miller and Yamamori develop at some length. They also explain how upward mobility fuels progressive Pentecostal social concern, so that "Pentecostals no longer see the world as a place from which to escape . . . but instead as a place they want to make better."[46]

Drawing on Max Weber's theory of the Protestantism work ethic, Amy Sherman identifies tangible economic benefits Pentecostalism yields for Mayan Indians in Guatemala's highlands. Whereas a traditional Cristo-pagan background might hold families back economically (through, for example, the financial burdens of the *fiesta* system or folk Catholicism), conversion to Pentecostalism integrates believers into the formal economy, providing better occupations and social mobility, less reliance on fatalism, and improved education, medical care, and agricultural practices.[47] In sub-Saharan Africa Pentecostalism also challenges aspects of traditional life and culture holding back economic development. These include helping individuals shake off negative structures and groups that place them at an economic disadvantage (for example, kinship, arranged marriage, being anchored to communities), creating autonomy, while awareness of the transnational nature of their faith leads to a broader and more enlightened world view. These new benefits have direct economic impact on individuals, and in an African society marked by inequality and little social mobility, Pentecostalism helps individuals foster and pursue aspirations.[48]

These economic benefits lead Isabelle Barker to challenge Karl Polanyi's view that social dislocation caused by liberal economies and self-regulated markets inevitably creates countermovements seeking self-protection, eventually forcing government to intervene and regulate laissez-faire capitalism. Instead, through its own social services and assistance programs, work ethic, and a world view helping make sense of economic turmoil, Pentecostalism equips believers to survive neoliberal economic restructuring (and in the process, unnervingly for secular progressives, it embeds and validates neoliberalism).[49]

Aside from how it benefits the individual it seems Pentecostalism also has the potential to yield an economic impact on wider spaces, even at the national level. William Kay notes the contribution of Pentecostalism to Korean nation building,[50] while Olufanke Adeboye asks if Pentecostalism's contribution to Korea's economy might be replicated somehow in Nigeria. Although he is not convinced, Adeboye highlights the movement's role in building numerous schools, medical centers, and hospitals, while the Redeemed Christian Church of God provides employment to highly skilled professionals such as technicians, medical personnel, and administrators.[51] Paul Gifford's study of Kenya develops this theme further, comparing churches with the nongovernmental organization (NGO) sector. Both proliferated in the country during the 1990s (with 5,000 NGOs registering between 1990 and 2007 and 8,520 churches registered by 2007). Both channeled money into the local economy and as such were "significant conduits of resources, all tax free," providing opportunity for middle class graduates in a stagnant economy.[52] In the Philippines, too, corruption and bribery means the country's wealth remains in a few hands, signifying "the flow of finance for charitable enterprises is a valuable resource for what is still essentially a poor country."[53]

Gifford spends considerable time exploring the prosperity gospel's impact on Kenya. Here the prosperity and success motifs have often replaced foundational Christian doctrines, while the historic Protestant denominations have been so influenced by this version of Pentecostalism that they too place considerable emphasis on success, victory, and "overcoming" (whether obstacles, challenges or the devil and his works). This message has moved beyond the church to influence Nairobi's middle class and, indeed, the country as a whole. In some churches congregants face considerable pressure to tithe, while substantial funds are raised through spin-off industries controlled by pastors who are religious entrepreneurs. Many of these ministries have a substantial media presence, which necessitates considerable resources (the constant need to solicit donations to stay on the air, of course, lends itself particularly well to fundraising and the prosperity gospel).[54]

This emphasis on prosperity is widespread in other parts of Africa, notably Nigeria, where one observer expresses disquiet about the movement's inability to effect economic and political change in the country.[55] In Cameroon it has also thrived because, it is argued, it provides a useful survival strategy in dire economic circumstances.[56] Indeed, the controversial prosperity message is widespread (although not universally accepted) throughout global Pentecostalism in both rich and poor countries. Some, while not endorsing the prosperity message, point out its utilitarian aspects. Kay notes how it provides "energy and hope to those within the slums: God does not want you to be poor because he loves you too much."[57] Miller and Yamamori detail a conversation in which one observer explained how the prosperity message gives people hope and changes how they think and act.[58] (Hope is a key feature of the theology of Yonggi Cho,[59] an architect and champion of the prosperity gospel.) Barker suggests within the widening gaps between "rich and poor and between hard work and economic reward, miracle religion is an invaluable resource."[60]

However, raising church funds is not just about prosperity. Apart from funding church and other ministries, such as social programs, it can also have an important bearing on political engagement. For example, self-sufficiency provides autonomy for churches and leaders on the political stage. Thus, the autochthonous nature of Brazil's UCKG, which does not rely on external funding, permitted one bishop to denounce publicly the evils of neoliberalism.[61] This self-sufficiency is at odds with some churches' dependence on external funding. For example, in post-Soviet Russia and Ukraine an emphasis on establishing as many Pentecostal churches as possible (all funded from the United States), rather than on developing self-sufficiency, resulted in many of those new churches closing just a few months later.[62] Pentecostalism is noted for its success in raising and distributing funds for mission work. However, with it comes the expectation that the ministry will work toward self-sufficiency rather than being dependent over the long term.

SOME OBSERVATIONS

The above snapshot survey demonstrates just how far global Pentecostalism has moved on from the apolitical and otherworldly stereotype common a few decades ago. Without losing their sense of the heavenly, Pentecostals, by and large, are thoroughly *this*-worldly, practical and concerned with the here and now, engaging the political and economic spheres at various levels.

Pentecostals engage in politics for a number of reasons. In parts of the world, particularly where Christianity is in decline, they seek to defend Christian mores and family values when perceived to be under threat from encroaching secularism (for example, Lewi Pethrus' Swedish Christian Democrats, Australia's Family First party, or the British Christian Party, headed by a Pentecostal). Another important motive is to defend sectarian interests, particularly in regions where Protestants represent a religious minority, such as Catholic Latin America. For this reason Latin American Pentecostals have often preferred liberal over conservative parties, the latter traditionally favoring the Catholic Church. Latin American postindependence liberalism, in seeking modernization and waning to curb Catholicism's role as a societal actor, created the political conditions necessary for allowing Protestants into the continent from the late nineteenth and early twentieth centuries.[63] (Interestingly, Brazil's UCKG partially took over the Liberal Party, providing the denomination with a political infrastructure and networks, although the UCKG also retains representatives in other parties).[64] Aside from supporting existing structures and parties, however, Pentecostals have also formed their own political parties and contested elections to protect freedoms and interests. Thus, in Colombia Pentecostals sought and won representation to the body tasked with drawing up a new constitution in 1991 and were directly responsible for enshrining guarantees of religious freedom and protection. This success served as a springboard for elections to congress later that decade.[65] Another important example is in Nigeria, where Pentecostals fearing encroaching Islamization have become heavily involved in Nigerian politics.[66]

Aside from defending sectarian freedoms or Christian mores, getting involved in politics is often driven by theological considerations. Mention has been made of progressive Pentecostalism's strong theological focus on holistic ministry. Meanwhile, in the 1980s and early 1990s some influential North American pentecostal leaders ditched their theology of an imminent rapture and embraced a version of postmillennialism sometimes referred to as kingdom theology (or Kingdom Now), emphasizing engagement with and capture of the social and political realms to help establish the Kingdom of God on earth (and in the process hasten the Second Coming).[67] Within this context Harvey Cox discusses how Pat Robertson's shift from pre- to postmillennialism paved the way for him to seek the Republican nomination for the U.S. presidency in 1988 (there is little point, Cox observes, seeking election for president, or running for the local school board for that matter, if the Second Coming is right around the corner).[68] Some observers have sought to caricature this theology as inherently right wing,[69] and it is true some expressions of and personalities associated with dominionism and theonomy lean politically that way. However, Bruce Barron warns against automatically stereotyping in this manner, explaining how some kingdom theology proponents are driven by strong social concerns.[70] In this regard some expressions of kingdom theology represent a mirror image of liberation theology. Meanwhile, the Pentecostal academy is increasingly bringing Pentecostal theology to bear on the political sphere, producing distinctly Pentecostal political theologies.[71]

There are also pragmatic reasons for Pentecostal political engagement. Freston suggests Brazil's Edir Macedo mobilized Pentecostals to vote against Lula's presidential candidacy because he represented a threat to Macedo's media empire. (Macedo later softened his stance toward Lula, and mention has been made of his support for Lula's successor Dilma Rousseff in the 2010 elections.) Other pragmatic motives Freston details include pastors seeking to secure finances for their churches or even providing an outlet for social upward mobility for themselves and their families through a political career.[72] Sometimes politics can provide an alternative source of patronage. Thus David Maxwell traces the transformation of the Pentecostal Zimbabwe Assemblies of God Africa (ZOAGA), led by Ezekiel Guti, from non-nationalist and apolitical denomination to strong supporter of President Robert Mugabe (Maxwell notes how at times ZOAGA's leaders sounded "more like chest-thumping politicians than men of God.")[73] Mugabe, for his part, reciprocated, and this patronage provided Guti with religious autonomy so that he was no longer reliant on external networks, although the move also caused some divisions within ZOAGA.[74] Guti later switched his support to opposition leader Morgan Tsvangirai, leading Mugabe to withdraw favor.[75]

This example of Pentecostal leaders expressing strong support for a socialist like Mugabe, albeit for pragmatic reasons, challenges a common stereotype of Pentecostals as inherently conservative and favoring the political right. At this stage it is worthwhile discussing the concept of Pentecostal "apoliticism" a little further, as the word evokes different meanings depending on how it is used (or who uses it). Historically an apocalyptic eschatology emphasizing an imminent rapture contributed to pentecostal political quiescence. Things can only get worse, it is argued, so why seek to change society at all?[76] In this sense, then, Pentecostals were (and some still are) apolitical. Meanwhile, the word apolitical can also mean to be *anti*-political – that is, the difference between being politically quiescent and firmly rejecting the notion of Pentecostal involvement in a worldly issue such as politics.[77] Being apolitical is also sometimes a vote for the status quo.

For revolutionaries in 1980s Central America, however, Pentecostalism's moral conservatism, a Manichaean rejection of communism, and a right-wing U.S. televangelist's support for the Contras, all combined so that apolitical became code for describing Pentecostalism as a counterrevolutionary movement that leaned to the right. (In

Marxist-inspired revolutionary socialist thought, of course, there is no place for neutrality, which itself is perceived as reactionary and politically motivated.) Some observers suggested apolitical Pentecostals served as a useful social prop and bulwark for regimes favored by Washington.[78] This goes some way to explaining why Fidel Castro's regime early on hounded Cuban Pentecostals on the basis of their resignation, otherworldliness, and pacifism,[79] or why Sandinista repressed Pentecostals because of their apoliticism (that is, unwillingness to participate in the revolutionary process), or why Pentecostals were treated the way they were in some Iron Curtain countries.

Thus, in the 1980s it was common for some on the revolutionary left to juxtapose liberation theology's progressivism with Pentecostal apoliticism. While the former sought to "conscientize" the masses and mobilize them against social and economic structures, Pentecostals were regarded as distinctly *unrevolutionary*. Hence, apolitical denoted not embracing the *right kind of politics* (i.e., revolutionary politics) but instead embracing *the politics of the right*. Others, notably Catholics alarmed by an invasion of the "sects" likewise caricatured Pentecostals as North American Republicans.[80]

However, a global survey of Pentecostal politics demonstrates how this is far from the case. Certainly many U.S. Pentecostals are Republican, but many also vote Democrat. Across the world there are Pentecostal voters and politicians of most political hues. Consider Harvey Cox's encounter with Benedita da Silva, or the irony of da Silva's Workers Party coming to power with a Pentecostal vice president.[81] In Chile it is true that Pentecostal leaders supported General Pinochet, but there is evidence that grassroots Pentecostals by and large backed the socialist Salvador Allende.[82] Mention has already been made of how Chile's left-of-center government has received important Pentecostal support for many years. In Nicaragua approximately one-third of classical Pentecostals supported the Sandinistas enthusiastically (and many still support a leftist political agenda). One, Miguel Angel Casco, was elected to parliament on a Sandinista ticket. Zambia's Frederick Chiluba was a trade unionist, while many trade union leaders in rural Brazil are Pentecostal.[83] Meanwhile, in South Africa the ACDP rejected the Iraq War.[84] These and many other examples demonstrate how impossible it is to stereotype Pentecostals as politically homogenous or inherently rightist. Consider how, during the 2010 meeting of the Society for Pentecostal Studies, the presidential address called for a constructive pentecostal engagement with, even crafting of, liberative theology in the pursuit of social justice.[85] The speaker is a professor at Pat Robertson's Regent University, illustrating a wide spectrum of Pentecostal politics in one institution alone. Economically, too, Pentecostalism exhibits considerable diversity, whether middle-class, urban neo pentecostal megachurches, classical Pentecostal churches serving poor, marginalized and disinherited communities in city slums across the developing world, or churches with dirt floors in rural Africa.

Perhaps it is Pentecostalism's alternative approach to ameliorating the needs of the poor that has most frustrated those seeking structural economic change through revolution. The West and neo-pentecostal megachurches aside, in the developing world Pentecostalism is very much a church of the poor. Pentecostals do not go around vocalizing a preferential option for the poor because they *are* the poor.[86] As such, liberation theologian Mario Aguilar regards Pentecostals as a potential ally.[87] However, he misses the point. Petersen explains how Pentecostals are creating their *own* alternative structures – a new paradigm through which to do politics and help the poor and disinherited.[88] This chapter has discussed how this paradigm has proved effective; its opiate has done more than provide an avenue of escapism. Thus Miller and Yamamori recall a theologian in Argentina who quipped, "[w]hile liberation theology opted for the poor, the poor opted for Pentecostalism," going on to describe its potential to replace a lackluster social gospel and fading liberation theology.[89] Hence, although Pentecostalism and liberation theology both appeal to the poor, in many respects they are rivals, opposites, one offering amelioration through revolution, the other via revival and the this-worldly benefits it offers.[90] Thus, in a curious mirror image of the Marxist international, "this transnational community of believers apparently erodes national difference all the while allowing for local distinctions and, as such, ironically represents a religion-based variant of Marx's workers of the world."[91]

That is not to say Pentecostalism always gets it right. Miller and Yamamori ask whether Pentecostalism can have an impact on many of the problems the world faces, responding: "Our answer to this question is a qualified 'yes,' acknowledging that some expressions of Pentecostalism may actually retard social transformations."[92] Although mapping out some of the positive economic benefits Pentecostalism offers individuals in sub-Saharan Africa, Samuel Zalanga argues that a naïve theology promulgated in parts of the continent are economically detrimental. These include a theology of demons and spiritual warfare, exonerating postcolonial elites from their economic failures, the defeatism associated with constantly labeling Africa a demonic stronghold, and a self-fulfilling prophecy of Africa as a cursed continent. All are marks of a theology that is "significantly pre-reformation, pre-scientific, and pre-enlightenment."[93] Zalanga also questions the widespread dominionist claims about taking one's nation for Christ, asking pertinently why "Christian Zambia" failed to achieve the economic success of non-Christian countries such as Japan and China.[94] Another observer asks why, after the largest explosion of Pentecostalism across Africa and despite all their postcolonial language of a new birth, spiritual warfare, and capturing the country for Christ, Nigerian Pentecostals have totally failed to transform the country.[95] (For the believer there is a danger here of reductionism, a point the author is acutely aware of and seeks to disavow.) Gifford lists the reasons for Africa's plight, including slavery, colonialism, geography, and trade terms. At the top of his list, however, are the continent's elite, stating how in Kenya at least Pentecostal leaders belong to that same elite.[96]

Neither have Pentecostals always covered themselves in glory when in office. Virginia Garrard-Burnett details at length the military atrocities carried out under Guatemala's Ríos Montt.[97] For their part, Ríos Montt and his followers have argued that he was unaware of such atrocities or else powerless to stop them but have conceded errors.[98] Nonetheless, in all his weekly sermonizing he never criticized the military.[99] There were also human rights abuses under Zambia's Frederick Chiluba, while Nicaraguan Pentecostal parliamentarian Guillermo Osorno allegedly sold his favors so many times to political parties that he earned the nickname "Pastor Soborno" (in Spanish *soborno*, which sounds similar to his surname, means "bribe").[100]

In the arena of formal politics, Pentecostalism's fortunes have been mixed. Some of the literature discussed in this chapter highlights several highly successful electoral results and effective politicking. However, at the other end of the scale Pentecostal attempts to win power have fared poorly, while some have been electorally insignificant. Reasons include fragmentation and rivalry among Pentecostals and voting systems that do not play out particularly well for Pentecostals in some countries,[101] and Freston discusses at length Pentecostals inability to secure the corporate vote. There is also the problem of having to appeal beyond the sectarian vote to attract a wider electorate. This is especially true in countries where Pentecostals and Protestants represent a tiny minority of the population, notably Western Europe, where they are unlikely ever to secure anything like the formal power enjoyed in the Pentecostal powerhouses of Brazil or Guatemala. Thus, a breakthrough for the Sweden's Christian Democrats, founded by and composed mainly of

Pentecostals for a long time, only came, in part, through a shift away from its sectarian image.[102]

Despite some of its problems, sociologist David Martin believes Pentecostalism "delivers enough to be the most immediate vehicle of hope for the hopeless."[103] Martin has produced considerable work demonstrating how this mobile, globalized movement represents an important force for cultural change, democratization, and pluralism,[104] citing examples of how in ethnically divided Transylvania Pentecostalism has brought Hungarians and Romanians together, while in China it serves as a parallel Cultural Revolution that the government is unsure how to handle.[105] Others make similar observations. An ethnographic study demonstrates how many Pentecostals in Guatemala are engaging in and enacting good citizenship seriously.[106] In multi-ethnic, multireligious Singapore Pentecostalism demonstrates the unique potential to be a "peaceful harbinger of pluralism."[107] Miller and Yamamori describe the many social ministries run by progressive Pentecostals as "some of the most innovative social programs in the world."[108] Pentecostals, it seems, appear to be particularly effective and powerful when seeking to engage politics from the bottom up, although in some parts of the world they have also seen considerable successes when working from the top down. In the developing world especially, given the widespread failure of politics there, Pentecostalism "offers a capsule of hope and mobility. This capsule is sustained by moral reform, hard work, opportunity for participation and mutual support, in an alliance with a belief in a providence that will bring salvation here and now as well as hereafter."[109]

Notes

1   For example, see Jay Beaman, *Pentecostal Pacifism: The Origin, Development, and Rejection of Pacific Beliefs among the Pentecostals* (Hillsboro, KS: Center for Mennonite Brethren Studies, 1989), and Paul Alexander, *Peace to War: Shifting Allegiances in the Assemblies of God* (Telford, PA: Cascadia, 2009).

2   Allan Anderson, *An Introduction to Pentecostalism* (Cambridge: Cambridge University Press, 2004), 261.

3   Amos Yong, "Pentecostalism and the Political – Trajectories in Its Second Century," *Pneuma: The Journal of the Society for Pentecostal Studies* 32:3 (2010), 333–36.

4   Calvin L. Smith, "Latin American Pentecostalism and the Academy" in Calvin Smith, ed., *Pentecostal Power: Expressions, Faith and Impact of Latin American Pentecostalism* (Leiden and Boston: Brill, 2010), 1–5.

5   Harvey G. Cox, *Fire from Heaven: The Rise of Pentecostal Spirituality and the Reshaping of Religion in the Twenty-First Century* (Reading, MA: Addison-Wesley, 1995), 165.

6   David Stoll, *Is Latin America Turning Protestant? The Politics of Evangelical Growth* (Berkeley: University of California Press), 181.

7   Stoll, *Is Latin America Turning Protestant?*, 207–9.

8   "Historical Overview of Pentecostalism in Guatemala," Pew Forum, Washington, DC (2006), http://pewforum.org/Christian/Evangelical-Protestant-Churches/Historical-Overview-of-Pentecostalism-in-Guatemala.aspx (accessed August 28, 2011).

9   Paul Freston, *Evangelicals and Politics in Asia, Africa and Latin America* (Cambridge: Cambridge University Press, 2001), ch. 18. Kindle edition.

10 Paul Freston, *Protestant Political Parties: A Global Survey* (Aldershot: Ashgate, 2004), 83–91.

11 Isabel Apawo Phiwi, "President Frederick Chiluba and Zambia: Evangelicals and Democracy in a 'Christian Nation'" in Terence O. Ranger, *Evangelical Christianity and Democracy in Africa* (Oxford: Oxford University Press, 2008), 105.

12 Freston, *Evangelicals and Politics*, ch. 1.

13 Marcos Simas, "Brazil's Evangelicals Make Voting Bloc Debut," *Christianity Today* (November 2, 2010), http://www.christianitytoday.com/ct/2010/novemberweb-only/53-21.0.html (accessed September 5, 2011).

14 Joshua Young-gi Hong, "Evangelicals and the Democratization of South Korea Since 1987," in David Halloran Lumsdaine, ed., *Evangelical Christianity and Democracy in Asia* (Oxford: Oxford University Press, 2009), 185–233.

15 Allan Anderson and Edmond Tang, eds., *Asian and Pentecostal: The Charismatic Face of Christianity in Asia* (Regnum: Oxford, 2005), 9. See also Kim Sung Gun, "Korean Protestant Christianity in the Midst of Globalization: Neoliberalism and the Pentecostalization of Korean Churches," *Korea Journal* 47:4 (2007), 147–70.

16 Timothy S. Lee, "Beleaguered Success: Korean Evangelicalism in the Last Decade of the Twentieth Century" in Robert Buswell, Jr., and Timothy S. Lee, eds., *Christianity in Korea* (Honolulu: University of Hawaii Press, 2006), 330–50.

17 Discussed by Freston in *Protestant Political Parties*, 92–97. Mbeki's quote is taken from his 30 December 1999 Cape Town parliamentary speech (available at the University of South Africa website, http://www.unisa.ac.za/contents/colleges/docs/tm1999/tm063009.pdf, last accessed 26 March 2014).

18 "Historical Overview of Pentecostalism in South Africa," Pew Forum, Washington, DC (2006), http://pewforum.org/Christian/Evangelical-Protestant-Churches/Historical-Overview-of-Pentecostalism-in-South-Africa.aspx (accessed September 5, 2011).

19 Gregory Melleuish, "Religion and Politics in Australia," *Political Theology* 11:6 (2010), 909–27.

20 Clemencia Tejeiro Sarmiento, ed., *El Pentecostalismo en Colombia: Practicas Religiosas, Liderazgo y Participación Política* (Bogota: Universidad Nacional de Colombia, 2010).

21 Roberto Zub, "The Evolution of Protestant Participation in Nicaraguan Politics and the Rise of Evangelical Parties," in Paul Freston, ed., *Evangelical Christianity and Democracy in Latin America* (Oxford: Oxford University Press, 2008), 97–129.

22 Dario Lopez Rodriguez, "Evangelicals and Politics in Fujimori's Peru," in Freston, *Evangelical Christianity and Democracy in Latin America*, 131–61.

23 Joel Halldorf, "Lewi Pethrus and the Creation of a Christian Counterculture," *Pneuma: The Journal of the Society for Pentecostal Studies* 32:3 (2010), 354–68.

24 Juan Sepulveda, "Another Way of Being Pentecostal," in Smith, *Pentecostal Power*, 60.

25 Calvin L. Smith, *Revolution, Revival and Religious Conflict in Sandinista Nicaragua* (Leiden and Boston: Brill, 2007).

26 David. S. Lim, "Consolidating Democracy: Filipino Evangelicals Between People Power Events, 1986–2001," in Lumsdaine, *Evangelical Christianity and Democracy in Asia*, 235–84.

27 Cable 05MANILA5130, http://wikileaks.org/cable/2005/11/05MANILA5130. html (accessed September 5, 2011).

28 Freston, *Evangelicals and Politics*, ch. 17.

29 Freston, *Protestant Political Parties*, 127–28.

30 Freston, *Evangelicals and Politics*, ch. 18, and *Protestant Political Parties*, 90.

31 Freston, *Evangelicals and Politics*, ch. 1.

32 Kevin Lewis O'Neill, *City of God: Christian Citizenship in Postwar Guatemala* (Berkeley: University of California Press, 2010).

33 Discussed in Calvin Smith, "Pneumapraxis and Eschatological Urgency: A Survey of Latin American Pentecostal Theology and Its Outworking" in Smith, *Pentecostal Power*, 192–93, 197–99.

34 Amos Yong, *In the Days of Caesar: Pentecostalism and Political Theology* (Grand Rapids, MI: Eerdmans, 2010), 11–14.

35 William K. Kay, *Pentecostalism* (London: SCM, 2009), 302.

36 Kay, *Pentecostalism*, 125.

37 Doug Petersen, *Not By Might Nor By Power: A Pentecostal Theology of Social Concern in Latin America* (Oxford: Regnum, 1996).

38 Donald E. Miller and Tetsunao Yamamori, *Global Pentecostalism: The New Face of Christian Social Engagement* (Berkeley: University of California Press, 2007).

39 Edward L. Cleary and Hannah W. Stewart-Gambino, eds., *Power, Politics and Pentecostals in Latin America* (Boulder, CO: Westview, 1998).

40 Lidia Susana Vaccaro de Petrella, "The Tension Between Evangelism and Social Action in the Pentecostal Movement," *International Review of Mission* 75:297 (1986), 34–38, and Joseph Eldridge, "Pentecostalism and Social Change in Central America (Honduran Case Study)," *Towson State Journal of International Affairs* 25:2 (1991), 10–21.

41 Daniel Míguez, "Opio Rebelde: Los Programas Pentecostales de Rehabilitación de Adictos la Argentina," *PentecoStudies* 4 (2005) http://www.glopent.net/pentecostudies/online-back-issues/2005/miguez2005.pdf/view?searchterm=opio%20rebelde (accessed on 26 March 2014).

42 Manuel A. Vázquez, "Saving Souls Transnationally: Pentecostalism and Gangs in El Salvador and the United States," (conference paper presented at Lived Theology and Community Building Workgroup, University of Virginia,

October 12–14, 2001) http://www.livedtheology.org/pdfs/m_vasquez.pdf (accessed September 18, 2011).

43 Discussed by Cecilia Loreto Mariz and Maria das Dores Campos Machado, "Pentecostalism and Women in Brazil," 41–54, and Carol Ann Drogus, "Private Power or Public Power: Pentecostalism, Base Communities, and Gender," 55–75, both in Cleary and Stewart-Gambino, *Power, Politics and Pentecostals.*

44 Allan Anderson, "Pentecostalism in Asia: Indigenous Oriental Christianity?" *Pneuma: The Journal of the Society for Pentecostal Studies* 22:1 (2000), 127.

45 Kay, *Pentecostalism,* 107.

46 Miller and Yamamori, *Global Pentecostalism,* 30.

47 Amy Sherman, *The Soul of Development: Biblical Christianity and Economic Transformation in Guatemala* (Oxford: Oxford University Press, 1997).

48 Samuel Zalanga, "Religion, Economic Development and Cultural Change: The Contradictory Role of Pentecostal Christianity in Sub-Saharan Africa," *Journal of Third World Studies* 27:1 (Spring 2010), 43–62.

49 Isabelle V Barker, "Charismatic Economies: Pentecostalism, Economic Restructuring, and Social Reproduction," *New Political Science* 29:4 (2007), 407–27.

50 Kay, *Pentecostalism,* 99.

51 Olufanke Adeboye, "'Arrowhead' of Nigerian Pentecostalism: The Redeemed Christian Church of God, 1952–2005," *Pneuma: The Journal of the Society for Pentecostal Studies* 29:1 (2007), 24–58.

52 Paul Gifford, *Christianity, Politics and Public Life in Kenya* (London: C. Hurst & Co., 2009), 160.

53 Kay, *Pentecostalism,* 99.

54 Calvin L. Smith, "Televangelism" in Adam Stewart (ed.), *A Handbook of Pentecostal Christianity* (DeKalb: Northern Illinois University Press, 2012), 205–208.

55 Ruth Marshall, *Political Spiritualities: The Pentecostal Revolution in Nigeria* (Chicago: University of Chicago Press, 2009).

56 Robert Akoko, "New Pentecostalism in the Wake of the Economic Crisis in Cameroon," *Nordic Journal of African Studies* 11:3 (2002), 359–76.

57 Kay, *Pentecostalism,* 118.

58 Miller and Yamamori, *Global Pentecostalism,* ch. 6.

59 Veli-Matti Karkkainen, "'March Forward to Hope': Yonggi Cho's Pentecostal Theology of Hope," *Pneuma: The Journal of the Society for Pentecostal Studies* 28:2 (2006), 253–63.

60 Barker, "Charismatic Economies," 422.

61 Freston, *Evangelicals and Politics,* ch. 1.

62 Christopher March and Artyom Tonoyan, "The Civic, Economic, and Political Consequences of Pentecostalism in Russia and Ukraine," *Society* 46:6 (2009), 510–16.

63 Smith, *Revolution, Revival and Religious Conflict,* 48–53.

64 Freston, *Evangelicals and Politics,* ch. 1; *Protestant Political Parties,* 8, 147–49.

65 Gina Marcela Reyes and Clemencia Tejeiro, "Participacion politica de los movimientos e iglesias pentecostales," in Sarmiento, *El Pentecostalismo en Colombia*, 215–28.

66 Yong, *In the Days of Caesar*, 10–11.

67 Bruce Barron, *Heaven on Earth? The Social and Political Agendas of Dominion Theology* (Grand Rapids, MA: Zondervan), 74–84.

68 Cox, *Fire From Heaven*, 289.

69 Sara Diamond, *Spiritual Warfare: The Politics of the Christian Right* (Boston, MA: South End Press, 1989), 111–46.

70 Barron, *Heaven on Earth?*, 74–84.

71 Notably Yong, *In the Days of Caesar*.

72 Freston, *Evangelicals and Politics*, ch. 1.

73 David Maxwell, "Catch the Cockerel Before Dawn: Pentecostalism and Politics in Postcolonial Zimbabwe," *Africa: Journal of the International African Institute* 70:2 (2000), 266.

74 Ibid., 267ff.

75 Kay, *Pentecostalism*, 151.

76 Discussed in Calvin L. Smith, "Revolutionaries and Revivalists: Pentecostal Eschatology, Politics and the Nicaraguan Revolution," *Pneuma: The Journal for the Society of Pentecostal Studies* 30 (2008), 55–82.

77 Hannah Stewart-Gambino and Everett Wilson, "Latin American Pentecostals: Old Stereotypes and New Challenges" in Stewart-Gambino and Cleary, *Power, Politics and Pentecostals*, 233.

78 Calvin L. Smith, *Revolution, Revival and Religious Conflict in Sandinista Nicaragua* (Leiden and Boston: Brill, 2007), 85–93.

79 Theron Corse, *Protestants, Revolution, and the Cuba-US Bond* (Gainesville: University of Florida Press, 2007), 74–75.

80 For example, Florencio Galindo, *El 'Fenomeno de las Sectas' Fundamentalistas: La Conquista Evangelical de America Latina* (Estella, Navarra, Spain: Editorial Verbo Divino, 1994).

81 Raúl Zibechi, "How Brazil Benefits From Being World's Most Pentecostal Country" (2008), http://www.brazzil.com/articles/197-october-2008/10120-how-brazil-benefits-from-being-worlds-most-pentecostal-country.html (accessed September 7, 2011).

82 Edward L. Cleary and Juan Sepulveda, "Chilean Pentecostalism: Coming of Age," in Clearly and Stewart-Gambino, *Power, Politics and Pentecostals*, 97–122. Also Freston, *Evangelicals and Politics*, ch. 23.

83 Freston, *Evangelicals and Politics*, ch. 1.

84 Freston, *Protestant Political Parties*, 96.

85 Estrelda Alexander, "When Liberation Becomes Survival," *Pneuma: The Journal of the Society for Pentecostal Studies* 32 (2010), 337–53.

86 Veli-Matti Kärkäinnen, "Mission, Spirit and Eschatology," *International Association for Mission Studies* 15:31 (1999), 73–94.

87 Mario Aguilar, *The History and Politics of Latin American Theology*, vol. 3.

88 Doug Petersen, "Latin American Pentecostalism: Social Capital, Networks, and Politics," *Pneuma: The Journal of the Society for Pentecostal Studies* 26:2 (2004), 293–306.

89 Miller and Yamamori, *Global Pentecostalism*, 12.
90 Smith, *Revolution, Revival and Religious Conflict*, 262–71.
91 Barker, "Charismatic Economies," 426.
92 Miller and Yamamori, *Global Pentecostalism*, 31.
93 Zalanga, "Religion, Economic Development and Cultural Change," 59.
94 Ibid., 51.
95 Marshall, *Political Spiritualities*.
96 Gifford, *Christianity, Politics and Public Life in Kenya*, 250.
97 Virginia Garrard-Burnett, *Terror in the Land of the Holy Spirit: Guatemala under General Efraín Ríos Montt, 1982–1983* (Oxford: Oxford University Press, 2010).
98 Joseph Anfuso and David Sczepanski, *He Gives – He Takes Away: The True Story of Guatemala's Controversial Former President Efrain Rios Montt* (Eureka, CA: Radiance Publications, 1983).
99 Stoll, *Is Latin America Turning Protestant?*, 203.
100 Freston, *Protestant Political Parties*, 111–14.
101 Freston, *Evangelicals and Democracy in Latin America*, 16.
102 Freston, *Protestant Political Parties*, 38.
103 David Martin, *The Future of Christianity* (Farnham, Surrey: Ashgate, 2011), 65.
104 David Martin, *Tongues of Fire: The Explosion of Protestantism in Latin America* (Oxford: Blackwell, 1990); *Pentecostalism: The World Their Parish* (Oxford: Blackwell, 2002).
105 Martin, *Future of Christianity*, 72–75.
106 O'Neill, *City of God*.
107 Tan-Chow May Ling, *Pentecostal Theology for the Twenty-First Century: Engaging with Multi-Faith Singapore* (Aldershot, UK: Ashgate, 2007), xxi.
108 Miller and Yamamori, *Global Pentecostalism*, 6.
109 Martin, *Future of Christianity*, 203.

Further Reading

Attanasi, Katy, and Amos Yong, eds., *Pentecostalism and Prosperity: The Socio-Economics of the Global Charismatic Movement*. New York, Palgrave Macmillan, 2012.
Burgess, Richard. *Nigeria's Christian Revolution: The Civil War Revival and Its Pentecostal Progeny (1967–2006)*. Milton Keynes, UK: Regnum, 2008.
Kessler, Christal, and Jürgen Rüland. *Give Jesus a Hand! Charismatic Christians: Populist Religion & Politics in the Philippines*, Manila: Ateneo de Manila University Press, 2008.
Murphy, Liam D. *Believing in Belfast: Charismatic Charisma after the Troubles*. Durham, NC: Carolina Academic Press, 2010.
Oosterbaan, Martijn. *Divine Meditations: Pentecostalism, Politics and Mass Media in a Favela in Rio de Janeiro*. Amsterdam: Amsterdam School of Social Science Research, 2006.
Steigenga, Timothy J. *The Politics of the Spirit: The Political Implications of Pentecostalized Religion in Costa Rica and Guatemala*. Lanham, MD: Lexington Books, 2001.

10 The Cultural Dimension of Pentecostalism
ANDRÉ DROOGERS

INTRODUCTION

The scope of this chapter is to draw the map of the pentecostal cultural landscape and make an inventory of actors and factors, patterns and processes. The expansion of Pentecostalism amid profound changes in the world will first lead to a discussion of two recent trends in the world cultural situation: a change in perspective and a recognition of the human capacity for meaning-making. Subsequently four aspects of the relationship between Pentecostalism and culture receive attention: that Pentecostalism appears to offer a "portable identity," the question of the degree to which continuity and rupture with the surrounding culture occur, the conversion process, and a repertoire model of a church or community. A section on the methodology of the study of the cultural dimension of Pentecostalism appears before the concluding summary.

TWO TRENDS

Religions, including Pentecostalism, inevitably inhabit cultural contexts. Faith seeks to dialogue with culture. Although Pentecostalism presents itself primarily as a faith experience with the Holy Spirit, in its manifestations it is part of a cultural environment. Believers are marked by their culture, just as they seek to influence it. Joel Robbins characterizes Pentecostalism as "a powerful driver of radical cultural change."[1] Pentecostalism's exponential expansion cannot be understood without taking the cultural dimension into account. During Pentecostalism's relatively short history, the cultural situation in the world has changed drastically. Pentecostalism has been subjected to these changes, just as it is an active player in them.

Two trends are relevant when discussing Pentecostalism's cultural dimension. The first is a change in humanity's perspective on culture and cultures in the world; the second regards a change in the anthropological concept of culture.

As to the first trend, there has been a change in focus from the localized and bounded culture to global and diffuse cultural processes. Three worldwide cultural and social processes are occurring:

- *Modernization*: the process by which the results of science and technology are applied in society, causing profound changes (e.g., industrialization, secularization, urbanization, migration, and mass communication)
- *Globalization*: the process by which the world is experienced as one single place (e.g., as visible in politics, mass media, travel, tourism, and migration)
- *Transnationalization*: the process that establishes multistranded identity links, notwithstanding national borders (e.g., relations between migrants of similar ethnic or religious origins across different countries)

These processes have become part of daily life in many parts of the world. Although global, they manifest themselves primarily in locally experienced changes. Initially the West seemed to be the motor of modernization, but gradually multiple modernities[2] have emerged, in different continents, ending the Western monopoly. Transnationalism has reduced the relevance of national boundaries, showing the emergence of links across nation-states.[3] Thus, a global and transnational perspective has gained preponderance over a Western and national focus.

The modern, global, and transnational can be distinguished as different processes, but they cannot be separated, because they are intermingled. They represent three ways of looking at similar phenomena. When construing their life and identity, people nowadays experience and draw from the three processes.

Pentecostalism responds to these processes, is carried on their wings, and has put them at its service. Modernization has created the conditions for pentecostal expansion, but Pentecostalism has produced its own ways of modernizing and created its own style of modernity. Pentecostals have moreover redefined local traditional customs and even in cases demonized them, producing their own modern views on them.[4]

Though Pentecostalism has its origins in the Northern hemisphere, the Western-Northern perspective is passé with the current Southern majority[5] and with Southern Pentecostals now marking presence in the West and North. Not only have migrants taken the pentecostal message with them when moving north, they have established megachurches in Northern-Western countries. This inversion has also contributed to a self-conscious pentecostal version of modernity.[6] Having their own brand of modernity, Pentecostals feel part of a global movement, their faith being an important factor on the global religious market. Moreover, Pentecostalism is now a flourishing transnational movement, linking people on a religious basis beyond national frames of reference.

In sum, the change in perspective situates local pentecostal churches in a worldwide framework. Globalization is manifest at the local level, which is why it has also been labeled "glocalization."[7] Even megachurches, with their worldwide outreach, have to operate at the local level. As far as the three processes are concerned, Pentecostals, in their day-to-day practice as believers, live a mixture of all three, in ever-changing composition. Their case does away with former stereotypical views that located the global initiative with modern Western/Northern culture, looking at the Rest from the perspective of the West, the Rest being expected to follow the example and model of the West. The Rest has now come to the West, in its own right.

Second, and parallel to this change in perspective and focus, the anthropological concept of culture has gained new connotations. Traditionally the emphasis was on localized cultures, each viewed as a more or less autonomous set of customs. In view of the change in perspective that modernization, globalization, and transnationalization brought, culture is now seen as the universal human capacity to give meaning to reality. Because the traditional boundaries were perforated, human beings were ready to use this universal cultural capacity to be able to operate in the expanding world. Practically speaking, people have learned which repertoires can be consulted for which situations, nearby and faraway, from the village level to the global dimension, from the neighborhood gossip to the world news.

Religions cannot escape these trends, and Pentecostalism is a striking illustration of the way religion, even at the local level, can be part of modern, global, and transnational processes – not merely being submitted, but as an active contributor. Pentecostalism also shows how people everywhere use their cultural capacity for meaning-making to redefine their basic beliefs and their way of life, adding new repertoires, such as the pentecostal world view. Pentecostalism is part of the new opportunities and solutions in people's dealing with a world that has expanded and presents itself as extremely dynamic – and often also as problem ridden.

Across former cultural boundaries, Pentecostalism is a new way of belonging, beyond the usual cultural and national categories. Its proposal has proved extremely attractive. Nowadays half a billion people, in the most diverse cultural environments, take part in a variety of churches and networks, all with their own history, size, organization, leadership, theological emphases, ritual preferences, ecumenical views, and political opinions. These new believers make new sense of their lives in a profoundly transformed world. The old categories often were no match to the new experiences. Pentecostalism offers a new way of dealing with modernity. Its core beliefs fit the new contexts, just as it comes with practical solutions to the afflictions that are part of this new world.

Pentecostal variety adds to its attraction. Thus Pentecostalism includes house communities and megachurches, established churches and brand new communities, churches where the charismata have become routinized, and recently founded groups where the Spirit blows at gale force. A special type of Pentecostalism is the charismatic movement, active in mainstream churches, offering church members spiritual renewal from within. Another striking type is that of the travelling evangelists, operating as transnational religious entrepreneurs.

The wide variety of pentecostal manifestations produces a number of paradoxical dilemmas that reflect the many styles in different churches.[8] Thus the belief in the Holy Spirit rehabilitates the individual believer, and yet leadership can become stronger than the authority of the individual's experience with the Spirit. Collective expressions of spontaneity, as in prayer and speaking in tongues, are common practice, yet they may ultimately be subject to the pastor's control of the ritual. Experience is primal, yet strict doctrine may prevail. Similarly the sinful world is avoided, and yet it is where believers recruit converts and combat evil. Pentecostal faith has apocalyptic characteristics, and yet the here and now is most important. Women often are the majority of the flock, and yet their access to leadership positions is limited. All these options can lead to one-sided convictions, just as they allow new converts and old hands to follow their own preferences in meaning-making. Differences between churches reveal the many ways of dealing with these dilemmas. Conflicts and schisms have occurred because of them. They also have nourished unilateral stereotypes of Pentecostalism, coined by outsiders, sometimes emphasizing the contrast with their own non-pentecostal churches.

This wealth of pentecostal phenomena and meaning-making has received attention from social scientists. Studying the cultural dimension is one way of entering this field. The general anthropological knowledge of culture and cultures has already proved helpful. Just as varied as the phenomena are, different approaches have been followed in studying them. The spectacular growth has stimulated research on Pentecostalism, yet the explanations given for the pentecostal success differ according to the theoretical model adopted. Some students follow functionalist lines (pentecostal faith is socially and psychologically useful in times of modernization and individual turmoil), others adopt a Marxist approach (Pentecostalism is opium of the people), or a neo-Marxist point of view (Pentecostalism compensates for the limited access to economic means of production, offering control of religious means of production), just as there have been symbolic and theological studies (the pentecostal belief system is attractive in itself). Corporeal conditions have received attention (the pentecostal faith saves not just the soul but also especially the body, constantly addressing the senses). Research on globalization and transnationalism has added to this debate by emphasizing Pentecostalism's capacity to adapt to changing circumstances and yet remain true to its identity. More recently, aspects other than Pentecostalism's rapid growth are receiving attention, such as gender and family conditions, or its rituals, or the role of migrant churches.

A PORTABLE IDENTITY

Pentecostalism offers a "portable identity," as David Martin has put it.[9] He describes Pentecostalism as "a religious 'movement' accompanying and facilitating the movement of people."[10] He refers to "the radical disturbance of roots" and "the accelerating compression of time and space in contemporary global society as people move about,"[11] both creating niches for the pentecostal message.

Admittedly, the global scope was present in Pentecostalism from the early beginnings, even in local communities such as in Azusa Street, Los Angeles (1906), and simultaneously in some other continents, as Pentecostalism very rapidly gained presence in several parts of the world.[12] When Pentecostalism took off, cultural boundaries were already being perforated and cross-cultural contacts were becoming the rule. From the nineteenth century onwards, the cultural situation in the world was changing rapidly under Western expansion. Industrialization came with a need for raw material, cheap labor, and new markets. Western colonial projects, including slavery, served these goals. Alongside the colonial setup, the expansion of classical Christianity through the missionary movement was already well under way.

Globalization thus has roots in the nineteenth and early twentieth century. During the last two centuries the world has been becoming one place. More or less autonomous cultures, although always subjected to external influences, were subject to unprecedented change. Former boundaries and traditions lost their meaning. Even when people stayed where they lived, modernization, driven by science and technology, impacted the environment.

Modernization came with evermore rapid transport, thereby facilitating migration and missionary outreach. Means of communication and mass media expanded in this process, preparing the way for the electronic church. Medical applications changed the world's demographic situation. Urbanization was irreversible and megacities emerged. Many people lost their social roots and tended to individualize. The twentieth-century war and genocide machines used modern technology and produced an unprecedented number of victims. The face of the earth was changing and cultures were affected by these global processes.

That Pentecostalism emerged under these conditions was, in hindsight, not coincidental. Even though the average Pentecostal would affirm that the Spirit made it happen, it can be said that the cultural, social, economic, and political circumstances were rather providential.

First, more than ever, there was a need for religious solutions and answers. Modernization did not just bring progress for all but also caused turmoil, unrest, and new forms of affliction. Not everybody had their share in the increasing wealth. Thus, developing countries paid part of the price for the developed countries' success. The global changes elicited redefinitions of the meaning of life. The pentecostal message was effective in dealing with the new situation. With its emphasis on prayer and healing, Pentecostalism offers instant solutions to day-to-day affliction. Where no doctor is, the pentecostal healer brings compensation. The pentecostal message also introduces a moral frame of reference that helps people find their way in an unfamiliar world.

Second, communication and transport have become easier. With new media available, the world as one place invited efforts to make it one religious place indeed. The command to go "into all the world" (Mk. 16:15) and "teach all nations" (Matt. 28:19), given in the Mediterranean world, could now find a maximal and literal realization. Modernization offered the means for a global presence. The portable identity could be offered on a worldwide scale.

Contrary to predictions that emerged in the sixties, modernization, despite its supposedly scientific secular world view, did not cause religion's end but appeared to stimulate religious initiatives instead – the spectacular growth of the global pentecostal flock being a case in point. Conversion meant a new start. Demanding a personal decision, it matched growing individualism. Whereas it could sever kinship ties,[13] at the same time believers encountered a new family of brothers and sisters, kin in the Spirit. Pentecostal leaders made natural and implicit use of group dynamics, even in large church buildings or stadium campaigns, giving individuals a feeling of belonging. Besides, believers could feel themselves part of a global movement, thus integrating themselves into the new world society. The pentecostal portable identity could also serve as an entry ticket to the capitalist system, although it can as well be said that it may hamper development and that corruption and self-enrichment are not absent from the pentecostal world. The widespread conviction of a global war between God and the devil is another expression of the transnational and public radius of action of the pentecostal movement, linking personal misfortune to the global drama.[14]

The pentecostal community served as a gateway to the new world. Through the churches, access to the new resources sometimes was facilitated, whether in medical help, literacy training, housing, or employment finding. The erosion of former boundaries ended relatively homogenous cultural and religious conditions and gave Pentecostalism the opportunity to occupy its own niche in the new plural society. As its ideals tend to a new religious, social, and cultural homogeneity, the church community could serve as a laboratory for a new social experiment. The 24/7 claim on the faithful and the paying of tithes reinforced its impact.

In sum, the pentecostal expansion can in part be explained from the prevailing circumstances under which it emerged. There was a large market eagerly waiting for a fitting, practical identity. Pentecostalism thus is a modern religion, born under modern circumstances, even though it does not fully reflect modernity and is critical of certain moral aspects of modern society and culture.

However, this thesis needs some qualification. Other religious movements have spread under similar circumstances, which raises the question why converts have preferred a pentecostal spiritual identity over others on the religious market. Besides, there were converts who, because they belonged to middle and upper classes, profited from the new circumstances, rather than suffering under them, and yet they became Pentecostals. As a consequence there must be exclusive characteristics proper to pentecostal religious views and practices that converts deemed attractive. What was so idiosyncratic in Pentecostalism's offering a portable identity on the religious market?

A basic element in pentecostal belief is the open access to the Spirit's gifts. As an organizing principle this means that every believer has her role to play, backed by the Spirit's manifestations. The multiplicity of roles open to pentecostal members corresponds to the democratic availability of the Spirit. A nobody in society is appreciated in church for what she is, spiritually speaking.

However, to complicate this explanation, the unique characteristics appear to borrow their exclusivity from the interpretation given them, more than from the phenomena as such. Although presented as the exclusive trademark of Pentecostalism, the charismata, as the Spirit's gifts, can also be viewed as belonging to a cultural class of corporeal sensorial manifestations that are not a pentecostal or Christian monopoly, but occur in other cultural and religious settings, albeit with different meanings. Religions, such as Pentecostalism, may present themselves as exclusive, yet in comparison show similarities in their use of human experiences with the transcendental. This makes the pentecostal ritual practice not as innovative as it seems. In fact conversion is made easier when the charismata, often central to the conversion experience, correspond to earlier known "sensational forms."[15] Conversion can also be seen as an example of the universal schema of a rite of transition, using universally recognizable bodily symbols to express the fundamental change that is taking place. A rite de passage expresses the change but may also bring it about. In that sense as well, conversion is an example of initiation rites.[16]

The emphasis on corporeal experience, combined with a particular pentecostal interpretation, serves to convince converts. In principle the pentecostal identity refers theological cognitive discourse, and thereby clerically sophisticated, trained leadership, to a second rank place. Correspondingly the discourse does not use exclusive elite language. This makes the message understandable to all. The readily comprehensible dualism that is present in Pentecostalism – between good and evil, God and devil, salvation and peril, before and after conversion – also helps get the basic message across. The new world can be approached and understood with the help of this dual matrix. The traditional past can be eliminated. Where eschatological millenarianism is part of the pentecostal – or even the preceding religious – repertoire, this takes a radical global form, a break not just with the past but also with the present, and that at the level of humanity.[17] The strong dualism also serves as the believers' antidote against outsiders' negative labeling of pentecostal followers as sectarian, fanatical, or weird. The appeal to universal human experience, even though loaded with Pentecostalism's exclusive interpretation, serves to spread the message and to convince potential converts.

This internal potential of pentecostal religion, appealing to universally recognizable experiences, can only find application in contexts in which external factors serve as a seedbed and, therefore, must be understood as connected with these factors. Thus, such unique beliefs as the emphasis on the Spirit – although corresponding to the basic dualist human experience just mentioned – must nevertheless be combined in any explanation of pentecostal success with a reference to the external context, with its particular cultural, social, political, and economic conditions, reinforced by the combined modernizing, globalizing, and transnationalizing processes. Neither basic human dualism, nor Pentecostalism's uniqueness nor the equally unique external setting, can by itself exhaustively explain pentecostal expansion.

It must be admitted that the picture given so far of pentecostal identity represents the ideal situation. Access to the charismata, although including variations on universal experiences and therefore widely available, is, in practice, not as democratically shared as idealized. Persons with charisma, in the secular sense of having a strong personality, may become more important than the Spirit's charismata. In reality, in the long run, tendencies in church organization, including strong leadership, seem to make some believers more equal in their access to the Spirit than others.

Nowadays, Pentecostalism operates as a global movement, no longer restricted to a North-South axis, but also operating along the South-North, South-South, and East-East links. Its capacity to connect with universal human corporeal experiences, even though marked by traditional meanings and despite being presented in a "converted" pentecostal form, permits such a wide application. Reversed mission has become part of its strategies, seeking to evangelize especially secularized Europe, once the cradle of the missionary movement. In a revised form, the Christian message is thus returned to its origins. Even though the intention is stronger than the actual result, the inverted direction is a sign of the autonomy of Southern pentecostal churches viewing the world as their domain. It makes of Pentecostalism a true transnational movement.

RUPTURE AND CONTINUITY

How do Pentecostals deal with general cultural and social processes characteristic of the societies in which they operate? What are Pentecostalism's culture politics at the local, national, and world levels, including their modern, global, and transnational aspects? In view of their dualist blueprint for society and culture, and also taking into account the global war they are waging against the devil, pentecostal churches pretend to play a public role and are ready to face combat. How does their presence affect culture and society at all levels?

Central to this debate is the question whether only rupture characterizes the pentecostal position, or whether continuity is present as well in pentecostal culture politics and in a convert's decision.[18] The degree to which Pentecostalism's radical lifestyle matches modernity's equally radical transforming role is part of this debate. If the external world is experienced as evil and as the devil's domain, how do Pentecostals nevertheless find ways to operate in it? When a national church seeks to plant a branch in another country, the culture politics regard two cultural contexts, of both countries, and the question about the cultural dimension becomes more complex. Taking all these aspects into account, how do Pentecostals face their cultural surroundings?

The anthropological debate on these questions reveals the influence of historically grown theoretical presuppositions. The traditional focus on more or less autonomous cultures, as integrated unities, has nourished the conviction that cultures show resilience when exposed to factors that seek to change them. The new is not supposed to substitute the old easily but is thought to be accommodated according to the criteria of the old framework, guaranteeing its continuity and persevering order. Thus, for a long time, the local culture remained the primary setting for the anthropological view, even when the effects of modernization, globalization, and transnationalization were already gaining visibility.

Nowadays, however, the local arenas are understood to be the scene of global dramas. Besides, disjuncture is taken to be the rule, instead of persisting order. The question of pentecostal cultural politics, and its possible contribution to rupture or continuity, must be discussed against the background of this shift in the scholar's outlook.

The fact that conversion introduces the believer to a radically different lifestyle seems to reinforce rupture. However, the search for continuity then becomes even more relevant. Undoubtedly the pentecostal message critiques anything that does not fit the world view and ethics that it propagates. Conversion often involves a severing of kinship ties, commonly connected with local customs. Compromising would be viewed as treason in the all-out war against the devil. Conversion as a radical break with the past also regards the convert's previous religion. Whether the person's former world view is one of the world religions – even including large sectors of traditional Christianity – or a tribal, syncretistic, or popular religion, the verdict is absolute. Divinities, ancestors, nature spirits, and saints are redefined as demons, deserving to be fought or exorcized.

Yet, interestingly, here is a first sign of continuity. The position taken usually does not include a denial of the existence or power of such demonic beings. On the contrary, their force is feared and fought. The previous world view thereby is indirectly part of the new conviction, even though in a critical manner.

Another sign of continuity comes from the fact that the human apparel for religious expression is limited in nature. Behind the seeming limitless diversity of religious expressions, common elements are present, as was clear in the previously mentioned universal background of charismata, and as the phenomenological study of religions has shown. The human body disposes of a number of capacities to experience and express the sacred, including extrasensory experiences such as trance, vision, and ecstasy. Although any religion in which the universal religious tools are used will attach an exclusive and idiosyncratic meaning to the believer's concrete experience, this does not eliminate the similarity with other religions' practices.

This applies to Pentecostalism as well, even though Pentecostals do not like the term "religion" or "ritual," being phenomena that the "others" are thought to have. Interestingly, any convert, despite the radical nature of her move, will use part of the previous religion's practice, albeit assigned a totally different meaning set. Thus a medium of an Afro-Brazilian religion, after being converted into a pentecostal church, will use part of the previous bodily ritual practice, despite this church's fierce way of combating Afro-Brazilian spirits as demons. Similarly in other contexts, a pastor may take on characteristics and roles of the traditional healer who he despises.

However, even less controversial elements may make for some form of continuity with other religions. Thus the organization of a pentecostal church may be inspired by that of mainstream churches from which it recruits its members, despite criticism of these churches. The basic democratic access to the gifts of the Holy Spirit would seem to find its natural translation in a rather horizontal way of organizing church life, yet the vertical dimension of, for instance, the Catholic Church has inspired church founders to copy elements from it, including bishops and cathedrals. Another example of such continuity between mainstream and pentecostal churches is the family model, suggesting kinship between sisters and brothers in faith.

Widening the scope, there may also be continuity between the pentecostal way of life and that prevalent in the surrounding society.

Cultural elements may be as normal in the believers' community as they are outside it. Although Pentecostalism offers women many opportunities for empowerment, the patriarchal tendencies that a literal reading of the Bible suggests may coincide with similar gender views in wider society.[19]

Church leaders may adopt clothing habits that in society command respect, such as wearing three-piece suits, even in a tropical climate. In using public space, street evangelists may copy behavior of profane street vendors. When operating as a group, the secular public demonstration model may prevail. Also the way in which the communication codes of pop concerts and television shows are copied in church services is an example, even more so when churches operate their own TV or music channel. "Why should the devil have all the pretty tunes?" is an early Methodist aphorism. In all these cases continuity is sanctified by a form of meaning-making that emphasizes rupture. Whatever the activity, the public space is subjected to conversion by purification and sanctification, transforming it into sacred territory, won over the devil.

This form of hallowed continuity may also find a political expression. Where Pentecostals are elected by their fellow believers into political assemblies, sometimes joining existing political parties for that purpose, the local political customs are embraced, in exceptional cases even including corruption, despite the exclusive moral stance and the criticism of the sinful secular state that formed the reason to become active politically.[20]

Continuity with capitalist consumer society can be detected in as far as prosperity gospel or sow-and-reap approaches are used, suggesting that givers to God will receive ample material and physical blessings. However, there are also interpretations of prosperity that stress the gift exchange between believer and God – sometimes an extension of traditional tribal or even universal exchange practices – or that include a critique of uncontrolled consumerism, new wealth being on principle put at the service of faith.[21]

In sum, whereas Pentecostals seek rupture in a personal, cultural, and also eschatological sense and would certainly deny any continuity between them and the territory that the devil still occupies, they cannot escape symptoms of continuity. In practice, they have to deal with a relatively large number of repertoires: their own, those of the society and culture they are surrounded by, including the constellation of modern, global, and transnational dimensions. Continuity exists but is made acceptable by a change in meaning. Accordingly there is a need for constant ritual reconfirmation of the boundaries, as in baptism, speaking in tongues, exorcism, and altar calls, precisely because continuity is the undertow in the wave of ruptures. Ironically, the harmless forms of continuity, as in organization, clothing, and consumption, are being ignored by the faithful, despite the fact that these link them to the profane world. What counts for them is Pentecostalism as the cult of disjuncture.[22]

CONVERSION

In discussing conversion we are getting close to the believer's individual faith, as a day-to-day experience, yet influenced by what happens in culture and society, at all levels and with all its worldwide dimensions. Conversion, if looked at from a cultural perspective, may contain a combination of rupture and continuity that is similar to Pentecostalism's position with regard to society and culture. What has been said earlier of the church institution and its culture politics persists, in an adapted form, at the individual level. Although conversion is experienced as an incisive rupture, continuity may exist in latent or more manifest forms. Much depends on how conversion is viewed.

The scholarly discussion on conversion has known a number of approaches, depending on the background of the author and the aspect selected.[23] To theologians and believers, biblical cases of conversion, especially Saul/Paul's on the road to Damascus, are authoritative. There is an emphasis on the unique, once-in-a-lifetime, decisive and incisive experience, quick as lightning but preparing for eternity.

Another perspective is that of the church-sect typology, dominated by mainstream views, in which conversion was considered problematic, being the passage from church to sect. Here psychological, social, or cultural problems were supposed to cause the convert's step, as if it were an abnormal or even pathological thing to do. Other explanations take their starting point either with the person or the community, allowing for different emphases on individual freedom and social control.

In studying conversion, authors may differ in the attention given to either supply or demand in the conversion process. Converting churches sometimes supply a specific ideal model of conversion, with its own codes for language and behavior, which converts learn to apply. In preparing for conversion, people may consult a number of repertoires that in some way supply models of conversion, either having their origin in religious institutions, in converts' biographies and testimonies, or in mass media stereotypes. Some authors stress the convert's passive attitude; others show how the convert actively makes her conversion process, dealing with available events, symbols, and meanings. Authors from so-called rational choice theory[24] have emphasized the convert's calculating attitude that weighs advantages and losses and decides accordingly. Conversion can thus be presented as a cognitive decision, yet there may also be a focus on the corporeal sensory aspects of the process, for example, when conversion is linked to the experience of charismata. It has also been viewed as part of a believer's religious career and life history, conversion being one of the stages.

Conversion can also be linked to changes in society or culture and to the pressure that actors and groups may experience. Thus the cumbersome position of ethnic groups was thought to prepare for conversion, whether at home (massive group conversion), in migration (migrant churches), or even in permanent wandering (gypsies). Another example of a societal condition is the process of individualization in modern society, allowing people to move beyond control of kin groups or religious institutions and stimulating development of their own preferences. The reverse is formed by cases in which individual freedom is experienced as a burden, allowing so many choices that a leading framework is direly needed, found in conversion. An important consequence of individualization is that the convert's relation with the new church may be unstable, conversion losing its supposedly permanent effect.

Becoming part of a church is a way of adopting the culture politics of that church, including its view of the current world cultural situation. The convert is introduced into the corporate culture of the pentecostal community that she is entering. Conversion is a cultural change. Part of a group's culture is its attitude towards the outside world. The do's and don'ts that are part and parcel of these culture politics will influence the convert's way of life. Although the ins and outs of the church's culture politics will not make themselves felt on all occasions and are not necessarily part of a believer's self-understanding, potentially they are always there.

THREE REPERTOIRES

The map of the culture politics of a church can be drawn with the help of a repertoire model. The cultural dimension of a pentecostal church is the result of the constellation of repertoires regarding the transcendental, internal, and external domains.[25] These repertoires may change over time. They rule behavior but may also adapt to changes in behavior. The three types of repertoires can be distinguished but not separated. They influence each other. Together they form the corporate culture of a

Repertoire	Principal power relations
Transcendental	Believers – God, Jesus, Spirit, Satan
Internal	Believers – Leadership
	Believers – Believers
External	Believers – Nonbelievers
	Believers – Other types of Believers
	Believers – Culture, Society

community and its culture politics. Each repertoire comes with its own set of power relations – power being the capacity to influence behavior.

Thus the pentecostal transcendental repertoire is characterized by emphasis on the presence of the Holy Spirit, the need for a conversion experience as access to salvation and the Spirit's gifts, and the expected victory of God over Satan. Of course, other elements can be added, and each church will make its own selection from the broad repertoire of pentecostal views and practices. In terms of this repertoire, the believer relates herself to the transcendental, with possible emphases on either God the Father, Jesus the Son, or the Holy Spirit. The experience with charismata, being the manifestation of the transcendental, may decisively impact a person's life. The believer feels overpowered as well as empowered. The particulars of this repertoire may color her views on the internal organization of the church as well as on her cultural surroundings.

The repertoire that rules the internal relations within the community includes the way it is organized, how leadership is exercised, and what labor division is used. The forms of leadership may vary, from CEO-like leaders of internationally operating megachurches to plural, decentralized leadership in other churches. Gender is often an organizing principle, with formal male leadership over a preponderantly female membership – women acting as informal leaders. In the pentecostal case an inbuilt tension exists, because both the leadership and the membership may appeal to authority stemming from their experience with the Spirit. Legitimization through the Spirit is open to all, unless the leadership claims exclusive and authentic access. The internal repertoire also determines how the ritual side of community life takes form and which place the charismata receive, including corporeal expressions. Views on the internal organization may change in the course of a community's history. Thus, if a community's success is such that a local initiative expands nationally or even internationally, the internal repertoire changes accordingly. There may also be changes over the generations, a third generation church often showing routinization and institutionalization. Such a situation may provoke a revival, leading to a split-off, and starting a new cycle.

The repertoire that rules the external relations comprises the culture politics of the community. The relation with the outside world, including other religious groups and secular authorities, is defined. As mentioned, this view may be marked by dualism, opposing the community of the saved to the sinful world. In the case of a local community, the repertoire will contain other elements than when we deal with a nationally or globally operating church. A particular case is the action a church may develop in society, such as when a development program is started or when a church becomes politically active.[26]

These three repertoires are constantly tested and adapted, which shows their interconnectedness. This will not necessarily lead to a coherent system. Contradictions may remain, without being solved. This is given with the dynamics of any organization, especially when growing. Expansion and subsequent institutionalization alter the repertoires of any church. Institutionalization may lead to a more strict control of the charismata, bodily expressions being reserved to certain times and places, thus losing their spontaneity. Order is hardly ever served by spontaneity, although in a controlled form it can be an asset in the hands of church leaders seeking church growth. However, even without a situation of growth there may be contradictions between the three repertoires, especially because each of the three dimensions offers choices that lead to differing emphases. Much depends on whether the attitude toward the Spirit is that of submission or manipulation, whether the internal organization tends to be either horizontal or vertical, and whether the sinful world must be condemned unconditionally or could allow value compromises.

The three repertoires are interrelated. A typical example of this is the prosperity gospel, seeking transcendental support for internal behavior that results in success in external relationships. Taken together the three repertoires also determine how the power relations are organized in the corporate culture of a community or church. The exercise of power is the synthesis of the mutual influence between repertoires. The need to guarantee a certain degree of order may be an important factor in arranging the repertoires.

In pentecostal settings a basic tension is that between the Spirit's power and human power. There is usually an ideal justification of both, with a practice that may show slight or fundamental deviations from the ideal. Nevertheless, not only the charismata, as visible in believers' behavior, but also charisma, as a personal leadership quality, may influence the power constellation. A leader's power may also be based on the church's rules or may even be of a hereditary nature, in the case of a dynasty of pastors. Even though ideally Scripture and the faithful's experience through the Spirit are decisive, in practice those in power may, on purpose or not, adapt the repertoires to the needs of their regime. This development may mark a church's history. It may change views on the transcendental repertoire, including the divine.

METHODOLOGY

Some methodological instruments for researching Pentecostalism's cultural dimension should be included in the student's toolkit.[27] In the preceding, the emphasis was on the interconnectedness of processes, perspectives, and repertoires, from the local to the global levels. Nowadays the cultural dimension is modern, global, and transnational, even when it is observed at the local level. This asks for a proper research methodology.

In view of the role played by the three discussed repertoires, there is a plurality of aspects. Even when research is limited to local churches, global influences should be taken into account. When a globally operating church is under consideration, with a more complex internal organization and extensive external contacts, multisited research is recommended. In all cases, rupture and continuity with regard to the cultural dimension must be included. The same tension will also be present in the way conversion, including its cultural aspects, is understood in specific church settings.

The model of the three repertoires may serve to map the dynamics that characterize a church, independent of its size. It represents an empty form that can be filled out by concrete cases. Each of the repertoires can be identified, and subsequently the connections between the three can be described. Together the three repertoires represent the portable identity of the believer of a church. Recruitment is ruled by the views on the external relationships of the group. The researcher may find it profitable to observe from the convert's position, who has to learn the internal repertoire in striving for full membership. Or she may identify with a member on (usually) his way for leadership. Both researcher and member will have to find their way in the corporate culture. The precise link between the repertoires can be a fascinating topic to study, showing the group's cultural dynamics.

In choosing methods, an important choice is that between quantitative and qualitative methods. Focus on church growth and marketing questions stimulates quantitative research. Policy makers usually demand to be fed with statistics. Surveys serve this purpose, producing data in a relatively short time. Their preparation, application, and analysis are a technical specialist's job, and their design should not be underestimated.

Qualitative research may help prepare survey design, just as it may check on and follow up quantitative work. However, qualitative methods may also be used in their own right. Its methodology can be adapted in the course of a project's application. All unquantifiable data can be generated using techniques such as open interviews, participant observation, and the collection of life histories and conversion narratives. Whereas the quantitative researcher avoids any personal involvement, the qualitative researcher often finds her most important tool in her personality. However, the non-pentecostal qualitative researcher will in her contacts be subjected to conversion efforts, because her participation will be understood as sincere interest.

CONCLUSION

The cultural dimension of Pentecostalism is intimately connected with the global cultural changes of the past two centuries. The effects of modernization, globalization, and transnationalization mark the rise of Pentecostalism, just as they have been marked by this new global religious movement. The cultural identity of Pentecostals reflects the characteristics of the worldwide global changes. The emphasis on an exclusive and idiosyncratic identity raises the question to what degree pentecostal faith and conversion demand a rupture with the cultural setting or allow some form of continuity. This is the case because becoming a Pentecostal is a way of participating in the modern world. The cultural dimension of Pentecostalism can furthermore be analyzed as the combined result of its transcendental, internal, and external repertoires. Finally, studying the cultural dimension demands proper methodological tools.[28]

Notes

1   Joel Robbins, "Anthropology of Religion," in Allan Anderson, et al., eds., *Studying Global Pentecostalism: Theories and Methods* (Berkeley: University of California Press, 2010), 156.
2   Shmuel N. Eisenstadt, "Multiple Modernities," *Daedalus* 129 (2000), 1–29.
3   Andreas Wimmer and Nina Glick Schiller, "Methodological Nationalism and Beyond: Nation-State Building, Migration and the Social Sciences,"

Global Networks 2 (2002), 301–34. Also, Ulrich Beck, *The Cosmopolitan Vision* (Cambridge: Polity, 2006), 24–33.

4 Ruth Marshall, *Political Spiritualities: The Pentecostal Revolution in Nigeria* (London and Chicago: University of Chicago Press, 2009).

5 Philip Jenkins, *The Next Christendom: The Rise of Global Christianity* (New York: Oxford University Press, 2002).

6 E.g., Kim Knibbe, "'We Did Not Come Here as Tenants, But as Landlords': Nigerian Pentecostals and the Power of Maps," *African Diaspora* 2 (2009), 133–58.

7 Roland Robertson, *Globalization: Social Theory and Global Culture* (London: SAGE, 1992), 173–74.

8 André Droogers, "Paradoxical Views on a Paradoxical Religion," in Barbara Boudewijnse, et al., eds., *More than Opium: An Anthropological Approach to Latin American and Caribbean Pentecostal Praxis* (Lanham: Scarecrow, 1998), 1–34.

9 David Martin, *Pentecostalism: The World Their Parish* (Oxford: Blackwell, 2002), 24.

10 Martin, *Pentecostalism*, 23.

11 Ibid.

12 Allan Anderson, *An Introduction to Pentecostalism* (Cambridge: Cambridge University Press), 35–38, 64–69.

13 Linda van de Kamp, *Violent Conversion: Brazilian Pentecostalism and the Urban Pioneering of Women in Mozambique* (Leiden and Amsterdam: Africa Study Centre and VU University, 2011).

14 Birgit Meyer, "Pentecostalism and Globalization," in Anderson, et al., *Studying Global Pentecostalism: Theories and Methods*, 115–18.

15 Meyer, "Pentecostalism and Globalization," 122–23.

16 Diane Austin-Broos, "The Anthropology of Conversion: An Introduction," in Andrew Buckser and Stephen D. Glazier, eds., *The Anthropology of Religious Conversion* (Lanham: Rowman and Littlefield, 2003), 1–12.

17 Robbins, "Anthropology of Religion," 160.

18 Joel Robbins, "On the Paradoxes of Global Pentecostalism and the Perils of Continuity Thinking," *Religion* 33 (2003), 221–31.

19 Elizabeth Brusco, "Gender and Power," in Anderson, et al., 74–92.

20 Ari Pedro Oro, "Ascension et déclin du pentecôtisme politique au Brésil," *Archives de Sciences Sociales des Religions* 149 (2010), 151–68.

21 Robbins, "Anthropology of Religion," 171.

22 Robbins, "Anthropology of Religion," 161–62.

23 Henri Gooren, *Religious Conversion and Disaffiliation: Tracing Patterns of Change in Faith Practices* (London: Palgrave MacMillan, 2010), and Miranda Klaver, *"This is my Desire": A Semiotic Perspective on Conversion in an Evangelical Seeker Church and a Pentecostal Church in the Netherlands* (Amsterdam: Pallas and VU University, 2011), 76–79.

24 For an overview of the debate on rational choice theory, see Grace Davie, *The Sociology of Religion* (Los Angeles: SAGE, 2007), 67–88.

25 André Droogers, "The Power Dimensions of the Christian Community: An Anthropological Model," *Religion* 33 (2003), 263–80.

26 Frans H. Kamsteeg, *Prophetic Pentecostalism in Chile: A Case Study on Religion and Development Policy* (Lanham: Scarecrow, 1998).

27   See Droogers, "The Power Dimensions," 275–78; Klaver, *"This is my Desire,"* 31–39.

28   I gratefully acknowledge comments by Miranda Klaver and Kim Knibbe on an earlier draft of this chapter.

Further Reading

Coleman, Simon. *The Globalisation of Charismatic Christianity: Spreading the Gospel of Prosperity.* Cambridge, Cambridge University Press, 2000.

Corten, André, and Ruth Marshall-Fratani, eds. *Between Babel and Pentecost: Transnational Pentecostalism in Africa and Latin America.* London: Hurst, 2001.

Hüwelmeier, Gertrud, and Kristine Krause, eds. *Traveling Spirits: Migrants, Markets and Mobilities.* London: Routledge, 2010.

Meyer, Birgit. *Translating the Devil: Religion and Modernity among the Ewe in Ghana.* Edinburgh: Edinburgh University Press, 1999.

Westerlund, David, ed. *Global Pentecostalism: Encounters with Other Religious Traditions.* London and New York: Tauris, 2009.

11 Sociological Narratives and the Sociology of Pentecostalism

MICHAEL WILKINSON

INTRODUCTION

The sociology of Pentecostalism, not surprisingly, closely resembles developments in the sociology of religion. Following the founding sociologists, scholars have developed various theories to explain the relationship between religion and society. The explanations, however, are filled with debate, and the differences vary most notably between European and American sociologists. Grace Davie points out that the development of secularization theory, more in line with European thinkers, and rational choice theory, favored by Americans, has defined the sociology of religion.[1] However, rather than seeing these explanations as accurate for their particular cases (secularization in Europe and competitive free markets in America), sociologists have continued to argue from both sides of the Atlantic for their particular interpretation to be taken as the global model. Both positions, says Davie, are partially right and partially wrong. In other words, there is no need for one theory to win. Davie does push for the development of empirically rich case studies, following the Weberian tradition, to be applied in a global and comparative fashion. David Martin's work on global Pentecostalism is one of her prime examples. However, I think that while Davie is accurate about the conflict among these different thinkers, she may underestimate the willingness of some sociologists to recognize the legitimacy of the other side.

Meredith McGuire and James Spickard, in a similar fashion, outline a somewhat expanded explanation for the development of the sociology of religion.[2] Utilizing the idea of narratives instead of theoretical paradigms, they add two other stories in the sociology of religion: including secularization and rational choice theory, they recognize reorganization of religion and individualization. They also point out that one other narrative, globalization, is in proto-form. While sociologists such as Roland Robertson, John Simpson, and Peter Beyer are influential and offer sustained analyses of religion and globalization, this particular narrative is still developing and requires some attention among scholars of Pentecostalism.

There are several strands that make up this chapter. First, I will make some comments about the development of sociological thinking and the role of networks for the construction of competing narratives. Second, I will outline the fairly well-developed narratives in the sociology of religion and illustrate how pentecostal studies reflect these accounts. Third, I will offer some reflection on the need for pentecostal studies to take seriously the globalization literature as they develop a global pentecostal narrative. While the globalization literature is still relatively in its infancy (in spite of the massive amounts of literature published on the topic), sociologists of global Pentecostalism ought to make a contribution to the field and also benefit from detailed, comparative, and empirically rich descriptions of the movement. Furthermore, accounts for the way in which Pentecostalism has emerged, developed, and changed in different social contexts ought to be a valuable resource for understanding other important sociological questions about the role of religion in global society. Although it is not possible to review all the literature, I will highlight a number of key authors and representative works to illustrate the major narratives in the sociology of religion.

SOCIAL NETWORKS AND THE CONSTRUCTION OF NARRATIVES

Sociology, generally speaking, is concerned with two enterprises: description and explanation. On the side of description, empiricism has long shaped the discipline with key methodological debates about sociology as a social science, the objective/subjective role of researchers, the limits of positivism, and questions about reflexivity and epistemology. On the explanation side there are long-standing debates about the relevance of classical theories from the works of Marx, Weber, and Durkheim, with a divide between those who believe we have nothing to learn from the founders to those who argue that the classics are still worth reading. Sociology has moved through various stages of embracing, rejecting, and modifying older theories. Contemporary theorists are focusing on explanations for understanding multicultural societies, gender, race and ethnic relations, the body, and globalization. Theory, generally speaking, refers to a series of interrelated assumptions about the nature of social relations, social structures, human agency, social institutions, stratification systems, and social change. However, notwithstanding the aims of sociology to describe and explain, there is much disagreement over the various interpretations, which raise important questions about sociological knowledge.

Randall Collins is critical of the traditional views shaping the evolution of sociological theory and argues that the formation of intellectual knowledge occurs in social networks often competing or conflicting with other groups.[3] Collins critiques the generally held views that knowledge is simply the function of the brain, the product of the genius, a cultural product, or relative, fluid, and unfixed. Rather, argues Collins in a convincing fashion, all knowledge is rooted in social networks of intellectual communities, where ideas are formed in relation to other competing networks of knowledge. The value of Collins's work is his focus on the social process of knowledge formation and the role key individuals play in putting forward explanations of social life. These explanations, however, are not simply straightforward observations about social reality. Rather, they are explanations based on specific assumptions often in conflict with competing viewpoints. Whereas sociologists have developed long-standing theoretical paradigms to articulate these assumptions, another way to think about theoretical paradigms is to use the language of social narrative.

Christian Smith writes an engaging and provocative critique of social theory that attempts to account for human motivation and social action.[4] The moral philosophy and epistemology of Charles Taylor and the anthropology of human personhood by Mary Douglas shape his assumptions. He argues that in spite of the many cultural differences worldwide and throughout history, there is a common structure of human personhood that orders human culture. This common structure is based on the idea that all humans are believers and that social life is based on sets of basic assumptions and beliefs. These assumptions about moral order – how life ought to be lived – have consequences for social reality. For example, all social institutions, he argues, express and animate these moral orders. Furthermore, sociologists need to take seriously their own assumptions and commitments as they relate to their sociological work.

To further his argument, Smith focuses on narratives as a form of communication that organizes human action into meaningful relations. Beyond the basic elements of characters, plot, and meaning, human beings construct and tell "stories" that, in turn, shape those who communicate these narratives. Societies, he argues, are organized by narratives that shape social interaction and generate culture and social institutions. Throughout history humans have lived by various narratives including what he refers to as the American experiment narrative, the militant Islamic resurgence narrative, the Christian metanarrative, the capitalist prosperity narrative, the progressive socialism narrative, the expressive Romantic narrative, the scientific Enlightenment narrative, and so on. Each of these "stories" constructs an ideal about the composition, direction, and interpretation of human life. Smith is not suggesting that we all live by one grand narrative. Rather, his point is that humans cannot live without stories, big stories that tell us what is real and significant, who we are, where we are, what we are doing, and why. Narratives are similar in form, structure, and function but vary according to particular cultural moral orders, often leading to conflict between those life-shaping narratives.

Likewise, sociologists construct narratives to make sense of social reality. They offer theoretical explanations or "narratives" for the various social descriptions they present. The main sociological narratives, according to Smith, are Liberal Progress, Ubiquitous Egoism, and Community Lost. It is this last narrative, Community Lost, which has had considerable impact on the sociology of religion. The Community Lost narrative is rooted in German and English Romanticism and is shaped by a reaction against the rationalism and skepticism of the Enlightenment. It is a narrative characterized by nostalgic tragedy evoking melancholy and dissent for those who have told it and lived it. It is not a dominant myth in sociology now but shaped many areas of research and underlying assumptions in the areas of urban and community sociology, immigration, and religion, especially the secularization thesis.

There are several implications for understanding the sociology of Pentecostalism. First, the various debates and critical issues in pentecostal studies are directly related to the development of sociological theories. Key figures and intellectual networks in sociology strongly influence the explanations offered about pentecostal-charismatic Christianity. These explanations about pentecostal communities are based on the underlying assumptions of competing sociological frameworks. More specifically, the development of the sociology of Pentecostalism in the past fifty years reflects the underlying assumptions of conflict and disagreement within the larger field. In sum, the development of sociology is structured by the social location of intellectual networks where ideas are formed, often competing with other socially structured networks. Second, the ideas generated by these intellectual communities form narratives that shape those who tell the stories as well as the explanations offered for social reality. Third, narratives are never neutral and in general offer a vision of how life ought to be.

MAJOR NARRATIVES IN THE SOCIOLOGY OF RELIGION AND IMPACT ON PENTECOSTAL STUDIES

There are four dominant narratives that have shaped the sociology of religion over the past 100 years. These narratives have captured the many issues of sociologists of religion from the emergence of modernity, secularization, the decline of religion, the institutionalization of religion, sectarian religion, theories of deprivation, church growth and decline, privatization, denominational life, congregations and communities, religious identity, individualized religion, fragmentation of religious life, spirituality, open religious markets and the churching of America, and the expansion of Christianity throughout the world. Likewise, scholars of Pentecostalism are shaped by the assumptions of these narratives and the sociologists associated with these views. These four narratives are secularization, religious markets, religious organization, and religious individualization.

Secularization and the Institutionalization of Religion

The longest standing debate among sociologists of religion is secularization. Secularization has a long history in the discipline and takes numerous forms. It is important to recognize that although secularization is severely critiqued by some sociologists, there is among many more a commitment to fleshing out the assumptions of their theories. Among the most notable proponents of secularization are sociologists such as Max Weber, Peter Berger, Bryan Wilson, David Martin, Karl Dobbelaere, and Steve Bruce. It is not possible to evaluate all of the theories or the criticisms. However, what follows is an assessment of the main contours and the way in which these ideas have shaped pentecostal studies.

At the center of Max Weber's work is the concept of rationalization, which he argued was the key characteristic of Western societies. Rationalization increasingly came to shape the major social institutions of politics, economics, law, and religion. Rationalization was deemed to be a historical process by which social life, especially with the emergence of modern social institutions, was increasingly characterized by a "means-end" orientation as it related to social action.[5] Weber made rationalization and social action central to his work as he accounted for the transition from traditional community life to modern, impersonal, and a rationalized social world.

The application of rationalization to religion is in *The Protestant Ethic and the Spirit of Capitalism* where he examined the relationship between religion and economics.[6] Specifically, Weber saw religion, especially Calvinism, advancing the principles of modernity and transforming religion itself through the appropriation of rational means including technique and science with religious justification in economic activities. The transformation of religion and society was thought to lead to an iron cage whereby modern Western society would be characterized by disenchantment. As the world becomes more rationalized, it leads to innovation and the development of nonrationalized symbolic forms. To survive this modern world, some people practice magic, the basic form of religion, or some gain special powers, which he called charisma. Charisma, for Weber, is a form of authority "applied to a certain quality of an individual personality by virtue of which he is considered extraordinary and treated as endowed with supernatural, superhuman, or at least specifically exceptional powers or qualities."[7] The instability of charisma, however, leads to its routinization with organized religion taking on a stable hierarchy and permanency. Sects are the prime example of religious groups resisting routinization and, through a process of adaptation or innovation, maintain a more traditional or anti-modern stance. Research on sectarian religious groups often focused on deprivation theories to explain why they remained in tension with modernity.

O'Dea elaborated on this process as institutionalization and described a number of dilemmas religions experience over time.[8] O'Dea argued that institutions needed and suffered most from institutionalization. However, the process also created other tensions. O'Dea identified five important tensions that leaders had to navigate. They included the following challenges. First, mixed motivation among the followers and leaders was thought to bring about compromise and weakened the organization. Second, religious organizations faced the dilemma of keeping the symbols alive so that the next generation would come to understand and experience what was important to the emerging movement. Third, religious movements faced the challenge of moving from relatively simple organizational principles to a more elaborate bureaucratic system, which may negatively affect motivation among followers. Fourth, religious groups face the challenge of translating the general ethos into more concrete ethical principles, which may lead to forms of legalism or the tension between the "letter of the law" versus the "spirit of the movement." Finally, O'Dea elaborated on power and its consolidation within the organization and offices of leadership as a dilemma. Each of these dilemmas of institutionalization was understood to be both blessing and curse and required careful management among religious leaders.

It is not surprising then, that much of the research on Pentecostalism and the interpretations offered are shaped by the assumptions of rationalization, sectarian religion, charisma, deprivation, and institutional dilemma.[9] Each of these explanations is rooted in a specific narrative of social reality: secularization and the loss of traditional religion, including its authority in the modern world. The most sustained sociological treatment of charisma, institutionalization, and Pentecostalism is Margaret Poloma's research on the Assemblies of God and David Martin's work on secularization and Latin American Pentecostalism. Each of these authors deserves some treatment here.

David Martin's *A General Theory of Secularization*, considered a classic in the field, argues for a more empirically based assessment.[10] Martin examined historical patterns throughout various regions offering a multidimensional explanation for his observations. An important contribution is his view that secularization and modernization are not universally exported in a linear fashion. Rather, there are particular ways in which these twin social processes occur, specific ways in which religions respond, and unique ways in which religious innovation occurs. One of the primary arguments Martin made was that under processes of modernization, religion does not simply disappear and decline. Rather, some religions under the constraints of modernization and secularization are replaced by other newly formed religions, the case being Pentecostalism replacing Methodism. Pentecostalism becomes a primary example for Martin as he offers his empirical evidence to support his theoretical assumptions.

In *Pentecostalism: The World their Parish*,[11] Martin continues his argument from his book *Tongues of Fire*[12] in which he accounts for the apparent resurgence of religion, especially outside of the West, and particularly among Pentecostals. Generally, his argument is as follows. Pentecostalism emerged in the late nineteenth and early twentieth century out of the Holiness and Methodist traditions. Initially, Pentecostalism was not considered an important factor on the religious landscape. Most sociologists were concerned with accounting for the impact of modernity on Western social life and the demise of religion. Quietly, Pentecostalism grew to become one of the most substantial shifts within Christianity and among the world's religions. Martin explains the impact of Pentecostalism within Christianity and more importantly the ability of Pentecostals to adapt and succeed in a modern and globalizing world through adaptation and innovation.

Martin picks up on his complex theory of secularization that questions views of the inevitable decline of religion, arguing for detailed comparative analysis of the interaction between religions and the dilemmas of modernity. Martin is sympathetic but not uncritical of

Pentecostals. More importantly, he takes seriously the role of religion as a cultural resource that enables practitioners to engage the world. Pentecostalism, while growing, does have its exceptions. Martin discusses the different cultural receptivity factors between North America, Europe, and those regions primarily in the southern hemisphere. Martin examines the impact of rationalization, privatization, differentiation, pluralism, religious monopoly, and religious volunteerism and the consequences for religion and society, pointing to why Pentecostalism is a significant movement globally except in Europe.

His work consists of case studies that examine the impact of modernization in Latin America, Africa, and Asia and the corresponding religious and cultural interactions with these sweeping global changes. The Latin American case deserves some attention. Martin argues that Pentecostalism aided the transition in Latin America from a premodern to a postindustrial society, not unlike the role Methodism played during the industrial revolution in Britain. In a Weberian fashion, he views the theology of Pentecostalism as a catalyst for a new world order that fits well with a pentecostal dynamic and system of ideas. Pentecostalism enables people to become modern global actors, and quite successful ones as well. Latin American Pentecostals may be mostly poor, but they are disciplined and world affirming, which contributes to a new pentecostal ethic. This ethic engages Pentecostals with contemporary global realities like the new global economy. Furthermore, because Pentecostalism is a renewal movement, the process of bureaucratization and routinization is always challenged by pragmatic flexibility, which is an advantage for the pentecostal entrepreneur. Martin concludes that Pentecostalism mobilizes the culturally and socially despised of the world, carrying them from the margins to modernity, illustrating the ability of Pentecostalism to appropriate and localize a version of Christianity in its own social space.

While Martin's work focuses on critiquing several assumptions of secularization, Margaret Poloma's research picks up on O'Dea's institutionalization views and applies them to the Assemblies of God. There are two significant books by Poloma that examine the effects of institutionalization on charisma. The first book is *The Assemblies of God at the Crossroads* in which Poloma shows how charismatic experiences such as speaking in tongues, healing, and prophecy are related to the growth of the Assemblies of God (AG).[13] However, the success of the denomination and its move toward a more stable, bureaucratic, and hierarchical organization contribute to specific tensions, inconsistencies between beliefs and practices, accommodation to the larger culture, support of conservative politics, ambivalence toward women in ministry, and a fear of the experiences that contributed to its growth. As the AG attempts to navigate institutional dilemmas, Poloma is pessimistic about its future as the denomination becomes more focused on the qualities of rationalization over charisma.

In the second book on the AG, Poloma and Green find some hope for the denomination, especially among those congregations who are experiencing new waves of divine love with the result of a renewed commitment to engaging the community in some benevolent way.[14] This is where the authors show that institutional dilemmas are not determined but always in negotiation or managed in some way. The authors review AG history, structure, and role of charisma on the basis of interviews, observations, and congregational surveys. They then move into an evaluation of institutional dilemmas, including mixed motivation and experience, doctrine, power and administration, Spirit-baptism, the role of prayer, prophets and healers, and finally, several chapters focus on the sociology of love, altruism, and benevolence, or what Poloma and Green call "Godly Love."

There are several points that require some comment. First, the book offers an important evaluation of the AG, one of the largest of the classical pentecostal denominations born out of the Azusa Street Revival, 1906–09. The history of the AG is rooted in the racial division that eventually led to the demise of the revival that initially was racially inclusive. For William Seymour, the African-American leader, racial reconciliation was a key sign that the Spirit had visited them and revival had come to Southern California. However, it was not long before racial division led to the end of the revival and out of it was born a white pentecostal denomination – the AG. This is an important aspect of the story as the AG has since sought reconciliation with African-American Pentecostals. It is also part of the discussion on how love may be connected to social justice and racial reconciliation.

Second, Poloma and Green offer an important observation on the different types of congregations emerging within the AG. Specifically, the authors identify four types as traditional non-English congregations, evangelical congregations, renewalist or charismatic congregations, and alternative congregations. Each of these types is defined and described with examples from their study. The typology proves helpful for understanding that congregations are not homogenized and are more diverse than perhaps recognized. There is no single type of AG congregation, and generalizations need to be nuanced with the denomination's growing diversity. Poloma and Green also nuance the role of institutionalization showing how the various tensions are important matters for pastors and church leaders as they attempt to navigate them. The authors seem to be less deterministic than the earlier view of institutionalization presented in the 1989 book by Poloma. In other words, there is always room for negotiating these tensions, and a fresh infusion of perceived divine love may be what is needed.

This emphasis on altruism or "Godly Love" represents another important contribution. Godly Love is defined as "a dynamic interaction between human responses to perceptions of divine love that affects personal lives, interrelationships with others, and social institutions."[15] Godly Love revolves around a perceived divine/human love interaction, which is consequential in such a way that experiencing God's love benefits others. The objective of Poloma and Green is to contribute to a growing conversation in the sociology of love by showing how Pentecostalism, which fosters divine/human experiences, motivates people to act in benevolent ways. The charismatic impulse within Pentecostalism is relatively understudied and may even be underestimated among scholars for understanding the role of the spirit among Pentecostals with its accompanying role of love in action. Overall, Poloma and Green offer an update on the AG while moving the discussion in a new direction with the introduction of an interactional love concept or, as the authors prefer, "Godly Love."

Market Models

Probably the most influential of theories in sociology in the latter half of the twentieth century are those related to exchange theory, economic and game theory models, and rational choice theories. Sociology of religion is particularly influenced by rational choice and market theories of religion through the work of Roger Finke and Rodney Stark. *Acts of Faith* by Stark and Finke received the 2001 book of the year award from the American Sociological Association (sociology of religion section).[16] Stark and Finke also won awards for *The Churching of America* in 1993 from the Society for the Scientific Study of Religion.[17] The market model, or rational choice theory, argues that the demand for religion or the gods in society are always high, but the providers change. Secularization is not the end of religion but only the end of certain providers. Secularization is replaced by religious revival or renewal. Eventually, Stark came to critique his early views of modified secularization and argued that secularization is the most incorrect theory and ought to be forgotten. Rational choice theory and secularization theory represent two important debates in the sociology of religion, and with different representatives from each group, the conflict is palpable.

In the fall of 1999 Stark published "Secularization, R.I.P." and argued that sociologists of religion have been duped by the assumptions of the theory for far too long.[18] The theory no longer made sense, and the empirical evidence continued to call for its end. The *Sociology of Religion* journal followed up Stark's paper with Steve Bruce's provocative article "Christianity in Britain, R.I.P." in 2001.[19] Bruce maintained that the empirical evidence supported the secularization thesis and it was still a valid theory as Christianity in Europe continued to decline. These two articles represent the competing assumptions of two theories in sociology with secularization as the "old paradigm" and a market model relying on a different set of theoretical assumptions and the application of economic exchange concepts like supply and demand to religion. The result is not the end of religion but the shift in religious providers as the less worldly and more vital groups take their place in the religious market. From the secularization of some religious groups comes the birth of new groups. Secularization leads to religious innovation. The assumption is that the demand for religion is always high although the providers are ever changing.

One of the better examples of a market model applied to Pentecostalism is the book *Global Pentecostalism* by Miller and Yamamori.[20] The authors offer an exceptional introduction and overview of holistic ministry by Pentecostals outside North America and Europe. Students and those unfamiliar with Pentecostalism will especially find this a valuable resource. The book covers a wide range of ministry activities in Africa, Asia, and South and Central America, offering some important comparative data not found elsewhere. The breadth of coverage is impressive, and those scholars intending to research in greater detail social ministry by Pentecostals will have an important base to begin. The book includes an overview of the various issues surrounding the study of Pentecostalism, a definition of "progressive Pentecostalism," an overview of programs serving children and youth, individual and social transformation, the role of the Holy Spirit in ministry, social mobility, structural/organizational characteristics, and some reflections on the future of social engagement. There are several points raised in the book that deserve some comment.

The book explores an emerging and growing aspect of Pentecostalism that focuses on holistic ministry. Progressive Pentecostalism refers to those who seek to holistically address the spiritual, physical, and social needs of their community. It does not refer to any particular political movement. However, the authors also want to counter a view of Pentecostals as wholly otherworldly, waiting for the return of Christ to the exclusion of social ministry. Progressive Pentecostalism, on the other hand, affirms the return of Christ but also argues that they are called to engage their communities. And, according to the authors, they are doing so through programs on AIDS, poverty, health, addictions, education, economic development, counselling, policy change, and the arts.

Another argument made in the book is that progressive Pentecostalism represents a movement in line with the social gospel movement of the early twentieth century and the liberation theological movement that followed. More specifically, it is argued that while the social gospel movement is dead and liberation theology is declining in influence, there is a gap to be filled and it may partly be done so by Pentecostals. However, these Pentecostals are quite different from those involved in the previously mentioned movements. Progressive Pentecostals are on the whole nonpolitical, opting instead to challenge governments and social policies from the ground up as they attempt to build the Kingdom of God one person at a time. Furthermore, the evidence from their research shows not only that pentecostal activism has replaced other movements but also that it supports the view that secularization no longer makes sense. As the authors state: "In our view, the emergence of Progressive Pentecostals is simply one more nail in the coffin of secularization theory."[21]

A third observation revolves around the view that researchers ought to take seriously and attempt to explain the world view of Pentecostals based on a theology of the Spirit and the Kingdom of God. Whereas theologians may find this odd (i.e., taking seriously the theology of a group to account for its activities), this is quite novel among sociologists and the long-standing tradition of explaining away the role of religion or reducing it to some sort of delusional behavior sectarian stance, material deprivation, or market demand.

Reorganization

In the 1970s and 1980s, much attention was given to questions of congregational growth and decline – attention that stemmed from the discovery that mainline Protestant churches were declining while conservative Protestant churches were growing. For example, Dean M. Kelley's book *Why Conservative Churches are Growing* offered an explanation that also sparked controversy.[22] Kelley argued that conservative churches were growing because they offered their members a clear sense of purpose, whereas liberal churches were declining because they did not. Conservative churches were strong because they were strict and placed high demands on their members. Liberal churches were weak and declining for the opposite reasons. Kelley's ideas were critically evaluated and tested in a series of studies on church growth and decline over the next decade as sociologists attempted to understand what was happening. For example, in *Understanding Church Growth and Decline* the contributors explored in detail why conservative churches were growing, the future of the churches, the role of pastors, and the demographic and contextual factors that shape growth and decline.[23] The relationship between demographic changes and church growth/decline was given much attention and became an important area of investigation. It was not the only factor discussed but proved to be an important one.

One of the influential studies to link social change and growth and decline issues with a congregational study was R. Stephen Warner's *New Wine in Old Wineskins*.[24] Warner examined the transition in a mainline congregation from more liberal views and leadership to a more conservative and evangelical style of leadership with pronounced growth as a result. Interestingly, Warner's work contributed to an important shift in the 1990s among sociologists to make the congregation the central unit of analysis in American religion. Warner argued that a paradigm shift was needed in the sociology of religion, a shift that placed emphasis on the flexibility of religious organizations in an open market.[25] Furthermore, Warner argued for research on congregations to illustrate the relationship between adaptability and flexibility as well as the central role of congregations in American life.

The narrative of religious reorganization is related to social change and congregational/church issues. The main point of the narrative is that with the advent of the modern world, religion is reorganized and takes new forms. Under the "old paradigm," religion is associated with state forms, official expressions, denominations, and generally the end of religion. Robert Wuthnow, in the *Restructuring of American Religion*, describes some of these changes and explores a series of questions around the end of denominationalism, the growth of small groups, and the role of congregations.[26] Wuthnow identified a variety of resources or "capital" that sustained congregations, giving them the ability to make cultural contributions to society including social, cultural, emotional, and spiritual. These resources included social capital, which referred to congregational activities that brought people together as they shared their lives with each other in personal and intimate ways while establishing strong bonds. Healthy congregations relied on social capital to generate trust in relationships with each other.

Cultural capital referred to congregational activities such as singing, learning, and performing music. Members of congregations produce culture, which in turn shapes those who participate in them. Cultural capital contributes to the identity of congregations or the fairly consistent ways in which people think, feel, and act. Healthy congregations are resourced through important shared cultural activities. Emotional capital referred to the ways in which members expressed feelings, encouraged sharing of personal problems, provided emotional support, and shared life experiences. Emotional capital is likewise an important resource for healthy congregations and also includes the ways in which members negotiate conflict and difference and learn to forgive. Spiritual capital focused on group activities revolving around worship, praying, reading scripture, meditating, fasting, discussing faith, and reflecting. Spiritual capital is an important resource available for congregations as they work through some important challenges and opportunities.

Whereas earlier research focused on the growth and decline of denominations, a new call was made to examine the reorganization of religion and the emergence of congregations as the central organizing principle of American religion. Congregations had many kinds of resources to adapt to social change, and understanding the ecological relationship between congregations and communities required detailed attention. The growth of congregational studies in America is illustrative of this narrative, and many studies have focused on pentecostal and charismatic congregations as adaptive and flexible local communities utilizing the kinds of capital discussed earlier to meet the needs of local communities.[27]

A good example of sociological research on a neo-pentecostal congregation is the work of Gerardo Marti and his book *Hollywood Faith: Holiness, Prosperity, and Ambition in a Los Angeles Church*.[28] Marti's work highlights the various assumptions of congregational studies and how congregations illustrate the ability of religion to adapt to social change. In particular, Marti examines a neo-pentecostal congregation located in Hollywood. The congregation is multicultural with 2,000 members, mostly involved in the entertainment industry. Marti shows how the congregation assists its members by accommodating to the entertainment industry through music styles, technology, and attempts at sanctifying the entertainment industry, and by serving people who have succeeded or failed in the business. The result is a fascinating read of the ways in which the neo-pentecostal message of prosperity facilitates the accommodation and adaptation process for Americans seeking a career in the entertainment industry.

Individualization
The fourth narrative in the sociology of religion is individualization. This particular narrative highlights the autonomy of the individual and the

proclivity for spirituality over religious organization. What characterizes research in this area is the role of the individual who pragmatically self selects in an eclectic fashion, often from a variety of religious beliefs and practices, a form of religion. The primary focus here is the relationship between religion and the individual, spirituality, personal experience, religion as therapeutic, identity, the body, and the construction of the self.

Danièle Hervieu-Léger is one of the key sociologists to capture this shift in her book *Religion as a Chain of Memory*.[29] Unlike secularization or market model theorists or congregational studies, Hervieu-Léger attempts to redefine religion in late modernity or what some might call postmodernity. One of the major problems of late modernity, argues Hervieu-Léger, is that social life is fragmented with one consequence being that people have no memory of a religious past yet are still attempting to address questions of meaning. Late modernity contributes to a new religious response to the social worlds people inhabit, not the end of religion as some secularization proponents argue. However, religious revitalization does not necessarily mean a return to a previous organizational form. Rather a new space is opened up for dealing with the questions surrounding the nature of modern social life and the role of religion. So, while the older ways of doing religion disappear and more people lose memory of the past, the modern world creates a need for spirituality and a new space opens up that religion fills.

Hervieu-Léger's work is important, and yet few scholars of Pentecostalism have picked up on her ideas. One in particular is David Lyon, who explores the shift from modernity to postmodernity.[30] Although Hervieu-Léger does not use the term postmodernity, Lyon argues that her description of contemporary social life fits well his view of postmodernity. What Lyon offers is an exceptional study of religion and postmodernity with a focus on the contemporary charismatic movement, particularly the so-called Toronto Blessing, as he illustrates how this new movement captures postmodern sensibilities.

In his book *Jesus in Disneyland*,[31] Lyon says postmodern society is characterized by an emphasis on personal spiritual authority as opposed to doctrine, church, religious leaders, or historical/traditional elements. The "self" is the reference point for one's spirituality. Two qualities characterize postmodern religion: consumption, whereby one shops for religion, and experience, which is highly therapeutic. The primary example of Lyon's analysis is the Toronto Blessing. In the early 1990s renewal meetings saw thousands of people from all across Europe and

North America coming to Toronto in what was described as either a genuine transformative experience of the Father's love or worse, a mass case of hysteria. Lyon employs important concepts to show how the charismatic movement deconstructs notions of religion by appropriating a more deregulated, constantly moving, new meaning system with its focus on the therapeutic. Charismatic Christianity is successful because it navigates people through massive social and cultural change, providing signs for pilgrims searching for direction in a postmodern world.[32]

All of these narratives have developed along important intellectual networks. Some of them are more organized with key scholars and have developed sustained research programs. In many ways, they all are linked to the sociological issues of the twentieth century, notably the nature of modern life, secularization (as decline, loss of authority, rationalization, or innovation), and the role of religion (sectarian, growing, strong, local, experiential). Likewise, pentecostal studies and sociologists who have studied Pentecostalism have picked up on these themes in numerous ways. However, much of the sociology of Pentecostalism is still dominated by secularization and market narratives. In spite of the pluralization of narratives, there remains a stronghold in these two areas. Yet, very interesting research is facilitating our understanding of congregations as important resources for Pentecostals. Very little sustained research has examined the nature of Pentecostalism from a postmodern perspective.

THE DEVELOPMENT OF GLOBALIZATION AS A SOCIOLOGICAL NARRATIVE AND THE IMPLICATIONS FOR PENTECOSTAL STUDIES

Globalization represents another important theoretical development especially since the 1990s. However, this does not mean there is a single coherently developed research agenda focusing on its application to Pentecostalism. This is not surprising because there is no single theory of globalization and there is considerable debate about when globalization began, who if anyone is responsible for it, whether it means new freedoms or injustice, if it is stoppable, or if something is gained or lost. Furthermore, there are questions about whether or not it is possible for a narrative of global society to offer a new story that substantially moves scholars beyond the classic secularization theme or the market story. From this perspective, the developments of religion in North America and Europe are simply diffused throughout the world without considering the ways in which religion generally and Pentecostalism particularly adapts to local contexts.

There are some important ways in which sociologists have examined globalization focusing on its economic, political, and cultural features.[33] Religion, when discussed, is often referred to as a form of protest against the capitalist system, a political protest group typically studied as fundamentalism, or a cultural resource and often a globalizer. Some studies examine the impact of migration as religions move from one location to another contributing to social change, pluralization, and religious change.[34] In many cases there is a lack of theoretical sophistication about globalization and Pentecostals especially when global is referenced solely with worldwide growth. The result is that any discussion about Pentecostalism as a global movement often means it is everywhere, but globalization is far more than the range or scope of space across the planet.[35] Globalization also calls researchers of Pentecostalism to pay attention to how it is transformed across cultures, including North America, where increasingly it is shaped by hybridization.[36]

In conclusion, I offer the following observations for the development of pentecostal studies rooted in the theoretical debates about globalization. First, globalization is about the worldwide spread of modern structures like modes of production, governance, knowledge, and cultural identities. Peter Beyer argues that a religion system (or ways of being religious including a variety of religious forms) is also spreading.[37] However, these various structures are not developing evenly and in many ways are adapting to local contexts referred to as glocalization by Roland Robertson.[38] In many cases, especially at the level of cultural identities and religion, the process of globalization contributes to hybrid forms. A globalization optic assumes the following for pentecostal studies. First, Pentecostalism in global society takes a variety of forms – hence, the idea of many Pentecostalisms. Second, the varieties of Pentecostalism are often placed side by side creating some conflict about the nature of Pentecostalism, which raises questions about what Pentecostals believe and what they practice or orthodoxy and orthopraxy. These issues are also matters of authority; who gets to say who is a pentecostal and who is not, or who is in or out. Finally, sociologists of global Pentecostalism must provide detailed, empirically and historically rich descriptions of Pentecostalism that comparatively account for sameness and difference across the globe. This also includes the impact of globalization on North America and Europe to understand the changing nature of Pentecostalism in our contemporary world.

Notes

1 Grace Davie, "The Evolution of the Sociology of Religion: Themes and Variations," in Michele Dillon, ed., *Handbook of the Sociology of Religion* (Cambridge, UK: Cambridge University Press, 2003), 61–75.

2 Meredith B. McGuire, *Religion: The Social Context*, 5th ed. (Belmont, CA: Wadsworth Thomson, 2002). See ch. 8 coauthored by McGuire and Spickard.

3 Randall Collins, *The Sociology of Philosophies: A Global Theory of Intellectual Change* (Cambridge, MA: Harvard University Press, 2000).

4 Christian Smith, *Moral, Believing Animals: Human Personhood and Culture* (New York: Oxford University Press, 2003).

5 Max Weber, *Economy and Society*, 2 vols. (Berkeley: University of California Press, 1978).

6 Max Weber, *The Protestant Ethic and the Spirit of Capitalism* (New York: Charles Scribner's Sons, 1958).

7 Max Weber, *Economy and Society*, vol. 1, 241.

8 Thomas O'Dea, "Five Dilemmas in the Institutionalization of Religion," *Journal for the Scientific Study of Religion* 1 (1961), 30–39.

9 For a classic historical example, see Robert M. Anderson, *Vision of the Disinherited: The Making of American Pentecostalism* (New York: Oxford University Press, 1979).

10 David Martin, *A General Theory of Secularization* (New York: Harper & Row, 1978).

11 David Martin, *Pentecostalism: The World Their Parish* (Oxford, UK: Blackwell, 2002).

12 David Martin, *Tongues of Fire: The Explosion of Protestantism in Latin America* (Oxford, UK: Blackwell, 1990).

13 Margaret Poloma, *The Assemblies of God at the Crossroads: Charisma and Institutional Dilemmas* (Knoxville: University of Tennessee Press, 1989).

14 Margaret Poloma and John Green, *The Assemblies of God: Godly Love and the Revitalization of American Pentecostalism* (New York: New York University Press, 2010).

15 Poloma and Green, *The Assemblies of God*, 47.

16 Rodney Stark and Roger Finke, *Acts of Faith: Explaining the Human Side of Religion* (Berkeley: University of California Press, 2000).

17 Roger Finke and Rodney Stark, *The Churching of America, 1776–1990: Winners and Losers in Our Religious Economy* (New Brunswick, NJ: Rutgers University Press, 1993).

18 Rodney Stark, "Secularization, R.I.P.," *Sociology of Religion* 3 (1999), 249–73.

19 Steve Bruce, "Christianity in Britain, R.I.P.," *Sociology of Religion* 2 (2001), 191–203.

20 Donald E. Miller and Tetsunao Yamamori, *Global Pentecostalism: The New Face of Christian Social Engagement* (Berkeley: University of California Press, 2007).

21 Miller and Yamamori, *Global Pentecostalism*, 37.

22 Dean M. Kelley, *Why Conservative Churches Are Growing* (New York: Harper, 1972).

23 Dean R. Hoge and David A. Roozen, *Understanding Church Growth and Decline: 1950–1978* (Cleveland: Pilgrim Press, 1979).
24 R. Stephen Warner, *New Wine in Old Wineskins: Evangelicals and Liberals in a Small-Town Church* (Berkeley: University of California Press, 1988).
25 R. Stephen Warner, "Work in Progress Toward a New Paradigm for the Sociological Study of Religion in the United States," *American Journal of Sociology* 5 (1993), 1044–93.
26 Robert Wuthnow, *The Restructuring of American Religion: Society and Faith since World War II* (Princeton: Princeton University Press, 1990).
27 For European developments similar to congregational studies, see the work in empirical theology, especially Mark J. Cartledge, *Testimony in the Spirit: Rescripting Ordinary Pentecostal Theology* (Surrey, England: Ashgate, 2010).
28 Gerardo Marti, *Hollywood Faith: Holiness, Prosperity, and Ambition in a Los Angeles Church* (New Brunswick, NJ: Rutgers University Press, 2008).
29 Danièle Hervieu-Léger, *Religion as a Chain of Memory* (New Brunswick, NJ: Rutgers University Press, 2000).
30 David Lyon, *Jesus in Disneyland: Religion in Postmodern Times* (Cambridge, UK: Polity Press, 2000).
31 Lyon, *Jesus in Disneyland.*
32 For comparison, see Margaret Poloma, *Main Street Mystics: The Toronto Blessing and Reviving Pentecostalism* (Walnut Creek, CA: Altamira Press, 2003), that deals with some issues raised from a postmodern perspective but is still shaped by issues of institutionalization.
33 Malcolm Waters, *Globalization*, 2nd ed. (New York: Routledge, 2001).
34 Peggy Levitt, *God Needs No Passport: Immigrants and the Changing American Religious Landscape* (New York: New Press, 2007); Michael Wilkinson, *The Spirit Said Go: Pentecostal Immigrants in Canada* (New York: Peter Lang, 2006).
35 Michael Wilkinson, "What's 'Global' about Global Pentecostalism?" *Journal of Pentecostal Theology* 17 (2008), 96–109.
36 Michael Wilkinson, "Religion and Global Flows," in Peter Beyer and Lori Beaman, eds., *Globalization, Religion and Culture* (Leiden, Netherlands: Brill Academic Books, 2007), 375–89.
37 Peter Beyer, *Religions in Global Society* (New York: Routledge, 2006).
38 Roland Robertson, *Globalization: Social Theory and Global Culture* (London: Sage, 1992).

Further Reading

Corten, Andre, and Ruth R. Marshall-Fratani, eds. *Between Babel and Pentecost: Transnational Pentecostalism in Africa and Latin America.* Bloomington: Indiana University Press, 2001.
Lehmann, David. *The Struggle for the Spirit: Religious Transformation and Popular Culture in Brazil and Latin America.* Cambridge: Polity Press, 1996.

Soothill, Jane E., *Gender, Social Change and Spiritual Power: Charismatic Christianity in Ghana*. Leiden: Brill, 2007.

Stålsett, Sturla J., ed. *Spirits of Globalization: The Growth of Pentecostalism and Experiential Spiritualities in a Global Age*. London: SCM Press, 2006.

Steigenga, Timothy J., and Edward L. Cleary, eds. *Conversions of a Continent: Contemporary Religious Change in Latin America*. New Brunswick, NJ: University of Rutgers Press, 2007.

12 Pentecostal Spirituality

DANIEL E. ALBRECHT AND EVAN B. HOWARD

Pentecostalism is a renewal movement that emphasizes the experience of God.[1] Certainly, Pentecostals reflect on theology. Certainly, Pentecostals maintain structures of ecclesiastical life. However, what is most distinctive about Pentecostals is not their theology or their ecclesiastical structure, but rather their sense of the experience of God. This being the case, it is appropriate to identify Pentecostalism particularly as a form of "spirituality."

Christian *spirituality* speaks of the lived experience of faith. Whereas theology examines our understanding of God, spirituality considers our more encompassing experience of God. [2] Christian spirituality has taken many different forms throughout the history of the church. We can, for example, speak of Methodist spirituality, Carmelite spirituality, Reformed spirituality, and pentecostal spirituality. Each community experiences God in a manner appropriate to its history and culture. For Pentecostals, however, the relationship between the tradition and spirituality is particularly significant, because both the identity of the tradition and the nature of spirituality as a field of interest are similarly focused on the lived experience of God. Pentecostalism is a movement of the *Spirit*, and spirituality is fundamentally about life in the Holy *Spirit*. More than a collection of kindred denominations and organizations, more than breakthrough of doctrine, Pentecostalism is a spiritual movement, a movement united in its experience of "life in the Spirit."

But just what is pentecostal spirituality? What does lived relationship with God look like for a pentecostal congregation, or for individual pentecostal Christians, or for the pentecostal-charismatic movement as a whole? These are the questions we intend to address in this chapter. In the first part we will provide an overview of pentecostal spirituality by looking at their beliefs, practices, sensibilities, and values. Then in the second part of the chapter we will consider more closely the character of Pentecostalism as a form of "renewal." We will look at the themes of restoration and continuity in the history of the pentecostal-charismatic movements. Do Pentecostals understand their own experience of God as a restoration of a divine-human relationship lost for centuries, or is it merely a matter of a renewal of aspects of spirituality that have always been present in some form throughout the history of the church? Reflection on this particular question will bring us around again to a final summary of what is most distinctive or characteristic of pentecostal spirituality as a whole.

PART ONE: AN OVERVIEW OF PENTECOSTAL SPIRITUALITY

Relationship with God incorporates various elements that shape the character of that relationship. There are *beliefs* that condition our view of God and our approach to the work of God in our lives. There are *practices*, both corporate and private, that serve as vehicles through which relationship with God is mediated and which contribute to the experience of God itself. There are *sensibilities*, habitual attitudes, or capacities for being affected in certain ways, which predispose a given community to notice or respond to the Spirit of God in a distinct manner. And then there are *values* that govern our sense of what is important to notice, to experience, or to do. By reviewing these four elements we can acquire an overall sense of what the spirituality of Pentecostalism is like.

BELIEFS

Chapter 13 of the present volume is devoted to a treatment of pentecostal theology, summarizing the "state of the art" of recent pentecostal theological research. Consequently, we will touch lightly on beliefs, drawing attention to four aspects of doctrine that directly influence pentecostal spirituality. These aspects express a fourfold devotion to Jesus Christ as Savior, Spirit Baptizer, Healer, and Coming King (fivefold if Sanctifier is distinguished from Jesus' roles as Savior and Spirit Baptizer).

By proclaiming Christ as Savior, Pentecostalism stands alongside evangelical and revivalist Protestantism, emphasizing the importance of conversion as entrance into the Christian life. For these, Christianity is not a matter of mere doctrinal precision, denominational allegiance, or religious duty. The Christian faith is about a fundamental conversion to Jesus Christ and an experience of the regenerating work of the Holy Spirit. For example, both Aimee Semple McPherson, a pentecostal evangelist and Don Gelpi, a Catholic charismatic theologian, place conversion at the forefront of pentecostal spirituality.[3]

For Pentecostals, however, Jesus Christ is not only the Savior but also the Spirit-Baptizer and Sanctifier. The Spirit of Christ is not merely a quiet presence received through regeneration but an active force experienced on an ongoing basis as a result of their immersion in the Spirit. While many Pentecostals emphasize the "subsequent" character of this experience of the Holy Spirit after initial conversion to Christ, others interpret further experiences of the Spirit as the natural working-out of what was worked-in through regeneration. The point in either case is that Pentecostals expect the Holy Spirit to speak to them, to touch their hearts through strong emotions, to reveal something of God to them through ideas and pictures that come to their minds or through dreams, to pray through them in sighs, groans, and in unknown languages, and to transform them ever more closely in holiness to the image of Christ.

Pentecostals also expect Christ to Heal. The Jesus who healed those who came to him with their infirmities on earth is the same Jesus who heals those who come to him today. Pentecostals interpret the coming of Christ and the Spirit as an infusion (or perhaps "invasion") of the supernatural kingdom of God into this world. Through the work of Christ and the Holy Spirit, people can be delivered from disease, spiritual oppression, strongholds of sin, and unnecessary suffering. This doctrine profoundly shapes their experience of God on a day-to-day basis.

Finally, Pentecostals anticipate Jesus's soon return as the Coming King. Pentecostalism emerged in the late nineteenth century amid a great deal of millennial interest. At that time, conferences on holiness, healing, and the return of Christ were often sponsored by the same organizations, attended by the same people, and welcomed the same preachers. A deep longing for power – victorious power over sin and power for effective witness – characterized the spiritual heart of many. When they experienced the power of God in the pentecostal revivals of the early twentieth century, many Pentecostals saw this as an "end times" restoration of the church. Consequently, their hope for divine encounter, healing, and powerful experience of God was fueled not only by doctrines of conversion, the Spirit, and healing but also by a belief in the soon coming of Christ.

PRACTICES

When we speak of pentecostal *practices* we mean, for example, the way pentecostal Christians worship and the way they perform their personal devotions – in short, those behaviors and activities that characterize their lived relationship with God. Some of these practices, such as the act of singing or Bible reading, are common to other Christians. Others, such as praying in tongues, are more distinctive to Pentecostalism.

We begin with corporate practice because that is where Pentecostals begin. Oliver McMahan writes: "Pentecostals and charismatics focus much of their activity within the worship setting of the church. Spirituality is frequently defined within the context of a church service more than a devotional closet."[4] A pentecostal worship service is "ground zero" for examining pentecostal corporate practice and, consequently, pentecostal spirituality. Although terms such as "rite" or "liturgy" may not be common among Pentecostals, they are very helpful for describing the elements and structure of pentecostal corporate spiritual practice, and we will use them here. The term "liturgy" designates a larger set of rites and practices as a whole, for example, the entire pentecostal Sunday service or evangelistic meeting. "Rites," then, are the particular practices or sets of practices and actions that transpire within liturgy. The giving of a prophetic "word" or the taking of an offering would be considered individual rites within the larger context of the liturgy of a gathering.

A flexible threefold structure often frames pentecostal services, revealing what we might call "foundational rites" or "macro-rites": worship in praise, pastoral message, and the altar service.[5] The term "worship" for Pentecostals with reference to a time of meeting generally identifies the first half hour or so of their gatherings. This portion of the service (called the "song service" or "preliminaries" in early pentecostal parlance) both lifts the congregants toward God in adoration and prepares their hearts for the hearing of the Word. Song, movement, and exclamations of praise are typical within the macro-rite of praise. The second macro-rite is a time of "Word." Here, the reading of Scripture and the sermon is primary, but other word-rites also appear in this portion of the service: testimonies, prayers, and the delivering of prophetic utterances are common examples. Indeed, regarding the latter, it has been said that if Martin Luther restored the "priesthood" of all believers, Pentecostals have restored the "prophethood" of all believers, emphasizing the universal availability of a direct revelation of God for the gathered body of believers.[6] The third macro-rite is the altar service. This portion of the service functions as a rite that calls for the response of the people and provides an opportunity for those who wish to have their needs met in a tangible way. As with their Holiness movement predecessors, Pentecostals make use of the altar area, or front section of the sanctuary, as a sacred space where conversion, reconciliation, healing, deliverance, and other forms of "doing business with God" are transacted.

Within this threefold macro-rite structure, a number of particular rites or practices are commonly performed, practices that are distinctive of pentecostal spirituality. There might be a minute or so of "singing in tongues" that arises during the macro-rite of praise. Or perhaps one might see the raising of hands or a few people "dancing in the Spirit." As mentioned, one might offer a prophetic utterance following the sermon, or perhaps a "word": a report (based on an intuitive perception of the activity of the Holy Spirit) that, for example, there are people present in this gathering who might be in need of prayer for some want. As the service moves to a time of response around the altar, it is common to see Pentecostals laying a hand on another as an expression of the ministry of healing. A person receiving prayer might experience being "slain in the Spirit" in which his or her body weakens and God is encountered more directly. What makes these individual practices or rites particularly "Pentecostal" or "Charismatic" is that they are perceived as anticipations of or responses to the active presence of the Holy Spirit. For example, liturgical dance becomes distinctly "Charismatic" when the dancers perceive the impulse of the Spirit or the congregation recognizes the Spirit's presence in or through the dance. Many of these smaller micro-rites should be considered "moveable parts" in pentecostal corporate spiritual practice, because their expression can appropriately appear in a number of places in the course of the pentecostal liturgy.

Sooner or later, the gathered service ends and people return home to their personal devotions. However, the corporate and the personal are exceptionally difficult to isolate in pentecostal spirituality. Individuals take the meeting home with them. What is experienced in community is developed in private. What is discovered in private is brought to the meeting next week. Nevertheless, a couple of practices characteristic of pentecostal personal spirituality deserve mention here.

One of the most distinctive practices of pentecostal spirituality is the practice of *glossolalia*, also known as "speaking in tongues," or "praying in the Spirit." Having scriptural roots primarily in passages in the book of Acts and in 1 Corinthians, tongues is a form of prayer in which one speaks (or, at times, merely "thinks") in a language unknown to the one praying, perhaps unknown to anyone. The apostle Paul speaks of tongues in terms of "the spirit praying" while the mind is "unproductive" (1 Corinthians 14:14), a description that appears to be suggestively supported in recent studies of cerebral activity during glossolalia.[7] For many Pentecostals, the practice of praying in tongues permits a unique expression of spiritual intimacy, as deep unconscious material flows through their "prayer language" to and from God.

Another practice that has received attention among Pentecostals is *fasting*. Even though fasting is not limited to the pentecostal community, Pentecostals have preserved a particular use of fasting that is rare these days, although it was common among Puritans and other Protestants from the seventeenth through the nineteenth centuries. Whereas fasting often has functioned, especially among Catholic and Orthodox Christians, as an ascetical practice oriented toward the purification of desire, Pentecostals see the restriction of food, following the lead of Old Testament portraits of fasting (with a nod to Acts 13:1), as a way of expressing an intensity of the pursuit of God. When Pentecostals get serious about desiring something from God, they fast, often for days at a time. This is true with regards to their personal devotions, and it is especially true of seasons of united prayer for a Holy Spirit revival. From Franklin Hall's *Atomic Power through Prayer and Fasting* (1946), to Derek Prince's *Shaping History through Prayer and Fasting* (1973), to Lou Engle and Catherine Paine's *Fast Forward: A Call to the Millennial Prayer Revolution* (1999), Pentecostals have made seasons of "prayer and fasting" an important part of their pursuit of God. Through fasting they offer concrete expressions of the longing for more of the Holy Spirit's influence in their lives.

SENSIBILITIES AND VALUES

By "sensibilities" we refer to certain habitual attitudes or predispositions that characterize a Pentecostal's relationship with God. By "values" we identify those concerns that are perceived as most important to Pentecostals. Sensibilities and values cannot be neatly separated: the pentecostal value for experience, for example, is lived out by means of a concretely trained sensitivity toward experience in both corporate and personal devotion. However artificial the categorization, it may help our understanding of pentecostal spirituality to describe a few of these sensibilities and values.

Pentecostal spirituality is hardwired to perceive and respond to the influences of the Holy Spirit. For example, if we examine the dynamics of pentecostal liturgy, it is possible to identify a number of distinct modes of sensibility present, many of which are oriented around the work of the Holy Spirit. There is a mode of celebration, characterized by spontaneity and expressiveness within the Spirit. There is a mode of contemplation, a "waiting on" or "being open to" the in the midst of the gathering. There is a mode of ecstasy, when the Holy Spirit moves and one experiences a flood of the Spirit's influence. And there is a mode of improvisation, following the Spirit's guidance from one moment of the gathering to the next. All of these "modes" of presence in a gathering are habitual attitudes, sensitivities embodied in the pentecostal worship or evangelistic service. Although these ways of being present in a worship gathering are not exclusive to Pentecostals, they are together demonstrative of a characteristically pentecostal relationship with God.[8]

More particularly, we can speak of the *orientation to experience* as a pentecostal sensitivity. The practice of repeating worship choruses for extended periods of time, the language of "worship" as being almost synonymous with entering into an experienced sense of the "presence of God," the oral (rather than written) character of pentecostal interaction, and the centrality of the baptism in the Holy Spirit, are only a few examples of this sensitivity built into the pentecostal mind and heart.

Another pentecostal sensitivity is their *faith* or *expectation* of God. Faith, or the expectation that God can or will heal/deliver/transform is quite common among Pentecostals. Within a gathering, this sensitivity can be seen in a mode of divine efficacy present in portions of the service, particularly in the altar service at the end of the gathering. Some branches of Pentecostalism (for example, the so-called faith churches) have identified themselves particularly around this sensitivity, emphasizing the value of understanding biblical principles and then of developing the "skills" of placing confident faith in those principles, thus assuring their concrete fulfillment in life.

Attention to the Holy Spirit is another pentecostal sensitivity. Whereas many capable Reformed Christians have developed the cognitive ability to notice the logical nuances of the Scriptures, capable Pentecostals have similarly developed an affective ability to notice the nuances of the Spirit. The New Testament speaks of the Holy Spirit leading, filling, convicting, comforting, and encouraging Christ's people. There is, in pentecostal culture, a kind of radical receptivity to this activity of the Spirit, a softness to changes in intuition and feeling that indicate the direction of the winds of the Spirit. Along with this attention to the Spirit more generally, there is specifically among Pentecostals an orientation toward the gifts of the Spirit, in particular the more demonstrative or "miraculous" gifts: tongues, prophecy, healing, miracles, and the like.

Another pentecostal sensitivity – or perhaps more accurately a pentecostal predisposition – is their sense of conflict or *spiritual warfare*. Pentecostals take the battle imagery of the Scriptures seriously.

It is simply part of their world view, especially in the Global South. Pentecostals see themselves as players on a battlefield of cosmic proportions. L. Grant McClung writes: "A review of the literature, history and oral stories of Pentecostalism reveal the centrality of the practice of exorcism in the expansion of the pentecostal and charismatic movements."[9] Although Pentecostals agree generally on the reality of the demonic, the need for sensitivity to spiritual warfare, and the power of God to deliver them from the clutches of Satan, there is a diversity of opinion regarding the particulars of demonology and the strategies for confronting evil spirits.

We can also consider the self-perception of Pentecostals as part of a *movement* (rather than a denomination or organization or religious society) as a sensibility of pentecostal spirituality. Although many early Pentecostals in America ultimately formed denominations (e.g., Assemblies of God), more significant was their own self-perception as participants in a work of the Spirit on this earth. While it has been common among Westerners to interpret Pentecostalism as a development of the Azusa Street Revival in Los Angeles in 1906, it is now proper to understand the origins of Pentecostalism as the emergence of kindred phenomena and interests globally. As Allan Anderson states, "there were revivals all over the world unconnected with North American Pentecostalism."[10] Pentecostals have tended to see themselves as part of "something big." Consequently, they behave less as an ecclesiastical structure and more as a cultural movement. Needless to say, this kind of a self-perception has implications for their spirituality, for example, in their sense of being in the center of and cooperating with God's renewing activity on earth.

In addition to the sensibilities of pentecostal spirituality, we can also identify a few basic values that guide or govern the way that Pentecostals conduct their relationship with God corporately and personally. Whereas some pentecostal values are characteristic of evangelical Protestantism more generally (for example, respect for Biblical authority), others are more characteristic of the pentecostal community.

The first of these is the importance of the *supernatural* and of the "power" of God. Immediately prior to the pentecostal revivals, Christians were eagerly seeking the power of God: power for abundant living, power for victory over sin, power for effective witness to the world. In the experience of the baptism in the Spirit, Pentecostals found that power. It is not a matter of denying the place of the natural, but rather of intentionally placing a focus on what is believed to be the supernatural.

A second value is the pentecostal value for *restoration*. Whether they speak of "revival," "renewal," or "restoration," Pentecostals emphasize God as a Restorer. Holiness Pentecostals emphasize the role of Christ entirely cleansing us from sin. They see the work of Christ and the Spirit restoring people in a threefold progression: salvation, sanctification, and baptism in the Holy Spirit (the "full gospel"). The value for restoration, combined with the value for the supernatural, serves to heighten pentecostal interest in healing. Whereas some might interpret Pentecostalism as an otherworldly expression of Christianity, Pentecostals in fact have expressed a very "embodied" faith – both through the use of their body in worship as well as in their belief in God's interest in the restoration of the human body through healing. We have discussed the pentecostal sensitivity to spiritual warfare, a sensitivity that is intimately connected with their sense of God's desire to restore Christians from their experiences of oppressiveness. Finally, pentecostal emphasis on restoration also extends to their approach to ordinary human suffering. For example, there is a tendency among some Pentecostals to expect God not only to restore humans from their bondages to sin, sickness, and Satan but also to restore a measure of prosperity to Spirit-filled Christians.[11]

A third pentecostal value is *participation*. Their emphasis on the ministry of the Holy Spirit, and particularly on the place of the gifts of the Spirit, obliges Pentecostals to understand themselves less as an ordered structure and more as a fluid, co-participating organism. God gives gifts to believers for the benefit of the whole body, and there is, along with this understanding, an expectation for believers to participate in the life of the body through the use of their gifts. Leadership in a congregation may arise at any moment as one sister or brother becomes the vehicle for the authoritative word or touch of God in the midst of a gathering. Similarly what Pentecostals term "ministry" commonly happens during the altar service, as people minister to one another in prayer. Ministry also happens as people take on appropriate roles in the local community of faith. As a result of this somewhat fluid recognition and release of others' contributions to the community, Pentecostals have a certain knack for improvisation. The value for participation and their ability to improvise makes Pentecostals particularly able to get things done quickly and adapt to new situations and environments.

Finally, it is important to acknowledge the pentecostal value of *missions*. Pentecostals see God as an empowering and a commissioning God. Once again, this cannot be entirely separated from their interest in restoration, participation, faith, and their sense of themselves as a movement. Their perspective is that the Holy Spirit has made available a new abundance to this world, which Christians are joyfully obliged to share with others. Christ sends them to share this new life with others, and then the Spirit empowers them to demonstrate the reality of this gospel through healing, deliverance, and other signs of the Holy Spirit. It is this value that makes pentecostal mission agencies some of the most strongly supported organizations in the Christian Church today.

Having looked at the beliefs, the practices, and the sensibilities of pentecostal spirituality, we repeat: it is appropriate to interpret Pentecostalism as a form of spirituality. The experience of God is a central part of all that Pentecostals think and do. It frames their beliefs, forms their practices, and informs their sensibilities and values. Whether we consider the dynamics of a pentecostal evangelistic or worship service, the nuances of personal devotion, or their sense of participation with a global movement of God, what is primary for Pentecostals is their consciousness that God has "broken in" to this world through the Spirit of Christ, invading it with an existentially real and tangible encounter with the Lord Jesus Christ himself.

PART TWO: PENTECOSTALISM AND HISTORY: RESTORATION, RENEWAL, OR REVITALIZATION

In this second part of this chapter we will consider more closely the character of pentecostal spirituality by exploring the themes of restoration and renewal. The subject of Christian spirituality has a long history. Yet the history of Pentecostalism is relatively short and is often viewed (particularly within their community) through a "restorationist" lens that highlights their discontinuity with the rest of that history. However, the charismatic movement saw things differently. Thus, the following questions will be examined in this part of the chapter: Should we understand Pentecostalism's experience of God as a radical (even eschatological) restoration of a divine-human relationship lost for centuries? Is it merely a matter of a renewal of aspects of spirituality that have always been present in some form throughout the history of the Church? Or is it something else?

We have already drawn near this topic as we have sketched out our overview of pentecostal spirituality. However, we must probe this issue further. We will divide our presentation into three sections. Under the first section ("Restoration") we will look at this theme from the perspective of the classical pentecostal restorationist lens, which has tended to see Pentecostalism in radical discontinuity with Christian history. Under the second section ("Renewal") we shall see how charismatic movements from 1960 forward saw themselves as part of a rich – although often ignored – history of Spirit-led phenomena. As earlier chapters of this volume demonstrate, strict distinctions of "Pentecostal" and "Charismatic" are problematic, particularly when our viewpoint is taken not simply from the United States but globally. Nonetheless, it is helpful in this case to distinguish two ways of approaching pentecostal-charismatic spirituality vis-à-vis the historic Christian Church and to use the North American history as an illustration of these distinctions. Finally, we shall propose a third term ("Revitalization") to describe more functionally how the pentecostal-charismatic movements have interacted with the traditions from which they have emerged.

RESTORATION: THE CLASSICAL PENTECOSTAL PERSPECTIVE

The first paragraph of the first entry in the first publication (September 1906) of the *Apostolic Faith*, a Los Angeles-based newspaper dedicated to the spread of the pentecostal revival, reads: "The power of God now has this city agitated as never before. Pentecost has truly come and with it the Bible evidences are following, many being converted and sanctified and filled with the Holy Ghost, speaking in tongues as they did on the day of Pentecost." Further in the same page we read:

> The meetings are held in an old Methodist church that had been converted in part into a tenement house, leaving a large, unplastered, barn-like room on the ground floor .... Many churches have been praying for Pentecost, and Pentecost has come. The question is now, will they accept it? God has answered in a way they did not look for. He came in a humble way as of old, born in a manger .... Jesus was too large for the synagogues. He preached outside because there was not room for him inside. This Pentecostal movement is too large to be confined in any denomination or sect. It works outside, drawing all together in one bond of love, one church, one body of Christ.[12]

In these few sentences we can identify a number of characteristics of the restorationist viewpoint of the pentecostal movement's relationship with church history.

The first item to note is the mention of "power." Many Christians have longed for the power of God, but for these Pentecostals power was not simply a blessing from God, but a sign with eschatological significance. Their study of the Scriptures had led them to believe that in the end times God would manifest his presence in a display of power. They believed that they were nearing those end times, and so to witness such an experience of God's power as they encountered in the pentecostal meetings at Azusa Street and elsewhere only confirmed their sense that "this was it!" This was a unique moment in history. The very "agitation" of the city (as never before) suggested the unique significance of the events.

The second item to note is the mention of Pentecost. Pentecost has come. We cannot minimize the importance of the biblical precedent of Acts 2 and 10 and elsewhere. When God wanted to do something new among the people of God, he poured out his Spirit on the people, giving them a powerful experience of himself. Those like Charles Parham and William Seymour, who in the first decade of the twentieth century examined the scriptures for wisdom about the Pentecost they sought, began to see these stories as normative patterns for the church of their time. They began to hope and to pray that God would send his Spirit on the earth as he did at the first Pentecost. And in September 1906 that is what they proclaimed: Pentecost has come. God is restoring the church to its primitive, apostolic purity.

The third point to notice is that Pentecost was confirmed with tangible "evidences": conversions, powerful experiences of sanctification, and moving experiences of being "filled" with the Holy Ghost.[13] Of particular importance was the sign of "speaking in tongues." Pentecostals saw the manifestation of speaking in tongues as a distinct sign of God's restoration of God's people in power to the fullness of the gospel. It has been an important pillar of the pentecostal restorationist perspective from that point on.

A fourth point to note is subtly embedded in the comments included after the first paragraph, such as "will they accept it?" "a humble way," "too large for the synagogues," and "too large to be confined." Restorationists perceived themselves in tension with traditional Christianity from the start. Even though many Pentecostals ended up forming "denominations and sects," their restorationist perspective saw the pentecostal movement as transcending those categories. There are denominations and other ecclesiastical organizations; however, *this* is something else.

Many Pentecostals, however, did not understand this restoration of the church to its primitive purity as a sudden transformation appearing in the twentieth century. Indeed, it was common to describe the restoration of the gospel as a progressive restoration, leading from Wycliffe and Luther (who restored Scripture and justification by faith) through

Wesley (who restored the doctrine of sanctification) and on to the present revival, which was understood to have restored the doctrine of the baptism and gifts of the Spirit. Thus Aimee Semple McPherson, evangelist and founder of the Foursquare, proclaimed in her classic restorationist sermon, "Lost and Restored": "Now the Church had not lost this 'all' at one time. The restoration came . . . as line upon line, precept upon precept, here a little and there a little, till today we are nearing the completion of this Restoration, and Jesus is coming soon to take His perfect Church."[14]

Finally, we should note that while the pentecostal movement saw itself in tension with traditional Christianity, it simultaneously understood itself as a restoration of the *unity* of the church. Through the renewal of the baptism and gifts of the Spirit, God was recollecting his people from all denominations and walks of life. God was inviting Christians of every stripe to join the church of the "full gospel" and was empowering his people to be sent to all parts of the world to usher in the harvest of the last days. It is important to see that the restorationists perceived themselves as a movement of church unity, not division.

RENEWAL: THE CHARISMATIC PERSPECTIVE

The charismatic movement (particularly that expression of it emerging in North America from the 1960s though the 1980s) is usually described as a Holy Spirit movement among mainline churches: Episcopalians, Roman Catholics, Lutherans, and so on. With earlier roots in the Latter Rain Movement, healing revivals, and the Full Gospel Businessmen's Fellowship, the charismatic movement witnessed the influence of the Spirit to populations that were largely unaffected by the earlier pentecostal movement. Charismatics share a number of constant characteristics with their pentecostal forebears: a focus on Jesus, an emphasis on praise, value for Scripture, belief that God speaks today, interest in spiritual gifts, and so on.[15] Nevertheless, when it comes to the self-perception of the movement in terms of their relationship with the historic Christian Church, the charismatic movement differs from classical restorationist Pentecostals. Charismatics generally do not see the outpouring of the Spirit so much as a divine restoring of a primitively pure church, but rather as a "renewal" of elements of spirituality present in the church throughout its history. Indeed, one term frequently used to refer to the charismatic movement is "the renewal." Whereas restorationist Pentecostals emphasized discontinuity with the church, Charismatics highlighted the continuity. The question we must ask to explore that distinction is this: How did the charismatic movement understand their relationship with the history of their own traditions?

The charismatic movement, as a *renewal*, was also a *recovery*. Led by mainline Protestant and Roman Catholic clergy and theologians, the movement was well equipped to examine the evidence for the continuity or the novelty of charismatic phenomena in history. And whereas in the early pentecostal revival a sense of novelty helped spread the movement, wise Charismatics knew that novelty would be viewed as a sign of danger and that documenting continuity would contribute to the spread of the Spirit among their own constituents. Consequently, especially in the 1970s and 1980s, a number of excellent historical surveys of charismatic phenomena were produced.[16]

So what did charismatic explorers discover in their quest for the charismatic in history? Space prevents a full summary of this material here, but we can venture a few comments by way of distinguishing the charismatic from the pentecostal perspectives. First, Charismatics found that they were *not alone*. Healings, tongues, prophetic utterances, and such had been present at various times and places throughout the history of the Christian Church. Often they were found on the fringes: in the monasteries and the groups bordering on heresy. They were clearly present, however, even in the experience and beliefs of some of the most respected Christians in history (like Irenaeus and Francis of Assisi). Furthermore, if they occasionally found spectacular phenomena in history, they encountered the more general pentecostal values and sensibilities (experience, attention to the Spirit, faith/expectation, participation, missions, spiritual warfare, and so on) frequently. Although, for example, attention to conflict with spiritual forces was not common to mainline Christianity of 1970, they found that it was common among desert mothers and fathers, Jesuits, and Puritans. Although the "modernist" world view had dominated the twentieth-century Protestant church with a value for reason and order, Charismatics discovered that a sense of experience (spirituality) was central to many Christians throughout history. A powerful recovery of the history of Christian spirituality gave Charismatics, along with mainline contemplatives and mystics, a sense of confidence in the possibility of an integration of their fresh experience of the living Spirit of Christ with their own historically rooted faith traditions.

A second discovery many Charismatics made in their historical explorations was that not only were they not alone in their experience of the Holy Spirit, but also they were not alone in their sense of living in the Spirit *in tension with their surrounding community*. Struggles between charisma and institution were commonplace in history. [17] Indeed, even the apostle Paul was pressed to reconcile believers struggling with their practice of the charismatic gifts. And yet the values, sensibilities, and practices of pentecostal spirituality would often reappear in times of renewal, when a dry or dead community would discover a new life in Christ. Gifts were not a guarantee of unity, yet they *were* valuable.

As such, the charismatic historical recovery found – and emphasized – a sense of continuity with the historic church. Along with the restorationists, Charismatics saw the experience of the baptism in the Spirit and the exercise of the gifts of the Spirit as a normative standard gloriously reintroduced to the people of God through the work of the Holy Spirit in their day. However, rather than interpreting this outpouring as an eschatological *restoration* of an ideal primitive church, they interpreted the outpouring as a welcome *renewal* of life to communities of faith.

REVITALIZATION: AN ALTERNATIVE UNDERSTANDING

Early restorationist Pentecostals have interpreted themselves through an eschatological paradigm, seeing the message of Pentecost as the expression of an end-time restoration of the primitive and pure Church of Jesus Christ. Later Charismatics utilized theological and church historical paradigms to interpret themselves as supporters of a renewal of neglected but valuable elements of historic Christian spirituality. We would like to propose a third paradigm that may help interpret the pentecostal movement vis-à-vis the larger historic church. Using the language of cultural anthropology, we would like to suggest the idea of "revitalization" as a way of looking at the relationship between the pentecostal movement, the historic church, and the emergence and ongoing development of a new Christian spirituality. [18]

Anthony Wallace's classic anthropological study of revitalization movements provides a useful guide for considering the process of pentecostal revitalization – that is, how the various elements of spirituality from a variety of groups that predated Pentecostalism combined and emerged as something unique. By revitalization we mean *a dynamic process* within which a group of people change by re-visioning and reshaping their understanding and living out of Christian spirituality. [19]

The fulcrum of a revitalization movement is a reformulation of the ways in which a group understands life and the world. Spiritual movements do not emerge in a vacuum; they occur in particular contexts. The worshipping community at Azusa Street and other similar early twentieth-century pentecostal "hot spots" around the globe provided intense social contexts. The sense of solidarity and togetherness produced in these venues were reinforced by rituals, attitudes, and values that increasingly distinguished the community from both the "world" and other strains of Christian spirituality. This unique sense of solidarity (called *communitas*)[20] allowed for the early seekers to participate in a common experience. It functionally democratized the field for all who attended.

Pentecostal experience of *communitas*, in turn, provided an environment that attracted people from different spiritual heritages, allowing them to experiment in the Spirit, sometimes mixing and merging elements of the heritages, which then served as the environment for a re-visioning of spirituality.[21] The people who came to the hot spots experienced the open mix of elements, and in this environment – charged with the Holy Spirit – they were enabled to become something new: to become Pentecostals. Wallace calls this re-visioning "mazeway reformulation." As a group reformulates their way of seeing, being, and understanding life and the world, a new vision of "reality" emerges. Proto-pentecostals experienced this change of "mazeway." The process of reformulating included a new or resynthesis of Christian spirituality. It ushered in a new coherent vision for and experience of spirituality and all of life.

The new configuration – that is, the reformulated spiritual "mazeway" – incorporated a new understanding of life in the Spirit. The notion of the life in the Spirit was "transmuted."[22] In fact, the view of life lived in the Spirit, and the baptism in the Spirit acted as a catalyst for the process of transmutation that brought with it a new vision of Spirit-filled spirituality, a qualitatively different experience.[23] Although we can find references to baptism in the Spirit in history and we find manifestations of tongues there as well, the link that was made by Parham and Seymour was new. Both speaking in tongues and Spirit baptism had been experienced as a part of other spiritualities. The emerging pentecostal spirituality, however, saw these two experiences linked, both part of one experience. This understanding was a new element within their way of conceiving reality, and it affected further changes that modified the constitutive relational structure of their way of relating to God.

Later, Charismatics experienced a similar process of *communitas* and transmuting "mazeway re-formulation." A sense of solidarity in intense communal experiences (welcoming a diverse participation) enabled them to begin to rethink the ways of viewing their faith. Their notion of the Holy Spirit and relationship with the Spirit was transformed (transmuted). While early Pentecostals emphasized their discontinuity with the church and later Charismatics emphasized their continuity, both were reformulating a set of diverse elements into a new, creative whole. Functionally, they were both "revitalization" movements, each being expressed in the contexts of its own place and time.

CONCLUSION

Pentecostal spirituality is about the lived experience of God, in the Spirit of Christ. It is a revitalized vision of the church and its relationship with historic Christianity, emphasizing the dramatic ministry of renewal and restoration that Christ brings to the people of God through the Holy Spirit. It is this experience and this vision that has fueled the expansion of Pentecostalism throughout the globe.

Notes

1 We will refer to all expressions of global pentecostal/charismatic/neo-charismatic or renewalist movements by the term "pentecostal."
2 See Walter Principe, "Toward Defining Spirituality," *Studies in Religion* 12:2 (1983), 127–41; Philip Sheldrake, *Spirituality and Theology: Christian Living and the Doctrine of God* (Maryknoll, NY: Orbis, 1998), 40–64.
3 See Aimee Semple McPherson, *The Foursquare Gospel* (Los Angeles: Echo Park Evangelistic Association, 1946); Donald Gelpi, *Experiencing God: A Theology of Human Emergence* (Lanham, MD: University Press of America, 1987), and *The Conversion Experience: A Reflective Process for RCIA Participants and Others* (Mahwah, NJ: Paulist Press, 1998). For evangelical spirituality more generally see, Evan B. Howard, "Evangelical Spirituality," in Bruce Demarest, ed., *Four Views on Christian Spirituality* (Grand Rapids, MI: Zondervan, 2012), 159–86.
4 Oliver McMahan, "Spiritual Direction in the Pentecostal/Charismatic Tradition," in Gary W. Moon and David G. Benner, eds., *Spiritual Direction and the Care of Souls: A Guide to Christian Approaches and Practices* (Downers Grove, IL: InterVarsity Press, 2004), 152–53.
5 Daniel E. Albrecht, "An Anatomy of Worship: A Pentecostal Analysis," in Wonsuk Ma and Robert Menzies, eds., *The Spirit and Spirituality: Essays in Honor of Russell Spittler* (New York: T & T Clark International, 2004), 70–82. It should be noted that this structure varies globally.
6 See Roger Stronstad, *The Prophethood of All Believers: A Study in Luke's Charismatic Theology* (Cleveland, TN: CTP Press, 2010).
7 For example, Andrew B. Newberg, Nancy A. Wintering, Donna Morgan, and Mark R. Waldman, "The Measurement of Regional Cerebral Blood Flow during Glossolalia: A Preliminary SPECT Study," *Psychiatry Research: Neuroimaging* 148 (2006), 67–71; Andrew Newberg and Mark Robert Waldman, *How God Changes Your Brain* (New York: Ballantine Books, 2009), 49.

8   Daniel Albrecht, "Variations on Themes in Worship: Pentecostal Rites and Improvisations," in Thomas F. Best and Dagmar Heller, eds., *Worship Today: Understanding, Practice, Ecumenical Implications* (Geneva: World Council of Churches Publications, 2004), 139–57.

9   L. Grant McClung, "Pentecostal/Charismatic Understanding of Exorcism," in C. Peter Wagner and F. Douglas Pennoyer, eds., *Wrestling with Dark Angels: Toward a Deeper Understanding of the Supernatural Forces in Spiritual Warfare* (Ventura, CA: Regal Books, 1990), 196.

10   Allan Anderson, "The Future of Protestantism: The Rise of Pentecostalism," in Alister E. McGrath and Darren C. Marks, eds., *The Blackwell Companion to Protestantism* (Malden, MA: Blackwell Publishing, 2007), 439. The Regional Studies in the present volume document this more recent interpretation.

11   Oral Roberts and G. H. Montgomery, eds., *God's Formula for Success and Prosperity* (Gary, IN: Abundant Life Publications, 1966).

12   *The Apostolic Faith (Los Angeles, CA)* 1:1 (September 1906), 1. For a fuller treatment of the Azusa Street Revival, see Cecil M. Robeck, Jr., *The Azusa Street Mission and Revival* (Nashville, TN: Thomas Nelson, 2006), 129–86.

13   This use of biblical and spatial language (e.g., "being filled," "in," "poured out," and so on) as ways of describing existential encounters with God is clarified nicely in M. M. B. Turner, "Spirit Endowment in Luke/Acts: Some Linguistic Considerations," *Vox Evangelica* 12 (1981), 44–63.

14   Aimee Semple McPherson, *This is That: Personal Experiences, Sermons, and Writings* (Los Angeles: Bridal Call Publishing House, 1919), 394–95.

15   For a more thorough treatment of the charismatic movement, see Peter D. Hocken, "Charismatic Movement," in Stanley M. Burgess and Eduard M. van der Maas, eds., *The New International Dictionary of Pentecostal and Charismatic Movements* (Grand Rapids, MI: Zondervan, 2003; rev. and expanded ed.), 477–519.

16   For example, George H. Williams and Edith Waldvogel, "A History of Speaking in Tongues and Related Gifts," in Michael Hamilton, ed., *The Charismatic Movement* (Grand Rapids, MI: Eerdmans, 1975), 61–113; Ronald A. N. Kydd, *Charismatic Gifts in the Early Church* (Peabody, MA: Hendrickson Publishers, 1984); Stanley M. Burgess's research is summarized in "The Holy Spirit, Doctrine of: The Ancient Fathers," "Holy Spirit, Doctrine of: The Medieval Churches," and "Holy Spirit, Doctrine of: Reformation Traditions," in *New International Dictionary of Pentecostal and Charismatic Movements*, 730–69; Kilian McDonnell and George T. Montague, *Christian Initiation and Baptism in the Holy Spirit: Evidence from the First Eight Centuries* (Collegeville, MN: Michael Glazier, 1994).

17   See Hans von Campenhausen, *Ecclesiastical Authority and Spiritual Power*, trans. J. A. Baker (Stanford, CA: Stanford University Press, 1969).

18   For a more detailed explanation of pentecostal spirituality as revitalization, see Daniel E. Albrecht, "Worshiping and the Spirit: Transmuting Liturgy Pentecostally," in Teresa Berger and Bryan D. Spinks, eds., *The Spirit in Worship, Worship in the Spirit* (Collegeville, MN: Liturgical Press, 2009), 223–44.

19   See Anthony F. C. Wallace's seminal work, "Revitalization Movements," *American Anthropologist* 58 (1956), 264–81.

20 See Victor Turner in "Variations on a Theme of Liminality," in Sally F. Moore and Barbara G. Myerhoff, eds., *Secular Ritual* (Amsterdam: Van Gorcum, 1977), 36–52. See also Edith Turner, *Communitas: The Anthropology of Collective Joy* (New York: Palgrave MacMillian, 2012), and Roberto Esposito, *Communitas: The Origin and Destiny of Community*, trans. Timothy Campbell (Stanford: Stanford University Press, 2011).

21 See Grant Wacker, *Heaven Below: Early Pentecostals and American Culture* (Cambridge: Harvard University Press, 2003), 9, on the "mix."

22 On "transmutation," see Don Gelpi, *Grace as Transmuted Experience and Social Process, and Other Essays in North American Theology* (Lanham, MD: University Press of America, 1988), 48.

23 See Donald D. Dayton, *Theological Roots of Pentecostalism* (Peabody, MA: Hendrickson Publishers, 1987), who traced the evolution and shifts in the concept of Spirit baptism in the nineteenth century.

Further Reading

Albrecht, Daniel E. *Rites in the Spirit: A Ritual Approach to Pentecostal/Charismatic Spirituality*. Sheffield: Sheffield Academic Press, 1999.

Burgess, Stanley M. *Peoples of the Spirit: A Documentary History of Pentecostal Spirituality from the Early Church to the Present*. New York: New York University Press, 2011.

Gelpi, Donald L. *Charism and Sacrament: A Theology of Christian Conversion*. New York: Paulist Press, 1993.

Howard, Evan B. *The Brazos Introduction to Christian Spirituality*. Grand Rapids, MI: Brazos Press, 2008.

Land, Steven Jack. *Pentecostal Spirituality: A Passion for the Kingdom*. London: Sheffield Academic Press, 1993.

Lindhardt, Martin, ed. *Practicing the Faith: The Ritual Life of Pentecostal-Charismatic Christians*. New York: Berghahn Books, 2011.

13 Pentecostal Theology

MARK J. CARTLEDGE

INTRODUCTION

The idea of pentecostal theology may seem like an oxymoron to some people: as if Pentecostals actually did theology proper, surely they are just concerned about ecstatic experience? Caricatures abound! Of course, it all depends on what we mean by theology, where it might be found, and by whom it is expressed. This essay acknowledges that within Pentecostalism, and even within broader Christianity for that matter, there are a variety of different kinds of theologies (ways of "speaking about God") addressing similar concerns in different ways. Some theologies focus on the horizon of the biblical text, others select a tradition within history and seek to retrieve it for today, while others focus on the contemporary horizon and seek to address issues of justice or ecclesial practice, sometimes with a revisionist agenda. Very often these different emphases combine because they are hardly ever exclusive. Walter J. Hollenweger famously argued that Pentecostals did not do theology in a standard Western mode but via songs, poems, testimonies, and dances.[1] In this way, he focused on the oral nature of theology as distinct from the literary forms of theology. This point has been well made and it is certainly the case that ordinary or everyday theology continues to reflect these modes. However, it is also the case that pentecostal denominations codified their theological beliefs in dogmatic statements of faith or in statements of fundamental truths, and these statements form a reading tradition within which theologizing occurs.

In recent years there has been an explosion of pentecostal theological scholarship, including attempts at articulating pentecostal and charismatic theology from a more systematic direction.[2] There are now various theological monograph series published by Brill, Deo, Eerdmans, and Paternoster, as well as a number of journals. This scholarship connects the ordinary spirituality of the pentecostal and charismatic movements with denominational and early pentecostal traditions and seeks to engage in a critical dialogue with broader Christian traditions and contemporary thought. It is this latter form of theology that forms the focus of this study. In other words, the aim of this essay is to sketch out the contours of recent pentecostal scholarship to define and describe the "state of the art" and suggest possible future trajectories. It does not seek to be exhaustive because, given the limitation of space, that is impossible, but it does seek to identify key thinkers in the field and illustrate their contribution. It will therefore focus on key monographs and full-length studies in the main. To achieve this aim, this essay will consider the areas of (1) biblical hermeneutics and theological method, (2) history and tradition, (3) culture and society, and (4) experience and practice. It will then conclude by making some critical observations and suggestions for possible future trajectories.

BIBLICAL HERMENEUTICS AND THEOLOGICAL METHOD

Pentecostal and charismatic scholars have largely inherited a commitment to treat the text of Scripture as both sacred (inspired by the Holy Spirit and thus carrying the authority of God) and relevant to contemporary life and witness. Thus engagement with Scripture is not just an intellectual exercise for the sake of extrapolating true propositions but a dynamic interaction with a living Word through which the Holy Spirit continues to speak today. Of course, such an encounter with the Bible is not a private matter, even if personal devotional reading is important (even for theologians); it is located within the context of the wider pentecostal community. For pentecostal scholars this wider context includes the broader scholarly community as well.

Two American Church of God (Cleveland, Tennessee) theologians have argued for a method of doing theology that works with a triad of sources: the text of Scripture, the community of the church, and the person of the Holy Spirit. All three sources are expected to work together to generate theological reflection and inform ecclesial decisions in relation to missiological praxis. The key illustration of how this method works has been articulated by John Christopher Thomas in relation to Acts 15 and the decision by the Jerusalem Council to include the Gentiles in the household of faith. First, attention is given to what had already taken place among the Gentiles: they had heard the gospel, believed, received the gift of the Holy Spirit, had their hearts purified by faith, and experienced signs and wonders (vv. 7–9). Second, attention is given to Scripture and James' choice of Amos 9.11–12 to argue that there is continuity between David and Jesus as David's fallen tent is both rebuilt and expanded to include the Gentiles. In other words the experience of the Spirit and the response to the gospel can be explained by this text. Third, in the light of these two aspects the whole group makes a decision together to include the Gentiles without requiring that they pass through Judaism (vv. 24–26). Testimony is given and received and this enables a group decision to be discerned. In the context of Acts 15, the Gentiles are allowed into the fellowship of the church provided that table fellowship is maintained, and to do this they are required to adopt specific attitudes toward Jewish food laws and sexual codes. The Holy Spirit is seen as acting through the text of Scripture, experiences such as signs and wonders, and the testimonies in the group.[3]

Kenneth J. Archer has built on this proposal in his work on pentecostal hermeneutics. He agrees with Thomas's reading of Acts 15 that there must be a dialogical and dialectical relationship between "the Scripture, Spirit, and reader/readers."[4] He argues for a contemporary pentecostal hermeneutical strategy that embraces a triadic negotiation for meaning, borrowing from semiotics and reader-response criticism. He integrates these insights within the Bible reading method of the early Pentecostals in the context of the community. The voice of the Holy Spirit is heard through the community and Scripture and permeates the hermeneutical process.[5]

For Archer, the manner of this pentecostal theology is narrative. This proceeds by understanding Scripture as the grand metanarrative with the Gospels and Acts as the centre of the story. The social doctrine of the Trinity is the central character with Jesus Christ at the very heart, thereby emphasising the gospel of Christ and its significance for the church and the world: the hub around which other theological themes revolve. Pentecostals have articulated this gospel in terms of the "full gospel," or "five-fold" gospel: Jesus as Saviour, Sanctifier, Spirit Baptiser, Healer, and Coming King, providing what Archer calls the central narrative convictions. These convictions flow out of the doxological community bestowing identity and affording guidance in the Christian life. Therefore, if this gospel is the hub, the pentecostal doctrines, beliefs, and practices are the wheel connected to the centre: Jesus Christ. Each dimension of the gospel is linked to the others and provides a way of reflecting on other themes such as ecclesiology and eschatology, being "held together around our missional story of the Social Trinity."[6]

It is important to mention the fact that during this period of discussion, from Thomas's first article in 1994 until the present, there have been a number of contributions that have considered this pentecostal trialectic. Another important contribution has been made by Amos Yong.[7] He brought together the acts of interpretation inspired by the Spirit and the objects of interpretation via the Word with the contexts of interpretation across various communities. These three features were interpreted by means of a Trinitarian and metaphysical framework using the philosophy of American pragmatics. It provides Yong not merely with a way of reading the Bible but also, similar to Archer, an overall (if heuristic) theological method. He argues for an approach that is (1) triadic insofar as it contains three moments: of the Spirit (in praxis and experience), of the Word (in thought and interpretation), and of the Community (in context and tradition). It is (2) trialectical insofar as these moments are interdependent and reciprocal, with each being informed and shaped by the other two for it to be itself. It is (3) trialogical insofar as each moment is submitted to the other two, even if the starting point can be any one of the three. This means that each moment is considered fallible and open to the correction of the other two in the ongoing process of interpretation and theological construction.

This trialectic has been mirrored in more charismatic, as distinct from classical pentecostal, circles, even if the denotation has been different. For example, Mark Stibbe, from the Third Wave Anglican tradition, has argued for a similar experiential connection between the horizon of the church and the biblical text. He takes as his starting point the text of Acts 2:16 in the Pentecost narrative and Peter's explanation, which states: "This is that which was spoken by the prophet Joel" (KJV). To interpret what God is doing in the midst of his church by his Spirit (the "this"), the church searches for biblical passages that illuminate the experience (the "that"). The church perceives what the Father is doing in its midst (John 5.19) and allows the Holy Spirit to guide readers to texts that illuminate that work.[8] Thus the communal story of the church is located and understood within the overarching narrative of Scripture. Stibbe argues that his approach has attempted to mediate between the conservative (meaning is located in the author's intention) and postmodern (meaning is located in the reader/s) approaches.[9] This means that there should be a harmony between Scripture and experience through which contemporary praxis is informed and directed.

Most recently, following a symposium held at Regent University, Virginia Beach, a collection of essays has been published that aims to build on these previous studies and advance the notion of a pneumatic hermeneutic. Mark J. Boda, Kevin L. Spawn, Archie T. Wright, Ronald Herms, John Christopher Thomas, and I contribute essays exploring new ways of thinking about such a hermeneutic. The volume is important for a promoting dialogue with sympathetic yet critical scholars of such an approach, with response essays from Craig C. Bartholomew, James D. G. Dunn, and R. Walter L. Moberly included in the volume.[10]

HISTORY AND TRADITION

There have been a number of studies seeking to retrieve the early pentecostal sources for the sake of both understanding pentecostal history and indeed seeking to reshape pentecostal and charismatic theology for today. A number of examples will suffice. Douglas Jacobsen has provided an overarching narrative of early American pentecostal theology by describing the beliefs of twelve key individuals from Charles Parham to Essek W. Kenyon. This historical study articulates a clear understanding of the emerging theology in this context and gives important background material for appreciating the nature of contemporary American pentecostal theology today.[11]

Steven J. Land has articulated a distinctly Wesleyan pentecostal theology of spirituality within a Trinitarian and eschatological framework, drawing on the work of Jürgen Moltmann, to provide a model for contemporary belief and practice.[12] Peter Althouse also reviewed early pentecostal eschatology and brought it into conversation with contemporary pentecostal theologians before using the work of Jürgen Moltmann to recast their theological contributions.[13] Similarly, Matthew K. Thompson has engaged with eschatology and brings early Pentecostalism and its antecedents into fruitful conversation with Eastern Orthodoxy and Jürgen Moltmann before offering constructive proposals.[14] Shane Clifton analysed the emergence of the Assemblies of God denomination in Australia and offered a constructive proposal for pentecostal ecclesiology.[15] Finally, William P. Atkinson analysed the controversial teaching of the Faith Movement regarding the "spiritual death" of Jesus and thus made theological contributions to anthropology, Christology, soteriology, and Trinitarian thought.[16] All of these studies have attempted to bring historical pentecostal and charismatic sources into constructive conversation with contemporary concerns.

Traditionally, pentecostal theologians have been concerned to articulate their distinct testimony of Spirit baptism, which has been considered an experience distinct from and subsequent to conversion. Recent theologians have also been interested in re-articulating the themes of conversion/justification, sanctification, and Spirit baptism. I shall illustrate these themes by considering the work of two theologians in particular: Frank D. Macchia and Edmund J. Rybarczyk.

Macchia attempted to provide a theology by means of the pentecostal distinctive of baptism in the Spirit. In this project he aimed to use the existing pentecostal metaphor, but instead of simply treating it as a second or third step within a pentecostal *ordo salutis*, he wished to treat it as a governing theological model (he affirmed it as both part of Christian initiation and in distinction from it – connected to it but following on from it).[17] In his hands the model expands considerably, and it becomes a way of reading other theological doctrines through the lens of pneumatology conceived by means of the metaphor of baptism. However, the model is also reshaped by an engagement with an eschatological framework, which situates it as part of God's overarching redemption and missionary goals. Indeed, a second framework is the doctrine of the Trinity, which provides resources for understanding pneumatology and in particular Spirit baptism as a Trinitarian act, because the persons of the Godhead are always united *ad extra* even allowing for the doctrine of appropriation, which would see Christ as the Spirit Baptiser. This understanding is subsequently framed in relation to ecclesiology because Spirit baptism is the origin and substance of the church's life, including its charismatic existence and mission in the world.[18] This has implications for ecclesial communion, anthropology, vocation, and the uniqueness of Christ, as well as for reinterpretation of classical ecclesiological signs and symbols. Finally, Macchia seeks to reinterpret Spirit baptism by means of divine love: Spirit baptism is explained as love's "second conversion," by which he means persons not only experience God's love in them but also transcend themselves by becoming "poured out" for others. If the first conversion turns Pentecostals toward Christ, this second conversion turns them toward the world in acts of loving service.[19]

Macchia's most recent book extends his influence by engaging with an important Western theological doctrine, namely justification, from a distinctly pentecostal perspective.[20] He does this by specifically reviewing the debate between Protestants and Roman Catholics and their ambivalence in finding a role for the Holy Spirit in the doctrine. He approaches the issue from the lens of Spirit baptism: the right relationship between the Creator and the creature within the covenant is established and sustained through a mutual indwelling. There is no justification apart from the fullness of life in the Spirit (2 Cor. 5.4–5), which also means framing it in relation to the Trinity. Even the forensic metaphor needs to be adapted to include the role of the Spirit as divine advocate and witness. He states: "The fact that justification brings life in the midst of death (Rom. 5.18) tells us that here we are dealing with something that transcends a mere legal acquittal. Justification in Scripture has legal overtones but cannot adequately be grasped by any legal metaphor. Righteousness is not *imputed*; it is *accessed* or *participated in* through faith and by the life of the Spirit."[21] Macchia sets the cross as an event of reconciliation within the broader context of the resurrection and Pentecost, and all are mediated by the Spirit in a communion of love. This means that justification and sanctification must be regarded as complementary and overlapping categories through which creation is "rightwised." It also means that pneumatology is not merely an appendage to the concept of justification because *all* soteriological categories are *both* in Christ *and* in the Spirit (1 Cor. 6.11) and indeed fully Trinitarian. Furthermore, the right relation established by justification is multifaceted and includes pardon, victory, vindication, and fellowship in divine *koinōnia*. This innovative approach demonstrates how pentecostal theologians are not merely interested in *charismata* and Spirit baptism but are engaging with the broader Christian tradition to contribute to theological discourse in general.

Rybarczyk illustrates how pentecostal theologians can interact with the Eastern theological tradition in creative ways.[22] He compares the notion of Christian transformation in both Orthodoxy and American Pentecostalism (Assemblies of God). In so doing, he considers aspects of both soteriology and anthropology as they intersect and overlap. Each tradition is interrogated first in terms of anthropology before salvific transformation is explored in detail. The Orthodox category of *theōsis* is brought into dialogue with pentecostal *ordo salutis*, and in particular sanctification, to ascertain how they might be understood as mutually enlightening. Both traditions consider Christian transformation to be essentially rooted in divine-human communion, and this influences and is influenced by their respective views regarding anthropology and the *imago dei*, the doctrine of God, and creation.

CULTURE AND SOCIETY

A number of theologians have attempted to engage with wider issues in society from a pentecostal perspective. Examples from culture and society, health care, politics, and science illustrate the kinds of interdisciplinary research in which pentecostal theologians are involved.

Hollenweger is one of the theologians to have used the phrase "intercultural theology" in the late 1970s.[23] He is the father of the academic study of Pentecostalism and set the agenda for the study of global Pentecostalism.[24] His concern was to investigate, analyse, and critique the

many and varied expressions of Pentecostalism to be found around the
world by focusing on culture as a key ingredient to understanding this
tradition. For Hollenweger, intercultural theology appropriates the cultural media outside of the theologian's own tradition, which serve as
resources for the task of doing theology. This is especially important
when seeking to advance non-Western forms of theological reflection. An
interest in society and culture has also offered resources for liberationist approaches from within the pentecostal tradition. For example, Eldin
Villafañe contends that the liberation of culturally identifiable oppressed
people groups, especially American Hispanics, is an aspect of the Spirit's
work in personal and social transformation.[25] This argument is based on
a social and cultural analysis of the Hispanic heritage and its sociopolitical dimensions. For Villafañe, pentecostal action must be regarded as a
form of pneumatically driven political discipleship. Similarly, Samuel
Solivan has argued for a Hispanic liberation theology in the context
of North America by using the concept of *orthopathos*, by which he
means a link to those who suffer; it is a third pole between orthodoxy
and orthopraxis, enabling identification with and solidarity among the
suffering community.[26] From a different context, Robert Beckford has
argued for the use of cultural analysis in relation to the black churches in
the United Kingdom.[27] From his analysis of racism and black resistance
he proposes a liberationist perspective on the basis of an action-reflection
model. Again, social and cultural perspectives combine to allow a critical engagement that seeks to inform concrete action.

Amos Yong is one of the leading theologians within Pentecostalism,
and his work has paid attention to the theology of religions using the
American pragmatist tradition in correlation with what he has termed
the "pneumatological imagination."[28] He has also written an overview
theology, which seeks to define the nature of pentecostal theology pro-
grammatically for the twenty-first century and addresses key theological themes in outline.[29] It is a theology that is biblically based, especially
informed by the narrative of Luke-Acts, pneumatologically orientated,
and christologically focused, as well as confessionally located by emerging out of pentecostal experience. It is an approach that is fallibilis-
tic, multiperspectival, self-critical, and dialogical. He believes that the
challenges to such a global theology in the context of late modernity
are to be found in relation to the wider Christian community, other
non-Christian religious traditions, and science.[30] The themes addressed
in conversation with different forms of Pentecostalism from around
the world include soteriology, ecclesiology, Trinity, public theology,
other religious traditions, and creation. This contribution provides a

theological agenda, which builds on his previous work and extends it in important directions. Two further contributions will be described to understand how this programme is pursued in more detail.

First, Yong has addressed the question of disability, and especially the condition of Down syndrome by means of pneumatology.[31] It is here that personal narrative and academic study combine, as Yong uses insights from his family experience of living with and caring for his younger brother, Mark, a person living with Down syndrome. Yong introduces the subject of Down syndrome and his theological approach, which uses what he calls the "pneumatological imagination" – that is, "an epistemic posture shaped in part by the biblical narratives of the Holy Spirit and in part by the Christian experience of the Holy Spirit."[32] The many tongues of Pentecost signal a diversity of witness and open up the possibility of valuing the narratives of people with disability. In a brief history of what we now call Down syndrome, and especially the changing nomenclature, Yong considers the question of institutionalisation and mental health. Here he demonstrates an ease with medical literature on the subject. This is developed by a survey of late modern discourses on disability via the social sciences and law, which have attempted to expose the discriminatory structures faced by people with disability. This discussion is supplemented by interaction with feminist, cultural, and world religious perspectives on disability. A theological anthropology is proposed that suggests the *imago dei* should be conceived in embodied, interdependent, and relational terms. An ecclesiology is subsequently advanced that is inclusive of disability as members of the broken body of Christ participate in catechism, sacraments, liturgies, and fellowship in the Holy Spirit, which empowers all for ministry within and beyond the boundary of the church. Traditional categories of soteriology are reviewed in the light of disability, including justification and healing. The book concludes by reconsidering eschatology via the lens of disability and challenges aspects of this doctrine that erase the effect of disability both in the *eschaton* and now. A dynamic theology of life after death is advocated (on the basis of Gregory of Nyssa's doctrine of *epectasis* – the soul's perpetual journey), that is inclusive of all people with disabilities in a way that preserves identity shaped by disability while allowing for redemptive transformation.

Second, in the publication of his Edward Cadbury lectures delivered at the University of Birmingham, United Kingdom, in 2009, Yong addresses the contribution that Pentecostalism makes to political theology.[33] Using the motif of the "many tongues of Pentecost," he considered the plurality of pentecostal political practices globally and their contribution toward a Christian theology of the polis. The distinctively pentecostal feature of this theology is an application of the Christocentric fivefold gospel popular among Wesleyan Pentecostals wherein Christ is viewed as Saviour, Sanctifier, Spirit Baptiser, Healer, and Coming King. These different lenses are used to view aspects of political theology: (1) salvation in relation to the demonic and the politics of worship, (2) sanctification in relation to culture and the church as an alternative polis, (3) a prophetic posture (connected to Spirit baptism) in relation to civil society and globalization, (4) healing in relation to health and economics, and (5) eschatology in relation to liberation movements and ecology. These different themes weave together to provide a distinctly pentecostal contribution that takes seriously the concrete realities of the different pentecostal communities from around the world. Thus ecclesiology, christology, and soteriology are given deeper and more sustained treatment as pentecostal and political theology dialogue.

EXPERIENCE AND PRACTICE

There are a good number of social science studies that have considered the nature of pentecostal and charismatic Christianity using empirical research methods and attending to religious experience and ecclesial practice. However, these studies frame their research within social scientific theories and concepts. Although these studies are often extremely illuminating and helpful, they do not contribute directly to the construction of *theological* discourse. Therefore, for the sake of this particular exercise, I shall focus on empirical studies conducted within or in relation to a theological agenda.

The use of empirical research methods within practical theological research has now become very well established. In fact one could suggest that this strand of practical theology is going from strength to strength. Pentecostals on the whole have not paid a great deal of attention to this approach because of their focus on the application of biblical models and texts or their attention to their own distinctive traditions.[34] However, there are some who have pioneered empirical research within this tradition. My own work used empirical research methods at a very early stage and engaged with the European tradition of empirical theology led by the Dutch Roman Catholic theologian Johannes A. van der Ven.[35] Using a modified version of van der Ven's empirical-theological research cycle, my study of glossolalia among members of the New Church movement in the United Kingdom used both qualitative and quantitative methods.[36] It explored the theology from below by listening to the voices of church members, as well as observing ecclesial practices and placing these practices within the overall ecclesial narrative to understand the nature and significance of the phenomenon. This local theology was brought into conversation with the extensive literature on the subject from biblical, theological, and social science sources, and a theoretical model of glossolalia was tested more widely using a questionnaire survey. This model was refined by an engagement with pentecostal scholarship to propose a construction that viewed glossolalia through Trinitarian, sacramental, and eschatological lenses.

Further reflection methodologically led to the publication of a practical theological text that illustrated both qualitative and quantitative studies.[37] It offers a detailed discussion of methodology from a pentecostal-charismatic perspective and gives examples of how empirical research within this framework can investigate the praxis of pentecostal and charismatic Christians. Chapters address concerns of great interest to the constituency, such as spirituality and worship, glossolalia, gender, prophecy, charismatic experience, the Toronto Blessing, and faith and healing. This book was the first, and remains the only, practical theological monograph approaching the field of pentecostal and charismatic studies using empirical methods.

My most recent study builds methodologically on this text and engages with the beliefs and values of pentecostal adherents to propose a rescripting of ordinary theology on the basis of qualitative data analysis.[38] It is a congregational study that seeks to map out the "views from the pews," so to speak, and listens in a disciplined and attentive manner to the ways in which a very multicultural congregation in an inner-city neighbourhood expresses and lives out its faith. It seeks to address three levels of discourse: (1) the ordinary expressions of the grassroots believers in their praxis; (2) the denominational and wider pentecostal tradition as it is mediated to them; and (3) academic theological discourse in dialogue with the social sciences as it seeks to give an account of this theology for the benefit of the congregation and the wider academy. This approach takes seriously the narrative structure of pentecostal ordinary theology as it is mediated through the medium of testimony. In this way it builds on and extends the idea that testimony is a legitimate form of theological discourse.[39] It addresses key pentecostal themes, such as worship, conversion, baptism in the Spirit, healing, life and witness, world mission, and the second coming, before suggesting a pentecostal ecclesiology emerging from these themes.

Others who have used empirical research methods within a practical theological paradigm include Stephen Parker.[40] He studied how

Pentecostals were led by the Holy Spirit in their congregational practices and focused on the subject of spiritual discernment. In this study he brought together ethnographic description and object relations psychology in mutual critical correlation, leading to a set of guidelines for use in evaluating the claims made with respect to the Spirit's guidance. William K. Kay has been a leading researcher of British Pentecostalism, combining history, theology and social psychology. He has produced two significant books in this genre. The first is based on a questionnaire survey of pentecostal ministers and explored items such as spiritual gifts, healing, the Toronto Blessing, general theological beliefs, and ethics.[41] The second book surveyed the beliefs and practices of the New Church movement. Building on earlier work, he explored the dynamics of charismatic activity, ministerial roles, church growth, and the use of *charismata*.[42] Cory E. Labanow's study of a Vineyard congregation in the United Kingdom uses a practical-theological approach and ethnography to investigate theological identity.[43] He places this congregation within the contemporary "emerging church" discussion and asks about the criteria used by the church to articulate a Christian identity that is relevant to its members and the wider community. This identity is then conceptualized in terms of religious parentage, safe places, growth and maturity, communication with contemporary culture, and reconstruction. Thus the study contributes to the discussion of ecclesiology in the context of contemporary society.

OBSERVATIONS AND FUTURE TRAJECTORIES

Finally, to consider an agenda for future pentecostal theological exploration, I make a few observations, ask some questions, and tentatively suggest some possible future trajectories.

It is interesting and hugely important that pentecostal theologians have embedded their spirituality within theological method. The captivity of post-Enlightenment theology to the role of reason and the need for respectability in the academy has in many cases forced the two apart. The advances in biblical hermeneutics and the need to articulate a theological method that is consonant with pentecostal sensibilities have meant that the role of the Holy Spirit within the process of theological thinking has once again found a place. To be sure, other theologians have made room for this feature, for example, Moltmann's "contemplative gaze," as a means of knowledge.[44] However, Pentecostals have placed the Spirit, if not centre stage, then at least on the stage. Of course there are problems as well with this retrieval of the role of the Holy

Spirit. One of the issues has to do with the nature of mediation. The Holy Spirit is always mediated within creation, and in the theological method that has been articulated the Spirit could be domesticated either by the Word or by the community of the church. There is a real danger here and further work is required to articulate a theology of mediation that complements the existing models that currently exist and are in use. The appeal to "direct unmediated" experience of the Holy Spirit has always been problematic and continues to be so.

It is important that Pentecostals retrieve their own traditions of thought not only to understand their theological identity but also to engage in critical appropriation of it. Recent theological scholarship has been at its most fruitful when it has attempted to revisit the early material to learn from its past. This has been most obvious in the Wesleyan pentecostal tradition, which has attempted to re-envision the fivefold gospel as a reading tradition for biblical and theological work. Other studies have attempted similar kinds of retrieval or comparison with different pentecostal traditions.[45] This retrieval of tradition raises some important questions, however. For example, why should this particular form of Pentecostalism be normative for other forms of Pentecostalism? Who decides which aspects of the tradition are essential to the identity of Pentecostalism and which are not? David A. Reed's study of Oneness Pentecostalism in the United States is an important example of how a dispute can be investigated to shed light on a contemporary theological conversation.[46] Similarly, should the doctrine of "initial evidence" – that is, glossolalia as the sign of a person having been baptised with the Holy Spirit as postconversion experience – be regarded as an essential truth for all pentecostal everywhere? Or again, how should pentecostal theologians relate to and appropriate the broader Christian tradition? We have seen that theologians are beginning to appropriate non-Protestant and non-Evangelical/ pentecostal sources, but what are the possibilities and restrictions in the appropriation of broader Christian tradition? Recent ecumenical conversations have been important in opening up such an engagement, but often the nature of these conversations are limited and lack official sanction by pentecostal denominations.[47]

My own area of practical and empirical theology is one that has come of age in the past twenty years or so. The *Journal of Empirical Theology*, as well as other practical theology journals, now publishes studies of pentecostal ecclesial life investigated from empirical perspectives. Nevertheless, this area is underdeveloped, and there is hardly a critical mass of pentecostal scholars working in this field. This state of affair is mirrored in the associated academic societies. Unfortunately key international academic societies outside of the *Society for Pentecostal Studies* have very few members who are also scholars engaged in constructive pentecostal theology using empirical research methods. I have suggested elsewhere that one reason for this lack of rigorous empirical work within the framework of theology is because pentecostal practical theologians are fundamentally wedded to an applied method of theology.[48] In this regard they have neither engaged with the broader academy of practical theology nor indeed with some of the more innovative thinking coming from pentecostal biblical hermeneutics and theological method noted. This weakness means that there is great scope for the development of pentecostal practical theology that takes seriously the theological praxis of pentecostal communities and their renewal.

This survey of recent theology has demonstrated that a few pentecostal theologians are creatively engaged in conversations with academic discourse outside of the domain of theology. This is a significant development and one that should be welcomed with enthusiasm. The leaders in this engagement are Amos Yong and James K. A. Smith, most notably with their Pentecostalism and science project,[49] but also with politics, economics, and health care issues. However, there are other kinds of discourse that are significantly underdeveloped, for example, in relation to social science. Some social scientists, sympathetic to Pentecostalism, sometimes use some theological ideas.[50] However, and importantly, the discourse being advanced is not really theology but sociology because ultimately sociological theory is being built, not theological theory. In addition, what about pentecostal contributions to aesthetics: music, the arts, and architecture? There have been some contributions to education, but again these have been limited and underdeveloped.[51] A full-blown pentecostal theology of education, even of theological education, is lacking and in need of articulation and discussion.

This naturally leads us to consider pentecostal theology and society. It is clear that a number of contributions have been made, especially from a liberationist perspective. This includes recent feminist contributions.[52] However, increasingly pentecostal theology must address issues of politics, economics, health care, third world development, and social justice broadly conceived. Work has begun in these areas, and there are initial studies and contributions that identify a concern and suggest the beginnings of some kind of pentecostal perspective. Nevertheless, it is not clear how such a pentecostal theology contributes to the overall discourse on a given subject and whether it is in fact taken as internal to Pentecostalism or external to it; in other words, whether it is part of a broader academic conversation. An area that does require careful and sustained treatment is theological ethics. Do pentecostal scholars have something distinctive to say to address some of the burning ethical questions of the day, such as ecology and global capitalism? What about a theology of peace and peace making? Paul Alexander has provided a study of pacificism within the American Assemblies of God tradition. Drawing on the earlier work of Jay Beaman,[53] he has retrieved the early pacifist tradition, which has been forgotten or marginalized in more recent times. He rehabilitates this pacifist narrative to challenge current assumptions about war, violence, and patriotism among Pentecostals in the United States.[54] This is an exciting and hugely relevant development and illustrates the kinds of possibilities by pentecostal theologians.

Finally, Pentecostalism is a global phenomenon and the centre of gravity is not the Western world but the non-Western. It is in African, Asia, and Latin America that the force of Pentecostalism is to be seen and in their transnational networks. Hollenweger was the first to draw the attention of the academy to the global nature of Pentecostalism and in its hugely diverse nature. Pentecostals in the non-Western world face a religious plurality that many in a Western context fail to appreciate, even with heightened migration and transnationalism. Amos Yong and Tony Richie are theologians who have attempted to address interreligious relations and their work suggests possible trajectories for future engagement.[55] It would be advantageous if Pentecostals from the non-Western contexts developed their thinking. Pentecostal theology in recent times has attempted to address this cultural and theological diversity, and there are a number of studies that articulate the different kinds of theology emerging from these different contexts.[56] Unfortunately, it has to be said that most pentecostal theology is still dominated by Western theologians. African, Asian, and Latin American voices can be heard, but they are not as clear as Western voices, especially from North America. This is understandable, given the fact that the United States in particular develops pentecostal theological talent like no other country and provides opportunities for nurture and employment. Therefore, the challenge for the pentecostal theological academy is to take seriously its responsibility for the nurture of non-Western scholars to advance intercultural pentecostal theology. In this way, the spirit behind the vision of Hollenweger would be advanced, even if the outcome might be somewhat different than his articulation of an intercultural theology among Pentecostals. Pentecostal theology has a bright and exciting future. It is definitely here to stay. The question is what kind of theology will it produce in the next fifty years? Only time will tell, but it is up and running and full of energy!

Notes

1   Walter J. Hollenweger, *Pentecostalism: Origins and Developments Worldwide* (Peabody, MA: Hendrickson, 1997), 18–19, 269–72.
2   For example, J. Rodman Williams, *Renewal Theology: Systematic Theology from a Charismatic Perspective*, combined ed., 3 vols. (Grand Rapids, MI: Zondervan, 1996); Keith Warrington, *Pentecostal Theology: A Theology of Encounter* (London: T & T Clark, 2008).
3   J. C. Thomas, 'Reading the Bible from within Our Traditions: A Pentecostal Hermeneutic as a Test Case', in J. B. Green and M. Turner, eds., *Between Two Horizons: Spanning New Testament and Systematic Theology* (Grand Rapids, MI: Eerdmans, 2000), 108–22; J. C. Thomas, "Women, Pentecostals and the Bible: An Experiment in Pentecostal Hermeneutics," *Journal of Pentecostal Theology* 5 (1994), 41–56.
4   Kenneth J. Archer, *A Pentecostal Hermeneutic for the Twenty-First Century: Spirit, Scripture and Community* (London: T & T Clark International, 2004), 145–47 (particularly 147).
5   Archer, *A Pentecostal Hermeneutic*, 156–91.
6   Archer, "A Pentecostal Way of Doing Theology: Method and Manner," *International Journal of Systematic Theology* 9:1 (2007), 1–14 (particularly 13). His work is further developed in *The Gospel Revisited: Towards a Pentecostal Theology of Worship and Witness* (Eugene, OR: Pickwick Publications, 2011).
7   Amos Yong, *Spirit-Word-Community: Theological Hermeneutics in Trinitarian Perspective* (Aldershot: Ashgate, 2002).
8   Mark Stibbe, *Times of Refreshing: A Practical Theology of Revival for Today* (London: Marshall Pickering, 1995), 5.
9   Mark Stibbe, "This is That: Some Thoughts Concerning Charismatic Hermeneutics," *Anvil: An Anglican Evangelical Journal for Theology and Mission* 15:3 (1998), 181–93.
10   Kevin L. Spawn and Archie T. Wright, eds., *Spirit and Scripture: Exploring a Pneumatic Hermeneutic* (London: T & T Clark Continuum, 2011).
11   Douglas Jacobsen, *Thinking in the Spirit: Theologies of the Early Pentecostal Movement* (Bloomington, IN: Indiana University Press, 2003).
12   Steven J. Land, *Pentecostal Spirituality: A Passion for the Kingdom* (Sheffield: Sheffield Academic Press, 1993). I attempted a similar exercise from a charismatic perspective in *Encountering the Spirit: The Charismatic Tradition* (London: Darton, Longman & Todd, 2006, and Maryknoll, NY: Orbis Books, 2007).
13   Peter Althouse, *Spirit of the Last Days: Pentecostal Eschatology in Conversation with Jürgen Moltmann* (London: T & T Clark Continuum, 2003).
14   Matthew K. Thompson, *Kingdom Come: Revisioning Pentecostal Eschatology* (Blandford Forum, UK: Deo Publishing, 2010).
15   Shane Clifton, *Pentecostal Churches in Transition: Analysing the Developing Ecclesiology of the Assemblies of God in Australia* (Leiden: Brill, 2009).
16   William P. Atkinson, *The Spiritual Death of Jesus: A Pentecostal Investigation* (Leiden: Brill, 2009).
17   Frank D. Macchia, *Baptized in the Spirit: A Global Pentecostal Theology* (Grand Rapids, MI: Zondervan, 2006), 153–54.

18 Macchia, *Baptized in the Spirit*, 155.

19 Macchia, *Baptized in the Spirit*, 280–82.

20 Frank D. Macchia, *Justified in the Spirit: Creation, Redemption, and the Triune God* (Grand Rapids, MI: Eerdmans, Pentecostal Manifestos, 2010).

21 Macchia, *Justified in the Spirit*, 6.

22 Edmund J. Rybarczyk, *Beyond Salvation: Eastern Orthodoxy and Classical Pentecostalism on Becoming Like Christ* (Milton Keynes: Paternoster, 2004).

23 See the discussion in Mark J. Cartledge and David Cheetham, eds., *Intercultural Theology: Approaches and Themes* (London: SCM Press, 2011).

24 Hollenweger, *Pentecostalism*, 129–31.

25 Eldin Villafañe, *The Liberating Spirit: Towards a Hispanic American Pentecostal Social Ethic* (Grand Rapids, MI: Eerdmans, 1993).

26 Samuel Solivan, *The Spirit, Pathos and Liberation: Towards an Hispanic Pentecostal Theology* (Sheffield: Sheffield Academic Press, 1998).

27 Robert Beckford, *Dread and Pentecostal: A Political Theology for the Black Church in Britain* (London: Society for Promoting Christian Knowledge, 2000).

28 Amos Yong, *Discerning the Spirit(s): A Pentecostal-Charismatic Contribution to Christian Theology of Religions* (Sheffield: Sheffield Academic Press, 2000), and Amos Yong, *Beyond the Impasse: Toward a Pneumatological Theology of Religion* (Grand Rapids, MI: Baker Books, 2003). These ideas were further developed in Amos Yong, *Hospitality and the Other: Pentecost, Christian Practices, and the Neighbour* (Maryknoll, NY: Orbis Books, 2008).

29 Amos Yong, *The Spirit Poured Out on All Flesh: Pentecostalism and the Possibility of Global Theology* (Grand Rapids, MI: Baker Academic, 2005).

30 For the discussion with science, see Amos Yong, *The Spirit of Creation: Modern Science and Divine Action in the Pentecostal-Charismatic Imagination* (Grand Rapids, MI: William B. Eerdmans Publishing Company, 2011).

31 Amos Yong, *Theology and Down Syndrome: Reimagining Disability in Late Modernity* (Waco, TN: Baylor University Press, 2007).

32 Yong, *Theology and Down Syndrome*, 11.

33 Amos Yong, *In the Days of Caesar: Pentecostalism and Political Theology* (Grand Rapids, MI: William B. Eerdmans Publishing Company, 2010).

34 See my discussion in Mark J. Cartledge, "Practical Theology," in Allan Anderson, Michael Bergunder, André Droogers, and Cornelius van der Laan, eds., *Studying Global Pentecostalism: Theories and Methods* (Berkeley, CA: University of California Press, 2010), 268–85.

35 Johannes A. van der Ven, *Practical Theology: An Empirical Approach* (Kampen: Kok Pharos, 1993).

36 Mark J. Cartledge, *Charismatic Glossolalia: An Empirical-Theological Study* (Aldershot: Ashgate, 2002).

37 Mark J. Cartledge, *Practical Theology: Charismatic and Empirical Perspectives* (Carlisle: Paternoster, 2003).

38 Mark J. Cartledge, *Testimony in the Spirit: Rescripting Ordinary Pentecostal Theology* (Farnham: Ashgate, 2010).

39   See Mark J. Cartledge, *Testimony: Its Importance, Place and Potential* (Cambridge: Grove Books, 2002).

40   Stephen E. Parker, *Led by the Spirit: Toward a Practical Theology of Pentecostal Discernment* (Sheffield: Sheffield Academic Press, 1996).

41   William K. Kay, *Pentecostals in Britain* (Carlisle: Paternoster, 2000).

42   William K. Kay, *Apostolic Networks in Britain: New Ways of Being Church* (Milton Keynes, UK: Paternoster, 2007).

43   Cory E. Labanow, *Evangelicalism and the Emerging Church: A Congregational Study of a Vineyard Church* (Farnham: Ashgate, 2009).

44   Jürgen Moltmann, *The Spirit of Life: A Universal Affirmation* (London: SCM Press, 1992), 199–205.

45   E.g., Kimberley Ervin Alexander, *Pentecostal Healing: Models in Theology and Practice* (Blandford Forum, UK: Deo Publishing, 2006).

46   David A. Reed, *'In the Name of Jesus': The History and Beliefs of Oneness Pentecostals* (Blandford Forum: Deo Publishing, 2008).

47   See Cecil M. Robeck, Jr., "Ecumenism," in Allan Anderson, Michael Bergunder, André Droogers, and Cornelius van der Laan, eds., *Studying Global Pentecostalism: Theories and Methods* (Berkeley: University of California Press, 2010), 286–307.

48   See Cartledge, "Practical Theology," 282, and Mark J. Cartledge, "Pentecostalism," in Bonnie J. Miller-McLemore, ed., *The Blackwell Companion to Practical Theology* (New York: Wiley-Blackwell, 2012), 587–95.

49   James K. A. Smith and Amos Yong, eds., *Science and the Spirit: A Pentecostal Engagement with the Sciences* (Bloomington, IN: Indiana University Press, 2010).

50   E.g., Matthew T. Lee and Margaret M. Poloma, *A Sociological Study of the Great Commandment in Pentecostalism: The Practice of Godly Love as Benevolent Service* (Lewiston, NY: Edwin Mellen Press, 2009).

51   E.g., William K. Kay, "Pentecostal Education," *Journal of Beliefs & Values* 25:2 (2004), 229–39.

52   E.g., Lisa P. Stevenson, *Dismantling the Dualisms for American Pentecostal Women in Ministry* (Leiden: Brill, 2012).

53   Jay Beaman, *Pentecostal Pacifism* (Hillsboro, KS: Center for Mennonite Brethren Studies, 1989).

54   Paul Alexander, *Peace to War: Shifting Allegiances in the Assemblies of God* (Telford, PA: Cascadia, 2009).

55   Yong, *Discerning the Spirit(s)*; Tony Richie, *Speaking by the Spirit: A Pentecostal Model for Interreligious Dialogue* (Lexington, KY: Emeth Press, 2011).

56   See Veli-Matti Kärkkäinen, ed., *The Spirit in the World: Emerging Pentecostal Theologies in Global Contexts* (Grand Rapids, MI: Eerdmans, 2009).

Further Reading

Anderson, Allan. *An Introduction to Pentecostalism: Global Charismatic Christianity.* Cambridge: Cambridge University Press, 2004.

Chan, Simon. *Pentecostal Theology and the Christian Spiritual Tradition.* Sheffield: Sheffield Academic Press, 2000.

Dayton, Donald W. *Theological Roots of Pentecostalism.* Peabody, MA: Hendrickson, 1987.

Hart, Larry. *Truth Aflame: Theology for the Church in Renewal.* Grand Rapids, MI: Zondervan, 2005.

Lord, Andy. *Network Church: A Pentecostal Ecclesiology Shaped by Mission.* Leiden: Brill, 2012.

Menzies, William W., and Robert P. Menzies. *Spirit and Power: Foundations of Pentecostal Experience.* Grand Rapids, MI: Zondervan, 2000.

Suurmond, Jean-Jacques. *Word and Spirit at Play: Towards a Charismatic Theology.* London: SCM, 1994.

Tan-Chow May Ling. *Pentecostal Theology for the Twenty-First Century: Engaging with Multi-Faith Singapore.* Aldershot: Ashgate, 2007.

Vondey, Wolfgang., *Beyond Pentecostalism: The Crisis of Global Christianity and the Renewal of the Theological Agenda.* Grand Rapids, MI: Eerdmans, 2010.

14 Pentecostalism and Ecumenism
WOLFGANG VONDEY

Pentecostalism is an ecumenical melting pot. Unlike the many existing churches and denominations that originated in deliberate response to splits and separations resulting from doctrinal and practical differences, pentecostal communities worldwide did not organize or institutionalize in conscious reaction to particular ecclesiastical patterns. Instead, global Pentecostalism has emerged in both continuity and discontinuity with various existing doctrines, practices, rituals, disciplines, spiritualities, and organizational forms, and the resulting character of pentecostal groups does not readily form a homogeneous ecumenical picture. This chapter elaborates on the relationship of Pentecostalism and ecumenism, beginning with early pentecostal hopes and understandings of Christian unity in North America, charting the frustration of such hopes, and explicating the revival of pentecostal participation in international ecumenical affairs since the latter half of the twentieth century. An exploration of the various ways that Pentecostals have approached interdenominational cooperation and ecumenical conversations precedes a survey of the current status of ecumenical encounters, from national discussions, to regional bodies, international discussions, participation in the World Council of Churches, and newer forms of ecumenical initiatives. This survey is complemented by a theological assessment of pentecostal approaches to the nature, purpose, and unity of the Christian churches. In conclusion, the chapter proposes that Pentecostals can and should continue to invest themselves wholeheartedly in the ecumenical enterprise, what they might receive in such participation, and what they might have to offer to the ecumenical movement in the twenty-first century.

EARLY PENTECOSTAL HOPES AND UNDERSTANDINGS OF CHRISTIAN UNITY

The ecumenical origins of the men and women who formed the newly established pentecostal groups in North America at the beginning of the twentieth century nourished an atmosphere of both hope and skepticism. Although it can be said "Pentecostalism started in most places as an ecumenical renewal movement in the mainline churches,"[1] the dynamics and conscious efforts toward renewal among pentecostal pioneers were characterized initially by a fundamental ecumenical optimism that was followed by confrontation and confusion.[2] The emerging pentecostal groups, which had not yet defined themselves in the existing ecclesiastical landscape, were denied the experience to develop their understanding of Christian unity in a mutually inclusive ecumenical setting.

Influential in charting the original optimism among Pentecostals was the diversity of churches, fellowships, and individuals confessing a similar experience of the Holy Spirit. This encounter was captured immediately by a theological imagery that was both restorationist and ecumenical. Labels such as Pentecostal, Apostolic Faith, or Latter Rain, commonly used among the groups, expressed not only the importance of continuity with Christian history but also the eschatological anticipation of a forthcoming universal ecumenical restoration of all of God's people.[3] The outpouring of the Holy Spirit was seen as the specific evidence of God's desire to bring unity to the churches and to proclaim the gospel to the ends of the earth. Mission and unity were inextricably linked among early Pentecostals who pointed back to the day of Pentecost only to point forward to the full realization of the kingdom of God.

Reflecting this ecumenical hope, Richard G. Spurling named one of the earliest pentecostal groups "Christian Union" in accordance with the vision to remain in fellowship with and to bring unity to all Christians.[4] In his influential writings on the Latter Rain, pentecostal leader David Wesley Myland proclaimed the entire goal of Pentecost as the oneness and unity of Christians brought about by God's Spirit.[5] William J. Seymour, pastor and leader of the Azusa Street Mission and Revival in Los Angeles, explained in his influential paper, the *Apostolic Faith*, that the pentecostal movement stands not only "for the restoration of the faith" but also for "Christian Unity everywhere."[6] Charles Fox Parham, a pillar of the early pentecostal movement, found himself confronted with a prophetic declaration that to live as a pentecostal was to live as "an apostle of unity."[7] Frank Bartleman, another important figure in the early years, declared unambiguously, "There can be no divisions in a true Pentecost. To formulate a separate body is but to advertise our failure as a people of God."[8]

Similar voices can be added from pentecostal leaders outside of North America. Thomas B. Barratt, who brought the pentecostal message to several Scandinavian countries, envisioned Pentecostalism as the "Very Revival Christ had in His mind when He prayed that *all His disciples might be one.*"[9] Gerrit R. Polman, the founder of the Dutch pentecostal movement, concluded in a similar vein, "The purpose of the pentecostal revival is not to build up a church, but to build up all churches."[10] The force of these ecumenical convictions cannot be separated from the revivals that occurred in broad ecumenical contexts during the late nineteenth and early twentieth centuries in Europe. Ecumenical contacts were encouraged by such well-known figures as the Anglican pentecostal leader in Great Britain Alexander A. Boddy, the Lutheran pentecostal leader in Germany Jonathan A. A. B. Paul, the French Reformed pastor Louis Dallière, the Belgian protestant writer Henri T. de Worm, and many other Pentecostals who saw themselves at the same time as ecumenical figures.[11] In Europe, and later with particular force in Latin America, Africa, and Asia, positive ecumenical attitudes were frequently the result of the influence of foreign missionaries and were often synonymous with the international and interdenominational origins of the participants themselves. Ecumenical Pentecostalism emerged as a melting pot of existing doctrinal traditions, liturgical practices, national and local ecclesiastical cultures, organizational structures, and spiritualities.

Theologically, the ecumenical impulse among early Pentecostals reflected a particular ecclesiological ethos.[12] The pentecostal groups hesitated to apply the title "church" or "denomination" to the movement. Pentecostals criticized the "formalism," "institutionalism," "ritualism," "ecclesiasticism," and "denominationalism" of existing "human organizations."[13] The heart of their ecumenical criticism was leveled at the existence of the "many different religious organizations each enclosed by its own particular sectarian fence."[14] The origins of pentecostal ecclesiology were deeply rooted in an ecumenical reading of history that informed both a deep-seated restorationist mind-set and vehement eschatological expectation. The dismissal of existing ecclesiastical patterns resulted from the conviction that the church was fundamentally an eschatological, not doctrinal, community and that the common trend toward denominational separation contradicted the eschatological vision of the gospel. Pentecostalism was seen as a movement in the church and among the churches, not a new church. More precisely, Pentecostals understood themselves as a movement in the process of *becoming* church. A particular community, denomination, or even the pentecostal movement as a whole was considered transitory and expected to be surpassed by the continued outpouring of the

Holy Spirit and the resulting restoration of Christianity. From an early pentecostal perspective, these expectations were synonymous with an understanding of the future direction of ecumenical unity.

THE FRUSTRATION OF AN ECUMENICAL MIND-SET AMONG PENTECOSTALS

The widespread ecumenical optimism among Pentecostals should not be mistaken for a naive or unadulterated attitude toward Christian unity. Apart from its ecumenical origins, Pentecostalism could not have emerged in as forceful a manner as it did on a global scale during the twentieth century. Nonetheless, the ecumenical impulses among pentecostal pioneers were often ambivalent, embracing the goal of Christian unity but questioning the means with which Pentecostals were to participate in ecumenical endeavors.[15] This ambivalence resulted from a number of internal and external factors that contributed to the shaping of the pentecostal movement in its early days. Four elements stand out with particular clarity.

Restorationist criticism. The primitivist or restorationist impulse among Pentecostals emerged as an emphasis on the need for a return to the practices of the apostolic community and was based on a critical attitude toward established churches and contemporary Christian practices.[16] Often associated with an emphasis on spiritual freedom, empowerment, and sanctification, Pentecostals lamented the fact that the established traditions stifled spiritual growth, de-emphasized the work of the Holy Spirit, and polluted the original forms of Christian fellowship. After all, it was for these reasons that a restoration of the apostolic faith was seen as necessary. And while the established churches were certainly seen as participating in the fulfillment of God's restoration of the world, they were also the primary contestants from which Pentecostals distinguished themselves. The perfectionist parentage and eschatological orientation of early pentecostal thought informed a critical stance toward any doctrine, practice, or community that seemed to promote spiritual ambiguity.[17] In light of the perceived urgency of the Lord's judgment, Pentecostals often drew a sharp line between the church and the world and included in the latter any community that did not distinguish itself sharply from the former. The result was a world view fostered by the demands of a Biblicist piety, the rigor of an unbridled apocalypticism, and the ardor of unprecedented manifestations of spiritual experiences that often prohibited rather than promoted efforts in Christian unity.

Persecution and rejection. Relatively quickly, Pentecostals found themselves at odds with the established traditions. Separation was often experienced among Pentecostals in the harsh reality of persecution and violent attacks at the hands of the established churches. The overwhelming targets were the practices and experiences that presented the most immediately accessible and tangible manifestations of the pentecostal revivals.

> Within a short time ... the Pentecostal revival became the object of scurrilous attacks. It was denounced as "anti-Christian," as "sensual and devilish," and as "the last vomit of Satan." Its adherents were taunted and derided from the pulpit as well as in the religious and secular press. Some leaders were actually subjected to violence. Those ministers and missionaries from the old-line denominations who embraced the doctrine of the Holy Spirit baptism were removed from their pulpits or dismissed by their mission boards.[18]

The revivals among Pentecostals were seen as immoral, childish, deluded, frivolous, insane, and even demonic.[19] Few critics actually sought to substantiate their judgments with concrete evidence. However, exceptions typically pointed to the controversial physical manifestations that accompanied the revivals and that earned Pentecostals the pejorative nickname "holy rollers."[20] This label was often indiscriminately used to describe the unorthodox practices of jumping, jerking, falling, rolling on the floor, and above all, the pentecostal commitment to Spirit baptism and speaking in tongues. In return, the more Pentecostals felt ostracized by the established traditions, the more their ecumenical hopes were frustrated. Restorationist criticism was fueled, new prejudices emerged, and the young pentecostal movement in North America soon entered a phase of ecumenical exclusivism.[21] The theological debate centered on the pentecostal challenge to the dominant cessationist principle, which rendered the pentecostal emphasis on the practice of spiritual gifts obsolete with the end of the apostolic age.[22] Coupled with a neglect to distinguish between the moderate, mainline Pentecostals and the more extreme manifestations of the movement, the World Christian Fundamentals Association cut its ties with the pentecostal movement in 1928 and contributed to an isolation of Pentecostals from ecumenical fellowship.[23] Most of these reactions were the result of rejecting pentecostal practices, spirituality, and worship; doctrinal divisions only confirmed rather than initiated the widening ecumenical separation.

Internal divisions. Pentecostal groups were plagued by internal debates, fractures, and divisions. The growing movement divided over disagreements on doctrine, personalities, church politics, and praxis.[24] Among the most detrimental issues ranked William H. Durham's teaching of the "finished work of Calvary," which rejected the idea of sanctification as a second crisis separate from salvation dominant among many Pentecostals, as well as divisions resulting from the controversy between Oneness and Trinitarian Pentecostals, and racial issues eventually dividing the Azusa Street leadership at a later point in the quarrel with Charles Parham.[25] By the second decade of the twentieth century, the movement had become a composition of several branches of pentecostal bodies that looked with suspicion at the inconsistencies, failures, and counterfeits that characterized some parts of the movement.[26] In the effort to provide order and coherence among those who called themselves Pentecostals, the theological concerns of the early movement were soon overshadowed by the structural demands of the rapidly expanding pentecostal communities. Distinctions of emphasis, formation of denominations and churches, and the establishment of organizational structures made concentrated ecumenical efforts among Pentecostals almost impossible.

Organizational demands and institutionalization. The unprecedented growth of the pentecostal movement, its manifold diversity, internal divisions, and isolation from the established traditions hastened the need to increase and improve organizational structures. In response, Pentecostals abandoned their initial rejection of traditional ecclesiastical patterns and organizational forms and adopted the label "church" or "assembly," thus entering the scene of American denominationalism.[27] The adoption of traditional ecclesiological classifications inevitably led to confrontation with others who adopted the same designations and nourished an ecclesiology of competition.[28] Although many Pentecostals remained adamant that the movement was not antagonistic but ecumenical in principle, the understanding of pentecostal ecclesiality had to be altered to allow for the existence of multiple "churches." This decision further consolidated internal divisions and the exclusivist attitude toward many non-pentecostal communities. Closer alignment with denominations and institutions critical of the ecumenical movement, such as the National Association of Evangelicals, led many Pentecostals to forsake the ecumenical conversations in which they had participated during the first half of the twentieth century.[29] During the middle of the twentieth century, the pentecostal movement reverted to a form of "spiritual" ecumenism, and its self-understanding as an active ecumenical contributor became ecclesiastically invisible. Pentecostal leaders abstained from formal ecumenical conversations with the emerging ecumenical movement, pastors and missionaries withdrew from ecumenical cooperation, congregational and institutional structures hardened, and the ecumenical fervor of the pentecostal pioneers was virtually eliminated.

ORGANIZED STEPS TOWARD INTERDENOMINATIONAL COOPERATION AND ECUMENICAL RELATIONS

Organized contributions to ecumenical conversations developed slowly after World War I. With the rise of the ecumenical movement since 1910, pentecostal denominations were sporadically involved in organized dialogue; some joined the Foreign Missions Conference of North America and the International Missionary Council and sent delegates to the annual conferences of these organizations, which contributed to the later formation of the National Council of Churches, United States, and the World Council of Churches (WCC).[30] However, the dominant frustration of the ecumenical mind-set among Pentecostals channeled the attention primarily toward the improvement of worldwide cooperation among themselves. In 1921, an International Pentecostal Convention was launched in Amsterdam, and before World War II plans were made for a world conference among Pentecostals. After the war, institutional relationships resulted initially from collaboration with churches and mission agencies engaged in relief efforts.[31] Ecumenical conversations developed gradually through cooperation with churches in neighboring countries. National fellowships were formed in North America, Central and South America, Great Britain, Germany, India, Africa, and Taiwan.[32] These national organizations contributed to the cooperation necessary to form and sustain an international fellowship among the different pentecostal groups, their diverse sociocultural backgrounds, practices, and theological emphases.

The first Pentecostal World Conference was organized in Zürich in 1947, followed by a second conference in Paris in 1949. Subsequent conferences were held every three years and significantly expanded the network among Pentecostals worldwide. An important result of the increasing worldwide conversation among Pentecostals was the formation of the Pentecostal World Fellowship, a global cooperative body as found in many other Christian groups, although without legislative authority over any national entity. Not all pentecostal groups attend the meetings, and the policies of large national pentecostal denominations in North America and Europe remain more influential factors in international cooperation.[33] Nonetheless, the pioneering efforts in international cooperation among Pentecostals carry a number of important implications. Most significant among these is the emergence of two central ecumenical figures, the British Pentecostal Donald Gee (1891–1966) and the South African Pentecostal David J. du Plessis (1905–87), who became one of the leading forces in the renewal of ecumenical commitment among Pentecostals worldwide.

Together, Gee and du Plessis organized the first worldwide conferences among Pentecostals and actively supported their organization; Du Plessis served as general secretary of the Pentecostal World Conference during the first decade, and Gee worked as editor of *Pentecost*, the chief periodical published by the Pentecostal World Fellowship.[34] These efforts gradually rebuilt interest in ecumenical conversations among Pentecostals. In addition, these and other representatives of the changing face of twentieth century Pentecostalism helped interpret the movement to those outside of the movement.[35] At the same time, Du Plessis's understanding of the ecumenical nature of Pentecostalism was at odds with the leadership of his own pentecostal denomination, and he was defrocked as a minister in 1962 until he was reinstated in 1980. During this period, he was able to expand significantly the trajectory of his ecumenical relations with the Roman Catholic Church, the WCC, and the charismatic movement.[36] Eventually, these conversations led to the first official ecumenical dialogue in which Pentecostals participated: it was between the Roman Catholic Church and Pentecostals, a pioneering event that became the model for subsequent ecumenical conversations between Pentecostals and other traditions.

Another important factor contributing to the increase of organized ecumenical conversations during the middle of the twentieth century was the transition in leadership among many pentecostal groups. The new generation of Pentecostals felt restricted by the anti-intellectual attitude, exclusivist mind-set, and lack of dialogue still dominant among many classical Pentecostals and fostered greater interest in establishing relations beyond local, and even national, boundaries. Some pentecostal groups in Latin America, in particular, developed a strong ecumenical vision and commitment. Eventually, a phase of ecumenical solidarity was initiated with the founding of national councils and organizations that promote interdenominational cooperation. These commitments became particularly visible when the first pentecostal churches, the Pentecostal Church of Chile and the Pentecostal Mission Church of Chile, joined the WCC in 1961.[37] This example was followed by several other churches in Latin America, Africa, and the United States.[38] Concerns about the visible exclusion of most pentecostal churches from official membership in the WCC has led to the formation of a Joint Consultative Group in 2000, a dedicated theological discussion between the WCC and Pentecostals that meets annually and has opened the doors for pentecostal contributions in various ecumenical programs and activities, particularly the work on unity, mission, evangelism, and spirituality and the commissions on Faith and Order and World Mission and Evangelism.[39]

A third influence contributing to a change in ecumenical attitude among Pentecostals is the development of pentecostal scholarship and the nurturing of successors to their ecumenical pioneers. The anti-intellectual attitude of many classical pentecostal groups did not equip them well to participate in ecumenical conversations and prejudiced them against what was perceived as an intellectual ecumenism with little practical impact. In response, the global expansion of the pentecostal movement and pioneering efforts in organized worldwide cooperation also increased conversations about an ecumenical pentecostal scholarship. The pioneering efforts of Walter J. Hollenweger brought widespread attention not only to Pentecostalism as an object of ecumenical interest but also to pentecostal scholarship as an ecumenical dialogue partner. Discussions at the ninth Pentecostal World Conference in 1970 led to the formation of the Society for Pentecostal Studies in the United States – a forum of scholars, teachers, ministers, and laypersons that opened up new opportunities to engage in various international ecumenical activities and to give greater visibility to pentecostal participation to both Pentecostals and non-pentecostal participants.[40] Du Plessis was active also in this venue, accompanied by Jerry L. Sandidge, and later Cecil M. Robeck, Jr., who became the successor of du Plessis in international pentecostal dialogues and has shaped the ecumenical character of the society as its president and editor of *Pneuma: The Journal of the Society for Pentecostal Studies*. In many regards, pentecostal scholarship has gained greater ecumenical recognition. In the 1980s, the society approved for its members to accept invitations from the commission of Faith and Order of the National Council of Churches.[41] Since then, the membership of the society has gradually expanded visibly beyond a purely pentecostal constituency, preconference sessions began to host informal conversations with Roman Catholics, and in 2001 an interest group in ecumenical studies was established that continues to serve as an organized ecumenical think tank among Pentecostals.[42] Similar societies, research networks, and publications have been established in Africa, Asia, Europe, Latin America, and Oceania. A large constituency of international pentecostal scholars participated in a widely attended ecumenical gathering in Brighton, England, in 1991.[43] The conference confronted the accepted stereotypes of Pentecostalism as both anti-intellectual and anti-ecumenical.

Nevertheless, the most significant factor in the current turn among Pentecostals toward visible participation in ecumenism is the world-wide expansion and transition of Pentecostalism into various forms that often differ sharply from the confines of the classical pentecostal denominations at the beginning of the twentieth century.[44] The diversification, institutionalization, and upward mobility of the pentecostal movement has also diversified and consolidated pentecostal participation in ecumenical endeavors. Membership in newly formed national councils, commissions, and fellowships worldwide contributes to reconciliation and organization among pentecostal churches, which in turn establishes a broader basis for ecumenical conversations with other traditions. The rise of pentecostal spirituality and practices in the established churches in the form of the charismatic movement further opened Pentecostalism to worldwide ecumenical recognition.[45] Some of these engagements are the result of the ecumenical fervor in the Catholic charismatic movement.[46] Others stem from the gradual shift in the center of attention from dominant Anglo-European concerns to global issues, which include in a large measure the presence of Pentecostals worldwide. Ecumenism among Pentecostals today must be characterized very much as a diversified global and international affair.

A SURVEY OF CURRENT ECUMENICAL ENCOUNTERS

At the beginning of the twenty-first century, Pentecostals are participating in a variety of forms in ecumenical affairs, often on the grassroots level but also in regional, national, and international contexts. In many places across the Global South, Pentecostalism continues to represent a particular challenge to the older historic churches.[47] Ecumenical conversations in these countries depend as much on the sociocultural engagement of pastors and ministers as on participation in existing national forums and organizations.[48] In the Western world, conciliar institutional dialogue is the more dominant form of ecumenical relations, and Pentecostalism has entered into several official conversations with the Roman Catholic Church, the WCC, the World Communion of Reformed Churches (WCRC), the Lutheran World Federation (LWF), the Baptist World Alliance (BWA), and other Protestant bodies.

The strong ecumenical commitment among Latin American pentecostal churches since the 1960s contributed significantly to the formation of the Latin American Council of Churches (CLAI) in 1982 and the all-Latin American Pentecostal Encounters (EPLA) since 1988 that eventually led to the founding of the Latin American Evangelical Pentecostal Commission (CEPLA) in 1990. Pentecostals are active in the Evangelical Union of Latin America (UNELAM), the Evangelical Christian Aid (ACE), the Evangelical Service for Ecumenical Development (SEPADE), and other ecumenical organizations, often connected with social, economic, and political emergencies in different countries. CEPLA has organized or facilitated pentecostal meetings at the national level in Bolivia, Chile, Costa Rica, Mexico, Venezuela, and elsewhere regionally. Transnational meetings of several Latin American Pentecostal consultations have also been convened by the WCC and in cooperation with CLAI in Brazil, Cuba, Peru, and Venezuela.[49] Pentecostal ecumenicity in these organized national efforts depends heavily on pentecostal base communities.[50] The work of these groups has found little support from large pentecostal churches and therefore does not represent all Pentecostalism in Latin America.

Ecumenical consultations and conversations including Pentecostals have taken place on a regional level in various parts of the world, but national discussions and organization have undergone a number of transitions especially in North America and Europe. The racially and doctrinally exclusive Pentecostal Fellowship of North America formed in 1948 was replaced in 1994 by pentecostal/charismatic Churches of North America, which includes African American Pentecostals.[51] Pentecostals have led in the formation of Christian Churches Together in the United States in 2001, a unique crossover organization formed to bridge the divisions between churches historically associated with the National Council of Churches and communities not so aligned.[52] The European Council of Churches received the first pentecostal church into its membership in 1984, and the Pentecostal European Fellowship was founded in 1987. The rise of the charismatic movement in the established churches has further contributed to a number of national dialogues involving pentecostal churches in Germany, Belgium, France, and the Netherlands.[53] African American Pentecostals and black churches in Britain and elsewhere in Europe have taken up the ecumenical challenges, although often not through the established conciliar channels.[54] In contrast, Africa and particularly Asia, although increasingly the host of international ecumenical dialogues, are still lacking national and transnational fellowships among Pentecostals, and an indigenous pentecostal identity emerges only slowly among the many pentecostal mission churches.[55]

The most significant long-term commitment is doubtlessly the international Roman Catholic-Pentecostal dialogue that emerged from the initiative of David du Plessis in 1972. The renewal of the Roman Catholic Church since Vatican II, coupled with its strong institutional support for ecumenical dialogue, the rise of the charismatic movement, and the development of Pentecostalism in the Latin American Catholic and the Hispanic communities in North America, further substantiated concrete efforts on both sides. The results of these conversations address a large number of topics.[56] The first round of discussions (1972–76) explored mutual concerns such as Spirit baptism and spiritual gifts, Christian initiation, and worship.[57] The second phase (1977–82), featuring a radically restructured pentecostal team, discussed questions of Scripture and tradition, faith and reason, speaking in tongues, divine healing, and the role of Mary. The third round (1985–89) produced the widely acclaimed document, *Perspectives on Koinonia*, including questions on the church, the sacraments, and the communion of saints. During the fourth quinquennium (1990–97), the dialogue tackled the difficult questions of evangelization, proselytism, and opportunities for common witness. The most recent phase (1998–2006) resulted in the massive document, *On Becoming a Christian*, focusing on conversion, faith and Christian initiation, Christian formation and discipleship, Spirit baptism and experience in Christian life and community.[58] The continuing dialogue has turned to some of the particular concerns among Latin American bishops and addresses the spiritual significance, pastoral implications, and discernment of spiritual gifts in the church. These conversations have significantly strengthened the ties between Pentecostals and the Roman Catholic Church, although they have also been met with significant criticism and skepticism on both sides.[59] Most significantly, the conversation has helped Pentecostals understand their own identity, consolidating the renewed ecumenical commitment among many Pentecostals, and has led to dialogue with other Protestant bodies.

Similarly influential and controversial has been the increasing involvement of pentecostal groups in the WCC. The Nairobi Assembly in 1975 made the charismatic renewal a central focus, and the Consultation on the Significance of the Charismatic Renewal for the Churches in 1980 brought pentecostal concerns to the center floor of discussion. Significant collaboration increased following the Assembly in Canberra, in 1991, with special attention given to the relationship of Pentecostalism and the charismatic movement.[60] Since the 1980s, Pentecostals have been fully integrated in the work of the Commission on Faith and Order and participate in national and international meetings and conferences.[61] The Faith and Order document, *The Nature and Mission of the Church* (2006), marks the first major ecumenical consensus statement with significant contributions from the pentecostal community.[62] The Joint Consultative Group with Pentecostals was confirmed at the latest Assembly of the WCC and focuses for the study period 2007–13 in particular on the marks of the church. Today, Pentecostals participate in more than forty national councils of churches.[63] The interaction between the rather diverse constituencies representing Pentecostals and the membership of the WCC present various intricate challenges to both sides.

Consistent efforts to strengthen ecumenical ties with other traditions have also led to official dialogue between Pentecostals and the WCRC (formerly the World Alliance of Reformed Churches). The first round of discussions (1996–2000) focused on mature theological themes such as the relationship between the Word and the Holy Spirit as well as the church and the world.[64] The meetings have continued in a second round and currently discuss issues related to experience in Christian faith and life with particular focus on worship, discipleship, community, and justice.

Conversations with the LWF have led since 2005 to official discussions on the question, "How do we encounter Christ?" This dialogue is concerned less with explorations of traditional doctrinal themes, which often force Pentecostals to speak a different theological language, than with allowing space for a genuine expression of faith from pentecostal voices. The focus on concerns with Christian experience has allowed for genuine explorations of an encounter with Christ in worship, proclamation, sacraments, and spiritual gifts.[65]

At this stage, with the exception of the international Roman Catholic-Pentecostal dialogue, ecumenical conversations with pentecostal participation serve primarily as mutual introductions. This is particularly important in the initial stages of informal conversations and opportunities not yet fully developed, such as meetings between Pentecostals and the Synodal Committee for Inter-Orthodox and Inter-Christian Affairs of the Ecumenical Patriarchate of Constantinople established in 2010 and potential conversations with the Mennonite World Conference and the Salvation Army. Dialogues with pentecostal participation typically include attending worship services of each tradition and reflection on those visits. While formal conversations and institutional dialogue continue to develop, much of the ecumenical atmosphere also draws attention to personal and informal meetings that are often perceived as less invasive and more genuine to the status quo of the participating traditions.

The most recent among those initiatives is the Global Christian Forum originating in 1998 and rapidly gathering representatives from all Christian traditions, including Pentecostals. Unlike traditional, formally organized dialogue, these conversations began by sharing the testimonies of each person's journey of faith and focus on establishing relationships.[66] The immediate intentions are not to forge doctrinal agreement or organizational unity but more modestly to contribute to mutual understanding, to overcome existing stereotypes, to encourage communication, and to foster ecumenical fellowship. Agendas for discussion arise from the group, and extended time is given for personal encounters and fostering relationships. Pentecostal participation in the conversations and in the steering committee has formed a new kind of ecumenical environment that responds not only to the limitations of traditional bilateral dialogues and the lack of informal opportunities for broader ecumenical gatherings but also to the dramatic shift of the churches worldwide toward the East and the Global South. The informal environment and testimonial conversations are more consistent with pentecostal forms of self-expression and promise to engage a greater pentecostal constituency in the future.

THE FUTURE OF PENTECOSTAL PARTICIPATION IN ECUMENISM

The changes in ecumenical attitudes among Pentecostals and the transition to new forms of ecumenical conversations reflect the massive changes that continue to take place in the pentecostal movement. Contemporary Pentecostalism is undergoing a transformational renewal on a global level that has taken the movement to the boundaries of its own identity by shifting focus away from issues relating to the major emphases of classical Pentecostalism and toward a global theological agenda that is of broad ecumenical significance.[67] The ecumenical character of Pentecostalism can be described as a manifestation of dominant, global theological developments that continue to shape Christian thought and praxis worldwide. Rather than debating topics that are of importance primarily within classical pentecostal circles, often emphasized by the framework of salvation, healing, Spirit baptism, sanctification, and the coming kingdom, contemporary forms of an ecumenically oriented pentecostal movement are characterized by a complex, multilayered, and globally diverse theological agenda.[68] In this sense, the transformation of Pentecostalism into a global movement demands not only a renewed understanding of what it means to be pentecostal but also a renewed understanding of global Christianity.

Despite the growth and diversification of Pentecostalism in ecu menical circles, ambiguity, uncertainty, and opposition to ecumenical relations prevail in many parts of the movement. The vast majority of Pentecostals worldwide do not participate in conciliar forms of ecumenism. The reasons range from fear and resentment, often coupled with a move away from the churches to which many Pentecostals once belonged and an exclusivist ecclesiology, to the influence of dominant anti-ecumenical attitudes in umbrella organizations, divisions on major issues within pentecostal circles, lack of training and familiarity with successful patterns of ecumenism, a widespread skepticism toward institutional forms of religion and ignorance toward ecumenical affairs, and a loss of orientation in ecumenical conversations dominated by theological patterns often foreign to Pentecostals. The optimism that characterized the movement at the beginning of the twentieth century has made room for a form of ecumenical pragmatism – a transitional phase on the way to more genuine pentecostal forms of engagement that include the development of organizational ecumenical structures and institutional support as well as a raised awareness and reception of ecumenical conversations at the grassroots level.[69] The future of ecumenical dialogue with Pentecostals undoubtedly moves beyond Anglo-European dominance to broader international participation and personal, multiracial, and communal structures that address the local, pastoral, sociocultural, and political concerns of a broad pentecostal constituency.

Investment in ecumenical dialogue is important for both Pentecostals and the ecumenical churches. For Pentecostals, a whole-hearted investment in the process can contribute significantly to a more complete understanding of what it means to be pentecostal in a global context. The origins and the current transition of the movement show that the understanding of Pentecostalism's global distinctiveness is synonymous with the movement's ecumenical identity. A renewed investment in ecumenical conversations can help overcome the glaringly undeveloped ecumenical ecclesiology among Pentecostals.[70] This includes surmounting the estrangement of Pentecostals from the creedal traditions and dominant formulations of doctrine in the established churches.[71] Ecumenical conversations also promise greater familiarity with the broad potential of a sacramental approach to reality despite often being seen as inimical to a pentecostal world view.[72] Finally, the ecumenical dialogue can help sharpen the pneumatological focus that has characterized the twentieth century of the ecumenical movement, and that is central to pentecostal thought and praxis. This could also present a starting point for a more comprehensive integration of pentecostal thought and praxis in the global theological agenda.

In turn, the massive transition of global Pentecostalism since the twentieth century also reflects the changes experienced during that time in the ecumenical movement. Pentecostalism is in many regards a manifestation of a broader ecumenical crisis that includes the structures, organization, comprehensiveness, and reception of ecumenical conversations. Pentecostal participation and leadership can produce new and fruitful forms of ecumenical dialogue that are able to bring clarity to definitions and procedures more akin to the diverse group of churches and fellowships in the global renewal movement. The worldwide representation of Pentecostalism, particularly in Latin America, Africa, and Asia, can restore the balance of international conversations and bring a renewed understanding of Christian unity that includes both the center and the margins of the global theological landscape.

Pentecostalism and ecumenism in the twenty-first century are two mutually interdependent endeavors. The organizational and structural weaknesses experienced in both the pentecostal and the ecumenical movement can only be alleviated by reciprocal international support.[73] The future of ecumenical conversations with Pentecostals does not lie in a numerical growth of the number of bilateral dialogues, although this is desirable. More important is the transformation of the existing status quo, including the provision of new and unprecedented opportunities, structures, and procedures for initiating ecumenical encounters and sustaining ecumenical relationships among churches and communities that do not always possess a solid footing in the historical traditions of Christendom. Pentecostalism brings to these relationships a sense of unity that embraces not only the established churches but also a vision for the currently emerging and not yet fully established groups and fellowships worldwide. What holds these communities together are various forms of understanding what it means to be pentecostal. These voices are as significant to the formulation of a pentecostal self-understanding as to the future of ecumenism. Individually they represent the confusing diversity and nuances of the global puzzle of the visually divided churches. Together they exhibit the colors and flavors of Christian faith and spirituality in the diverse contexts that form the contemporary Christian world.

Notes

1 Walter J. Hollenweger, *Pentecostalism: Origins and Developments Worldwide* (Peabody, MA: Hendrickson, 1997), 334.

2 Douglas Jacobsen, "The Ambivalent Ecumenical Impulses in Early Pentecostal Theology in North America," in Wolfgang Vondey, ed., *Pentecostalism and Christian Unity: Ecumenical Documents and Critical Assessments* (Eugene, OR: Pickwick, 2010), 3–19; Cecil M. Robeck, Jr., "Pentecostals and the Apostolic Faith: Implications for Ecumenism," *Pneuma: The Journal of the Society for Pentecostal Studies* 9:1 (1986), 61–84; Veli-Matti Kärkkäinen, "'Anonymous Ecumenists?' Pentecostals and the Struggle for Christian Unity," *Journal of Ecumenical Studies* 37:1 (2000), 13–27.

3 Donald W. Dayton, *Theological Roots of Pentecostalism* (Peabody, MA: Hendrickson, 1987), 23–8.

4 Charles W. Conn, *Like a Mighty Army: A History of the Church of God, Definitive Edition* (Cleveland, TN: Pathway, 1996), 12–14.

5 D. W. Myland, *The Latter Rain Covenant and Pentecostal Power with Testimony of Healing and Baptism* (Chicago: Evangel, 1910), 111.

6 William J. Seymour, "The Apostolic Faith Movement," *Apostolic Faith* 1:1 (1906), 2.

7 Charles Fox Parham, *Kol KareBombidar: A Voice Crying in the Wilderness* (Baxter Springs, KS: Robert L. Parham, 1902; reprint 1944), 61.

8 Frank Bartleman, *Azusa Street* (South Plainfield, NJ: Bridge Publishing, 1925, reprint 1980), 68.

9 Thomas B. Barratt, *In the Days of the Latter Rain* (London: Simpkin, Marshall, Hamilton, Kent, 1909), 145. Emphasis original.

10 See Cornelis van der Laan, *Sectarian against His Will: Gerrit Roelof Polman and the Birth of Pentecostalism in the Netherlands (Studies in Evangelicalism)*, Book 11 (London: Scarecrow, 1991), 268.

11 Ibid., 105–30; Hollenweger, *Pentecostalism*, 334–49; David Bundy, "Pentecostalism in Belgium," *Pneuma: Journal of the Society for Pentecostal Studies* 8:1 (1986), 41–56.

12 Wolfgang Vondey, "The Denominations in Classical and Global Pentecostal Ecclesiology: A Historical and Theological Contribution," in Paul M. Collins and Barry Ensign-George, eds., *Denomination: Assessing an Ecclesiological Category, (Ecclesiological Investigations)*, Book 11 (New York: Continuum, 2011), 100–16.

13 William F. Carothers, "Position of the Old 'Movement,'" *Weekly Evangel* 127 (February 19, 1916), 5.

14 L. M. Conway, "United We Stand, Divided We Fall," *Weekly Evangel* 185 (April 14, 1917), 5.

15 Jacobsen, "The Ambivalent Ecumenical Impulses," 4–13. See also Harold D. Hunter, "Global Pentecostalism and Ecumenism: Two Movements of the Holy Spirit?" in Vondey, *Pentecostalism and Christian Unity*, 20–33.

16 Grant Wacker, "Playing for Keeps: The Primitivist Impulse in Early Pentecostalism," in Richard T. Hughes, ed., *The American Quest for the Primitive Church* (Urbana: University of Illinois Press, 1988), 196–219.

17 D. William Faupel, *The Everlasting Gospel: The Significance of Eschatology in the Development of Pentecostal Thought* (Sheffield: Sheffield Academic, 1996), 44–76.

18 John T. Nichol, *Pentecostalism* (New York: Harper & Row, 1966), 70.

19 Cf. Horace S. Ward, "The Anti-Pentecostal Argument," in Vinson Synan, ed., *Aspects of Pentecostal-Charismatic Origins* (Plainfield: Logos International, 1975), 99–122.

20 See Cecil M. Robeck, Jr., "Sanctified Passion or Carnal Pleasure? A Review Essay," *Pneuma: The Journal of the Society for Pentecostal Studies* 29:1 (2007), 103–11.

21 Kärkkäinen, "Anonymous Ecumenists," 17–18.

22 Jon Ruthven, *On the Cessation of the Charismata: The Protestant Polemic on Postbiblical Miracles* (Sheffield: Sheffield Academic, 1993), 13–17.

23 Stanley H. Frodsham, "Disfellowshiped!," *Pentecostal Evangel* (August 18, 1928), 7. Cf. Vinson Synan, *The Holiness-Pentecostal Movement in the United States* (Grand Rapids, MI: Eerdmans, 1971), 205–07.

24 Cf. Robert Mapes Anderson, *Vision of the Disinherited: The Making of American Pentecostalism* (New York: Oxford University Press, 1979), 192–94.

25 See William J. Seymour, *The Doctrines and Discipline of the Azusa Street Faith Mission of Los Angeles, California* (n. p., 1915), 10, 12–13.

26 Synan, *The Holiness-Pentecostal Movement*, 141–63.

27 Vondey, "Denominations in Classical and Global Pentecostalism," 140.

28 Wolfgang Vondey, *Beyond Pentecostalism: The Crisis of Global Christianity and the Renewal of the Theological Agenda* (Grand Rapids, MI: William B. Eerdmans Publishing Company, 2010), 155–59.

29 Cecil M. Robeck, Jr., "The Assemblies of God and Ecumenical Cooperation 1920–1965," in Wonsuk Ma and Robert P. Menzies, eds., *Pentecostalism in Context: Essays in Honor of William W. Menzies* (Sheffield: Sheffield Academic, 1997), 107–50.

30 Cf. Robeck, "The Assemblies of God and Ecumenical Cooperation."

31 Jeffrey Gros, "Pentecostal Engagement in the Wider Christian Community," *Mid-Stream: The Ecumenical Movement Today* 28 (1999), 26–47.

32 Jerry L. Sandidge, *Roman Catholic/Pentecostal Dialogue (1977–1982): A Study in Developing Ecumenism*, 2 vols. (Frankfurt: Peter Lang, 1987), vol. I, 6.

33 Walter J. Hollenweger, "Two Extraordinary Pentecostal Ecumenists: The Letters of Donald Gee and David Du Plessis," *Ecumenical Review* 52:3 (2000), 391–402.

34 Robeck, "Pentecostals and the Apostolic Faith," 65–66; Hollenweger, "Two Extraordinary Pentecostal Ecumenists," 391–92.

35 M. Robinson, "David du Plessis – A Promise Fulfilled," in Jan A. B. Jongeneel, et al., eds., *Pentecost, Mission and Ecumenism: Essays on Intellectual Theology: Festschrift in Honour of Professor Walter J. Hollenweger* (Frankfurt: Peter Lang, 1992), 143–55.

36 Ibid., 149.

37 Carmelo E. Alvarez, "Joining the World Council of Churches: The Ecumenical Story of Pentecostalism in Chile," in Vondey, *Pentecostalism and Christian Unity*, 34–45.

38 Sandidge, *Roman Catholic/Pentecostal Dialogue*, I:13–14.

39 Huibert van Beek, "Pentecostals-Ecumenicals Dialogue," in Andre Droogers, Cornelis van der Laan, and W. van Laar, eds., *Fruitful in This Land: Pluralism, Dialogue and Healing in Migrant Pentecostalism* (Geneva: WCC, 2006), 81–92.

40 Cecil M. Robeck, Jr., "Pentecostals and Christian Unity: Facing the Challenge," *Pneuma: The Journal of the Society for Pentecostal Studies* 26:2 (2004), 329–31; Sandidge, *Roman Catholic/Pentecostal Dialogue*, I:16–18.

41 K. Houghland, "Pentecostals and NCC Begin Dialogue," *Christian Century* 104:3 (1987), 87–89.

42 Vondey, *Pentecostalism and Christian Unity*, ix–x.

43 Harold D. Hunter and Peter D. Hocken, eds., *All Together in One Place: Theological Papers from the Brighton Conference on World Evangelization* (Sheffield: Sheffield Academic Press, 1993), 262–65.

44 Donald E. Miller and Tetsunao Yamamori, *Global Pentecostalism: The New Face of Christian Social Engagement* (Berkeley: University of California Press, 2007), 1–38; Murray W. Dempster and B. D. Klaus, eds., *The Globalization of Pentecostalism: A Religion Made to Travel* (Oxford: Regnum, 1999), 3–123.

45 Allan H. Anderson, *An Introduction to Pentecostalism* (Cambridge: Cambridge University Press, 2004), 249–53.

46 Hollenweger, *Pentecostalism*, 159–65.

47 Cecil M. Robeck, Jr., "The Challenge Pentecostalism Poses to the Quest for Ecclesial Unity," in Peter Walter, Klaus Krämer, and George Augustin, eds., *Kirche in ökumenischer Perspektive: Kardinal Walter Kasper zum 70. Geburtstag* (Freiburg: Herder, 2003), 306–20.

48 Richard Shaull and Waldo Cesar, *Pentecostalism and the Future of the Christian Churches: Promises, Limitations, Challenges* (Grand Rapids, MI: Eerdmans, 2000); Carmelo E. Alvarez, *Pentecostalismo y liberación: Una experiencia latinoamericana* (San Jos: Editorial Departamento Ecuménico de Investigaciones, 1992).

49 Alvarez, "Joining the World Council of Churches," 35–43; Bernardo Campos, *De La Reform Prostestante a La Pentecostalidad de La Iglesia: Debate sobre el Pentecostalismo en América Latina* (Quito: Ediciones Consejo Latinoamericano de Iglesias, 1997).

50 Roger Cabezas, *CLAI: Experiencia de un ecumenismo latinoamericano de base* (Lima: CLAI, 1982).

51 Frank Macchia, "From Azusa to Memphis: Evaluating the Racial Reconciliation Dialogue among Pentecostals," *Pneuma: The Journal of the Society for Pentecostal Studies* 17:2 (1995), 203–18.

52 http://www.christianchurchestogether.org. Accessed March 1, 2014.

53 Paul van der Laan, "Guidelines for Ecumenical Dialogue with Pentecostals: Lessons from the Netherlands," in Vondey, *Pentecostalism and Christian Unity*, 46–65; Sandidge, *Roman Catholic/Pentecostal Dialogue*, I:352–59.

54 Allan H. Anderson and Walter J. Hollenweger, eds., *Pentecostals after a Century: Global Perspectives on a Movement in Transition* (Sheffield: Sheffield Academic Press, 1999), 33–107.

55 John M. Prior, "The Challenge of the Pentecostals in Asia, Part One, Pentecostal Movements in Asia," *Exchange: Journal for Missiological and*

Ecumenical Research 36:1 (2007), 6–40; Allan H. Anderson, "The Struggle for Unity in Pentecostal Mission Churches," *Journal of Theology for Southern Africa* 82 (1993), 67–77.

56   Sandidge, *Roman Catholic/Pentecostal Dialogue*, I:60–279.

57   The documents of the dialogues from 1972–197 can be found in Vondey, *Pentecostalism and Christian Unity*, 101–98.

58   "On Becoming a Christian: Insights from Scripture and the Patristic Community. The Report from the Fifth Phase of the International Dialogue between Some Classical Pentecostal Churches and Leaders and the Catholic Church (1998–2006),"in Wolfgang Vondey, ed., *Pentecostalism and Christian Unity*, vol. 2, *Continuing and Building Relationships* (Eugene, OR: Pickwick, 2013), 95–216.

59   Cecil M. Robeck, Jr., "Lessons from the International Roman Catholic-Pentecostal Dialogue," in Vondey, *Pentecostalism and Christian Unity*, 82–98.

60   Hollenweger, *Pentecostalism*, 377–84.

61   Gros, "Pentecostal Engagement," 33–35.

62   See the pentecostal reflections on the text in Vondey, *Pentecostalism and Christian Unity*, 231–68.

63   Huibert van Beek, *A Handbook of Churches and Councils: Profiles of Ecumenical Relationships* (Geneva: World Council of Churches, 2006).

64   See the report in Vondey, *Pentecostalism and Christian Unity*, 199–227. Cf. Frank D. Macchia, "Spirit, Word, and Kingdom: Theological Reflections on the Pentecostal/Reformed Dialogue," *Ecumenical Trends* 30:3 (2001), 33–39.

65   Institute for Ecumenical Research, The David du Plessis Center for Christian Spirituality, and The European Pentecostal Charismatic Research Association, eds., *Lutherans and Pentecostals in Dialogue* (Strasbourg: Institute for Ecumenical Research, 2010), 7–21.

66   Huibert van Beek, ed., *Revisioning Christian Unity: The Global Christian Forum, Studies in Global Christianity* (Oxford: Regnum, 2009); Richard Howell, ed., *Global Christian Forum: Transforming Ecumenism* (New Delhi: Evangelical Fellowship of India, 2007).

67   Vondey, *Beyond Pentecostalism*, 1–15.

68   Wolfgang Vondey, *Pentecostalism: A Guide for the Perplexed* (London: Bloomsbury, 2013), 9–27; Amos Yong, *The Spirit Poured Out on All Flesh: Pentecostalism and the Possibility of Global Theology* (Grand Rapids, MI: Baker Academic, 2005), 167–202; Dempster and Klaus, *The Globalization of Pentecostalism*, 127–258.

69   Wolfgang Vondey, "Presuppositions for Pentecostal Engagement in Ecumenical Dialogue," *Exchange: Journal for Missiological and Ecumenical Research* 30:4 (2001), 344–58.

70   Wolfgang Vondey, "Pentecostal Ecclesiology and Eucharistic Hospitality: Toward a Systematic and Ecumenical Account of the Church," *Pneuma: Journal of the Society for Pentecostal Studies* 32:1 (2010), 41–55.

71   Wolfgang Vondey, "Oneness and Trinitarian Pentecostalism: Critical Dialogue on the Ecumenical Creeds," *One in Christ* 44, no. 1 (2010): 86–102.

72 Chris W. Green and Wolfgang Vondey, "Between This and That: Reality and Sacramentality in the Pentecostal Worldview," *Journal of Pentecostal Theology* 19:2 (2010), 243–64.

73 Wolfgang Vondey, "Appeal for a Pentecostal Council for Ecumenical Dialogue," *Mid-Stream* 40:3 (2001), 45–56.

Further Reading

Gros, J., E. McManus, and A. Riggs. *Introduction to Ecumenism.* New York: Paulist Press, 1998.

Moltmann, J., and K.-J. Kuschel, eds., *Pentecostal Movements as an Ecumenical Challenge.* , London: SCM Press, 1996.

Wainwright, G. "The One Hope of Our Calling: The Ecumenical and Pentecostal Movements after a Century." *Pneuma: The Journal of the Society for Pentecostal Studies* 25 (2003), 7–28.

15 Pentecostal Mission and Encounter with Religions

VELI-MATTI KÄRKKÄINEN

INTRODUCTION: MISSION AT THE HEART OF THE SPIRIT MOVEMENT

No doubt, pentecostal mission has been a success story if we look at numbers. Statistics are impressive, even staggering![1] However, numbers are numbers. They only tell so much – and numbers do not do theology. Still, numbers matter in terms of inviting both Pentecostals and others to reflect theologically and missiologically on the shape and distinctive features of Pentecostalism as a missionary movement.[2] Why do Pentecostals focus so much on mission? What is the missionary agenda? What are the underlying motifs – or resources? This kind of critical and constructive theological reflection on mission has not been the hallmark of Pentecostalism for the simple reason that Pentecostals have been more "doers" than "thinkers." Rather than writing theological treatises, first Pentecostals produced evangelistic tracts.[3]

Only recently have pentecostal theologians and missiologists begun this reflective work, including mission in relation to other living faiths. Undoubtedly Pentecostals – along with the Roman Catholic Church – are the most widely spread Christian movement among various cultures and religions. That fact alone would necessitate a careful look at missiology and the theology of religions.[4]

The centrality of mission, evangelization, and social concern among Pentecostals is wonderfully illustrated by the "mission statement" of the Apostolic Faith Mission, in Los Angeles, California. Claiming to be standing in the long line of biblical "apostolic" life energized by the Holy Spirit, their self-identification put it like this:

THE APOSTOLIC FAITH MOVEMENT Stands for the restoration of faith once delivered unto the saints – the old time religion, camp meetings, revivals, missions, street and prison work and Christian Unity everywhere.[5]

Inspired by this robust missionary ethos, at the beginning and many decades thereafter, pentecostal "missionaries were for the most part inexperienced although they had one common qualification: an overwhelming conviction that they had been filled with the Holy Spirit to spread their message to the furthest corners of the earth. And this is what they did, defying the conventions of the time and, in some cases, laying down their lives for their cause."[6]

This missionary enthusiasm by and large still persists as is evident in the declaration on evangelism adopted in 1968 and subsequently affirmed several times by the Assemblies of God, the largest white pentecostal denomination in the United States. In it they declared "[t]hat the Assemblies of God considers it was brought into being and built by the working of the Holy Spirit as an instrument of divine purpose in these end times." It further declared that it recognized its mission "[t]o be an agency of God for evangelizing the world." Other pentecostal bodies have issued similar statements.[7]

A PROFILE OF PENTECOSTAL MISSION ETHOS

Scholarly consensus holds that whatever other reasons may help us understand the centrality of mission for Pentecostalism, it has everything to do with the two formative factors underlying the whole pentecostal spirituality: eschatological fervor and the crucial role of the Holy Spirit. These two factors are integrally related to each other. Pentecostals believe that they have been called by God in the "last days" (Acts 2:17) to be Christlike witnesses in the power of the Spirit. The hope in the imminent coming of the Lord has energized pentecostal churches and movements in their worldwide missionary enthusiasm and activity. Pentecostals have consistently taught that the church must be ready for the coming of the Lord by means of faithful witness and holy living.[8]

Although outside observers of Pentecostalism tend to overestimate the importance of speaking in tongues, it is also true that, particularly in the beginning of the movement, speaking in tongues, coupled with eschatological urgency and evangelistic burden, resulted in an expectation of the soon-to-be-finished nature of the task of mission. Some of the earliest missionaries held an unwarranted optimism that speaking in tongues (*xenolalia*), a form of glossolalia in which human languages previously unknown to the speaker could be spoken, would be given by the Holy Spirit to help finish the evangelization of the world before the imminent return of Christ.[9] "So intensely did they expect the Second Coming of Christ that envisioning an additional decade – or even another century – for evangelization would have been inconceivable."[10] However, when few pentecostal missionaries ever claimed to have experienced xenolalia and were forced to learn the languages of those they wanted to evangelize and the end did not come, Pentecostals easily adopted the missionary methods of other Protestants.

When attempting a more specific list of factors behind pentecostal missions ethos, the American missiologist Grant McClung's intuitions seem to be right on target. He mentions seven such characteristics of pentecostal missions:[11]

- experiential and relational
- expressly biblical with a high view of inspiration of Scripture[12]
- extremely urgent in nature
- "focused, yet diversified," prioritizing evangelization, but not to the exclusion of social concern
- aggressive and bold in its approach
- interdependent (both among various pentecostal/charismatic groups and in relation to older churches and their mission endeavors)
- unpredictable as to the future

Similar kinds of characterizations have been posed by other pentecostal missiologists who have spoken of naive Biblicism, eschatology, individualism, total commitment, pragmatism, flexibility, a place for emotions, personal testimonies, establishment of indigenous churches as a goal of missions, demonstration of the power of the Spirit, and participation of all believers.[13]

When it comes to the actual praxis of the missions work, the so-called indigenous church principle has been a high priority from the beginning of pentecostal mission. This was, paradoxically, helped by the lack of funding especially in the beginning decades of pentecostal missions when a considerable number of missionaries went overseas without any pledged support. The "faith missions" approach was enthusiastically adopted by many pioneers both because of the biblical support of the idea and an intensive expectation of the Second Coming, but it soon gave way to a more traditional mission praxis.

Not surprisingly, Pentecostals have also been pragmatists in their approach to mission. Consequently, flexibility in choosing methods, strategies, and structures – or lack of structures – has been a brand mark of pentecostal missiology. In their mission and church structures, Pentecostals embrace all the possible variations from Episcopal (e.g., former Eastern Europe, Africa) to Presbyterian (mainly in the English-speaking world) to polities emphasizing total autonomy of local churches (Scandinavian Pentecostals and their mission fields, for example, in some Latin American countries).

THE DEVELOPMENT OF PENTECOSTAL MISSIOLOGY

What is the state of art in pentecostal reflection on the theology of mission? The first missiological treatise written by a prominent pentecostal theologian and practitioner did not appear until 1953, when Melvin L. Hodges produced the widely read book *The Indigenous Church*. Two decades later, he wrote a sequel to it under the title *Theology of the Church and Its Mission* (1977). Both of these books followed the paths explored by Evangelicals on mission theology and social action.[14] It was quite natural for Pentecostals to align themselves with Evangelicals, because the mainline ecumenical movement seemed too liberal both theologically and in its mission agenda.[15] Both Pentecostals and Evangelicals share conservative doctrinal views regarding the inspiration and authority of the Bible, the lostness of humankind without Christ, and justification by faith, as well as the priority of evangelism over social action. Recently, an increasing number of pentecostal theologians and missiologists have come to question the compatibility of their pneumatological distinctiveness with Evangelical beliefs about the Holy Spirit, yet they have not questioned their allegiance to the wider evangelical constituency.

It was not until 1991, when the major compendium of pentecostal missiology came out,[16] that some theologically serious perspectives were offered by a younger generation of pentecostal academics. This initial volume contains biblical, theological, strategic, cultural, and religious viewpoints on global pentecostal mission.

Along with their interest in the work of the Holy Spirit, some pentecostal exegetes have done serious work in the area of New Testament pneumatology, especially in Luke-Acts,[17] which has a lot of missiological potential. The Pacific Rim missionary Robert Menzies has written on distinctive features of Lukan pneumatology with a view to mission.[18] He argues that the church, by virtue of its reception of the pentecostal gift, is a prophetic community of empowerment for missionary service. His line of thought is developed and specifically focused on mission by Australian J. M. Penney, who contends that the reason Luke-Acts has been so dear to Pentecostals is that Pentecostalism – from inception a missionary movement – saw in the Spirit baptism of Acts 2 a normative paradigm for the empowerment of every Christian to preach the gospel. "Acts is more than history for the Pentecostal: it is a missionary manual, an open-ended account of the missionary work of the Holy

Spirit in the church, concluding, not with ch. 28, but with the ongoing Spirit-empowered and Spirit-directed gospel preaching of today."[19]

The latest major contribution to pentecostal missiology comes from the Korean couple Julie and Wonsuk Ma, long-term missionaries to the Philippines, who also have extensive experience in academic teaching and research in pentecostal missiology.[20] Their contribution has a great deal of relevance beyond pentecostal and charismatic movements. The Mas develop a robust and holistic account of the work of the Spirit of God, beginning from the Old Testament, in the work of the Spirit of Yahweh in creation. The turn to the Old Testament is a needed corrective to the one-sided focus on the New Testament often found in pentecostal circles. Hence, a pneumatological creation theology is developed first and only then does the work of the charismatic Spirit of God come to play, including signs and wonders.[21]

This kind of theology supports the care for the environment as an essential part of mission work and affirms the importance of theological anthropology as well. This Korean pentecostal theology also pays close attention to the social context of mission, particularly the Asian cultures (Chapter 6) and highlights the importance of tackling issues of oppression, poverty, and various forms of human abuse. An important part of the cultural task is to engage the diverse religious traditions of the continent (Chapter 7). Along with careful tackling of biblical, theological, cultural, and other basic missiological issues, the Mas also offer a detailed consideration of the praxis of mission work, including church planting (Chapter 8), church growth (Chapter 9), the role of women (Chapter 13), and similar issues, as well as a look into the future.

THEOLOGICAL INTUITIONS OF PENTECOSTAL MISSION

Although it would not be feasible – and perhaps not even useful at this time in its development – to attempt a full-scale pentecostal theology of mission from a movement that is only one century old, it certainly is a necessary task to attempt to discern key theological convictions and insights underlying the massive mission activities. This kind of sketch has to be based on key intuitions of pentecostal spirituality and theology at large, lest it suggests something external to the "core" of the movement. A tentative, suggestive presentation of leading theological motifs includes the following interrelated aspects:

- Jesus Christ and the Full Gospel
- The Holy Spirit and Empowerment

- Salvation and the Vision of Holism
- Church and the Spirit of *Koinonia*

Jesus Christ and the Full Gospel
Against the assumptions of uninformed outside observers, pneumatology does not necessarily represent the center of pentecostal spirituality. Rather, Jesus Christ is the center, with the Holy Spirit in relation to Christ. At the heart of pentecostal spirituality lies the idea of the "Full Gospel," the template of Jesus Christ in his fivefold role as Savior, Sanctifier, Baptizer with the Spirit, Healer, and Soon-Coming King.[22]

On this robust "Spirit-Christology" stands the Pentecostal missiological vision:

> Thus, the outpouring of the Spirit at Pentecost constituted the church as an eschatological community of universal mission in the power and demonstration of the Spirit. The tongues at Pentecost and Peter's subsequent sermon meant that the church in general and each Spirit-filled individual are to be and to give a witness to the mighty acts of God in saving humanity. This witness centers in Jesus Christ and must therefore be given in the power of the Spirit if it is to have continuity with his ministry and fulfill the promise of the Father through Christ. The "full gospel" of the Jesus who is Savior, Sanctifier, Healer, Baptizer in the Holy Spirit and coming King can and should be proclaimed in the fullness of the Spirit so that the kingdom will be manifested in the midst of the world in words and deeds.[23]

The term "Full Gospel" signaled to Pentecostals the desire to embrace "all" of Christ.[24] Observing the preaching and mission of other churches, Pentecostals wondered if older traditions were missing some crucial aspects of the Full Gospel.[25] The healing work of Christ is a case in point. Pentecostals were glad to hear Lutherans preach the gospel of justification by faith, and Methodists/Holiness movements highlight the importance of sanctification. What they did not hear in the preaching of other churches and their missionaries was the dynamic New Testament testimonies to the healing power of Jesus, the One who is the same yesterday, today, and tomorrow (Heb. 13:8).[26] The prioritization of the Christ and his Full Gospel does not of course mean downplaying the work of the Holy Spirit. Rather, it is to put pneumatology in the proper perspective.

The Holy Spirit and Empowerment
Whereas for most other Christians the presence of the Spirit is just that, *presence*, for Pentecostals the presence of the Spirit in their midst

implies *empowerment*.[27] While this empowerment often manifests itself in spiritual gifts such as speaking in tongues, prophecy, or healings, it is still felt and sought by Pentecostals even when those manifestations are absent. The main function of the pentecostal worship service is to provide a setting for an encounter with Jesus, the embodiment of the Full Gospel, to receive the (em)power(ment) of the Spirit.[28] As important as sermon, hymns, and liturgy are, they all take second place to the "meeting with the Lord," as Pentecostals put it.

Part of the texture of enthusiastic missions ethos is a spirituality that incorporates the importance of visions, healing, dreams, dance, and other archetypal religious expressions. The Harvard theologian Harvey Cox rightly remarks that "the reemergence of this primal spirituality came – perhaps not surprisingly – at just the point in history when both the rationalistic assumptions of modernity and the strategies religions had used to oppose them (or to accommodate to them) were all coming unraveled."[29]

Gifts of the Spirit such as prophesying, prayer for healing, and works of miracles are enthusiastically embraced and sought by Pentecostals. Belief in the capacity of the Spirit to bring about healing, whether physical or emotional/mental, is one of the hallmarks of Pentecostalism. A related belief is the Spirit-given capacity to engage in "spiritual warfare"[30] and to exorcise demonic spirits.[31]

Salvation and the Holistic Vision

In their search for a holistic vision and experience of salvation that includes not only the spiritual but also physical, material, and socio-relational, Pentecostals seem to echo the postmodern insistence on a holistic understanding of the body-mind relationship, as has been noted by some scholars of Pentecostalism[32] and pentecostal theologians.[33] The common features between the two movements include the principle of embodiment, search for holism, as well as the attention paid to "experientialism." Be that as it may, it seems that Pentecostalism "has succeeded because it has spoken to the spiritual emptiness of our time by reaching beyond the levels of creed and ceremony into the core of human religiousness.... Pentecostals have touched so many people because they have indeed restored something."[34] No doubt, in their yearning and search for a holistic account of the Full Gospel, Pentecostals came to embrace the notion of "holistic salvation" long before the term gained fame in some mainline theologies.[35]

In an important essay titled "Materiality of Salvation: An Investigation in the Soteriologies of Liberation and Pentecostal

Theologies," the Yale theologian Miroslav Volf, who comes originally from the Pentecostal Church of Croatia, former Yugoslavia, has argued that with all their differences, these two Christian movements share a vision of salvation in this-worldly, physical, material, embodied terms.[36] While neither of the movements, of course, leaves behind the eschatological, future-oriented hope, relegating salvation merely to the future will not do either. True, liberationists focus their efforts on sociopolitical (including gender) liberation, whereas for Pentecostals it is more about the individual's release from sicknesses and ailments, physical or emotional – however, not to the exclusion of sociopolitical dimensions either.

From early on, Pentecostals invested money and energy for building schools, hospitals, and orphanages. Although giving priority to evangelism and individual conversion, Pentecostals were never oblivious to social concern, even though that myth exists among outside observers of Pentecostalism.[37] With all its problems with "other-worldliness," Pentecostalism is also characterized by a commitment to social justice, empowerment of the powerless, and a "preferential option for the marginalized" tracing back to its roots at Azusa Street as a kind of paradigm of marginalization – a revival in an abandoned stable, led by an African-American preacher.[38]

At the same time, the idea of the materiality of salvation in the hands of too many Pentecostals and Charismatics has also turned into a gross materialistic search for financial and other benefits. Any visit to some pentecostal churches not only in the United States but also all over the global South from Africa to Asia to Latin America paints a picture that raises serious questions for any theologian and missiologist. Health and wealth are sometimes made the prime indicator of God's blessings, and spiritual techniques for reaching them are fine-tuned by ever-new itinerant charismatic preachers. Pentecostalism also at times suffers from the same kind of "spiritualist" reductionism that Volf sees indicative of many traditional theologies – namely, prioritizing the salvation of the "souls" to the point at which the wholeness of the human being as an embodied *imago Dei* is being missed. In pentecostal preaching and witnessing, you can hear simultaneously both voices: seeking for wholeness of salvation and emphasis on the salvation of the soul.

Church and the Spirit of *Koinonia*

Although only a few Pentecostals have joined the vibrant ecumenical conversation about communion theology,[39] in their aggressive and creative church planting work they have intuited the importance of communal dimensions and communities. Despite the lack of fully developed ecclesiology, a good case can be made for the claim that "[p]entecostal soteriology and pneumatology point ... unmistakably in the direction of an *ecclesiology of the fellowship of persons*."[40] Pentecostals speak of the church as a charismatic fellowship, a fellowship of persons, the body of Christ.[41]

On the other hand, in a dynamic opposition to this communion orientation, much of Pentecostalism, especially in the global North and as a result of missions work from the North, has tended to foster the hyperindividualism of the post-Enlightenment mentality.[42] That said, there is no denying the fact that a charismatically conceived communion theology, with an inclusive vision, has supported pentecostal missions' efforts and led to the mushrooming of communities that have experienced the multifaceted *koinonia* described in Acts 2:42–44, a dear passage to Pentecostals.[43]

PENTECOSTALS AND THE CHALLENGE OF RELIGIOUS PLURALISM

From Rejection of Interfaith Engagement to Cautious Dialogue

If not for other reasons, then because of their worldwide extension as a result of aggressive mission work, Pentecostals ought to pay close attention to the relation to other living faiths. Not surprisingly, for a long time Pentecostals took it for granted that the topic of religious plurality has little need for reflection, as the typical conservative-fundamentalistic exclusivism was taken for granted. No wonder, the wish of a sympathetic observer of Pentecostalism, Clark Pinnock, has not been materialized among masses of pentecostal missionaries: "One might expect the Pentecostals to develop a Spirit-oriented theology of mission and world religions, because of their openness to religious experience, their sensitivity to the oppressed of the Third World where they have experienced much of their growth, and their awareness of the ways of the Spirit as well as dogma."[44]

Aligning with the more conservative wing of the church, Pentecostals have also been the first to raise doubts about any kind of saving role of the Spirit apart from the proclamation of the gospel. Most often Pentecostals have either succumbed to the standard fundamentalist view of limiting the Spirit's saving work to the church (except for the work of the Spirit preparing for receiving the gospel)[45] or have ignored outright any reflection on what their otherwise strong insistence on the principle *spiritus ubi vult spirat* ("The Spirit blows where it wills," Jn

3:6) might mean in relation to other religions. Furthermore, with other conservative Christians, Pentecostals have been afraid of the dangers of recent "liberal" or pluralistic approaches to the issue.[46] A case in point is the warning from a teacher affiliated with Central Bible College of the Assemblies of God in the United States. According to this statement, a pluralistic approach poses a threefold problem: (1) it is contrary to Scripture; (2) it replaces the obligation for world evangelism; and (3) those who fail to fulfill the Great Commission are ultimately not living under the Lordship of Christ.[47]

An important impetus for prompting Pentecostals to begin engaging interfaith issues has come from ecumenical exchanges with older Christian traditions, beginning from the International Dialogue with Roman Catholics, which began in 1972.[48] There was a tentative discussion on the possibility of salvation for those not explicitly confessing faith in Christ during the second quinquennium (1978–82) of that dialogue although no unanimity was reached. Although they reported that both Catholics and Pentecostals believe that "ever since the creation of the world, the visible existence of God and his everlasting power have been clearly seen by the mind's understanding of created things" (cf. Rom 1:20; Ps 19:1–4), their perspectives diverged over the existence and/or meaning of salvific elements found in non-Christian religions.[49] Pentecostals insisted that there can be no salvation outside the church.[50] Most Pentecostals limit the saving work of the Spirit to the church and its proclamation of the gospel, although they acknowledge the work of the Holy Spirit in the world, convicting people of sin.[51] The rationale for this more exclusivist attitude is found in the fallen state of humankind and in a literal reading of the New Testament, which for Pentecostals does not give much hope for non-Christians.[52] Furthermore, Pentecostals, like many of the early Christians, tend to point out the demonic elements in other religions rather than common denominators.[53] However, there are some Pentecostals who would see a convergence toward the Catholic position that the Holy Spirit is at work in non-Christian religions, preparing individual hearts for an eventual exposure to the gospel of Jesus Christ.[54]

Emerging Pentecostal Interfaith Theologies

A decisively new turn in the brief history of pentecostal missiology has been taken by the release of two volumes by Amos Yong, originally from Malaysia, that advance a robustly pneumatological approach to mission and other religions.[55] Yong argues for a uniquely pentecostal pneumatology that, while holding on to the uniqueness of Jesus Christ and

Trinitarian faith, would also be open to acknowledging the ministry of the Holy Spirit outside the Christian Church. His goal is to develop criteria for discerning the Spirit of God and distinguishing that ministry from the work of other spirits in the world.

In his next important contribution to emerging pentecostal systematic theology, Yong continues the honing of a pneumatological approach to religions and "spirits" of religions.[56] He issues a call to all Pentecostals to work toward a public theology by engaging pentecostal pneumatology with interfaith dialogue. His thesis is that

> a pneumatologically driven theology is more conducive to engaging [interfaith issues] ... in our time than previous approaches. ... [R]eligions are neither accidents of history nor encroachments on divine providence but are, in various ways, instruments of the Holy Spirit working out the divine purposes in the world and ... the unevangelized, if saved at all, are saved through the work of Christ by the Spirit (even if mediated through the religious beliefs and practices available to them).[57]

In his latest major contribution to the developing pentecostal theology of religions, Yong taps into the theme of hospitality, enthusiastically embraced by much of contemporary interfaith conversations, as a way to help his movement engage the religious Other.[58]

The most recent contribution to emerging theology of religions by Pentecostals comes from Bishop Tony Richie of the Church of God (Cleveland, Tennessee), whose monograph both considers carefully typical objections posed by Pentecostals against the engagement of interfaith issues and seeks to constructs a viable approach to religions, building especially on the core pentecostal practice of testimony. Richie considers it important to pursue this task in the matrix of Pentecostalism's "strong heritage of evangelism and missions, generally conservative ethical and theological history, and undeniable multicultural variety."[59] He also takes lessons from some pentecostal pioneers in whose ethos Richie sees seeds of openness to religions while at the same time faithfully representing the pentecostal tradition.[60]

A growing number of pentecostal theologians are currently engaging the topic of interfaith engagement.[61] My own work in the field of interfaith studies has focused on developing a Trinitarian understanding of the role of the Spirit in the world. In this pursuit, the dialogue partners have been Protestant and Catholic colleagues outside Pentecostalism.[62]

Useful guidelines for the pentecostal engagement of living faiths and religious pluralism are provided by the Hispanic pentecostal theologian

Samuel Solivan. According to him, the following principles might help Pentecostals in this endeavor: (1) the fact that the Holy Spirit is the one who leads Christians to all truth; (2) the importance of identification with the poor of the world and the need to bring their distinctive voice into the dialogue; (3) the conviction of the prevenient workings of the Holy Spirit in every human being; (4) the empowerment of believers for witness by the Spirit; and (5) the diverse and pluralistic character of the Spirit's manifestations across racial, class, gender, language, and religious boundaries.[63] On this foundation, as a pentecostal pastor and academic theologian, Solivan is led to "examine the diverse ways the Holy Spirit is at work among other people of faith."[64] However, he does so critically because there are always pitfalls – such as relativization of the truth – in an approach to mission in which dialogue is the *main* vehicle.[65]

CONCLUDING REMARKS: CONTINUING TASKS AND CHALLENGES FOR PENTECOSTAL MISSION

The rapidly developing fields of pentecostal missiology and theology of religions are taking significant steps toward greater clarification and constructive maturity. In the midst of great numerical success in missions work, one of the impending tasks for Pentecostals has to do with the issue of suffering, a topic counterintuitive to much of the pentecostal ethos of "overcoming" and victory.[66] Rightly, the Indian pentecostal theologian Gabriel Reuben Louis laments that today's Pentecostalism is in danger of neglecting the "way of the cross" and instead looking for Christ's benefits mainly for the sake of this-worldly goods and enjoyment. Although the theme of suffering, he continues, "may not be that relevant for a Pentecostal theology in a rich and prosperous West ... [it is] in a poor and miserable Asia."[67] The omission or downplaying of the theme of suffering among Pentecostals is of course not limited to the Asian or Western contexts; similar kinds of charges have been leveled, for example, against African Pentecostalism.[68] Mindful of the importance of this theme, several pentecostal theologians and missiologists have begun to address more intentionally the theme of suffering in human life and Christian experience. The pentecostal biblical scholar and missiologist William W. Menzies, hence, suggests a theology of suffering for Pentecostals.[69] This task has been taken up by another pentecostal biblical scholar, Martin William Mittelstadt.[70] Focusing on the theme of suffering in the book of Acts is significant for more than one reason. First, Acts is by far the most popular book among Pentecostals and widely believed to be the *magna charta* of that movement's spirituality. Second, Acts is about mission. And third, the role of the Holy Spirit therein is profound and robust. Several other Pentecostals from various global contexts, including Puerto Rico[71] and Sudan,[72] have tackled the issues of suffering, poverty, injustice, and similar topics from a pentecostal perspective.

Other noteworthy tasks for pentecostal missiology include the relation of pentecostal grassroots spirituality to the spiritualities of living faiths. Pentecostalism, particularly in the global South, not unlike Roman Catholicism, is to a large extent a folk religion, with deep rootage in local cultures. What are the implications of that for the future of pentecostal mission, on the one hand, and the relation to other local faiths, on the other.

Several other academic and practical tasks could be listed, crucial to the future of pentecostal missions, including continuing reflection on the identity of Pentecostalism – "What makes Pentecostalism Pentecostalism?"[73] – both in relation to "spiritual cousins," Charismatics within the existing churches, and neo-Charismatics, pentecostal-type Christians among a bewildering number of independent movements in African Instituted Churches, in Chinese House Churches, and so forth. Do Pentecostalism, and its mission, represent a distinctively unique manifestation in Christian history, or is it rather an offshoot from a wider religious revival?[74]

Notes

1   Annual statistics provided in the January issue of the *International Bulletin of Missionary Research* give the most up-to-date survey of the spread of Christian churches and movements for each year, including Pentecostals. For a healthy cautionary note to Pentecostals not to glory in numbers, see Gary B. McGee, "Pentecostal Missiology: Moving beyond Triumphalism to Face the Issues," *Pneuma: The Journal of the Society for Pentecostal Studies* 16:2 (1994), 275–81.

2   The definitive current history of pentecostal missions is Allan Anderson, *Spreading Fires: The Missionary Nature of Early Pentecostalism* (Maryknoll, NY: Orbis, 2007). Also important is Anderson's *An Introduction to Pentecostalism: Global Charismatic Christianity* (Cambridge: Cambridge University Press, 2004).

3   See further Russell J. Spittler, "Suggested Areas for Further Research in Pentecostal Studies," *Pneuma: The Journal of the Society for Pentecostal Studies* 5:2 (1983), 39–56. The Nicaraguan Carlos Sediles Real ("Pentecostalisms in Nicaragua: General Aspects of Their Foundations, Growth and Social Participation," *Exchange: Journal for Missiological and Ecumenical Research* 36 [2007], 386–96) rightly attempts to discern key

themes of pentecostal theology of mission as they appear in songs, hymns, and choruses of worship and liturgy. Although not academic or discursive in nature, they allow an access to central theological intuitions.

4 See further my "Pentecostal Missiology in Ecumenical Perspective: Contributions, Challenges, Controversies," *International Review of Mission* 88:350 (1999), 207–25. For an informed outside observation and assessment of recent pentecostal missiology by the famous Latin American liberationist José Bonino Miguez, see his "Pentecostal Missions Is More than What It Claims," *Pneuma: The Journal of the Society for Pentecostal Studies* 16:1 (1994), 283–88.

5 *Apostolic Faith* 2:1 (September 1906).

6 Allan H. Anderson, "The Vision of the Apostolic Faith: Early Pentecostalism and World Mission," *Svensk Missionstidskrift/Swedish Missiological Themes* 97:3 (2009), 295–314 (295).

7 L. Grant McClung, *Azusa Street and Beyond: Pentecostal Missions and Church Growth in the Twentieth Century* (South Plainfield, NJ: Bridge Publishing, 1986), 166–72.

8 See further my "Mission, Spirit, and Eschatology: An Outline of a Pentecostal-Charismatic Theology of Mission," *Mission Studies* 16:1 (1999), 73–94.

9 Douglas Petersen, *Not by Might, Nor by Power: A Pentecostal Theology of Social Concern in Latin America* (Oxford: Regnum, 1996), 9ff. (with quotations from original sources); Gary B. McGee, "Pentecostal and Charismatic Missions," in James M. Phillips and Robert T. Coote, eds., *Toward the Twenty-first Century in Christian Mission: Essays in Honor of Gerald H. Anderson* (Grand Rapids, MI: Eerdmans, 1993), 41ff.

10 McGee, "Pentecostal and Charismatic Missions," 42.

11 L. Grant McClung, Jr., "Pentecostal/Charismatic Perspectives on a Missiology for the Twenty-First Century," *Pneuma: The Journal of the Society for Pentecostal Studies* 16:1 (Spring 1994), 11–21.

12 For a useful discussion, see Richard Burgess, "Nigerian Pentecostal Theology in Global Perspective," *PentecoStudies* 7:2 (2008), 29–63 (http://www.glopent.net/pentecostudies/2008-vol-7/no-2-autumn/burgess-2008/).

13 See further my "Missiology, Pentecostal and Charismatic," in Stanley M. Burgess and Eduard M. van der Maas, eds., *The New International Dictionary of Pentecostal and Charismatic Movements* (Grand Rapids, MI: Zondervan, 2002), 877–85.

14 For an evaluation, see Gary B. McGee, *This Gospel Shall Be Preached: A History and Theology of Assemblies of God Foreign Missions to 1959*, 2 vols. (Springfield, MO: Gospel Publishing House, 1986, 1989), vol. 2, 157–58.

15 McGee, "Pentecostal and Charismatic Missions," 43.

16 M. W. Dempster, B. D. Klaus, and D. Petersen, eds., *Called and Empowered: Global Mission in Pentecostal Perspective* (Peabody, MA: Hendrickson, 1991).

17 Some missiological insights can be gleaned from Roger Stronstad, *The Charismatic Theology of St. Luke* (Peabody, MA: Hendrickson, 1984), with its idea of the transference of the Spirit from Jesus to his followers.

18 Robert P. Menzies, *Empowered for Witness: The Spirit in Luke-Acts* (Sheffield: Sheffield Academic Press, 1994).

19   J. M. Penney, The Missionary Emphasis of Lukan Pneumatology (Sheffield: Sheffield Academic Press, 1997), 12.

20   Wonsuk Ma and Julie Ma, Mission in the Spirit: Towards a Pentecostal/ Charismatic Missiology (Oxford: Regnum International, 2010).

21   The American pentecostal theologian Steve Studebaker has issued a similar call to appreciate the Spirit's role as the principle of life and creation in his: "Christian Mission and the Religions as Participation in the Spirit of Pentecost," in Amos Yong and Clifton Clarke, eds., Global Renewal, Religious Pluralism, and the Great Commission: Toward a Renewal Theology of Mission and Interreligious Encounter (Lexington, KY: Emeth Press, 2011).

22   The classic study is Donald W. Dayton, Theological Roots of Pentecostalism (Grand Rapids, MI: Zondervan, 1987). It seems to me that the Full Gospel template, with a robust "Spirit-Christology," is a valid interpretation in spite of the important and useful criticism coming from the Singaporean Pentecostalist Tan-Chow May Ling (Pentecostal Theology for the Twenty-First Century: Engaging with Multi-Faith Singapore [Aldershot, UK: Ashgate, 2007], 102–03) according to which a robust Christological and Trinitarian focus may be missing in pentecostal theology.

23   Steven J. Land, Pentecostal Spirituality: A Passion for the Kingdom (Sheffield: Sheffield Academic Press, 1993), 60–61.

24   Materially, the pentecostal term Full Gospel carries the same meaning as the ancient term of "catholicity," the idea of wholeness and completeness (literally, "not missing anything"). For a theological discussion, see my "Full Gospel, Fullness of the Spirit and Catholicity: Pentecostal Perspectives on the Third Mark of the Church," Ecumenical Review (forthcoming).

25   Of course, the early Pentecostals at times were guilty of an ideological use of the term Full Gospel. They were not only sincerely concerned about the well-being of other churches but also sometimes used the Full Gospel template as a way of criticizing, making pejorative comments, and even condemning their "dead" spiritual life. That human fallibility, unfortunately, is not limited to Pentecostals alone; however, misuse of the term is hardly a reason to ignore its positive contribution.

26   Rightly, the Korean Samuel Yull Lee, Grace and Power in Pentecostal and Charismatic Theology (Apeldoorn: Theologische Universiteit Apeldoorn, 2002), 109–10, forges an integral connection between Christ, the Full Gospel, and healing of the body, a central theme to pentecostal spirituality. See further Vernon Purdy, "Divine Healing," in Stanley M. Horton, ed., Systematic Theology: A Pentecostal Perspective (Springfield, MO: Logion Press, 1999), 508–09.

27   In this distinction I am indebted to the Benedictine Catholic expert on pentecostal-charismatic movements, Fr. Kilian McDonnell, OSB, who was my mentor in postdoctoral studies.

28   See Daniel E. Albrecht, Rites in the Spirit: A Ritual Approach to Pentecostal/ Charismatic Spirituality (Sheffield: Sheffield Academic Press, 1999).

29   Harvey Cox, Fire from Heaven: The Rise of Pentecostal Spirituality and the Reshaping of Religion in the Twenty-first Century (Reading, MA: Addison-Wesley, 1995), 81–82.

30 Ogbu U. Kalu, "Preserving a Worldview: Pentecostalism in the African Maps of the Universe," *Pneuma: The Journal of the Society for Pentecostal Studies* 24:2 (2003), 122.

31 See further, Opoku Onyinah, "Deliverance as a Way of Confronting Witchcraft in Contemporary Africa: Ghana as a Case Study," in Veli-Matti Kärkkäinen, ed., *The Spirit in the World: Emerging Pentecostal Theologies in Global Contexts* (Grand Rapids, MI: Eerdmans, 2009), 181–202.

32 See especially Cox, *Fire from Heaven*, 299–301.

33 An important contribution here is Jackie David Johns, "Pentecostalism and the Postmodern Worldview," *Journal of Pentecostal Theology* 7 (1995), 73–96. Lately, however, more modest and self-critical remarks have emerged such as those found in John C. Poirier and B. Scott Lewis, "Pentecostal and Postmodernist Hermeneutics: A Critique of Three Conceits," *Journal of Pentecostal Theology* 15:1 (2006), 3–21.

34 Cox, *Fire from Heaven*, 81.

35 Amos Yong, *The Spirit Poured Out on All Flesh: Pentecostalism and the Possibility of Global Theology* (Grand Rapids, MI: Baker Academic, 2005), 82.

36 Miroslav Volf, "Materiality of Salvation: An Investigation in the Soteriologies of Liberation and Pentecostal Theologies," *Journal of Ecumenical Studies* 26 (1989), 447–67.

37 See further my essays: "Are Pentecostals Oblivious to Social Justice? Theological and Ecumenical Perspectives," *Missiology: An International Review* 29:4 (2001), 417–31; and "Are Pentecostals Oblivious of Social Justice: Theological and Ecumenical Perspectives," in Christoph Dahling-Sander, Kai M. Funkschmidt, and Vera Mielke, eds., *Pfingstkirchen und Ökumene* (Frankfurt: Lembeck Verlag, 2001), 50–65.

38 See the important discussion by the Hispanic pentecostal ethicist Eldín Villafañe, *The Liberating Spirit: Toward an Hispanic American Pentecostal Social Ethic* (Grand Rapids, MI: Eerdmans, 1993), 218.

39 See my "The Church as the Fellowship of Persons: An Emerging Pentecostal Ecclesiology of Koinonia," *PentecoStudies* 6:1 (2007), 1–15 (http://www.glo-pent.net/pentccostudies/2007). An exciting collection of essays on pentecostal ecclesiology focused on the Full Gospel template is Chris Thomas, ed., *Pentecostal Ecclesiology: The Church and the Five Fold Gospel* (Cleveland, TN: CPT Press, 2010). Similarly, "The Ecclesiology of the Pentecostal Churches," with Veli-Matti Kärkkäinen (guest ed.) is the theme issue of the *International Journal for the Study of the Christian Church* 11:4 (2011).

40 Peter Kuzmic and Miroslav Volf, "*Communio Sanctorum*: Toward a Theology of the Church as a Fellowship of Persons'" (pentecostal position paper read at the International Roman Catholic-Pentecostal Dialogue, Riano, Italy, May 21–26, 1985, 2) (unpublished manuscript with the author of this essay).

41 See further, V.-M. Kärkkäinen, *Spiritus Ubi Vult Spirat: Pneumatology in Roman Catholic-Pentecostal Dialogue (1972–1989)*, Schriften der Luther-Agricola-Gesellschaft 42 (Helsinki: Luther-Agricola Society, 1998), 100–21.

42 See Frank Macchia, *Baptized in the Spirit: A Global Pentecostal Theology* (Grand Rapids, MI: Zondervan, 2006), 203, 205.

43   In the third phase of the Roman Catholic-Pentecostal International Dialogue
the theme of communion was studied in some detail, leading to an important ecumenical document: *Perspectives on Koinonia: The Report from
the Third Quinquennium of the Dialogue between the Pontifical Council
for Promoting Christian Unity of the Roman Catholic Church and Some
Classical Pentecostal Churches and Leaders (1985–1989)*, available on the
website of Centro Pro Unione (Rome, Italy) (http://www.pro.urbe.it/dia-int/
pe-rc/doc/i_pe-rc_pento3.html); last accessed 12 March 2014.

44   Clark Pinnock, *Flame of Love: A Theology of the Holy Spirit* (Downers
Grove, IL: InterVarsity Press, 1996), 274.

45   A quick survey of pentecostal manuals shows this clearly: Ernest S. Williams,
Systematic Theology (Springfield, MO: Gospel Publishing House, 1953),
3n15; Ned D. Sauls, *Pentecostal Doctrines: A Wesleyan Approach* (Dunn,
NC: Heritage Press, 1979), 54; Guy P. Duffield and Nathaniel M. Van Cleave,
Foundations of Pentecostal Theology (Los Angeles: L.I.F.E. Bible College,
1983), 268–70; Aaron M. Wilson, *Basic Bible Truth: A Doctrinal Study of
the Pentecostal Church of God* (Joplin, MO: Messenger Publishing House,
1987), 115; Mark D. McLean, "The Holy Spirit," in Stanley M. Horton, ed.,
Systematic Theology: A Pentecostal Perspective (Springfield, MO: Logion
Press, 1994), 392. For this bibliographical note, I am indebted to Cecil M.
Robeck, "A Pentecostal Assessment of 'Towards a Common Understanding
and Vision' of the WCC," *Mid-Stream* 37:1 (1998), 31n40.

46   For an important comprehensive up-to-date discussion of the reasons why
Pentecostals have been very reserved about engaging the interfaith issues, see
Tony Richie, *Speaking by the Spirit: A Pentecostal Model for Interreligious
Dialogue* (Lexington, KY: Emeth Press, 2011), ch. 6. On pp. 26–29, Richie
briefly presents the main reasons for Pentecostals to reject interfaith engagement, including the dangers of compromised Christology, diminishing the
value of the Bible, distorted soteriology, and undermining of mission and
evangelization.

47   Harold Carpenter, "Tolerance or Irresponsibility: The Problem of Pluralism
in Missions," *Advance* 31:2 (1995), 19.

48   For a scrutiny of some relevant missiological and interfaith issues, see my
articles: "'An Exercise on the Frontiers of Ecumenism': Almost Thirty
Years of the Roman Catholic-Pentecostal Dialogue," *Exchange: Journal of
Missiological and Ecumenical Research* 29:2 (2000), 156–71; and "Culture,
Contextualization, and Conversion: Missiological Reflections from the
Catholic-Pentecostal Dialogue (1990–1997)," *Asian Journal of Mission* 2:2
(2000), 149–77.

49   *Final Report 1991–1997*, #20. All the final reports are available at the Centro
Pro Unione website at http://www.pro.urbe.it/dia-int/pe-rc/doc/i_pe-rc_
pento2.html. 03/12/2014

50   *Final Report 1978–1982*, #14.

51   *Final Report 1991–1997*, #20.

52   *Final Report 1978–1982*, #14.

53   *Final Report 1991–1997*, #21.

54   Ibid. Key interfaith issues were also touched in the International Dialogue
between the Reformed and Pentecostal Churches, started in 1996. For the

final report of the first phase, see "Word and Spirit, Church and World," *Final Report of the International Pentecostal-Reformed Dialogue*, available at the website of the World Alliance of Reformed Churches, http://pctii.org/cyberj/cyberj8/WARC.html; last accessed 12 March 2014.

55 Amos Yong, *Discerning the Spirit(s): A Pentecostal-Charismatic Contribution to Christian Theology of Religions* (Sheffield: Sheffield Academic Press, 2000), and *Beyond the Impasse: Toward a Pneumatological Theology of Religions* (Grand Rapids, MI: Baker Academic, 2003).

56 Yong, *Spirit Poured Out*, ch. 6.

57 Yong, *Spirit Poured Out*, 235–36.

58 Amos Yong, *Hospitality and the Other: Pentecost, Christian Practices, and the Neighbor* (Maryknoll, NY: Orbis, 2008).

59 Richie, *Speaking by the Spirit*, 3.

60 See also Richie, "Azusa-era Optimism: Bishop J. H. King's Pentecostal Theology of Religions as a Possible Paradigm for Today," *Journal of Pentecostal Theology* 14:2 (2006), 247–60.

61 For recent collection of essays relevant to interfaith issues by pentecostal theologians representing widely global diversity, see Kärkkäinen, *The Spirit in the World*, and Yong and Clarke, *Global Renewal, Religious Pluralism, and the Great Commission*.

62 See V.-M. Kärkkäinen, *Trinity and Religious Pluralism: The Doctrine of the Trinity in Christian Theology of Religions* (Aldershot, UK: Ashgate, 2004); "'How to Speak of the Spirit among Religions': Trinitarian 'Rules' for a Pneumatological Theology of Religions," *International Bulletin for Missionary Research* 30:3 (2006), 121–27; "The Uniqueness of Christ and Trinitarian Faith," in Sung Wook Chung, ed., *Christ the One and Only: A Global Affirmation of the Uniqueness of Jesus Christ* (Exeter: Paternoster, 2005), 111–35; "Trinity and Religions: On the Way to a Trinitarian Theology of Religions for Evangelicals," *Missiology* 33:2 (2005), 159–74; and "Trinitarian Rules for a Pneumatological Theology of Religions," in Michael Welker, ed., *The Work of the Spirit: Pneumatology and Pentecostalism* (Grand Rapids, MI: Eerdmans, 2006), 47–70.

63 Samuel Solivan, "Interreligious Dialogue: An Hispanic American Pentecostal Perspective," in S. Mark Heim, ed., *Grounds for Understanding: Ecumenical Responses to Religious Pluralism* (Grand Rapids, MI: Eerdmans, 1998), 37–45.

64 Ibid., 43.

65 Ibid., 44.

66 See my "Theology of the Cross: A Stumbling Block to Pentecostal-Charismatic Spirituality," in Wonsuk Ma and Robert P. Menzies, eds., *The Spirit and Spirituality: Essays in Honour of Russell P. Spittler* (London and New York: T & T Clark International, 2004), 150–63.

67 Gabriel Reuben Louis, "Response to Wonsuk Ma," *Cyberjournal for Pentecostal-Charismatic Research* 4 (July 1998) (http://www.pctii.org/cyberj/cyber4.html), last accessed 12 March 2014; this is a response to Wonsuk Ma, "Toward an Asian Pentecostal Theology," *Cyberjournal for Pentecostal-Charismatic Research* 1 (January 1997) (http://www.pctii.org/cyberj/cyber1.html), last accessed 12 March 2014.

68 See further J. Kwabena Asamoah-Gyadu, *African Charismatics: Current Developments within Independent Indigenous Pentecostalism in Ghana* (Leiden: Brill, 2006), 218, 228–32.

69 William W. Menzies, "Reflections on Suffering: A Pentecostal Perspective," in Wonsuk Ma and Robert P. Menzies, *The Spirit and Spirituality: Essays in Honour of Russell P. Spittler*, 141–49 (141). See also the important essay by the British pentecostal biblical scholar who has written extensively on healing, Keith Warrington, "Healing and Suffering in the Bible," *International Review of Mission* 95:376/377 (2006), 154–64.

70 Martin William Mittelstadt, *The Spirit and Suffering in Luke-Acts: Implications for a Pentecostal Pneumatology* (London and New York: T & T Clark International, 2004).

71 Samuel Solivan, *The Spirit, Pathos and Liberation: Toward an Hispanic Pentecostal Theology* (Sheffield: Sheffield Academic Press, 1998).

72 Isaiah Majo Dau, *Suffering and God: A Theological Reflection on the War in Sudan* (Nairobi, Kenya: Paulines Publications Africa, 2003).

73 See my "Identity and Plurality: A Pentecostal-Charismatic Perspective," *International Review of Mission* 91:363 (October 2002), 500–04.

74 For some aspects, see my "'The Re-Turn of Religion in the New Millennium': Pentecostalisms and Postmodernities," *Swedish Missiological Themes* 95:4 (Fall 2007), 469–96.

Further Reading

George, Geomon K. *Religious Pluralism: Challenges for Pentecostalism in India*. Bangalore, India: Centre for Contemporary Christianity, 2006.

Lord, Andy. *Spirit-Shaped Mission: A Holistic Charismatic Missiology*. Waynesboro, GA: Paternoster Publishing, 2005.

McGee, Gary B. *Miracles, Missions, and American Pentecostalism*. Maryknoll, NY: Orbis Books, 2010.

Pomerville, Paul. *Third Force in Missions: A Pentecostal Contribution to Contemporary Mission Theology*. Peabody, MA: Hendrickson Publishers, 1985.

Westerlund, David, ed. *Global Pentecostalism: Encounters with Other Religious Traditions*. London: I. B. Tauris, 2009.

Instead of a Conclusion: A Theologian's Interdisciplinary Musings on the Future of Global Pentecostalism and Its Scholarship

AMOS YONG

The following anticipates the future of global Pentecostalism in light of the preceding pages. Any speculation about the future is hazardous, not only because guessing is always unreliable but also, in this case, because of the unpredictability that modern pentecostal movements have repeatedly shown themselves to be. Further, as a theologian, I am neither a trained social scientist (and so have little knowledge of how to make future projections on the basis of present data) nor a prophet or son of one (despite my training in some aspects of the Bible)! However, these concluding pages will nevertheless ask about the pentecostal future by triangulating around three sets of questions: (1) How might pentecostal growth be tracked, much less defined? (2) What global, regional, and other trends may impact future developments? (3) How might pentecostal beliefs and practices inform as well as be affected by what happens? Its goal is to step back from the "trees" described in the chapters of this volume and ask about how the "forest" of modern and global Pentecostalism is changing as we peer into the middle of the twenty-first century.

First, the topic of pentecostal growth bring us back to the contested questions about who is counting and why, registered in the editors' introduction. There are many demographic sources, but even those that are generally reliable are careful to delineate the definitional issues precisely because there is no consensus about the movement, at least in global context.[1] There are a multitude of categories that have been included for various reasons:

- Certainly pentecostal churches that trace their origins back to the first decade of the twentieth century, usually via missionary connections to the Azusa Street Revival; these are often called "classical" pentecostal churches – but many are morphing in relationship to present trends.

- Those who are part of charismatic renewal streams in non-classical pentecostal churches, oftentimes in older Protestant denominations or in the Roman Catholic or various Orthodox Churches.
- Those in nondenominational, independent, and oftentimes evangelical churches and movements that embrace the ongoing charismatic manifestations of the Holy Spirit as part of the regular Christian life – although in many cases, these do not self-identify as either Pentecostal or Charismatic.
- Churches and movements indigenous to global South regions such as many African Independent Churches whose spiritualities regularly feature many of the charismatic expressions of the Holy Spirit – although, again, in most cases, these do not necessarily self-identify as Pentecostal or Charismatic.

There are other considerations, and many of the chapters, especially those in Parts I and II, discuss the relevant matters. These variations guarantee that the question about how to define "Pentecostalism" will persist into the foreseeable future.

Consensus is elusive, however, not only because demographers are disagreeable people. Rather, those who do self-identify as pentecostal may also be motivated to count differently. Some members of classical pentecostal churches might be more committed to a theological understanding of Pentecostalism, for instance, so that only those who are members of or adhere to classical pentecostal teachings concerning the baptism in the Holy Spirit with the sign or evidence of tongues-speech following are included. Others may be more wedded to a sectarian categorization to posit Pentecostalism as a challenge to certain features of a church otherwise believed to have accommodated itself to wider cultural influences. Many of these are Oneness or apostolic believers for whom "true Pentecostals" include not only belief in certain theological notions but also certain behavioral or presentational markers that set them off from "the world." On the other side of the spectrum, however, denominational leaders, particularly those involved in negotiating strategic interfaces with political and other social sectors, may be more inclined to adopt more inclusive views of Pentecostalism to secure the advantages related to larger size. On the more practical side, missionaries and others raising moneys for missionary work may also be predisposed to such larger numbers because these are more likely to generate enthusiastic support. The point is that the question of who is counting and why is relevant to the discussion of how Pentecostalism is defined even within classical pentecostal circles, and this in turn influences how pentecostal progression is tracked going forward.

To be sure, research on global and local pentecostal churches and movements will continue to accelerate in secular university environments so long as they continue to evince growth. When scholars approach this topic who are not themselves insiders to the religious groups or movements they study, they wrestle with classification matters for theoretical, methodological, and analytical reasons. Economists, for instance, will continue to be motivated to study pentecostal trends to better predict market forces, factors, and impacts,[2] whereas social and political scientists (as Calvin Smith's and Michael Wilkinson's chapters indicate) may be impelled to attend to Pentecostalism because population statistics have the capacity to affect democratic elections as well as other sociopolitical realities. To be sure, many, especially sociologists and anthropologists, will prioritize the self-understanding of insiders. However, even in these cases, identification of such for research will itself precede the ethnographic fieldwork that generates such insider perspective and qualitative data, so these then may arrive too late, so to speak, for purposes of adjudicating the terminological disputes. Yet such research will continue, and their publication and distribution will assuredly impact the ongoing discussion. The point is that although scholarly investigation on religious movements theoretically does not decide on normative questions of definition, their cumulative results, especially on a set of movements as complex and widespread as is global Pentecostalism, will inevitably affect, if not complicate, matters.

Yet the question of growth is confounded not only by who and how to count but also by wider globalizing factors.[3] As has been repeatedly mentioned throughout this book, the so-called secularization thesis appears to have been overturned by pentecostal-instigated revitalization worldwide.[4] Truth be told, however, in the West such revival and renewal is happening as much if not more because of immigrant groups than in established churches. Scholarly conjecture is that the dynamics of South-North and East-West migration motivate rather than discourage religious carry-over. When confronted with rapid sociocultural change, some degree of stability is sought and the religious dimension is the most portable in the immigrant context. Hence, migrants begin churches in the Euro-American West that mirror those "back home" so that these provide some semblance of continuity between their former and present lives. This phenomenon of "reverse mission" (see especially Jean-Daniel Plüss's chapter), hence, meets the needs first and foremost of immigrants rather than the established inhabitants of Europe and North America.[5] It remains to be seen how these trends will shift with the children of these immigrants, not to mention once migration trends reach an equilibrium (which they will as we move further into the twenty-first century).

Yet that immigrants are bringing their pentecostal spirituality with them means also that Pentecostalism is alive and well at least in certain regions of the global South. Part of the scholarly challenge on these fronts is to untangle the sociopolitical, economic, historical, and religious knots. The chapters especially in Part II press the following questions: To what degree is pentecostal spirituality flourishing across Asia, Africa, and Latin America because of specifically religious versus political, economic, or other reasons? Are the religious reasons separable from these other dimensions? To what degree will the continual modernization, urbanization, and secularization of the global South influence religious beliefs and practices? How will the dynamics of the global economy continue to shape religious lives? Will postcolonial developments have unanticipated religious consequences? How will the various forces of globalization – including advances in, accessibility of, and participation within technological, medical, and communicative networks – interface with pentecostal movements in the twenty-first century?[6] To be sure, it is not as if Pentecostalism will disappear, just as we know that religion itself has proven resilient in the secular West. However, its primary features will also almost certainly continue to evolve, even as what is now popular in secular environments is not traditional, classical, or established institutional forms of religiosity as such but more precisely postmodern modes of "spirituality" in its various guises.

Part of the unpredictability of globalization and its religious consequences is related also to broader religious factors, in particular how other Christian traditions continue to react and respond to the contemporary context. Primary among these, for those tracking pentecostal advance, is the continual adaptations of the Roman Catholic Church (RCC) in the third millennium. There are various reasons that the fortunes of the RCC are intertwined with that of global Pentecostalism, but I will mention only three. First, the embrace of charismatic renewal within the RCC has not only minimized outflow toward pentecostal churches but also revitalized its parishes.[7] Second, while the Catholic hegemony over certain parts of the world, including but not limited to Latin America, will continue to erode, this pluralization does not portend the disappearance of the RCC or its influence in these regions.[8] Last but not least, the appointment in 2013 of evangelical-friendly Argentinian Jorge Mario Bergoglio as Pope Francis will almost certainly sustain if not freshly endow the streams of charismatic renewal in the church. All of these elements suggest that growth in neo-pentecostal, charismatic, and neo-charismatic sectors will continue to complicate the global pentecostal picture.

As a theologian, however, I wonder both how the actual beliefs of pentecostal churches, regardless of their stripe, will be impacted by future developments and vice versa. This relates to the questions not only of how pentecostal believers will make a difference but also of how Pentecostalism will itself be transformed by wider forces. I comment along three lines as informed by the sorts of multidisciplinary data presented in this volume, even as I hopefully connect some of the dots registered in the foregoing.

First, earlier classical pentecostal fervor is being tempered as measured by the lessened eschatological urgency in the current generation when compared to those in the first half of the twentieth century. Sociological explanation will chalk this up to the routinization and rationalization that attends to all religious movements. Arguably, however, there are also explicitly theological reasons for such reconsiderations because the pages of the New Testament itself depict divergent eschatological orientations. However, the point is that insofar as eschatological sensibilities impact missionary commitments and practices, the emergence of different eschatologies in contemporary pentecostal theology will have diverse missiological implications. Not without reason, then, we are also seeing a proliferation of pentecostal mission theologies, as Veli-Matti Kärkkäinen's chapter documents. For those who believe that authentic Pentecostalism is marked by the Spirit's empowerment for traditional forms of missionary witness to the world, the redefinition of pentecostal missiology and the transformation of pentecostal mission practice signals a devolution from more pristine forms. Others will counter that the advent of more holistic mission theologies and practices actually more consistently manifests the potency of the "full-gospel" of the early modern pentecostal message to engage holistically with contemporary sociopolitical, economic, and even environmental and ecological concerns.[9] The point, however, is indisputable: it is unlikely that we will be witnessing agreement any time soon about pentecostal eschatology and missiology, and this itself is related to the flowering of pentecostal beliefs and practices in its second century.

Second, many of the chapters in this book highlight the theme of prosperity that is salient across pentecostal communities worldwide. Pentecostals of various stripes have been critical of this phenomenon in its many guises, and rightly so. However, such criticisms do not get at many of the factors that have shaped the present discussion. The connections between early pentecostal emphases on bodily healing and socioeconomic upward mobility have not been explored; the sociopolitical and economic implications of the biblical promises regarding the prosperity of believers have been neither studied in global (pentecostal) context nor resolved; and the this-worldly rather than otherworldly sensibilities of those in the global South have not been factored into the theological mix. The concerns about imbalanced teaching and abusive, extortionistic, and exploitative practices are certainly warranted; however, a balanced theological perspective must also heed larger soteriological considerations that those outside of the Euro-American West are confronting. Purely spiritual answers prominent in Western contexts do not adequately respond to questions that those in the majority world are asking. Instead, for indigenous cultures and others unwilling merely to spiritualize matters, spiritual forces are believed to interface adversely and auspiciously, as the case may be, with the physical, financial, and material world of human beings. Hence, the pentecostal full-gospel is, in this perspective, relevant, and it addresses real fears and hopes, including those related to human poverty and prosperity.[10] In short, pentecostal theologians need to take up this issue of prosperity as a central theme within their broader soteriological and theological considerations. What is the problem and how does the gospel provide a response? These are the issues underneath the debates about prosperity theology. Answers to these questions will influence the next generation of pentecostal churches as well as their impact on these wider social, political, and economic domains.

Last but not least, pentecostal theology is also currently undergoing ferment. For many, "pentecostal theology" is at worst an oxymoron (given the anti-intellectualism that has been popular and continues unabated in many segments of the movement) or at best limited to a theology of glossolalia, Spirit baptism, or mission. What Pentecostals are known for is not theological reflection but evangelistic and missionary praxis, or their spirituality. Yet a new generation of pentecostal theology is now emerging, as the last three or four chapters nicely portray. For these, the pentecostal contribution is no longer limited to initial evidence, much less to pneumatology (the theology of the Holy Spirit). Certainly, the pneumatological thread is dominant. However, the main reason for this is not only because of the centrality of the Holy Spirit in popular pentecostal beliefs and practices, but the discernment among the emerging generation of pentecostal theologians that the potential for their own contribution to the broader theological conversation at present is precisely in this pneumatological arena that has been most neglected by the Christian tradition. Hence, pentecostal theologians are now no longer theologizing only for their own movements and churches but also proposing new perspectives for the consideration of the church ecumenical (as Wolfgang Vondey's chapter accents) and the wider theological academy.[11] These projects are indicative of how global Pentecostalism is generating new perspectives on age-old questions; in these ways, pentecostal realities are inspiring multi- and interdisciplinary dialogue. Simultaneously, they also exemplify many of the definitional conundrums already discussed, even as they anticipate how present theological discourses may precipitate new trends going forward.

The final words of this book cannot provide final conclusion, largely because much of what appears in this book is practically dated even as it comes off the press. If researchers consulting these pages are catalyzed to ask fresh questions and to reconceive the next project design on Pentecostalism, the editors and authors of this volume will have considered their contributions a success. Pentecostal insiders who are likewise led to reconsider the significance of the movement and to revisit both theological and practical concerns will have comprehended the major thrusts of what the preceding documents. If Pentecostalism is a movement of the divine Spirit as its devotees claim, then the degree to which it is accurately described here ought to open up to its dynamic character, rather than provide an absolute template for any ideology. Similarly, scholarly work that registers rather than obscures such putatively divine realities will initiate wonder and urge cautious assessment, rather than mobilize reckless claims in the divine name. That is the spirit with which this work has been executed; may such also be the spirit in which it is received.

Notes

1   E.g., compare the discussions of the difficulty of how to count in the introduction to Stanley M. Burgess and Eduard M. van der Maas, eds., *The New International Dictionary of Pentecostal and Charismatic Movements* (Grand Rapids, MI: Zondervan, 2002), esp. xvii–xxiii, with Todd M. Johnson and Kenneth R. Ross, *Atlas of Global Christianity* (Edinburgh: Edinburgh University Press, 2010), esp. 100–07.

2   See, for instance, Katherine Attanasi and Amos Yong, eds., *Pentecostalism and Prosperity: The Socioeconomics of the Global Charismatic Movement*, Christianities of the World 1 (New York: Palgrave Macmillan, 2012).

3   See Chandler Im and Amos Yong, eds., *Global Diasporas and Mission*, Regnum Edinburgh Centenary Series (Oxford, UK: Regnum Books International, 2014).

4   As brought to the attention of the academic elite by Harvey G. Cox, *Fire from Heaven: The Rise of Pentecostal Spirituality and the Reshaping of Religion in the 21st Century* (Reading, MA: Addison-Wesley, 1995).

5   See Claudia Wahrisch-Oblau, *The Missionary Self-Perception of Pentecostal/ Charismatic Church Leaders from the Global South in Europe: Bringing Back the Gospel*, Global Pentecostal & Charismatic Studies 2 (Leiden: Brill, 2009); cf. Babatunde Aderemi Adedibu, "Reverse Mission or Migrant Sanctuaries? Migration, Symbolic Mapping and Missionary Challenges of Britain's Black Majority Churches," *Pneuma: The Journal of the Society for Pentecostal Studies* 35:3 (2013), 366–84.

6   That many of these questions are inextricably interwoven can be seen in the essays in Monique Ingalls and Amos Yong, eds., *The Spirit of Praise: Music and Worship in Global Pentecostal-Charismatic Christianity* (University Park, PA: Penn State University Press, 2015).

7   See Edward L. Cleary, *The Rise of Charismatic Catholicism in Latin America* (Gainesville, FA: University of Florida Press, 2011).

8   See Cecil M. Robeck, Jr., "Creative Imagination and Ecumenism: Implications of Changing Demographics," the 2013 Figel Address on Ecumenical Dialogue, Catholic University of America, Washington, DC, February 4, 2013, http://washtheocon.org/for-the-public/figel-address/ (accessed June 13, 2013). Thanks to my coeditor for pointing me to this paper.

9   As argued in the chapters in parts III and IV of Amos Yong, ed., *The Spirit Renews the Face of the Earth: Pentecostal Forays in Science and Theology of Creation* (Eugene, OR: Pickwick Publications, 2009).

10 As I discuss throughout, but also concentratedly in the seventh chapter, of my *In the Days of Caesar: Pentecostalism and Political Theology – The Cadbury Lectures 2009*, Sacra Doctrina: Christian Theology for a Postmodern Age series (Grand Rapids, MI, and Cambridge, UK: William B. Eerdmans Publishing Company, 2010); see also Estrelda Alexander and Amos Yong, eds., *Afro-Pentecostalism: Black Pentecostal and Charismatic Christianity in History and Culture*, Religion, Race, and Ethnicity Series (New York: New York University Press, 2011), for discussions of related matters by African-American pentecostal scholars and theologians.

11 For a glimpse of how these theological discourses are unfolding, see my books, *The Spirit Poured Out on All Flesh: Pentecostalism and the Possibility of Global Theology* (Grand Rapids, MI: Baker Academic, 2005), and *Spirit of Love: A Trinitarian Theology of Grace* (Waco, TX: Baylor University Press, 2012). For a succinct statement, see my article, "Pentecostal and Charismatic Theology" in Chad Meister and James Beilby, eds., *The Routledge Companion to Modern Christian Thought* (New York and London: Routledge, 2013), 636–46. Further commentary on current trends is provided by Wolfgang Vondey and Martin W. Mittelstadt, eds., *The Theology of Amos Yong and the New Face of Pentecostal Scholarship: Passion for the Spirit*, Global Pentecostal and Charismatic Studies 14 (Leiden and Boston: Brill, 2013).

Name Index

Abrams, Minnie, 16, 23, 25, 26n11, 30n77, 78
Adams, Leonard P., 78–79
Adeboye, Olufanke, 182, 192n51
Adedibu, Babatunde Aderemi, 320n5
Adelaja, Sunday, 99, 144
Adogame, Afe, 108n31, 110n53
Aduboffour, Samuel B., 148n8
Aguilar, Mario, 187, 193n87
Ahonen, L., 108n35
Aikman, David, 36–37, 170n23, 27
Akoko, Robert Mbe., 150, 192n46
Albrecht, Daniel E., ix, 7, 235, 251n5, 252n8, 18, 253, 308n28
Alexander, Estrelda, 91n20, 92, 186–87, 193n85, 320n10
Alexander, Kimberly Ervin, 271n45
Alexander, Paul, 91n22, 189n1, 268, 271n54
Alfaro, Sammy G., 131n32
Allen, A. A., 87
Allen, John, 10
Allende, Salvador, 186
Althouse, Peter, 9, 49n60, 258, 269n13
Alvarado, Juan, 126
Alvarado, Román, 126
Alvarado, Rosario, 126
Alvarez, Carmelo E., 30n80, 290n37, 291n48–49
Anderson, Allan, 9–10, 14, 18, 25n2–4, 28n47, 30, 34, 46n6, 7, 15, 47n17, 48n34, 35, 36, 49n52, 65n7, 148n6, 149n36, 150, 168n3, 170n24, 189n1, 2, 190n15, 192n44, 212n1, 213n12, 213n14, 19, 242, 252n10, 270n34, 271, 271n47, 54, 292n55, 306n2, 307n6
Anderson, Robert Mapes, 47n17, 147n3, 232n9, 290n24
Anfuso, Joseph, 194n98

Angley, Ernest, 177
Annacondia, Carlos, 38, 123
Araica, Alberto, 130n12
Archer, Kenneth J., 256, 269n4–6
Argue, Donald, 86
Arnott, Carol, 38, 42
Arnott, John, 38, 42
Asamoah-Gyadu J. Kwabena, 34, 48n34, 46, 49n51, 148n10, 149n26–27, 150n43, 312n68
Ashcroft, John, 175
Assimeng, Max, 145, 150n48
Atanasov, Miroslav A., 108n29
Atiemo, Abamfo, 133, 148n5
Atkinson, María, 120
Atkinson, William P., 258, 269n16
Attanasi, Katherine, 149n29, 194, 319n2
Atteberry, Thomas, 28n40, 29n68
Au, Connie Ho Yan, 47n26
Auilar, Mario, 186
Austin-Broos, Diane, 213n16
Avila, José Joaquin "Yiye", 117, 123

Babalola, Joseph, 134
Baëta, C. B., 148n6
Baez-Camargo, Gonzalo, 122
Ball, H. C., 119
Barker, Isabelle V., 181, 183, 192n49, 60, 194n91
Barratt, Thomas Ball, 16, 20–21, 25, 26n13, 27n34, 28n55, 29n61, 36, 93–97, 106n10, 107n12, 22, 274, 289n9
Barrett, David B., 50n68, 70, 168n1, 169n12, 170n22
Barron, Bruce, 184, 193n67, 70, 225
Bartholomew, Craig C., 258
Bartleman, Frank, 14, 16, 18–20, 26n10n13, 27n36, 29n74, 274, 289n8
Bastian, Jean-Pierre, 112, 118, 129n3, 6

Subject Index

Acts29, 155
addiction, 42, 226
African American (Black), 14, 21–22,
    40, 71, 73–83, 86–89, 90n13, 108n27,
    121, 124, 223, 283
African Christian Democratic
    Party, 178
African independent/initiated/
    indigenous/instituted churches
    (AIC), 33, 133–38, 306, 314
African National Congress, 178
African spirituality, 136
African traditional religion, 135–36
African Universal Church, 82
Afro-Brazilian religion, 205
afrocentrism, 40
Aladura Churches, 133
alienation, social, 14
altruism, 223–24
Alpha Program, 37, 42, 44
Amistad Cristiana Church, 117
anointing with oil, 138, 141–42, 146
anthropology, 14, 44, 121, 198, 204, 249
anti-intellectualism, 280
apocalyptic, 18, 118, 185, 198, 276
apostles, 35, 37, 43, 274
Apostolic Church in Great Britain, 97
Apostolic Church of Ethiopia
    (ACE), 61–64
apostolic churches (Oneness), 16, 314
Apostolic Faith, 16, 114, 274, 276
Apostolic Faith Mission, 75, 77–78,
    90n13, 133, 137, 294
Apostolic World Christian Fellowship
    (AWCF), 60
Assemblea Christiana, 101
Assembleias de Deus (Brazil), 121
authority, (spiritual), 229
Azusa Street (Mission), 19–21, 24, 31–32,
    44, 54, 58, 66n12, 74–75, 77, 93,

109n44, 114, 119, 124, 125, 133, 136,
    242, 246, 249, 274, 294, 301, 313

baptism in the Holy Spirit (Spirit
    baptism), 1, 18, 23, 24, 33, 36, 45, 52,
    55, 76, 94, 98, 107n22, 115, 242–43,
    250, 258–59, 264, 284, 286, 318
baptism in the name of Jesus (Jesus'
    name baptism), 56, 62, 76, 98
baptism of suffering, 110n48
Baptist Charismatic St. Olav's Church,
    110n49
Baptist World Alliance (BWA), 282
Berlin Declaration (*Berliner Erklärung*),
    21, 103, 109n44
biblical hermeneutics, 255–58, 265, 267
biblicism, 296
Billy Graham Evangelistic Association
    (BGEA), 117
blood of Jesus, 63–64
Bolshevik Revolution, 108n23
Bonnie Brae Street, 75
Born Again Fellowship (China),
    159–60, 165
Boxer Rebellion, 161
Brazilian spiritists, 40
Brotherhood of Pullman Porter, 83

Campus Crusade, 86
Catholic mysticism, 45
cell groups/churches, 44, 102
Central Bible College, 303
Centre of Black and White Christian
    Partnership, 99
charisma, 210
charismatics, xiii, 3, 8, 32, 34, 36–37,
    44, 86–87, 98, 105, 110n49, 126, 133,
    138, 141, 143, 164, 198, 230, 247, 249,
    264, 284
charismatic leadership, 164–66

Titles in the Series (*continued from page iii*)

THE CAMBRIDGE COMPANION TO PAUL TILLICH
edited by Russell Re Manning (2009)
9780521859899 hardback, 9780521677356 paperback

THE CAMBRIDGE COMPANION TO JOHN HENRY NEWMAN
edited by Ian Ker and Terrence Merrigan (2009)
9780521871860 hardback, 9780521692724 paperback

THE CAMBRIDGE COMPANION TO JOHN WESLEY
edited by Randy L. Maddox and Jason E. Vickers (2010)
9780521886536 hardback, 9780521714037 paperback

THE CAMBRIDGE COMPANION TO CHRISTIAN PHILOSOPHICAL
THEOLOGY
edited by Charles Taliaferro and Chad Meister (2010)
9780521514330 hardback, 9780521730372 paperback

THE CAMBRIDGE COMPANION TO MUHAMMAD
edited by Jonathan E. Brockopp (2010)
9780521886079 hardback, 9780521713726 paperback

THE CAMBRIDGE COMPANION TO SCIENCE AND RELIGION
edited by Peter Harrison (2010)
9780521885386 hardback, 9780521712514 paperback

THE CAMBRIDGE COMPANION TO GANDHI
edited by Judith Brown and Anthony Parel (2011)
9780521116701 hardback, 9780521133456 paperback

THE CAMBRIDGE COMPANION TO THOMAS MORE
edited by George Logan (2011)
9780521888622 hardback, 9780521716871 paperback

THE CAMBRIDGE COMPANION TO MIRACLES
edited by Graham H. Twelftree (2011)
9780521899864 hardback, 9780521728515 paperback

THE CAMBRIDGE COMPANION TO FRANCIS OF ASSISI
edited by Michael J. P. Robson (2011)
9780521760430 hardback, 9780521757829 paperback

THE CAMBRIDGE COMPANION TO CHRISTIAN ETHICS, SECOND EDITION
edited by Robin Gill (2011)
9781107000070 hardback, 9780521164832 paperback

THE CAMBRIDGE COMPANION TO BLACK THEOLOGY
edited by Dwight Hopkins and Edward Antonio (2012)
9780521879866 hardback, 9780521705691 paperback

THE CAMBRIDGE COMPANION TO NEW RELIGIOUS MOVEMENTS
edited by Olav Hammer and Mikael Rothstein
9780521196505 hardback, 9780521145657 paperback

THE CAMBRIDGE COMPANION TO THE CISTERCIAN ORDER
edited by Mette Birkedal Bruun (2012)
9781107001312 hardback, 9780521171847 paperback

Made in United States
Orlando, FL
06 July 2024